The Royal Institution of Chartered Surveyors is the mark of property professionalism worldwide, promoting best practice, regulation and consumer protection for business and the community. It is the home of property related knowledge and is an impartial advisor to governments and global organisations. It is committed to the promotion of research in support of the efficient and effective operation of land and property markets worldwide.

Real Estate Issues

Series Managing Editors

Clare Eriksson	Head of Research, Royal Institution of Chartered Surveyors
John Henneberry	Department of Town & Regional Planning, University of Sheffield
K.W. Chau	Chair Professor, Department of Real Estate and Construction, The University of Hong Kong
Elaine Worzala	Director of the Carter Real Estate Center, College of Charleston, U.S.A.

Real Estate Issues is an international book series presenting the latest thinking into how real estate markets operate. The books have a strong theoretical basis – providing the underpinning for the development of new ideas.

The books are inclusive in nature, drawing both upon established techniques for real estate market analysis and on those from other academic disciplines as appropriate. The series embraces a comparative approach, allowing theory and practice to be put forward and tested for their applicability and relevance to the understanding of new situations. It does not seek to impose solutions, but rather provides a more effective means by which solutions can be found. It will not make any presumptions as to the importance of real estate markets but will uncover and present, through the clarity of the thinking, the real significance of the operation of real estate markets.

Further information on the Real Estate Issues series can be found at: http://eu.wiley.com/WileyCDA/Section/id-380013.html

Books in the series

Greenfields, Brownfields & Housing
Development
Adams & Watkins
9780632063871

Planning, Public Policy & Property Markets
Adams, Watkins & White
9781405124300

Housing & Welfare in Southern Europe
Allen, Barlow, Léal, Maloutas & Padovani
9781405103077

Markets & Institutions in Real Estate &
Construction
Ball
9781405110990

Building Cycles: Growth & Instability
Barras
9781405130011

Neighbourhood Renewal & Housing Markets:
Community Engagement in the US and UK
Beider
9781405134101

Mortgage Markets Worldwide
Ben-Shahar, Leung & Ong
9781405132107

The Cost of Land Use Decisions:
Applying Transaction Cost Economics to
Planning & Development
Buitelaar
9781405151238

Urban Regeneration & Social Sustainability:
Best Practice from European Cities
Colantonio & Dixon
9781405194198

Urban Regeneration in Europe
Couch, Fraser & Percy
9780632058419

Urban Sprawl in Europe:
Landscapes, Land-Use Change & Policy
Couch, Leontidou & Petschel-Held
9781405139175

Transforming Private Landlords
Crook & Kemp
9781405184151

Planning Gain
Crook, Henneberry & Whitehead
9781118219812

Real Estate & the New Economy:
The Impact of Information and Communications
Technology
Dixon, McAllister, Marston & Snow
9781405117784

Economics & Land Use Planning
Evans
9781405118613

Economics, Real Estate & the Supply of Land
Evans
9781405118620

Management of Privatised Housing: International
Policies & Practice
Gruis, Tsenkova & Nieboer
9781405181884

Development & Developers:
Perspectives on Property

Guy & Henneberry
9780632058426

The Right to Buy: Analysis & Evaluation of a
Housing Policy
Jones & Murie
9781405131971

Housing Markets & Planning Policy
Jones & Watkins
9781405175203

Office Markets & Public Policy
Colin Jones
9781405199766

Challenges of the Housing Economy:
An International Perspective
Jones, White & Dunse
9780470672334

Mass Appraisal Methods: An International
Perspective for Property Valuers
Kauko & d'Amato
9781405180979

Economics of the Mortgage Market:
Perspectives on Household Decision Making
Leece
9781405114615

Towers of Capital: Office Markets & International
Financial Services
Lizieri
9781405156721

Milestones in European Housing Finance
Lunde & Whitehead
9781118929452

Making Housing More Affordable:
The Role of Intermediate Tenures
Monk & Whitehead
9781405147149

Global Trends in Real Estate Finance
Newell & Sieracki
9781405151283

Housing Economics & Public Policy
O'Sullivan & Gibb
9780632064618

International Real Estate:
An Institutional Approach
Seabrooke, Kent & How
9781405103084

Urban Design in the Real Estate Development
Process: Policy Tools & Property Decisions
Tiesdell & Adams
9781405192194

Real Estate Finance in the New Economy
Tiwari & White
9781405158718

British Housebuilders: History & Analysis
Wellings
9781405149181

European Housing Finance
Lunde
9781118929452

Dynamics of Housing in East Asia
Renaud
9780470672662

Planning Gain
Crook
9781118219812

Dynamics of Housing in East Asia

Dynamics of Housing in East Asia

Bertrand Renaud

Fellow of the Weimer Graduate School of Advanced Studies
in Real Estate and Urban Land Economics
Homer Hoyt Institute
USA

Kyung-Hwan Kim

Professor of Economics at Sogang University in Seoul
Vice-Minister, Ministry of Land, Infrastructure and Transport
Republic of Korea

Man Cho

Professor at the KDI School of Public Policy and Management in Seoul
Visiting Scholar, Institute of Real Estate Studies
National University of Singapore
Singapore

Library of Congress Cataloging-in-Publication data applied for.

ISBN: 9780470672662

A catalogue record for this book is available from the British Library.

Wiley also publishes its books in a variety of electronic formats. Some content that appears in print may not be available in electronic books.

Set in 10/13pt Trump Mediaeval by SPi Global, Pondicherry, India
Printed and bound in Malaysia by Vivar Printing Sdn Bhd

1   2016

Contents

Preface

This book offers the first genuine comparative study of the dynamic interactions between the housing sector and the wider economies of six East Asian countries: China, Japan, South Korea, Hong Kong, Singapore and Taiwan. These economies currently account for more than 30% of global housing assets and share important physical, cultural and institutional features that distinguish them as a group from other countries and create a unity of analysis. A comparative study of East Asia would also contribute to redressing the conspicuous imbalance between the overwhelming flow of academic research about the USA and a few other Western real estate markets on one side, and the rest of the world on the other.

Our comparative analysis has three complementary dimensions. First, an analysis of the institutional origins of these six housing system explains commonalities in their origins, their significant structural differences, and how these systems work at the present time. Second, the econometric analysis of housing price volatility and price cycles provides quantitative evidence of the significant differences across the six East Asian housing systems, and between East Asian and Western housing markets as well. Third, we present an analysis of the incentives and behavior of six key players (or participating groups) that are always present in housing cycles, but which have not been investigated jointly in previous studies of these cycles.

There have been twists and turns on the road toward the completion of this book. The idea for a comparative study of housing in East Asia goes back to an international real estate seminar at the Weimer School in Florida, several years after the outbreak of the 1997 Asia Financial Crisis (AFC). While there, two of us discussed the merits of a comparative study of East Asian housing that would go well beyond a 2000 book, on real estate during the AFC, in which we had cooperated. We agreed that the Asian Financial Crisis had suggested that East Asian housing markets behave differently from Western markets.

During the decade of the 2000s, East Asian real estate research was growing rapidly in scope, depth and quality, which provided further motivation as well as technical support for our interest in a comparative study. A major step forward was made for our comparative study at a conference on global housing held in Cambridge, UK, in 2010, in the aftermath of the Global Financial Crisis. During that conference, Kyung-Hwan met Senior

Commissioning Editor Madeleine Metcalfe and discussed with her his research ideas, as well as a course on real estate and financial cycles that he had developed at the Singapore Management University during his sabbatical leave from Sogang University. She asked if he would be interested in doing a book for the Wiley-Blackwell Series in Real Estate. We responded by submitting a joint proposal, expecting that the partnership of three economists with complementary research interests and significantly different policy experiences should produce a better book than any one of us could do individually.

The global financial crisis (GFC) of 2007–2008, and the associated Great Recession of 2009, have drastically changed the views of macroeconomists about the central place of housing in the dynamics of advanced economies. For us, the GFC provided another impetus to our interest in the comparative dynamics of housing in East Asia during this new crisis, a decade after the 1997 Asia Financial Crisis. This time, again, housing volatility in East Asia had been visibly different from Western economies, and that of the US in particular. In fact, seen from East Asia, the GFC was really a broad and deep Western financial crisis, triggered by the crash of the seemingly minor US housing subprime sector.

A growing flow of comparative research on the dynamic interactions between price volatility in real estate markets, and the stability of national economies and their financial systems in high income economies, has been coming from leading international institutions such as the Bank for International Settlements in Basel, the Organization for Economic Cooperation Development (OECD) in Paris, the International Monetary Fund in Washington and the European Central Bank in Frankfurt. Of particular interest to us was IMF research on the differences among housing cycles, credit cycles and business cycles, and the interactions between these three types of cycles in (mostly) Western economies. Associated with this research was the global debate on desirable responses to housing price volatility and appropriate macro-prudential policies. This new comparative research reinforced our view that the macroeconomic dimensions of housing volatility in East Asia is a much-needed complement to the academic research on microeconomic analyses of housing and the real estate sector. We also felt that a better understanding of the channels of interactions between housing and the macroeconomy, and the mechanisms of causation, would be necessary.

A critical milestone in the genesis of the book has been the joint policy research report led by Man for the Korea Development Institute on *Real Estate Real Estate Volatility and Economic Stability: An East Asian Perspective* (2013). Two important components of the present book took shape during the preparation of this KDI monograph. First, we adopted the conceptual framework needed to organize our thinking about the interactions between housing, the national economy and the global economy, in the six open economies of East Asia. This framework is graphically presented in Figure 7.9. Second, the quantitative findings on housing price behavior and price cycles across East Asia, compared with Western economies of the KDI report, have become Part III, on the drivers of East Asian housing cycles. We thank KDI for the financial support and permission to publish some parts of our research monograph in this book.

Markets are embedded in specific institutions. To explain the drivers behind the quantitative findings of our KDI research report, it was clear that detailed attention had to be given to both the institutional origins of each of these six housing systems and their respective housing price and output dynamics today. The context of our quantitative findings needed to be probed, because there is no unique, universal economic model applicable everywhere and at all times; the context should dictate the selection of the appropriate economic model (Rodrik, 2015).

Also, without an understanding of the origins of today's East Asian housing systems, how could we hope to address questions such as:

- Why is Taiwan the only East Asian economy to have experienced several market-driven housing cycles since the 1970s?
- Why are the distributive impacts resulting from the performance of housing systems of Singapore and Hong Kong almost diametrically opposite?
- What are the historical and institutional reasons behind why the Korean government is intervening so constantly in housing markets, even now?
- Why was Japan the only East Asian country to experience a very damaging multiple asset price bubble in the 1980s with its impact drawn out over decades?
- How are the institutional legacies of the pre-1978 central planning era shaping the present dynamics of China's housing?

Housing institutions are remarkably path-dependent over the long term in any country, and major breaks with past institutional arrangements are rare. The biggest breaks typically occur during the growth take-off decades when a modern housing system is emerging. Being an East Asian latecomer to economic development, China's massive privatization of housing in 1998–2003 stands out due to its magnitude and its far-reaching impacts. In fact, China's housing privatization should be acknowledged as one of the two major reforms that have changed the course of economic development in China. The other institutional reform of fundamental historical significance for China has been the implementation of the agricultural "household responsibility system" that occurred in the early 1980s, when China was still predominantly a rural economy and its level of urbanization was about 20%.

Identifying critical moments in the development of East Asian housing institutions has led us to re-evaluate research findings on East Asian urban development since World War II. Understanding the development of the six housing systems, and the mechanisms of causation between housing sector behavior and macroeconomic performance, has to bring together the findings of real estate studies, macroeconomic analyses, and of the political economy of development in these systems. Bertrand took the lead on this dimension of the project, as he was the most experienced with the institutional details in different countries.

One attractive benefit of the analytical organizing framework already adopted for our KDI policy research report is that this research review had to integrate widely spread academic research that was becoming both deeper and increasingly more focused over time. Space constraints have prevented detailed reporting of the quantitative and institutional evidence gathered. By necessity, the chapters presenting each country's analysis are more intuitive than quantitatively formal. As a partial remedy, the long list of references documents the extensive research that has been carried out. We hope that this information will be of value to readers who want to deepen their own understanding of individual country cases, and might also wish to expand further the present comparative analysis.

During the econometric analyses of Part III, we were concerned by the limits imposed on the comparative results by the fact that the first consumer-driven (as opposed to state-driven) housing cycle emerged fully in China only after 2003. We decided to turn this constraint into an opportunity, and to deepen our understanding of China's housing dynamics by analyzing the incentive and behavior of the six key players that drive China's housing price and output outcomes. These six are:

- the central bank that regulates interest rates and is controlling the emergence of the housing finance system;
- the central government, with its direct role in fiscal policies and in the regulation of housing and the real estate industry;
- local governments, which usually play a key role in the performance of local housing markets of most countries;
- households, with their rising incomes, changing expectations and degree of willingness to rely on housing finance credit;
- the incentives and ability of banks and other lenders to provide such housing credit;
- the national real estate industry with its pervasive oligopolistic behavior at the city level.

As a comparator for the Chinese six-factor analysis, we choose Korea, given our in-depth knowledge of its housing system. To minimize the length of the book, we also decided to combine the analysis for China and Korea with the institutional analysis already done for the other four countries, for which a similar analysis would certainly be doable.

Our comparative study could not have been carried out without the assistance of numerous friends and colleagues. Among many others, our sincere thanks go to Deniz Igan, Seko Miki, Son Jae-yong, Chang Jin-Oh, Chen Ming-Chi, Phang Sock-Yong, Lum Sau Kim, Deng Yongheng, Wu Jing and Liu Hongyu. Kye Sera provided research assistance on econometric analysis. We also thank Pieter Bottelier for his valuable comments on the China chapter. This list is embarrassingly incomplete, and we apologize to the numerous colleagues whose help should have been recognized. We are also grateful to KDI for allowing us to use some of the materials in our KDI monograph for our book.

We would like to thank Madeleine Metcalfe for inviting us to submit our book proposal and managing the entire project. We hold a special debt of gratitude to Harriet Konishi, formerly of Wiley-Blackwell, for encouraging us to persevere at a crucial time when we had misgivings about the wisdom of our project, given its expanding demands and mounting delays. We thank Viktoria Vida for monitoring the day-to-day progress of our manuscript. We also want to recognize the high degree of professionalism and commitment of Saravanan Purushothaman and Revathy Kaliyamoorthy of SPi Global, for their work on a critical stage of production of our book during weeks when their personal and professional lives were so deeply disrupted by the 100-year flood in Chennai, India, whose severity forced their relocation to the city of Pondicherry.

Last, but not least, in an era when the contributions of women to society can only grow and lead to greater fairness and prosperity in every way, we dedicate this book to our respective daughters, Hyun-Jeong Kim and Keunjoo Cho, and grand-daughter Ariana-Sua Adabi.

Part I

Foundations and Emergence of Modern East Asian Housing Systems

1

Introduction: Motivations of the Study

1.1   The first comparative study of housing dynamics across East Asian countries

The Global Financial Crisis (GFC) of 2007–2009 and its aftermath have demonstrated the large impact that housing volatility can have on the stability of the national economy in highly urbanized, high-income countries, where housing has become the most important class of real assets and is often larger than financial assets. This study explores the two-way interactions between housing and the macroeconomy in six East Asian economies: China, Hong Kong, Japan, South Korea, Singapore and Taiwan. The analysis focuses on the risks that real estate price and output volatility might create for the stability and performance of the national economy.

The study focuses on three main questions. First, how have the growth models followed by East Asian economies shaped the organization and dynamics of the housing sectors that we observe today? Second, has housing volatility in East Asian economies differed from Western experiences in recent decades? And, do sources of risks for the wider economy as well as transmissions channels differ in East Asia?

We draw upon leading current frameworks in development economics, real estate finance, real estate cycles and urban economics to understand the common features that these six economies share. We also identify the factors that make the performance of their housing systems different at times, including during the 1997 Asian Financial Crisis (AFC) and during the Global Financial Crisis (GFC) a decade later. To complement usual econometric analyses of housing cycle analyses, we shall also consider

Dynamics of Housing in East Asia, First Edition. Bertrand Renaud,
Kyung-Hwan Kim and Man Cho.
© 2016 John Wiley & Sons, Ltd. Published 2016 by John Wiley & Sons, Ltd.

how the structure of the incentives embedded in the institutions of these countries has been shaping the behavior of the six key players who actually drive housing and real estate cycles everywhere, usually in different ways in each case.

What distinguishes this study from previous studies of East Asian real estate is its genuinely comparative nature. Previous international books on national housing systems have presented country-specific information in collections of individual chapters, whose contents and quality are determined by the ability of the book's editors to recruit leading national experts to write them. These books do not provide readers with a common analytical framework that can deepen their understanding and increase their own analytical independence of judgment about the performance of the countries covered. Usually, the contributors are leading specialists in their own countries, yet the best use we can make of such work is to consult each country's chapter for its factual content, and for the individual authors' insights into the dynamics of their national housing markets, usually during the latest decade. Implicit analytical frameworks differ, and so does the internal organization of each case study. One ambition of the present study is to offer its readers the opportunity to develop their own views on the similarities and contrasts between the drivers of these six housing systems.

1.1.1   Why East Asia?

Since the GFC and the Great Recession of 2008–2009, international research and policy discussions have focused intensely on the Western countries that have been highly impacted by the GFC. However, East Asian housing systems are also worth studying on their own merits, because these economies have been among the most dynamic ones in the world for decades, and also they produce a major share of global housing output.

By now, East Asian housing systems represent about one third of the world's housing output. The East Asian share of global GDP (measured in PPP terms in the IMF's *World Outlook*) rose from 12.8% of world GDP in 1980, to 23.8% in 2010, and it was approaching 25% in 2015, as seen in Figure 1.1. In the absence of global estimates of the total value of housing, we can infer from national GDP data that the six East Asian housing systems make up at least 30% of global housing output – probably more. The reason why the East Asian share of global housing is considerably larger than their share of global GDP is because, in highly urbanized countries, the *values* of annual housing output and of total existing housing assets are much higher than in low-income and middle-income economies, where household incomes are lower by multiples and the housing sector remains a much smaller part of the economy.

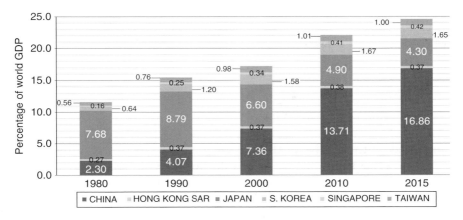

Figure 1.1 East Asian shares of world GDP, 1980–2015.

1.1.2 Why focus on housing and not on every type of real estate in the economy?

Real estate is the quintessential non-traded sector of an economy. Providing services to local business and consumers, the sector's performance in terms of prices, levels of output and volatility is woven into the structure and performance of the overall economy. The real estate industry is composed of different residential and non-residential sectors, each with its own distinct cyclical behavior. We focus on housing because, together with financial assets, housing is one of the two largest asset classes in every high-income economy. Moreover, between these two major classes of assets, housing volatility has had by far the largest and longest lasting impact on macroeconomic stability in high-income economies, due to the leveraged nature of housing investment.

The focus on housing is also motivated by the GFC. During the three decades of the Great Moderation from the early 1980s to 2007, the variability of total output in the US economy fell by more than 50%, and inflation declined by two-thirds (Bernanke, 2004). During that period, many macroeconomists found it convenient to lump together all forms of asset price changes in highly aggregated conceptual models, whether these assets were financial assets, like stock market securities, or tangible assets, such as residential or non-residential real estate assets. The GFC and the Great Recession of 2008–2009 have drastically altered perceptions of the capacity of property markets to influence developments in the macroeconomy, in the banking system, and in labor markets.

The main types of non-residential real estate assets are: offices, retail, warehousing and industrial. Except for warehousing and industrial real estate, these are closely linked to local urban employment. Commercial real estate is the second largest RE asset class after housing, but it is considerably smaller. A rare estimation of the composition of US urban real estate assets in 1989 was that housing represented 79% of all real estate assets, offices 8.5%, retail 7%, and warehousing and industrial 5.5% (Hartzell *et al.*, 1994). In spite of the much greater role that land plays in the value of real estate assets in East Asia than in the US, there is no obvious reason why the composition of urban real estate assets in East Asia would differ greatly from the basic US mix of 80% residential and 15% non-residential offices and retail real estate assets, with 5% going to the rest of real estate.

The various types of real estate assets have different cyclical properties. The volatility of each type depends crucially on the interactions between the rationality of investors' expectations and the structural characteristics of each real estate type, which are asset durability, investment lags behind shifts in demand and supply, and demand elasticity. Typically, in the US, office cycles and multi-family housing cycles are more volatile, and have shorter peak-to-trough duration than the dominant detached housing sector. Is that also true in East Asia, given that multi-family housing units prevail in high-density EA cities? Should we expect the cyclical characteristics of housing and commercial RE to be behaving more similarly in East Asia than in Western countries? If the supply of housing in East Asia is inelastic for institutional and physical reasons, existing analytical models of real estate cycles lead us to expect more price volatility than in Western economies as a consequence (Wheaton, 1999).

1.2   Distinguishing features of East Asian economies

There is a genuine unity of analysis in focusing on East Asia. The six economies share three important characteristics that justify calling them East Asian (EA) economies, to differentiate them from Western economies or from South-East Asian and South Asian groupings. First, they have very high rural and national population densities, which are multiples of most Western economies.

Second, in spite of significant differences in local cultures, these societies share a deep Sinitic heritage, especially from Confucianism, that has had a lasting impact on the governance of their public and private institutions as well as on prevailing norms of public and private behavior. Vietnam is the only other East Asian society left out of the study, for lack of suitable information.

Third, during the second half of the 20th century, the governments of these societies have successfully pursued development strategies and implemented industrial policies that have resulted in the highest sustained economic growth rates in the world over several decades, together with the fastest rates of urbanization on record. In spite of its detached geographic location at the crossroad of South-East Asia, Singapore belongs to the group of East Asian economies, because of its dominant cultural heritage, institutions and economic performance.[1]

1.2.1   Impact of high East Asian population densities on economic growth and urbanization

The high population densities of East Asian economies have played a major role in their urbanization. Urbanization is central to economic development, in which it has three basic functions. First, the concentration of population allows an economy to carry out a greater variety of manufacturing and service activities, with more efficient economies of scale.

Second, transportation systems are more efficient within cities and metropolitan regions, compared to the high costs of transportation over longer distances in rural areas. In fact, the economic and spatial size of a city is usefully defined by the size of its internal labor market and the maximum feasible travel distance for the daily journey to work in that city.

Third, many cities play a strategic role in meeting the physical services and institutional requirements of international trade, and the important share of export-oriented industrialization has accentuated the concentration of population in major metropolitan areas during East Asian economic growth take-offs. The modern economic geography of trade developed by Krugman, Fujita, Venables and others has significantly deepened and refined our understanding of these three drivers of urban change (Duranton, 2009).

The evolution of the national population densities in China, Japan, Korea and Taiwan is graphically presented in Figure 1.1. These gross national densities under-represent their urban reality by very large margins. Both Japan and Korea are mountainous countries, where only about a fifth of the land is flat enough for agriculture or for cities with slopes of less than 15°. Similarly, the gross national density misrepresents the distribution of population in China. The "380-millimeter isohyet line" (or 15-inch isohyet) of annual rainfalls permitting agriculture is of major significance for understanding the geography and history of China. Only 43% of China's territory lies east and south of this isohyet line, but 90% of China's population was concentrated there in 2000. Excluding the city economies of Hong Kong and Singapore, Taiwan has the highest gross densities of the four EA economies, but it is somewhat less mountainous than Japan or Korea, and 45% of its land can be cultivated or used for cities. Figure 1.2 also shows how these

---

[1] The case of Singapore illustrates the general finding that civilizations and cultures, through the institutions that they foster, have a greater impact than geography in explaining a country's rate of economic development. See Rodrik *et al.*, 2002.

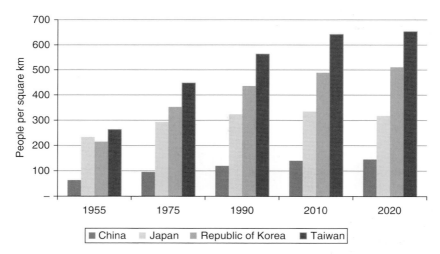

Figure 1.2   East Asia: high and rising gross population densities, 1950–2020.

high national population densities have risen further in every EA economy until 2010, but these densities are projected to stabilize by year 2020.

The most conspicuous trait of East Asian economies is very high *rural* population densities. EA rural densities have been multiples of the rural densities found in Western economies and other regions of the world. National statistics differ significantly across countries in their criteria of what constitutes a town or a city, but everywhere they define urban areas explicitly or implicitly by their density. In East Asia, concentrations of rural population reach high densities that would be called urban elsewhere. On the other hand, urban population densities in the (administratively defined) cities of East Asia are closer in magnitude to the urban densities found in Western cities. Yet East Asian urban densities remain higher which, among its variety of impacts, contributes to the higher relative cost of floor space, everything else being equal. The successful EA growth strategies that followed from the 1950s have built on these high rural densities and the economies of scale that they permit, even in the early stages of development of labor intensive industrialization.

In contrast with the consistently high EA densities, population densities vary greatly across Western countries. Figure 1.3 shows the level and increase over time of gross densities in six Western countries in 70 years. Among Western countries, only the Netherlands has gross densities comparable to those of Korea or Taiwan, but a favorable qualifier is that there are no mountains in the Netherlands, and that it is a very flat country. Somewhat similarly to East Asia, high and rising Dutch densities, and the need to maintain the system of polders in rural areas, have led to strong communal practices towards land in both rural and urban areas and public value recapture in urban

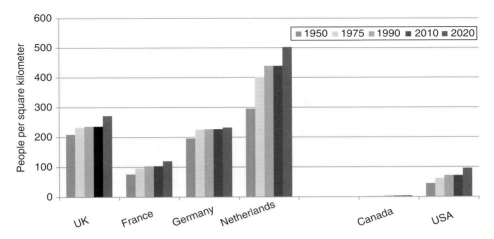

Figure 1.3   Gross population densities in six Western countries, 1950–2020.

development (Needham, 2007). At the other end of the Western spectrum, Canadian gross densities are so low that they do not even show in Figure 1.3. In 2010, the size of the total population of Canada, with 33.4 million people living on 9.09 million km^2, was of the same magnitude as that of the special municipality of Chongqing in Sichuan, China, with its 28.8 million people living on 82 000 km^2, which is 110 times less land.

Increases in urban densities have important impacts on housing, yet the economic consequences of high densities remains to be analyzed across countries, or even over time within one country. One pressing question is whether real housing prices follow a non-linear trajectory that becomes *steeper* as high population densities continue to rise. This issue faces every East Asian country, and several Western countries with high densities, such as the UK, the Netherlands and Germany. For the UK, Miles (2012) argues that the 'impact of further rises in *per capita* income and in population is non-linear and will be increasingly on price[2]." As levels of population densities, sizes of cities and household incomes keep rising, so also do concerns for the environmental sustainability of cities and the demand for green development. We cannot ignore that, between 1950 and 2010, the total population of the six EA countries increased 2.33 times from 665 million in 1950, to 1,553 million in 2010 (UN Population Division, 2012).

---

[2] Suggestive of the rising non-linearity of land prices in East Asia, Hyundai Corporation paid 10.55 trillion Won (US $10bn) for a 79 000 m^2 plot in the Gangnam district of Seoul. "Investor dismay over land purchase for HQ" *Financial Times*, p. 15, Friday 19, September 2014.

1.2.2 Significance of the Confucian cultural legacy for East Asian institutions and policies

From the 1950s to the 1980s, East Asian cultural and political legacies have shaped the emergence of national real estate systems through the balance between public and private property rights in land use, policies followed toward the development of the financial system and housing finance, and other economic and urban choices. The social and political thoughts and beliefs behind these choices become clearer by considering the impacts of the Sinitic cultural legacy on these societies, compared with Western and other societies.

East Asia, as a civilization, "*comprises countries which in the past have embraced the classical Chinese language and script as a principal medium for their high culture, and which in some significant degree have embraced both Mahayana Buddhism and neo-Confucianism. Four countries meet all these conditions: China, Korea, Japan and Vietnam. This, no more and no less is East Asia. [...] This high culture provided the cultural norms of the educational systems [...]. It is the network that provides common ground for the diverse ethnic groups of China, Japan, Korea, and Vietnam, and unites these extremely diverse individual cultures*" (Ramsey, 2013).

The ideals of the Confucian tradition have had deep and lasting impacts on both the public and the private spheres. Their influence remains present today, even after decades of very rapid economic development, so compressed in time.

Contrasting political and social traditions in East and West, a leading Western scholar points to, "*a specific and distinctive commitment to public service and humanistic scholarship in ways not typically associated with traditions deriving from Semitic religions. [...] For Confucians the applicable criterion was the greater good of the commonalty. [...] and since the model for the commonalty was the family, the essential criterion has been whether economic activity, including capitalist activity, served the long-term interests and values of the family or, by extension, the state as a whole*" (de Bary, 1988, p. 118).

Included in these values, views of the law in traditional East Asia have differed from those in the West.

Confucian legacies that have played an immediate role in the very rapid economic growth of East Asia are a very strong emphasis on education, life-long learning and personal diligence, which has resulted in a level of human capital that was considerably higher than would be predicted based on the level of *per capita* GDP alone. Respect of family, social hierarchies, and an emphasis on proper social interactions and group loyalty, have also meant a strong emphasis on the common good. Civil service systems have recruited the best students on merit through competition, which means that the civil service has enjoyed a high degree of prestige, and also that social mobility has been high, especially during the economic take-off. The Confucian concept of the "benevolent ruler" has also been used in support of authoritarian governments during the economic take-off. Long traditions of detailed record-keeping has meant that the quality of economic and social information has also been high, considering the *per capita* GDP level. Given these conditions favorable to development, the critical factor has become the choice of economic strategies and the quality of their implementation over time.

1.2.3 The "Developmental State" and its role in East Asian economic growth take-offs

A major impact of the Sinitic tradition in the economic sphere has been the emergence of the "developmental state", which gained strength first in Japan in the pre-World War II period, and then spread across the emerging East Asian economies during the post-war decades. One concise description is that, "*the secret of development in our world seems to lie in the combination of the rationality of the market in allocating scarce resources, and the strategic guidance of the state in charting the development course in a comprehensive way, while keeping the state's relative autonomy over the interests of specific groups*" (Castells *et al.*, 1990). The concept of the "developmental state" was first articulated by Johnson (1982) in his influential study of the political economy of Japan's industrialization between 1925 and 1975. Chalmers Johnson has summed up the main features of the developmental state across East Asia as follows:

"*My contention is that the Japanese, Koreans and Taiwanese have put together the political economy of capitalism in ways unprecedented in the West...[These are]: (1) financial control over the economy; (2) labor relations; (3) the degree of autonomy of the economic bureaucracy; (4) the degree to which the state has been captured by its main economic clients; (5) balance between incentive and command in economic guidance; (6) special private sector organizations... and (7) the role of foreign capital*" (Johnson, 1982).

Expanding upon Johnson's analyses, Wade (2004) found that the East Asian success in "governing the market" had three main outcomes: very high levels of productive investment, relatively more investment in certain key industries, and exposure of many industries to international competition. These outcomes resulted from economic policies, incentives, controls and risk-spreading mechanisms that came from a strong and proactive government.

Public interventions, which we shall revisit later from an urban and housing sector perspective, included:

- redistribution of agricultural land in the early post-WWII period;
- controlling the financial system and making financial capital subordinate to industrial capital;
- maintaining stability in the key economic parameters that affect long term investment – exchange rate, interest rate and the general price level;
- managing the impact of foreign competition and prioritizing the use of scarce foreign exchange;
- promoting exports;
- promoting technology acquisition;
- providing assistance to specific industries.

The developmental state achieved different production and investment outcomes from that which would have resulted under free market policies. Critically, such public actions would not have been possible without a specific organization of the state *and* of the private sector during the economic take-off. East Asian success combined a strong public administration and a strong private sector, in contrast with other developing countries that either have had a weak state or a weak private sector, or both (Lindblom, 1977; Riggs, 1964).

1.3   Organization of the book

To better understand the interactions between housing and the wider economy in East Asia, the study goes deeper than econometric studies comparing housing cycles, financial cycles and business cycles, which take the underlying institutions shaping these cycles as given and focus on measurable and testable quantitative outcomes (Igan *et al.*, 2011). We proceed in three complementary ways.

First, we look back at the emergence of modern mass housing markets across East Asia during the growth take-off period, to learn how these decades have laid the foundations of current EA housing markets, because understanding the origins of these housing systems throws considerable light on how they work today.

Then, within the constraints imposed by data limitations across countries, we use established econometric techniques for the study of cycles to investigate the secular and cyclical components of East Asian housing prices, as well as their volatility in comparison with Western housing systems.

Finally, to investigate the specific source and channels of interactions between housing and the macroeconomy, a third level of analysis investigates the distinct behavioral incentives of the six key players that shape housing cycles in different ways in different economies. These six players are the central bank, the central government, local governments, households, banks, and developers. The interactions over time between these six players determine the risks of a boom-bust cycle. These interactions are best understood at the country level and we focus on China given the widespread interest in the implications for the wider economy of a housing downturn in this new market system. We also focus on S. Korea as a comparator to China in terms of extremely rapid development, except for scale.

1.3.1   *Part I: Foundations and emergence of modern East Asian housing systems*

Part I shows how the foundations of present EA housing systems were laid during the decades of fastest industrialization and urbanization of these countries, known as the "economic growth take-off stage", and then proceeds to analyses of the individual dynamics of present housing systems in Japan, Taiwan, Hong and Singapore. Part I shows the validity of the observation that "knowing how something originated often is the best clue to how it works" (Deacon, 1997).

The comparison of the emergence of organized mass housing systems in other East Asia several decades ago, during their growth take-offs, throws considerable light on the recent emergence of a new housing system during China's own growth take-off stage, which has just come to an end. Clearly, this "growth take-off stage" holds a central place in Part I – but what is it? Development economics finds it significant to distinguish two main stages in the long-term economic growth and development of a country (Rodrik, 2005). First, there is a rather rapid growth take-off stage, until the economy reaches a *per capita* GDP of around $10000 PPP dollars (Brülhart and Sbergami, 2009; Eichengreen *et al.*, 2013).

The second stage of development is marked by a shift in growth regimes to a slower, sustained long-term growth, during which a country reaches a high income level and becomes fully urbanized. Between these two stages lies a critical "growth transition", often called by development economists the "middle-income trap", because it is economically and politically a risky transition that many countries have failed to manage successfully. China is currently going through this uncertain and risky growth transition. The other five EA economies did not fall into their own middle-income traps, and they are now advanced economies. The ratio of their urban population is between 80% and 100%, which also means that their housing assets now constitute the largest class of assets in the economy, above financial assets.

The impact of economic growth regimes on the organization of housing systems in East Asia has been very significant throughout the development of these housing systems. Chapter 2 presents the urban and housing dimensions of the development policies that drove urban growth take-offs that were exceptionally rapid and powerful across East Asia. Chapter 3 then discusses the transition of traditional East Asian vernacular housing system into modern mass housing urban systems, driven by the spatial transition from a historical "Von Thünen urban dynamics" to the modern "Krugman urban dynamics" of industrialization and the growth take-off. Far from leading to identical housing systems, the differences in the growth strategies adopted by individual East Asian governments at the start of the growth take-off resulted in four very distinct types of housing strategies, whose effects are still being felt today. One benefit of looking back at the emergence of modern housing systems across East Asia in Part II is to show that, far from being unique to China today, the peak rates of urban concentration that characterize the earlier EA growth take-offs also led to skyrocketing land and housing prices which, in turn, induced strong and lasting public policy responses, especially in Japan and South Korea.

When discussing the transition from pre-industrial vernacular housing to the organized urban mass housing markets of today, Part I highlights characteristics of EA housing systems that differentiate them from western housing systems in four areas:

- the regulation of land use and urban planning;
- financial sector policies and housing finance;
- housing taxation and subsidies; and
- the direct provision of public housing.

1.3.2   *Part II: Current East Asian housing systems*

Five of the six East Asian economies are today high-income, advanced societies with large, deep and internally differentiated housing systems. Only China remains a middle-income, only partially urban economy that expects a considerable increase in its urban population over two decades. Chapter 4 first provides a regional overview of the six housing systems. It then compares and contrasts the impact of the 1997 Asia Financial Crisis, and then that of the Global Financial Crisis a decade later. The severity of the impacts of these crises, two decades apart, was clearly different for the six EA housing systems taken as a group. These impacts differed significantly between countries, as well as during each crisis. Three country groupings emerge for both crises. Korea, Hong Kong and Singapore were the most impacted each time, in terms of housing prices and GDP, but the AFC resulted in bigger downturns in housing prices than during the GFC. China and Taiwan were essentially unaffected. The behavior of Japan's housing and other real estate stands apart, because the two crises occurred when Japanese housing markets were still in decline in the prolonged aftermath of the burst of Japan's multiple asset price bubbles in 1990. Remarkably, Taiwan is the only EA country to come out virtually unaffected by either crisis.

To understand better how each country reacted differently to the two crises, Chapter 5 analyses the institutional structure and contrasts the behavior and dynamics of the Japanese and the Taiwanese housing systems, where the capital region in Taiwan and the six largest cities in Japan behave differently and are more volatile than the rest of the national system in these two countries. Chapter 6 then compares and contrasts the city-states of Hong Kong and Singapore.

The case studies of China and Korea are postponed until Part IV, to avoid covering these two housing systems in detail twice. The rationale for this decision is to complement the quantitative analyses of the drivers of East Asian housing cycles that is carried out in Part III, based on mainstream econometric analysis of cycles, with a less common approach to investigating drivers of cycles in the remaining two cases of China and Korea from an institutional perspective. This less common approach focuses on the incentives and behavior of the six key players already mentioned that are actively shaping any housing cycle.

We expect this complementary approach to be especially useful for our understanding of China's new housing system, where housing prices data are limited in time and space, because the Chinese housing system has changed fundamentally with the housing privatizations of 1998. This far-reaching historical reform has transformed the dynamics, not only of housing, but of the entire Chinese economy. It also led to the great housing boom of 1998–2012. Given its very rapid transformation and the structure of its housing system, Korea is a useful conceptual comparator for China. Another reason is our better access to, and familiarity with, the needed information about the behavior of these six players in Korea over a much longer period of five decades.

1.3.3   *Part III: Drivers of East Asian housing cycles: evidence and analysis*

Using established econometric techniques for the study of cycles, Part III investigates quantitatively the trend and cyclical component of East Asian housing prices, as well as their volatility in comparison with selected Western housing systems, at the national level, in capital cities and selected other large cities (which, taken together, will also be described as "primate" cities).

Due to data constraints that are only too frequent, the analysis focuses on price movements and does not cover housing output volatility. Even then, housing prices are not measured in a consistent manner across countries. Moreover, the periods of time for which consistent housing price index series (HPI) exist vary from country to country. These time series can even differ in length from city to city. Part III is, therefore, divided into two complementary parts.

Chapter 7 describes the quantitative evidence available on the six EA housing systems, and makes basic comparisons with the cyclical behavior and volatility of selected major Western housing systems. First, it provides an overview of the magnitudes of the housing price cycles that were observed across East Asia over four decades, and presents basic comparative statistics of the difference in the volatility of housing prices across East Asian capital cities during the decades of the 1990s and 2000s. The chapter discusses the limitations of recent statistical methods of defining an asset price cycle, its peak, trough and duration. It uses a heuristic approach to identify 11 cycles in housing prices across major EA cities. It also compares these cycles with selected Western countries and cities, and shows that, while EA cycles are of similar amplitude to Western cycles, they tend to be of shorter duration.

Based on national statistics, house prices have been relatively stable for the EA countries during the last decade of the global housing boom, compared with those of the US and European countries, which have often been significantly volatile. This finding is confirmed by comparing price movements along their long-term trends for the capital cities of EA countries with selected US cities (Los Angeles, Las Vegas, and Washington DC) using the Hodrick-Prescott filtering method.

In a revealing comparative graphical analysis, Chapter 7 then examines the individuality of national housing cycles and the specific dynamics of housing prices in each East Asian capital. Using the same methodology and a uniform format of presentation, this section identifies separately for each market housing price boom-bust episodes and changes in housing prices for periods as long as the housing price indices (HPI) of each country allow. Particular attention is given to the impact of the 1997–98 AFC and the 2007–2009 GFC. The housing markets graphically analyzed are:

- Seoul for Korea;
- Taipei for Taiwan;
- Singapore;
- Hong Kong;
- Tokyo for Japan;
- Beijing for China.

The final section of Chapter 7 examines the institutions and regulations that shaped the cycles presented in the previous section. It discusses the channels of interactions between housing and the wider economy in the open economies that characterize East Asia today. It also identifies the six key players in their housing cycles, that are investigated in Part IV for China and for Korea. Given the major role of housing finance in cycles, we compare the key features of EA mortgage markets and discuss features of these mortgage markets that tend to increase price volatility. Chapter 7 also discusses the wide range of government interventions in East Asian housing, and examines the relationship between the extent of real estate regulations and the supply price elasticity of housing, and their impact on price volatility.

Chapter 8 complements the graphical evidence presented in Chapter 7, with econometric analyses of the drivers of EA price cycles. First, it reviews the shared conceptual foundations of housing cycle models. The next section quantifies the role of market fundamentals in EA price cycles. It compares unconditional measures of housing price volatility between East Asia and 15 Western countries, and also at the city level with US cities. Housing price models are estimated to investigate the quantitative impact of three variables representing market fundamentals: GDP as a proxy of household incomes, the user cost of capital in housing investment, and the ratio of residential investment. In the case of Korea, for which appropriate data are available, it is also possible to estimate the respective impacts of each of these three variables on the ratio of housing prices to rents in the Seoul Capital Regions and the rest of the country.

The third and final section of Chapter 8 is devoted to the analysis of two-way interactions between housing and the macroeconomy. It tests the Granger causality in each East Asian country between four macroeconomic variables: housing prices, GDP as proxy for income, the volume of credit and the level of long-term interest rates through Granger tests. Chapter 8 also tests for co-integration between these same variables, and compares the results for East Asia with those from a prior analysis for 16 OECD countries, to test the significance of housing in these economies. It also examines whether the dynamics of the housing sector and that of the macroeconomy significantly track each other.

1.3.4   Part IV: The six actors of housing cycles in China and in Korea

The third level of analysis of East Asian cycles investigates the distinct behavioral incentives of the six key players in housing cycles, and how their interactions may increase the risks of a boom-bust cycle. These six players are:

- the central banks, with their varying degree of monetary policy independence in setting monetary policies and interest rates in particular;
- the central governments, with their politically determined priorities in fiscal and also monetary policies;

- local governments, which play a major direct role in the regulation and performance of housing markets;
- households, with their savings behavior and critically important housing market expectations;
- banks and other housing lenders that collect household savings and fund investment in housing and related assets;
- real estate developers, who provide the new supply of housing.

This focus on the actors of cycles mitigates data limitations, helps to identify major sources of instability, and reveals factors behind the quantitative measurement of changes in the level of risk.

In contrast with the earlier supply-demand framework, the analysis of national housing cycles focusing on the six key actors of housing cycles leads to country-specific analyses. The two countries chosen are China and Korea, for almost opposite reasons. In the case of China, the focus on the six players in housing cycles can help overcome data gaps and housing price index quality issues. These were encountered earlier in the cyclical analyses that included only two megacities of the coastal region of China – Beijing and Shanghai – when the rapidly growing urban system of China is of continental scale and currently includes more than 660 cities. Here, the six actors are defined as operating nationwide and impacting these cities in different degrees. Korea is used as a comparator country, where we have full access to national data of known quality.

Studying China through the behavior of these six actors is especially needed because of the implicit assumption of standard quantitative cycle analyses, namely that the housing institutions of all the countries analyzed are fully market-based, stable and broadly comparable. This is not yet the case in China. The post-1998 structure of the new Chinese housing markets still reflect four important legacies from the administrative command system of the pre-1978 Maoist era, whose impacts on the dynamics of housing and of the entire urban system are now part of Chinese public policy debates. The duality of Chinese labor markets and urban migration patterns is shaped by the discriminatory *hukou* registration system.

The constitutional amendments of 1988, redefining property rights, have created an abrupt discontinuity between rural and urban property rights, which is deeply affecting urban land use, and housing in particular. Another lasting legacy of the central planning era is that local governments have a monopoly over land use, and typically continue to intervene in every land use decision, whether public or private. Another large distortion in local housing and other urban activities results from the very imbalanced allocation of mandated expenditures and revenue sources in the 1994 intergovernmental fiscal reforms of 1994, which has driven local government into increasingly speculative activities and capital mis-allocation. The resulting hypothesis is that the transmission channels of shocks between housing and the macroeconomy may be different in China from the channels in the five other East Asian economies; and even more so from those encountered in advanced Western market economies, as recently analyzed by Muellbauer (2012).

A benefit from studying China in greater depth is to gain a clearer picture of the Chinese housing system at its critical growth transition between the just-completed economic take-off stage and the targeted, but still uncertain, move to a different path of sustained long-term growth. The focus on the key actors of cycles should facilitate our understanding of the channels of interactions between housing and the macroeconomy, which are very different in China from the usual channels of housing market systems. What can we learn about the likelihood in China of a very costly Western-style twin housing and banking crisis, like the Global Financial Crisis of 2007–2009? The degree of stability of the Chinese housing and real estate sector has become a global concern, now that China is growing into the largest economy in the world.

In the case of Korea, Chapter 10 first reviews housing stability in terms of both construction and price cycles, including three episodes of rapid price changes. Then we highlight key housing issues in a new era of deep socio-economic changes in South Korea. Having set this context, Chapter 10 then proceeds to the analysis of the six key players of cycles. It shows how the behavior of some of these players has changed significantly from earlier decades, and is bringing housing to a crossroads in terms of an adequate match between a rapidly shifting housing demand, with rapid population aging and a rising income inequality.

1.3.5   Part V: Conclusions

The concluding Chapter, 11, offers two perspectives. First, looking back, it sums up the lasting differences in the structure of EA housing markets, through their institutions and regulations that continue to shape East Asian housing cycles and make them distinct from Western cycles. It also reviews how different the dynamics of China's housing markets might be from the five other East Asian systems, based on the insights gained.

Looking forward, a significant part of the concluding chapter outlines five new structural challenges facing all six East Asian housing markets:

- The impact of rapid population aging on the composition and price dynamics of the housing stock.
- The worsening income and wealth inequality.

- Rising household debt levels; slower GDP growth rates.
- And climate change, with its differentiated impact on green growth management across high-income EA cities, where urban population growth and urban population decline will occur simultaneously in different parts of the national urban system.

How deep will the impact on housing of this new environment be, with so many unknowns never previously experienced anywhere in the world?

2

Growth Take-Offs and Emerging EA Housing Systems

Organized, modern housing systems emerged during the growth take-off decades of East Asian economies. Institutionally, the growth take-off period is the time when the basic legal and regulatory frameworks, as well as the information systems of the real estate sector, develop. This is the period when large, organized urban markets and a new real estate industry emerges under the compounded impacts of fast urban population growth and rapidly rising urban incomes, especially in the largest metropolitan regions, which are the engines of industrialization, international trade and national development across East Asia. As Andrew Sheng notes in his study of the lessons of the 1997 Asian Financial Crisis and of the Global Financial Crisis a decade later, "… Markets are social institutions that are self-organized and path dependent. No one designed the market economy, but one of the principal participants is the government, as owner, regulator, and protector (in some cases predator) of property rights. This path dependency is why we need to look at history" (Sheng, 2009).

Chapter 2 proceeds as follows: first, it compares the exceptional East Asian growth experience with the rest of global experience. It contrasts the high economic growth rates during the take-off stage with the slower growth rates during the second stage of sustained growth, during which East Asian economies were becoming fully urbanized and reached high income levels. Having set East Asian growth in the global development context, this chapter then examines the characteristics of East Asian growth from a specific urban and spatial perspective. Until recently, this perspective, which is central to understanding of the dynamics of housing, had been absent from the analyses of East Asian growth by international economists.

Dynamics of Housing in East Asia, First Edition. Bertrand Renaud,
Kyung-Hwan Kim and Man Cho.
© 2016 John Wiley & Sons, Ltd. Published 2016 by John Wiley & Sons, Ltd.

Three specific aspects of East Asian urbanization deserve special attention. First, owing to their very high growth rates, East Asia economies have also had the highest tempos of urbanization on record. The tempo of urbanization is a measure that has long been used by demographers to characterize the speed of population concentration in cities, which has multiple impacts on housing. Second, these high rates of economic growth and high tempos of urbanization were accompanied by exceptionally large land price increases during the growth take-offs across East Asia. In that respect, the experience of latecomer China, with very high rates of land prices during its great housing boom of 1998–2012, was not significantly different from other East Asian experiences three or four decades earlier. Thirdly, similarities in the foundations of East Asian development have affected how large-scale, organized real estate markets emerged. However, these six housing systems differ among themselves as much as they do from Western housing systems.

2.1   East Asia and the global experience with growth and development

2.1.1   *Exceptional performance of East Asian economies since World War II*

International research now shows that one should distinguish two main stages in the long-term growth and development of a country (Rodrik, 2005). First there is the ability to initiate economic growth and reach a middle-income status. This growth take-off stage might be intuitively characterized as "catch-up" industrialization, with advanced economies. Second, there is the ability to sustain growth over the long run and reach the status of a high-income, deep economy. In between lies a political and economically difficult "growth transition", when the economic policies that had been successful during the take-off stage have to be replaced by new policies that are better suited for the long-term growth of a much larger and diversified economy. This growth transition is also politically treacherous, because the public and private interests that benefitted during the growth take-off decades often object to necessary policy and institutional changes that are less favorable to them. This is why this important transition has become popularly known as the "middle-income trap" (Gill and Kharas, 2007; Eichengreen *et al.*, 2013).

The growth take-off stage is particularly important for housing and real estate systems, because a major dimension of that development stage is an endogenously high rate of urban growth and large-scale urban concentration, as the modern economic geography of trade, led by Krugman, has now clarified. The expanding two-way interactions between housing and the macroeconomy led to powerful structural changes and the transition from small-scale vernacular housing, with its long historical roots in East Asia, to large, organized, urban mass housing systems that drive the housing cycles that we seek to understand better.

Following the destruction of World War II, reconstruction and development became a priority around the world. The ideological confrontations of the Cold War added momentum to this new concept of economic development, and proved to have a direct impact on the choice of housing system. Quite a number of developing countries were able to initiate rapid growth. Strikingly, however, none outside East Asia were able to sustain this growth to reach the status of advanced economies.

In a two-year study, the Commission on Growth and Development (2008) found that only 13 out of more than 150 countries of all sizes have experienced sustained high growth, which the Commission defined as 7% real GDP growth per year for more for 25 years or longer. All six East Asian economies are part of this small elite group of 13 development take-off successes.[1] After an initial stage of successful growth, most of these countries then got caught in "the middle-income trap". A slow and unstable growth followed their initial period of very rapid growth. Today, this is precisely the concern regarding China's ability to implement successfully the political and economic reforms necessary to extend the remarkable growth take-off during the period 1980–2010 into a new stage of sustained long-term growth.

2.1.2   The changing context of East Asian growth 1950–2010

Before proceeding to analyses of the housing sector, a brief economic history of the region will sharpen our understanding of the changing context of East Asian growth over time. For East Asia, the post-World War II period, between the 1950s and the 1980s, saw the economic take-off of the four economic dragons of South Korea, Taiwan, Hong Kong and Singapore[2]. The Japanese economy was already quite advanced. Yet Japan also experienced very much higher rates of growth during the decades of the 1960s and 1970s than it ever experienced during the pre-WWII decades. It is also during that period that Japan completed its urbanization and then experienced the massive, multiple asset price bubble of the 1980s that is analyzed in Chapter 5. The growth strategies that these five EA economies pursued led to extremely high rates of income growth and a powerful speed of urbanization that generated considerable construction employment, caused massive stress on cities and durably shaped their real estate institutions.

---

[1] These 13 economies are: Botswana; Brazil; the People's Republic of China; the Hong Kong SAR; Indonesia; Japan; the Republic of Korea; Malaysia; Malta; Oman; Singapore; Taiwan; and Thailand. This study is also known as the Spence Report after its director, Nobel laureate Michael Spence.
[2] For concise, yet insightful, analyses of the political economy of the take-offs in these four economies, see Vogel (1993).

The international context was quite different from today where the globalized financial system is such a large factor in the stability of emerging economies (Rey, 2014). Initially, the post-WWII global trading system was fragmented by high trade barriers and was dominated by the USA, which accounted for over 27% of world GDP and 38% of world trade in 1950, with 55% of all trades made in US dollars. The security umbrella and political support from the US, as well as access to its markets and those of Europe, played a critical direct and indirect role in East Asian take-offs.

In contrast, the socialist centrally planned economies (CPE) were playing a very limited role in the global economy, as they mostly engaged in a small volume of state trade among themselves. Their small global trade footprint contrasted greatly with their population size, which was more than a third of the world's total population in 1991 when the Soviet system collapsed. The geography of trade resulted in very different urban and housing systems in centrally planned socialist economies, including China until 1978 and North Korea until now.

Across market East Asia, one effect of manufacturing exports as a major engine of growth was to stimulate the rapid growth of export-oriented cities. The emergence of organized real estate markets during that first period was heavily influenced by government interventions, so that the housing and real estate fluctuations in prices and output that occurred during that first period differ from more familiar market-led western cycles. East Asian housing volatility during that period was often affected by direct government interventions.

East Asian take-off policies gave a low priority to housing, except in Hong Kong and Singapore, where housing was an integral component of building the city infrastructure which, for these city economies, also means that of the entire economy. Housing was also seen as a critical element of labor welfare and social stability in these two small, totally open economies. In contrast, Japanese and Korean policies aimed to divert resources away from households, in favor of investments in manufacturing and the related national infrastructure. As will be detailed in Chapter 5, only Taiwan had neutral policies toward housing.

Meanwhile, in centrally planned Maoist China, prevailing low housing standards deteriorated further between 1949 and 1979 under a series of internal political crises and misconceived economic policies. In contrast to the take-off years in the five other East Asian economies between 1950 and 1980, closed Communist China, which stood on the other side of the Cold War, went through now well-documented catastrophic economic policies, such as the Great Leap Forward. Political and economic conditions reached a nadir during the 1966–1976 decade of the Cultural Revolution (Liu and Wu, 1986; Vogel, 2011). During that decade, the level of urbanization actually fell in China, as shown by the negative tempo of urbanization during that decade (see Figure 2.2).

The second development period, in the 1990s, was quite different from the take-off decades between 1950 and 1980 for the national real estate systems of East Asian economies. The five EA market economies had, by now, transitioned successfully from middle-income to high income fully-urbanized economies. Their now very large housing systems had become a major element of their national economic performance.

Externally, the structure of the world economy began changing profoundly in the 1980s. The first global real estate cycle in commercial real estate, led by Japan, occurred between 1985 and 1994, a full decade ahead of the global housing boom of 1996–2007 in the run-up to the GFC (Renaud, 1997). Housing and real estate fluctuations, which had been closely regulated by government interventions, became more similar to Western real estate cycles. During this second period, financial systems and real estate markets became increasingly deregulated, especially in the aftermath of the 1997 Asia Crisis (Renaud, 2003). Meanwhile, China was finally experiencing its own growth take-off.

Connecting these two periods, the 1980s were a decade of major discontinuities across East Asia on several fronts. This decade marks the start of the Deng Xiaoping reforms and China's reentry into the global economy, with major impacts on industrial supply chains and trade patterns within East Asia and across the world. Globally, financial liberalization, which had started in the early 1980s in the US and the UK, gained worldwide momentum, especially after the mid-1990s. The 1980s also saw the rapid globalization of trade in goods and services, supported by the IT revolution, the sharp fall of the transportation cost of goods (thanks to containerization and new shipping technologies), the deregulation of airlines and the decline in travel costs, as well as new trade agreements led by the World Trade Organization.

The internal collapse of the Soviet system during the late 1980s ended four tense decades of existential confrontation with the West, with isolated Stalinist North Korea remaining among the last holdouts. Socially, the 1980s were also the time when the Confucian cultural heritage slowly began to be seen by new urban middle-class generations with different eyes, which led to gradual changes in household behavior, with important demographic, social and political implications for housing (Ho, 2012).

Global trade flows were now growing at rates twice as high as world GDP. The accelerating globalization of trade and finance enlarged existing channels of global contagion and also created new ones, such as trade flows along the new international supply chains. These expanded, or entirely new, channels contributed in major ways to the Asia Financial Crisis of 1997, and then to the Global Financial Crisis, which started in 2007 but is not yet fully resolved by structurally better and more stable financial systems. It is now widely understood that high global growth rates prior to the GFC had been fed by huge increases in leverage and unsustainable household spending in Western economies (Mian and Sufi, 2014). The long-term outlook for the global economy and for East Asia has now changed significantly, as will be outlined in the concluding Chapter 11.

2.1.3 Similarly high growth rates across East Asia, but diverse income growth paths

Due to different initial conditions, there is more than one East Asian growth story. Using national data in constant 2000 US dollars, Figure 2.1 shows that the six EA economies fall into four groups, in terms of income growth paths as they were catching up with the US income level and, in some cases, overtook it.

During the period 1960–2010, Japan's *per capita* income caught up with that of the US by the late 1970s, and did better than the US after 1980, but drifted during the "lost decades" following the burst of the Japanese real estate and banking bubble in 1991. Hong Kong and Singapore, being city states unburdened by low-income rural hinterlands, have caught up with US incomes. Hong Kong did it first, benefiting from an initial industrial base that Singapore did not have, and also a more efficient investment pattern (Young, 1992). South Korea and Taiwan, which had *per capita* incomes lower

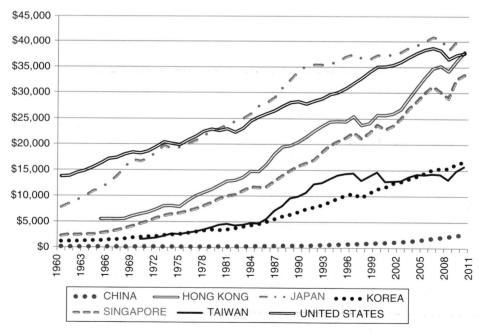

Figure 2.1 East Asia: rapid GDP *per capita* growth 1960–2011, but diverse paths (in constant 2000 US$).

or barely equal to those of African countries in the 1960s, became advanced economies enjoying sustained economic growth.

Finally, drawing upon the lessons of other East Asian countries, China experienced its economic take-off during the two decades of 1990–2010. Its domestic growth now has spillover effects across the global economy, which explains the global interest in the performance of the Chinese real estate sector[3]. China's high GDP growth rates during the period 1990–2010 have been described as a "miracle", but they are similar to those of Japan, then Singapore, Hong Kong and, finally, Taiwan and South Korea during their respective economic take-offs. What truly differentiates China from the rest of East Asia is its scale.

During the decades 1950–1980, Japan led in relying on the "developmental state" to achieve very high rates of economic growth. Long before World War II, Japan had become a world power. Devastated by World War II, Japan's level of urbanization fell sharply from 37.9% in 1940 to 27.8% in 1945. By 1953, Japanese aggregate output had regained its peak pre-war income level, yet Japan was still a mixture of developing and developed country features, with about 40% of its labor force still employed in agriculture. Then, Japanese growth rates became far higher than they ever were during the pre-war period[4]. During the period 1951–1973, the Japanese economy grew at an average annual rate of 10% in real terms. *"In a span of only five years, from 1965 to 1970, Japan actually doubled its industrial capital stock"* (Denison and Chung, 1976). In 1970, Japan's urbanization level of 72.2% had become comparable to those of high income Western economies.

2.2　East Asian growth policies from an urbanization and housing perspective

During the 1990s, economists widely debated the causes of rapid growth of the East Asian economies and the role that public policies played, especially regarding government interventions in industrialization (Chang, 2007). However, one consistently omitted dimension in these debates was the role of urbanization. In his Nobel Lecture, Paul Krugman comments that *"as late as 1990 international economists took virtually no notice of trade within countries, or of the location of production in space"* (Krugman, 2008).

---

[3] By 2010, China had become "the first or second trading partner of 78 countries with 55% of global GDP, versus just 13 countries with 15% of Global GDP in 2000" (IMF, 2011b).

[4] Multiple factors contributed to Japan's post-war recovery: successful domestic reconstruction with unanticipated American support; the "peace dividend" of a new constitution that prohibited rearmament and freed resources for productive investments; the early stages of implantation of its industrialization strategy at home; the resumption of international trade during the post-war recovery of the global economy under the Bretton Woods international system; and the trade windfalls of the 1950–53 Korean War.

By now, there is finally a convergence and greater consistency of interpretations of the EA growth take-offs, and an explicit recognition of the spatial impact of East Asian growth policies on the foundations of the housing and real estate systems that were emerging.

Initial conditions have had a significant role in the take-offs of Taiwan, South Korea, Hong Kong and Singapore. These societies had a better level of education than other countries, with much higher *per capita* incomes in terms of school enrolment and literacy rates, and virtually universal primary school enrollment for both men and women. Taiwan and South Korea also scored much better than countries with several times their *per capita* income in one of the first studies to use a broadly based index of socio-economic development across developing countries in the late 1950s and early 1960s (Adelman and Morris, 1967)[5].

2.2.1   East Asian policies successfully captured the benefits of the demographic transition

Two demographic factors have contributed to the steep East Asian growth take-offs compared to the rest of the world. First, capturing the growth *potential* of the demographic transition was conditional upon the implementation of appropriate development of economic and social policies. Second, there was a significant element of endogeneity between a rapid demographic transition, accelerating economic growth, and high rates of urban concentration.

At the time when East Asian growth take-offs were occurring, Western academic economists considered the contribution of population dynamics to economic growth as minor. Such views were not shared by Asian policy makers, who implemented policies that specifically targeted demographic conditions. Supporting East Asian views and policies, empirical research carried out after the 1990s has now yielded the diametrically opposite finding, that demographic transitions and the changing age structure have been major contributors to the East Asian growth take-offs, and that, "compared to the rest of the world, East Asia was the largest beneficiary of the population dynamics coming from the demographic transition"[6].

---

[5] This pioneering study includes a large number of social and institutional indicators, such as: the degree of labor market dualism; the level of urbanization; the scope of the middle class; social mobility; literacy; means of mass communications; cultural homogeneity; sense of national unity; and modernization outlook. Both Korea and Taiwan ranked in the most advanced group of developing countries, in spite of the fact that their *per capita* GNP in 1961 US dollars was $73 for South Korea and $145 for Taiwan.

[6] There is now a large literature on the interactions between population dynamics and economic growth. References on East Asia are: Ito and Rose (2010); Mason and Kinugasa (2008); Bloom and Williamson (1997); and Mason (2001).

East Asian government policy responses to rising population growth rates were systemic and effective. These policies changed the composition of urban housing demand over time. All East Asian countries, including Hong Kong, introduced *voluntary* family planning programs integrated with their public health systems: Japan in 1948, Taiwan in 1959, South Korea in 1962, and Singapore in 1966, just one year after independence. In 1980, the Chinese government announced and promoted nationwide its compulsory one-child-per-couple policy, which remained strictly enforced for 25 years in urban China. The timing and form of China's *mandatory* one-child policy, as well as its long-terms impacts, have now become quite controversial, and it was finally loosened in 2014.

Between 1960 and 1970, East Asian countries began to experience a sustained and sharp decline in their dependency ratios, resulting from a rapid fertility decline. The age structure turned increasingly favorable to faster growth, and the "demographic dividend" of a very favorable ratio of young active workers to individuals under 15 or over 60 fuelled rapid economic growth *per capita*. The demographic dividend sometimes had echo effects. Japan experienced its first peak in 1970, which coincided with its peak years of economic growth; then an echo effect peaked in 1990. Unfortunately, this relative second peak reinforced the great Japanese bubbles of the 1980s. In South Korea, the demographic dividend peaked during the 2000s, as it did in Taiwan. In Hong Kong, a sharp secondary peak occurred in 2010, due to migration interactions with the mainland. Singapore experienced local peaks in 1990 and 2010 (Mason and Kinugasa, 2008). In China, a sharp single peak occurred in 2010 and, by 2012, China recorded a fall in its working population for the first time.

An endogenous factor that furthered rapid economic growth is that improving dependency ratios and rising private investment in education worked together. EA families with fewer children and increasing household savings rates soon pursued strong private investment in education and human capital through intra-family transfers. This endogenous dimension of the demographic transition is seen as a secondary demographic dividend (Mason and Kinugasa, 2008).

2.2.2 Multiple benefits of land reforms for the development of the real estate sector

Fundamental land reforms, comparable to those that had occurred in Japan seven decades earlier, also played a central role in the higher degree of income and wealth equality in East Asia, compared to other developing countries. These successful land reforms also provided the legal, regulatory and institutional foundations of land administration systems that covered the entire national territory. East Asia did not experience the large, even systemic, problems of informal land occupancy and unclear land property rights encountered in most countries of Latin America, the Middle East, South Asia and Africa. The benefits of these land administration systems for the efficiency of urbanization were large and direct – they raised the speed of small and large, public as well as private investments. Much of these widely distributed rural land assets were converted into urban assets when real land prices rose much faster than real GDP, as the tempo of urbanization and urban concentration increased. China is the East Asian outlier, due to the ideological legacies on property rights left over from the Maoist era.

Japanese land and tax reforms were the first in Asia. They took place in 1871 and 1873 during the Meiji era, when Japan adopted the Prussian model of government, with its civil law legal system. Included in this Prussian model was also the most advanced form of municipal government in Europe at the time, with lasting consequences for housing and the real estate legal and regulatory system of cities. The Prussian civil law system was transferred later by Japan to its colonies of Taiwan (Formosa) and Korea.

Major benefits of these reforms for the real estate sector were the clarification of property rights and titles, the implementation of land registration, and land valuation systems. Reforms covered the entire national territory and permitted effective national and urban land use policies, as well as infrastructure policies. Operational land registries, valuation and brokerage laws also improved the efficiency and speed of a multiplicity of real estate transactions. Elsewhere in the developing world, clear and secure access to land remains a major cause of delays in infrastructure and investment projects, as is the case in India (Garg, 2007).

In South Korea, the modern foundations of today's land use system were laid by the Constitution of 1948 and the Farm Land Reform Law of 1949–1950, which established the principles of equity and a maximum farm land ownership of three *Jeongbo* (almost 3 hectares). Land reforms transformed South Korea from a nation of 19% landowners and 81% tenants in 1938, to 93% farm owners and 7% tenants in 1965. Other laws were also passed in parallel to create a comprehensive national land management system covering non-farm land and cities (Ban *et al.*, 1982). The rural-urban land conversion price dynamics during urbanization then played a major role in wealth allocation.

Similarly, Taiwan implemented its successful land reforms between 1949 and 1953, which drastically improved the distribution of incomes and made agricultural innovations easier and faster. Politically, this reform was presented as the implementation of Sun Yat-Sen's Three Principles of the People and was seen as a way to increase the legitimacy of the Kuomintang government. Technically, the work was led by the Sino-American Joint Commission on Rural Reconstruction.

The impact of the Taiwanese reform on the distribution of land parallels that of South Korea. In 1948, there were 56% owners and 44% tenants; by

1960, there were 86% owners and only 14% tenants. The maximum agricultural land holding was the same as in Korea, with three *chia*. Building on
this foundation, Taiwan's rural industrialization policies and macroeconomic policies led to the emergence of a strong and resilient SME sector, in
contrast with Japan and South Korea where the SME sector remains a weaker
industrial link even today – and now in China, as well (Koo, 1968). As a
result of its structural reforms and macroeconomic policy choices, Taiwan
was the only East Asian economy to experience an *improving* income
distribution during its economic take-off (Ho, 1978; Fei *et al.*, 1979).

In Hong Kong and Singapore, conditions at the start of the take-off were
very different from the other East Asian economies, given that neither
had a large hinterland of rural population. After the initial shock of being
completely cut off from their hinterland, these two city states faced
limited in-flows of immigrants. Government policies had to deal mostly
with the existing population and its natural growth. In both cases, the
government had systemic control of land use. In Hong Kong, government
has owned most of the land since the origin of the colony in 1841[7]. The
Hong Kong land market operates under a system of leases, initially
auctioned off by the government with land use regulatory conditions
attached (Bristow, 1987). In Singapore, state land ownership has increased
over time through the Land Acquisition Law of 1966, from 50% in 1965
to well over 75% of the territory today. Issues of income inequality and
social protections were addressed early through public housing programs,
and both cities might be described as "urban systems based on public
housing" (Castells *et al.*, 1990).

During the same decade, land reforms in China went in the opposite direction from market East Asia, and China abolished land markets through the
collectivization of agricultural land and the nationalization of urban land,
with the promulgation of the Land Reform Law in June, 1950. Meanwhile,
in North Korea, *"the nascent regime operated under the complete control
of the Soviet supervisors. The Soviet advisers drafted the land reform law
and Stalin himself edited the draft of the 1948 North Korean Constitution"*
(Lankov, 2013). North Korean cities, including the capital city of Pyongyang,
which had been leveled during the 1950–53 Korean War, were rebuilt under
Soviet physical urban planning principles during the 1960s and early 1970s,
when Kim Il-Sung was ruling. In retrospect, this was the best period of
economic growth in the entire DPRK history, as reflected in the DPRK
tempo of urbanization (see Figure 2.2).

---

[7] The Hong Kong land leasing system developed stepwise. Britain seized Victoria Island with
the 1842 Treaty of Nanking , which ended the First Opium War. At the end of the Second
Opium War, in 1860, Britain gained a perpetual lease over the Kowloon peninsula. In 1898, after
another armed conflict with China, Britain gained a 99-year lease over the "New Territories".
It is this 99-year lease that triggered the return of all of Hong Kong to China in 1997, under the
status of Special Administrative Region (SAR).

Except for a limited stock adjustment of urban population after 1978, the spatial structure of Chinese cities remained practically frozen until two critical amendments (influenced by Hong Kong's leasehold system), made in 1988 to the 1982 Constitution, restored the possibility of trading land use rights within Chinese cities. At that time, China's level of urbanization was still low, at 25%, and the rapid urban concentration of the take-off era was only starting. Unfortunately, these constitutional amendments have maintained the damaging duality in property rights between the collective ownership of rural land and the state ownership of urban land, with the state having the exclusive right to sell tradable land use right leases to various owners, including private developers. According to the Constitution, collective rural land can only be converted into tradable urban leases after having been acquired by the state which, in practice, means mostly provincial and local governments (Lin and Liu, 2007). The serious negative consequences of this duality for Chinese rural residents are discussed n chapter 9.

The absence of tradable land use rights is a fundamental obstacle to spatially efficient urbanization anywhere. However, the spatial structure of Chinese cities, as reflected in their land density gradients did not suffer too much for two serendipitous, yet negative reasons (Bertaud and Renaud, 1997). First, when the Communist land reforms occurred, China was still a rural economy, with a very low level of urbanization (well under 15%), and rather similar to Russia's urban level at the time of the 1917 revolution (see Figure 2.3). Second, a sequence of ill-conceived policies ensured that there would be very little investment in Chinese cities during three decades, and that urban population growth would remain low.

During the first decade of the PRC, planned industrial investments occurred westward, away from the traditional industrial centers of the coastal provinces. Policies and administrative incentives promoted spatial autarchy, and encouraged municipalities to be self-sufficient and to produce everything. Migration to cities was rigidly controlled, via the *hukou* registration system. The peculiar, and eventually tragic, policies of the Great Leap Forward (1958–60) triggered a massive famine that caused well over 36 million deaths (Yang, 2010; Dikötter, 2010). Later, during the 1966–1976 Cultural Revolution, the growth of cities ground to a halt and urbanization went into reverse. China's tempo of urbanization fell steadily after 1960, and even became negative during the decade of the Cultural Revolution.

2.2.3 *Coordination of spatial infrastructure plans with national growth strategies*

A central feature of East Asian industrialization strategies is that they combined conservative macroeconomic management with extensive and effective microeconomic interventions (such as credit allocation, public enterprises, administrative guidance, trade restrictions, and foreign exchange subsidies) to address market coordination failures at the early stages of industrialization. Using a trade and economic geography interpretation, these industrialization policies made it possible for private firms to realize the benefits of increasing returns to scale, and to benefit also from urban concentration with its knowledge spillovers, labor market pooling and specialized suppliers. Such a domestic industrial coordination strategy, directed by the financial and economic ministries, became popularly known within Japan as the "wild geese flying pattern."[8]

In addition to raising the returns to urban concentration, what was important for land use and every type of real estate development in Japan, South Korea, Singapore and Taiwan is that coordinated private industrial investments were complemented by formal national ten-year spatial development plans for the provision of national infrastructure and city-level trunk infrastructure investments. As a result, public infrastructure investments usually *anticipated* private industrial investments. In that respect, East Asian growth contrasts with India, where national and city level public infrastructure investments still lag considerably behind private investments, and are of very uneven quality across states and cities (Garg, 2007). Alone in East Asia during the three decades 1949–79, China was a severely mismanaged economy, spatially fragmented under ill-conceived autarchic Maoist policies.

Within large Japanese, South Korean and Taiwanese cities, local urban infrastructure was often financed through the recapture of rapid land price appreciation, using the technique of urban "land readjustment", which was first developed in Japan in an adaptation of a Prussian rural land consolidation technique, then transferred to South Korea and Taiwan during their colonial eras (Doebele, 1982). In Japan, during the peak period of high economic growth, the contribution of land readjustment projects increased from 22% of total national urban land development in 1972 to 40% in 1979 (Hebbert and Nakai, 1998).

The benefits of coordinating infrastructure investments with industrial investments have been a significant factor in East Asia's rapid take-off. Research shows that during a growth take-off, there is a desirable balance between public and private investments if a country is to achieve the highest productivity gains and returns to private investments. Peak returns appear to be reached when the aggregate ratio between private investments and public investments is about 60 : 40 during the take-off (Isham and Kaufmann, 1995).

---

[8] The "flying geese" model of industrialization, where a leading national industry, supported by government policies, pulls forward other related industries, is discussed in Akamatsu (1961). This image of a "flying geese development pattern" was later used quite differently by the Japanese media in discussions of the Asia-wide impact of large Japanese foreign direct investments (FDI), especially after the acceleration of overseas Japanese investments, triggered by the currency realignment of the 1985 Plaza Accord between the US, Japan, and the other G-7 economies.

The efficiency and public good benefits of investments can be significantly distorted, at the expense of both consumers and small and medium enterprises (SME)s, when excessive investments are actually done by state-owned enterprises (SOE) having access to preferential capital at subsidized rates for sustained periods of time. Relative over-investment occurred during the take-off of Singapore between 1965 and 1985. Young (1992) found that, during its take-off, Singapore invested significantly more than Hong Kong to achieve the same level of GDP growth. In Singapore, most of national savings were allocated by the government, which led to overinvestment by SOEs, in particular in housing by the Housing Development Board, and also in infrastructure (Lim and associates, 1988).

A problem of overinvestment in urban infrastructure and housing, comparable to that of Singapore in the early 1980s, has been occurring in China under the investment-led growth model that has dominated the take-off decades between 1990 and 2010. After boosting short-term growth numbers, these investments can lead to deadweight losses when new infrastructure facilities are not used to any significant degree within a reasonable period of time after their completion. Spatially, under the "Go West" policy after 1999, some types of investments across provinces, and also by sector, that aimed to speed up urbanization in Western provinces, became excessive, especially in infrastructure and real estate. The implicit losses can initially be masked by over-borrowing, which is reflected in a continuing rise in credit as implicit losses are rolled-over, as happened especially after 2009. This overinvestment problem has been less serious in the Chinese coastal provinces (Lee *et al.*, 2012).

2.2.4   Manufacturing exports favored employment concentration in large cities

The standard discussions of rapid growth in East Asia during the take-off speak of their "export-led growth". There is no doubt that the share of exports in GDP rose very rapidly, from about 10% of GDP in the early 1960s to about 30% of GDP in the mid-1970s for South Korea, and rose even higher in the smaller, more open Taiwan economy. However, Dani Rodrik has argued convincingly that such an explanation of rapid growth is, "*incomplete and quite misleading [...] It also has backward the causal relationships between exports, on the one hand, and investment and growth on the other*" (Rodrik, 1994, 1996).

The earnings from exports played a critical role in financing domestic investments, especially when domestic savings were initially quite low and US foreign aid was reaching its limits in Korea and Taiwan. Integrating the non-spatial Rodrik trade arguments with Krugman's geography of trade, one can see that exports played a critical role in funding the investments that permitted East Asian economies to capture fully the increasing return to scale of industrialization, together with those of rapid urbanization. Across East Asia, the export of manufactured goods to the most advanced economies also played a major role over time in bringing East Asian industrialization and *domestic* supply chains up to international standards, and accelerated the rate of domestic innovation and labor productivity (Westphal *et al.*, 1981; Rodrik, 1994).

2.3 East Asia has had the highest tempos of urbanization in the world

An aggregate measure of the speed of urban concentration, long used by demographers, is the "tempo of urbanization", which is the difference between the rate of growth of the urban population of a country and that of its rural population during a given time period (UN Population Division, 1974). A high tempo of urbanization means a high rate of urban concentration and, therefore, strong pressures on cities and the emerging national real estate system. East Asia has experienced very high tempos of urbanization, and South Korea reached some of the fastest tempos on record of 7.23 in 1965–70 and then again in 8.49 in 1985–90. China's highest tempo of urbanization was 5.59 in 2000–05 (Figure 2.2).

In addition to revealing major demographic transitions, the tempo of urbanization can also reflect major socio-economic disruptions in a country,

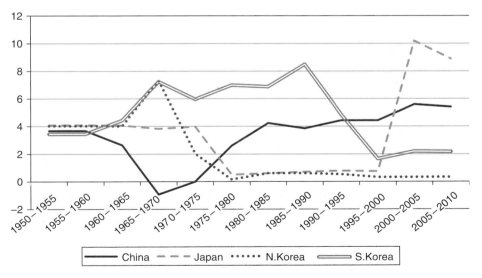

Figure 2.2 Tempos of urbanization 1950–2010 in China, Japan, North Korea, South Korea. *Source*: UN Population Division, World Urbanization Prospects 2011, Revision 2012.

as seen in Figure 2.2. In the case of China, the economic and political disruptions of the Maoist era are readily apparent in the sharp decline in the tempo of urbanization during the 1960s and 1970s, later followed by accelerating urban concentration after successful market reforms. In North Korea, the urban boom during the short modernizing period under the Kim Il-Sung rule was followed by the sharp decline of urbanization under the DPRK's extreme form of central planning in a closed economy, even before the collapse of the North Korean economy in the early 1990s.

Until now, prevailing economic and demographic modes of thinking have been based on a perpetual growth paradigm, but East Asia is changing. Japan's seemingly aberrant tempo of urbanization after 2000 is a forerunner of South Korea's and Taiwan's own rapid population aging. Japan's high rate of urban concentration ended around 1980, once it had become fully urbanized. The sharp spike in Japan's urbanization tempo during the period 2000–05 in Figure 2.2, with the extraordinarily high value of 10.78%, is an entirely new statistical pattern that reflects the fact that Japan has been the most rapidly aging country in the world until now. During the five-year period 2000–05, Japan's rural population shrank at the very high rate of –8.41% per year, while its urban sector grew at the slow rate of 1.78%. This was projected to fall further, to 0.65%, by 2015. Japan's national population has been falling since 2005. The implication is that Japan's housing sector is facing a very different future of low expectations. China, South Korea, and Taiwan are now following Japan's experience.

2.4   The 50% urban population marker signaled the arrival of the growth transition

China officially crossed its 50% level of population urbanization in 2011[9]. How does that moment compare with the experiences of other East Asia countries and Western countries? This 50% marker is not a mere demographic curiosity. On the contrary, this indicator signals multiple socio-economic changes in EA countries, which have a direct impact on the performance of the housing system. During the East Asian take-offs, urbanization has been led by labor-intensive, export-oriented industrialization, which has concentrated in

---

[9] In China, the social segregation created by the *hukou* registration system causes distortions of all kinds, including statistical ones. In the 2010 census, China's total population was 1,334 million, its urban population was 664 million, and the urban population ratio was 49.7%. Subtracting the "floating population" of 220 million of rural migrants denied an urban *hukou*, the urbanization ratio shrinks to an unrealistic ratio of 33.2%. This "floating population" lives in cities and has made major contributions to China's low-cost industrialization. The *hukou* system allows local governments to report misleading housing statistics and to minimize their social obligations toward workers, who are thereby denied major long-term benefits from their contributions to industrialization.

new and rapidly growing cities. This is most vividly illustrated in China by the new city of Shenzhen. It is during the take-off stage that the manufacturing core of modern East Asian economies has emerged. The 50% marker coincides with historical peaks in EA shares of manufacturing employment in the national labor force. This was also the case for the USA in 1920.

2.4.1   End of the dualistic economy and impact of Lewis turning point on East Asian cities

The highest tempos of urbanization and peak rates of urban concentration led to the rapid crossing of the 50% level of urbanization which, in East Asia, marked the transition to a different form of economic growth and urbanization. During that period, labor markets reached their Lewis turning point, and rising real wages fed an expanding housing demand and higher housing prices. Manufacturing production switched to higher value-added goods. The service sector expanded not only because of the growth of consumer demand from an expanding urban population with rising incomes. More importantly, with the transition away from labor-intensive manufacturing, to higher value-added manufacturing, the service sector also expanded, as new manufacturing goods included a rising share of *industrial services inputs* (Stanbach and Noyelle, 1983).

W. Arthur Lewis (1954) was the first economist to analyze the growth implications of the dualistic structure of developing economies, which is characterized by two distinct sectors – a dominant low-productivity agricultural sector with excess labor, and a small, higher-productivity manufacturing sector located in cities. The higher-productivity sector is profitable in part because of the surplus of labor that it can employ very cheaply, because of the low wages prevalent in the agricultural sector. The profitability of the modern sector promotes higher capital formation, which drives overall economic growth.

As the number of surplus workers shrinks, wages in the labor-intensive manufacturing sector begin to rise, profits begin to be squeezed, and investments in labor-intensive manufacturing begin to decline. At that point, the economy is said to be crossing its Lewis turning point. Jorgenson (1961) modeled this process of rural-urban labor transfer during the early stages of industrialization. Due to the differences between rural and urban productivity, Jorgenson's analysis concludes that the level of urbanization should basically follow a logistic curve. The Lewis turning point would coincide with the inflexion point in this urbanization curve and would be located at or around the 50% level of urbanization, depending on the specific pattern of productivity differentials between agriculture and manufacturing.

Once a country approaches, and then passes, its Lewis turning point, the interactions between housing and the macro-economy become stronger, through the expanding urban labor market channel. Rapidly rising housing prices puts pressures on urban wages, whose rise, in turn, weakens exports. In this manner, the non-traded housing sector now can have a direct impact on the performance of exports. When the Lewis turning point was reached in Taiwan and Korea, around the 50% urban population marker, wages began to rise rapidly, but rural-urban migration continued, as different industries, producing higher value-added goods, were developing. The pressures of rising incomes and a rapidly expanding urban population, together with expectations that such trends would continue, had a powerful impact on expectations for the rate of increase of land and housing prices. The situation had been similar in Japan during the 1960s and 1970s decades of very high growth, which fed the costly "myth of ever rising land prices".

A comparable pattern of rising wages and rapid inflation of land and housing assets has been occurring in China, and passed the 50% urban marker in 2011. In China, the effects of the Lewis turning point are accentuated by demographic aging and the declining share of the working population, which also means the end of the demographic dividend (Das and N'diaye, 2013).

2.4.2   The share of EA manufacturing employment peaked near the 50% urban marker

An important feature of the 50% urbanization inflexion point is that the highest shares of *manufacturing* employment in total employment and of manufacturing output in GDP occur toward the end of the take-off stage. During that transition, the economy also reaches its highest level of spatial concentration of manufacturing, as a new industrial core emerges. Beyond that point, as already outlined, manufacturing starts to diversify away from the production of labor intense goods, to higher value-added products, and to decentralize spatially across the urban system. Higher value-added goods include a higher share of industrial services inputs, which should not be lumped together analytically with consumer services. These consumer services are also expanding with rising urban population and incomes. This spatial and industrial transformation occurred in East Asian countries when they were crossing the 50% level of urbanization and were also experiencing their peak tempos of urbanization.

This industrialization and urbanization was also the case for the USA in the 1920s, when the country became more than 50% urban (Krugman, 2008; Kim, 1998). In Korea, the share of manufacturing employment peaked in 1975, as the urbanization curve was passing through its inflexion point. Japan had crossed its 50% urbanization marker around 1953, and its peak share of manufacturing employment occurred a few years later (Mills and Ohta, 1976). In China, these manufacturing and spatial transitions, with their powerful impact on housing and the entire the real estate sector, are currently occurring.

2.4.3   Transition to the second stage of sustained long-term development

The historical sequence of growth take-offs and peak rates of urbanization in Japan, Taiwan, South Korea and then in China is presented in Figure 2.3. China's crossing of the 50% marker has happened several decades after the other EA economies. As a latecomer to growth, China was able to draw from earlier East Asian experiences. Figure 2.3 reports only Japan's *second* crossing of the 50% marker. Japan had already reached this marker once, before WWII, but, the costs and devastations of the war drove Japan's economy backward, and its urban population had fallen to 35% in 1944. Japanese urbanization crossed the 50% marker after WWII for the second time in the 1950s. Afterwards, the extremely rapid growth of Japan's economy during its second stage of development caused much exaggerated US fears of "Japan as number one", challenging the supremacy of the US economy by 1980 (Vogel, 1978).

During the second stage of sustained long-term development, the urbanization level climbed well beyond the 50% level to 70% and higher, as the core-periphery structural dichotomy of the economy diminishes steadily. This process has been described as *"urban polarization reversal"* (Harry Richardson). Spatially, the second stage of sustainable growth differs from the urban concentration during the take-off, as it involves a spatial decentralization of manufacturing across the urban system, as occurred in the USA after the 1930s (Kim, 1998). Small-scale sectoral clusters in industry and services become pervasive across successful cities (Duranton, 2008).

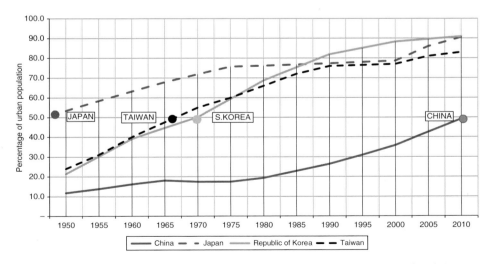

Figure 2.3   Growth take-off and 50% level of urbanization: Japan, Taiwan, South Korea, China, 1950–2010.
Sources: UN Population Division (2012), ROK MLTI ministry 2013, National Statistical Bureau, Taiwan.

During the second development stage, housing assets continue to accumulate and to become the largest asset class in the economy. This is why housing cycles begin to play a leading role in the stability of the economy.

To succeed, the transition to sustainable growth requires a mix of new governance and new policies, in order to manage the much larger, more diversified and spatially decentralized urban growth. A deepening of the institutions of the markets (Williamson, 1985) also requires very different political and administrative arrangements. To maintain growth and to avoid being caught in the middle-income trap, countries must also develop more flexible participatory political systems, responsive to the increasingly diverse range of values and preferences of a deep, post-industrial urban middle-class. These are very different from those of the traditional rural population of the early years of the take-off.

In parallel to the expansion of the real estate sector, the role of local governments in the national economy become larger and larger as urbanization progresses. Local government maintenance operations, and investments needed to manage urban assets, usually range between 20–30% of GNP in advanced OECD countries[10]. China's development sequence has been different from the rest of East Asia, due to the institutional legacies of the Maoist era, and Chinese local governments have been playing a central role, even during the take-off stage, as shown in the case study of China's take-off in Chapter 9.

2.5 Exceptionally powerful land price increases during East Asian growth take-offs

2.5.1 *Structural factors behind high rates of land price appreciation*

Across East Asia, the impact of the growth take-off on land prices was spectacular. The combination of high tempos of urbanization and the concentration of population in large, export-oriented metropolitan centers, together with rapidly rising incomes, led to exceptionally powerful land price increases during the growth take-off stage. Similar rates of land price inflation did not occur again beyond the growth transition during the second stage of long-term growth, even in Japan during its massive bubble in the 1980s.

Scarce land supply was made even more inelastic by restrictive land use conversion policies aiming to protect farm land in Japan, in South Korea, and now in China. In addition, in Japan, tax policies, strongly biased in favor

---

[10] The economic scale of land and property assets under the control of governments is often underestimated by a wide margin. However, some OECD countries have been developing national policy frameworks and instruments to support a better management of these assets. See Kaganova and McKellar (2006).

of farm land, interacted with inheritance taxes to encourage a widespread hoarding of developable parcels within major cities, as landowners kept their plots into farm land status inside these cities. On the demand side, the triple impact of the demographic dividend, the rise in wages and household incomes, and rapid migration to cities, was creating a strong demand for a greater number of housing units of larger sizes.

Land values across East Asia have been much larger multiples of GDP than in the USA. Even if we recognize that the ratio of the value of a stock of assets to a GDP flow is dimensionally flawed, the result remains informative for comparisons across countries, and also over time for the same country. For instance, aggregate land value in relation to GDP was 1.85% in South Korea in 1975, compared to 0.77% for the US in 1970 (Ingram, 1982). Even if land rent had been the same proportion of GDP in East Asia and in Western countries, high growth rates, of the order of 10%, during the take-off decades would have insured that land values would be a much larger ratio of GDP than in a Western economy growing at 3%, given widespread expectations that such growth rates would persist[11].

2.5.2 *Individual EA country experiences with land price inflation*

Land values skyrocketed everywhere during the East Asian growth take-offs. Beyond explanations of these rising land values, what matters the most for housing policies of today are the lasting institutional changes and policies that were adopted in response to the public's reactions to deteriorating housing affordability and the wealth redistribution that was occurring. Similarities in land and housing price appreciation across EA take-offs are worth highlighting in a single place before the individual country chapters.

In Japan, there have been three peaks in land prices: in 1963, in 1973, and then in 1988, during the great real estate bubble. The inflation-adjusted annual rate of increase of land prices in major cities reached a peak of 42% in 1963, when Japan was 62% urban (Noguchi, 1994). The pattern of land price increases according to types of land use reflected the structural development path of the urban economy. This sequence of land price increases shifted over time.

First, *industrial land prices* rose faster than other types of land use during the great period of manufacturing expansion of the late 1950s and early 1960s, when Japan's industrial base expanded five-fold. Then, during the 1970s, Japan's urban system kept expanding steadily, and the rates of *residential land price* increases led other types of land use and peaked in 1973–74.

---

[11] The present value V of a stream of rents r when the growth rate is g and the discount rate is i converges to $V = r/i-g$. The discount rate will vary by country, but reflects the level of the global cost of capital, and will be higher than the national GDP growth rate.

This land price boom was broken by the first oil crisis, and land prices actually fell briefly. Then, *commercial land prices* rose fastest in 1986–87, due to the interactions between the mismanaged liberalization of the financial system, and structural flaws specific to Japan, associated with the unusual role of land in Japan's corporate sector. Japanese corporate investments in commercial real estate abroad triggered the first global real estate boom of 1985–1994 (Renaud, 1997).

Commercial land prices played the leading role in the rapid inflation of every type of land prices during the Japanese bubble of 1985–1991. The value of land in every type of land use peaked in 1990–91. Since that time, Japanese land prices have been falling continuously until 2013. The massive wealth losses associated with land price declines have been key contributors to Japan's two decades of low or negative GDP growth and low deflation.

Taiwan has the highest gross population density of East Asia, and land costs represent 50% or more of the total cost of housing. Given Taiwan's high GDP growth rates, the rise of land and housing prices has been high over time, but the behavior of land prices has differed significantly from Japan and South Korea because, since the early 1960s, Taiwan's central government has pursued more free market macroeconomic policies and conservative financial sector policies, and has intervened little in the housing market, compared to Japan, Korea, Hong Kong or Singapore.

As a result, Taiwan has experienced four genuine land and housing prices cycles since 1970, whose four peaks have been in 1972–74, 1979–1980, 1987–1989 and 2004–2010. These four Taiwanese cycles have had short and sharp price booms, followed by downturns of longer duration (Chang and Chen, 2011). During the downturns, housing prices have declined more significantly than land prices, which is unusual. The sharpest *rate* of increase occurred during the 1987–89 boom.

In South Korea, powerful land prices increases during the take-off decades triggered lasting institutional change. Korean urban land prices increased 14.3 times nationally, and 29 times in Seoul between 1974 and 1998. The highest annual rate of aggregate land prices, adjusted for inflation, occurred in 1978, and reached a 64% annual rate of increase in major cities. The difference between South Korea, Japan and Taiwan is that the land price index for South Korea kept rising. There was no significant downturn with actual price declines. The three periods of very high rates of land price increases were 1964–70, 1975–80 and 1987–90.

The very high tempo of Korean urbanization and the high rates of urban population concentration, mostly in the Seoul metropolitan region, were clearly a leading factor behind national land price increases. As noted, South Korea holds the fastest tempo of urbanization on record, with 8.2% for the period 1985–1990. Another factor was the significant level of inflation, which increased incentives to convert financial assets into real assets.

The real rate of return (ROR) on land and real estate assets, after adjusting for inflation, was high and volatile, but its volatility was no deterrent, since the annual ROR on real estate assets did not become negative. In addition to high rates of rural-urban migration, financial repression was the second major factor, as favored corporations in "priority" sectors used part of the low interest rate loans they received from the then state-controlled banking sector to invest in real estate.

The land price boom of 1975–1980 led to a first strong public policy response in 1978. The "August 8 Speculation Control Measures" included heavy income taxes on the transfer of land and other forms of real estate, and the adoption of a land transaction reporting system in 30 geographical areas deemed "speculation-prone". Strong public control over land develop-ment processes was also created through the establishment of the Land Development Corporation and the Building Development Facilitation Law. Adjustments have been made over time, but government control over land development processes is still in force today.

A second, and even more powerful, public outcry occurred during the third price boom of 1987–90, when South Korea was already significantly urban-ized, urban incomes were already high and democracy was expanding. The two leading public policy issues were high rates of land price appreciation and the rapid concentration of land ownership. A Land Study Committee was created in 1989, to evaluate the implications of implementing of the concept of *Gongkaenyum or "Concept of Public Land"*, given the direct conflicts that such a concept had with the affirmation of private property rights by the Constitution (Son, 1994).

The recommendations of the Land Committee that were implemented include: limits on residential landownership; charges on development gain charges; excess land profit taxes; the Aggregate Land Tax (ALT), whereby an integrated land recording system would consolidate all the real estate holdings of an individual across the entire country; a new system of land assessment; reinforced transaction regulations over those created in 1975–1980; and the compulsory registration of all land transactions with the government.

Today, South Korea still has an extensive system of micro-management of the housing system. Administrative changes by decrees occur frequently. To "regulate" real estate cycles, administrative decrees affect the various real estate taxes and bank lending conditions, as well as land use planning and construction by developers.

China's economic growth take-off has produced a land and housing price inflation experience comparable to that of the five other East Asian econo-mies, but several decades later. During the period 2003–2011, which was China's decade of most rapid urbanization, the average annual compound rate of real, constant quality land price growth exceeded 20% per annum in eleven major cities (Deng *et al.*, 2012). The structural reasons behind the wealth redistribution and inefficiency effects of urbanization in China are discussed in Chapter 9.

In Hong Kong, the auction of state land lease system has permitted the public to capture a significant share of the land price appreciation. Because Hong Kong has a dual housing system, where 35% of the population still lives in public housing, high and rapidly rising housing prices have been felt most acutely in the private housing markets, which experienced a bubble in the 1990s that burst in 1997. However, Hong Kong avoided the costly combination of a real estate bust and a banking crisis like that in Japan or the USA, Spain and Ireland during the 2007–09 GFC. Thanks to the quality of risk-based banking regulations and mortgage lending regulations, the Hong Kong banking system was adequately capitalized to absorb the impact of the housing price bubble. Due the role of Hong Kong as a major global financial center, and to the increasingly strong impact of China buyers, private housing prices continue to rise in the city. For macroprudential reasons, Hong Kong financial authorities have been intervening actively into the housing market since 1997.

In Singapore, state intervention in both land supply and housing has been systemic, and an explicit part of national development plans, since 1965. To understand the dynamics of housing prices in Singapore, it is essential to differentiate between the source of supply of housing and the patterns of ownership of housing. The supply of housing has long been dominated by a public development agency – the Housing Development Board. However, there is now a small, growing supply of relatively higher quality units built by private firms.

As of 2009, only 21.7% of the entire existing housing stock had been built by the private sector, and the public sector had built 78.3% of Singapore housing. However, because 95% of the HDB-built housing stock has been privatized over time, the structure of housing *tenure* is quite different and, now, 94% of Singaporean housing units are owner-occupied. In terms of housing price behavior, Singapore has a tiered housing structure, and housing prices in the privately-built, privately-owned housing segment are considerably higher and quite volatile. Different housing price indices track Singapore's segmented housing market structure, as shown in Chapter 6. As in Hong Kong, the volatility of housing prices had become a major macro-prudential concern in Singapore even before the Asia Financial Crisis of 1997.

3

From Vernacular Housing to Organized Housing Systems

3.1 Housing transformation from a Von Thünen to a Krugman urban dynamic

The vernacular housing of East Asia has had a long and proud tradition, going back for millennia in China, Korea and Japan. In history, East Asian cities have often been larger and more sophisticated than Middle Eastern and European cities of the same period. However, these East Asian cities and urban systems were slowly growing as they were driven by pre-industrial administrative and agricultural forces, and the overall level of urbanization remained very low. Demographic growth was also low under traditional high fertility and high mortality rates.

One way to characterize the East Asian urban transformation that occurred throughout the 20th Century, and so strongly after World War II, is that East Asian cities moved from a pre-industrial von Thünen urban dynamic of agricultural markets, with high transportation costs and limited economies of scale, to a new Krugman industrial urban geography, of rapidly declining transportation costs interacting with large economies of scale, which generated rapidly rising urban incomes, stimulated rural-urban population migration and favored an initial population concentration into core manufacturing regions (Von Thünen 1826; Skinner, 1964; Krugman, 2008).

The impact on housing of the transition from a von Thünen to a Krugman urban world is so strong as to be called fundamental. In the von Thünen world, East Asian vernacular housing had construction materials, designs and spatial characteristics that reflected the local physical environment as much as traditional social organizations, where the extended family was the rule.

Dynamics of Housing in East Asia, First Edition. Bertrand Renaud,
Kyung-Hwan Kim and Man Cho.
© 2016 John Wiley & Sons, Ltd. Published 2016 by John Wiley & Sons, Ltd.

Large, deliberately organized urban mass housing systems that reflect the new Krugman urban economic dynamics emerged during the urban growth take-offs. New types of housing, capable of dealing with high urban densities and very rapidly rising land prices, were now based on new financing mechanisms, changing building technology using new industrial materials as incomes were rising rapidly, and the state-led development of the infrastructure.

The new housing focused predominantly on nuclear families and was supplied by an organized real estate industry capable of managing the production of the high-density integrated housing estates that have become characteristic of East Asian cities. The impact of the new Krugman urban world, and the rapid growth of urban services past the growth transition, was equally powerful on every other form of real estate, particularly on commercial real estate (Glickman, 1979; Dietz and Cutler, 1971; Raftery, 1991; Willis, 1995).

One simple and powerful, if rather abstract, way to represent the transformation from a von Thünen to a Krugman urban world is the logistic curve of urban growth associated with the rural-industrial model of economic development. The logistic curve of the ratio of urban population to total population is a quantitative representation of Arthur Lewis's model of labor markets in a dual rural-urban economy. This logistic curve covers the entire range of the growth and development of a country. At the low end of the urbanization curve, where urban ratios are much less than 15%, we have the traditional von Thünen rural economies, where vernacular housing prevails. The transformation of urban housing accelerates with industrialization between that initial point and the 50% urban marker. Chapter 2 emphasized the growth take-off stage as the period of crucial transformation of East Asian housing systems on the left side of the urbanization curve. At that point, many of the lasting features of large, organized mass housing systems have fallen into place. Beyond that, 50% urban marker some structural reforms may still be needed, but further housing reforms will tend to be more incremental, usually in the direction of market liberalization.

China officially crossed the 50% urban marker in 2011. The question of whether the Chinese economy has now reached its Lewis Turning Point has been the subject of research and policy debates. In spite of the great regional diversity of Chinese labor markets, the consensus is that this turning point has been reached (Knight, 2007; Zhang *et al.*, 2010). The implications of more rapid wage increases are important for the expanding Chinese housing demand and for higher value-added manufacturing (see Chapter 9).

Comparative research has validated the logistic curve of urbanization as a representation of the transformation of housing over the entire course of economic development. Initially, at low levels of industrialization and urbanization, on the left side of the urbanization curve in Figure 3.1, the weight of the housing sector in the overall economy is limited, and the share

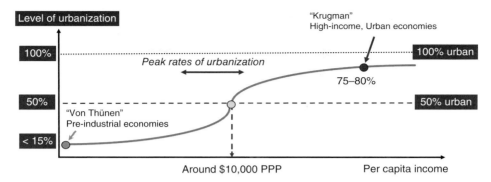

Figure 3.1 From a rural (von Thünen) to an industrial (Krugman) economy.
Source: Jorgenson (1961).

of new housing investment in GDP is low (of the order of 2–3%). During the growth take-off, this housing investment share of GDP rises to peaks around 8% at the 50% inflexion point, then declines again to around 3–4% at the upper end of the logistic curve, when urbanization has reach its saturation level in high income economies (Malpezzi, 1988).

In Singapore, which is known to have over-invested in housing prior to 1985, the share of housing investment in GDP peaked as high as 10%, and even slightly higher. The peak of the share of housing investment in GDP which occurs around the 50% urban makers was estimated to occur at US $8000, which is very similar to the latest findings on the location of the danger zone for the middle-income trap at around PPP $10,000 (Eichengreen *et al.*, 2013).

A conclusion deriving from the long-term urbanization curve is that housing systems are best compared at the same stage of development of the economy. Direct comparisons between China's overinvestment in housing, and the macroeconomic risks of the housing correction, which started in late 2013 with the Japanese bubble or the US subprime debacle, are inappropriate. On one side, we have China, a middle-income economy currently going through its peak rates of urbanization. On the other, we have the two high-income, fully-urbanized economies of Japan and the US, that made the major policy error of trying to sustain their national economic growth rate by boosting their now very large, but low productivity, real estate sector. Similar quantitative tools may be used for research on this housing over-investment, but the policy contexts are completely different.

A better comparison to make is between China today and Singapore in the years preceding the 1985 recession. Extreme differences in size aside, are there insights to gain for China from the major policy restructuring adopted by Singapore after 1985 to get back on its long-term economic growth path?

One impact of the housing transformation that occurred during the peak rates of urbanization during the growth take-off stage was the widespread demolition of obsolete vernacular housing sitting on high-value parcels of land. The zoning protection of the remnants of this vernacular housing did not occur until decades later. By now, the protection of vernacular housing is a top priority of high-income East Asian cities, where these areas are valued as major cultural assets, a core element of city identity, and also as an urban amenity that is increasingly important in the intercity competition for footloose high value-added services (Brueckner *et al.*, 1999).

3.2   Stylized facts of organized East Asian urban housing markets

In middle and high-income market economies, housing systems are driven by the household demand both for housing services and for housing as a major investment asset. In response to these two types of demand, there is now an organized production of services and new housing units provided by developers, builders, landlords and other homeowners selling the services from their housing assets. The inputs into the new production are land, finance, infrastructure, labor, and materials.

Household demand is driven mostly by incomes and demographic factors. International comparative research has shown that the structure of the demand for housing services is remarkably consistent and regular between developing countries and high-income countries. Housing demand elasticity is usually less than one. This leads to the interesting spatial pattern that, within a given city, the share of household expenditures declines for higher-income residents, but that across cities of different *per capita* incomes, the share of housing expenditures is higher in richer cities with a higher average income level (Malpezzi *et al.*, 1985). In other words, the level of housing consumption rises at least as fast, if not faster, than incomes across city markets.

A central element of housing demand is the tenure choice between owning and renting. A shared feature of East Asian housing policies during the growth take-off is their predominant policy emphasis on home ownership. It is only at relatively high income levels that explicit policies were developed for social rental housing. Coming from the centrally planned economy (CPE) end of the policy spectrum, China has a large legacy of social rental housing, even after the historical turning point of the housing privatization policies of 1998–2003.

Most of the largest distortions in housing systems are found on the supply side, except in socialist centrally planned economies like China, that interfered with the free demand for housing services by households and replaced it by bureaucratic criteria. What separates CPE housing from market housing is that CPE housing policies succeeded in creating important distortions on *both* the demand side and the supply side of their housing system. In spite of the privatization reforms of 1998, China's housing systems is still facing very important structural distortions, which are legacies of the Maoist era. In market housing, supply-side distortions can affect access to land, and to finance in particular. East Asian housing systems are no exception, and we therefore outline later in this chapter the impacts of land policies, financial policies, taxation and subsidies across East Asia, including the public supply of housing.

In emerging housing markets, typically there are three related sub-markets: the market for new housing units, the market for existing standard housing and the market for substandard housing. One shared characteristic of East Asian housing is that the informal housing markets that are such a large component of housing systems in other regions of the world never became as significant, even during the years of most rapid urbanization, when the price of housing was often rising faster than incomes. Even in South Korea, where the housing shortages left by the Korean War of 1950–53 were combined with the fastest rates of urbanization on record, the share of illegal or substandard housing, at its peak, represented about 4% of the country's population and about 8% of the urban population, with more than 70% in Seoul (Mills and Song, 1979). The organization of EA housing markets during the growth take-off was the cause of this positive outcome (see Chapter 2, Section 2).

The supply price elasticity of housing in a market city is a function of its land and non-land inputs (Phang *et al.*, 2012). In a given city, this elasticity depends on the relative shares of land and non-land inputs in total housing costs, the elasticity of substitution between land and non-land inputs (which is affected by planning rules on floor-area-ratios, technology and building economics), and also by the elasticity of land supply, as affected by rural-urban land use conversion regulations. We can make the following stylized observations about East Asian housing systems:

- The housing supply elasticity determines the level of house prices. Across East Asia, housing prices are high because:
  1. the supply price elasticity of housing tends to be low;
  2. the share of land in total unit cost is high overall and the highest in large cities; and
  3. the supply elasticity of land itself is low.
- Housing prices will be more volatile in response to a demand shock when housing supply elasticity is low. The impact of speculative behavior will be stronger and boom-bust cycles are more likely when supply is inelastic (Malpezzi and Wachter, 2002). We therefore expect East Asian price cycles to be rather volatile.

- During the recent housing bubble in the US, cities with inelastic supply had larger price run-ups and subsequent long, drawn-out crashes (Glaeser *et al.*, 2008). We expect similar differences across the urban systems of China, with about 665 administrative cities, Japan, with 160 cities, South Korea, with 55 cities and Taiwan, with 25 cities. Smaller, lower-tier cities are expected to have more elastic housing supplies than the very large top-tier cities.
- Land prices are usually more volatile than house prices during a cycle. Land prices are also pro-cyclical, so land price downturns are usually much more severe than housing price downturns. However, as we shall see in Chapter 5, Taiwanese land and housing prices appear to behave differently.
- A major land use inefficiency issue facing China is the absence of rural land market prices to establish fair and economically sound values of land. This issue does not exist in the five other EA economies where, apart from the impact of zoning rules, there is the usual continuity in the pricing of land across all forms of rural and urban land uses transitions, as observed in other market economies.

3.3   Four distinct East Asian housing strategies during the period 1950–1980

Shared initial conditions, and the pursuit of growth strategies based on rapid industrialization, did not lead to uniform East Asian housing strategies. In fact, housing development strategies have differed remarkably across East Asia during the decades following World War II. The housing sector received very different levels of priority in national economic strategies, and the supply of housing ended up being organized quite differently across the six economies. It would also be wrong to assume *ex-post* that East Asian housing policies were the products of full economic rationality, any more than they are in Western economies. These housing policies resulted from laws and regulations driven by prevailing political and social views at the time, around which frequent piecemeal decisions, made by highly interventionist "developmental states", accumulated over time. Given the path dependence of laws and institutions, these strategies continue to shape East Asian housing systems until today. Four very different types of national housing strategies could be observed across East Asia during the three decades following World War II, according to the interactions between macroeconomic strategies and housing policies practiced in each economy (Renaud, 2004).

3.3.1   Demand redirection and relative under-investment in housing

In Japan, after 1925, the redirection of household savings toward industrial investment also reflected the management of the economy as a war economy. Post-war reconstruction after 1945 saw the continuance of much of these policies (Lockwood, 1954; Mills and Ohta, 1976).

In the aftermath of the 1950–53 Korean War, South Korea followed the Japanese strategy of redirecting demand away from consumption, in order to speed up industrialization and infrastructure investment. Housing being a domestic, non-traded, non-industrial good, was also taken as part of "consumption."[1]

One consequence of demand redirection was a lagging supply of housing and urban services. Japan reached a basic quantitative balance between the number of households and the total number of housing units in 1973, but South Korea did it only in 2002. In both countries, this milestone was crossed well after the economic take-off stage. However, the "housing supply ratio", which is the ratio of the number of housing units to the number of households, is a weak and asymmetric policy indicator. When it falls below a value of 1.0, the ratio clearly signals that the housing shortage is severe but, when the supply ratio finally rises above one, this does not necessarily mean that housing conditions have finally become good. First, the number of households is endogenous to supply conditions; under bad supply conditions, the formation of new young households will be delayed. Second, this ratio says nothing about the quality of housing, which remained low in Japan well into the 1980s.

In both Japan and South Korea, relative under-investment in the housing sector was masked to casual observers by the visible high rates of housing construction in cities, in response to the very high rates of urbanization and rising household incomes. However, the level of housing services per household remained low, by international standards, compared with countries of comparable income levels.

3.3.2   Non- interventionist housing policies relying on market mechanisms

Different from the rest of East Asia, Taiwan followed distinctive non-interventionist housing policies and relied on market response mechanisms. This housing strategy was facilitated by Taiwan's balanced growth path, rising income equality, better endowed agricultural sector, rural industrialization, and the resulting better spatial distribution of its population[2]. Taiwan's central government had a policy of non-intervention in housing markets until its first, limited housing policy of 1975, in the aftermath of the recession triggered by the first global oil crisis. Beyond the land use framework set by the Constitution, land use and housing policies were the domain of local governments.

---

[1] In South Korea, the national real gross capital stock expanded during the period 1960–1985, at an average rate of 9.73% per annum, but the dwelling sector expanded the slowest of all major sectors, at 6.85% (i.e. 30% slower that the total capital stock (Pyo, 1988)). This relative underinvestment in housing during South Korea's economic take-off period, 1970–1986, was confirmed by Kim and Suh (1991).

[2] For key differences in the economic growth strategies of Taiwan and Korea, see Scitovsky (1986).

The details of the Taiwan story, and the impact of Taiwan's exceptional economic development policies on housing during its growth take-off on the present economy, are presented in Chapter 5.

3.3.3   *Large-scale public housing programs in support of a small open economy.*

When Hong Kong and Singapore adopted their public housing strategies, they were both refugee economies whose internal stability and economic success was far from being a foregone conclusion. They were very small, open economies, dependent on their international competitiveness in the international markets, so one way to maintain social stability, while keeping wages as competitive as possible, was to improve the housing environment of the workers. The choice was a non-ideological, pragmatic strategy of providing a public housing supply on a very large scale.

There was, however, a fundamental difference. In Hong Kong, the public supply of housing remained under public control. At its peak, up to half the population of Hong Kong lived in public rental housing, managed by the Hong Kong Housing Authority. In Singapore, the 1965 decision to enter into the public production of housing was driven by market failures and the inability of existing private developers to supply affordable housing on the scale deemed necessary. The government nationalized *de facto* the production of new housing by acquiring control over land use through: the Land Acquisition Act of 1966 and the Urban Redevelopment Authority (URA); control over housing construction through the Housing Development Board (HDB); and control over housing finance through the Central Provident Fund (CPF).

However, once produced, housing units were transferred into the private ownership of the occupant household, because home ownership was considered fundamental to the development of an integrated polity with a vested interest in the success of this new country[3]. Presently, over 80% of the Singapore housing stock was once publicly produced, but the private home-ownership rate is over 85%, and the share of public rental housing managed by the HDB is only 5%. The housing systems of today in Hong Kong and Singapore are compared in Chapter 6.

3.3.4   *Central planning's view of housing as a social good to be distributed by the state.*

In the 1950s, both China and North Korea took a central planning path to housing provision, modeled after state housing policies in the much more

---

[3] For an authoritative account of the Singapore long-term housing strategy, see Chapter 7, "A Fair, Not Welfare Society", in Lee, 2000. An in-depth comparative study of housing policy implementation in Hong Kong and Singapore during each city-state's growth take-off is provided by Castells *et al.* (1990).

urban Soviet system. In centrally planned economies (CPE), housing is considered a "distribution good" to be allocated by the state according to administrative criteria. Functionally, CPE housing is not a separate economic sector, as it is in market economies: housing production is entirely driven by state investment programs. Embedded inside state industrial investment programs, new housing is chronically under-supplied. The existing housing stock is severely under-maintained, as maintenance budgets are routinely cut in favor of new construction, while very small nominal rents are not meant to cover operating and capital cost recovery, as in market economies. Over time, these policies have led to increasingly severe housing shortages and very low urban housing standards. Low socialist wages were meant to cover only consumption goods, as the key assets for which households save in market economies – health services, education, housing and retirement – were expected to be entirely provided by the state (Renaud, 1991, 1995). In China, this labor and housing system became known as the "iron rice bowl."

During the East Asian growth take-offs, the dynamics of housing market cycles had been suppressed, or more or less regulated out of existence *de facto*, by public interventions in finance, land use and development regulations, and even the regulation of the construction industry itself[4]. Nonetheless, heavy regulation did not preclude episodes of housing output and price volatility, driven by domestic or international macroeconomic shocks. The exception to close central government control across East Asia was Taiwan, where the government not only followed balanced macroeconomic policies that were exceptional for the times, but also adopted market-oriented land use and housing policies. Taiwan has experienced four housing cycles since the 1950s, but no crisis resulting from a housing bust. We now examine the distinguishing features of East Asian housing policies regarding land use, housing finance, taxation and subsidies, and the direct public housing provision.

3.4 Patterns of EA government intervention in housing policies

There are four main ways through which national and local governments can, and do, intervene in the housing sector:

1. Through financial policies and the regulation of access to residential mortgage lending, which has a direct bearing on the effective demand for new housing and also the trading of the existing stock of units.

---

[4] In contrast, for an analysis of modern housing cycles in high-income Western economies, see Muellbauer (2012).

2. Through the taxation of housing, which affects the demand for housing assets, their use and their trading.
3. Through land use and urban planning that shapes directly the supply of new housing and its price level.
4. Finally, through social housing policies designed to insure a changing socially determined minimum level of consumption of housing, which may lead to the direct supply of public housing by national and/or local governments.

East Asian choices have emphasized the powers of the government for "the greater good of the commonalty", and the rationale for government intervention has been significantly stronger than in Western economies, especially during the decades of the economic take-offs, when EA economic growth reached very high levels (often above 10% per year) and the rapid growth of cities created high pressures on the organized housing systems that were emerging. The distinct housing strategies observed across the six East Asian countries led to a different mix of government interventions in each economy.

Given the incremental, and often myopic, nature of housing policy-making during these periods of extremely rapid urban growth, the degree of internal economic consistency of the overall housing policy frameworks that resulted was not always high. One contributing factor was the internal organization of each national government, and the very significant difference in perspective between economic and financial ministries (which ranked considerably higher in East Asian government hierarchies) and the physical planning orientation of infrastructure and urban ministries. With the unitary nature of all six EA governments, central governments dominated the policy-making process over local governments, with their usually much greater knowledge of the dynamics of urban processes and local housing conditions.

As EA economies reached higher incomes, the urbanization process slowed down and general understanding of this process by decision-makers improved. Consequently, a trend towards more market-oriented housing policies, with expanding consumer choices and greater autonomy of local governments, took place across the systems of cities of Japan, Korea, Taiwan, and now in China. The self-contained city states of Hong Kong and Singapore faced different constraints. However, given the path-dependency over time of institutions, laws and regulations, the six housing systems observed today across East Asia remain strongly influenced by the choices made during the emergence of their large, organized housing systems.

The detailed individual features of six EA housing systems, and how they now shape the interactions between housing and the wider economy, are presented in subsequent country chapters. Here, we only aim to characterize

EA government policies across the four main areas of government intervention into their housing systems during the historical transition from the traditional, East Asian pre-industrial vernacular housing systems, to the large, organized urban housing systems of today. Adjusting the usual economic order of housing policy discussions, we begin with land and urban planning, because land scarcity is the factor that most sharply differentiates East Asian economies from the great majority of Western economies and others across the world. Real estate property rights, and access to buildable land, are also the components of housing systems where the path dependency of institutional arrangements tends to be the most enduring over decades.

3.4.1   Land use and urban planning: a major concern across East Asia

The allocation of scarce land among different uses changed profoundly across East Asia. During the transition from the slowly evolving preindustrial agrarian and administrative Von Thünen urban systems of the Asian past to the new and dynamic Krugman environment of rapid industrialization and fast urban population growth, both the diversity and scale of competing land uses expanded drastically, with non-linear expansion of demand for urban space.

Given the non-reproducible nature of land, and the fact that the value of a land parcel at a given time is not only determined by its physical characteristics and its location (as it is in agricultural use), but also by the bundle of land use rights that are attached to it in urban and suburban use, public policy debates about the balance between public and private property rights, appropriate government powers of intervention, and what level of government should exercise, have all shifted over time (Whitehead, 1983). However, one constant feature of land policies across all of East Asia throughout the past seven decades is the strong emphasis on the communal component of property rights. Land use policies and instruments have emphasized public values in four areas:

- in land use and urban planning approvals;
- in government powers to intervene in the markets and to regulate private transactions;
- in property taxation and land use transitions; and
- in powers to use public lands and public finance to produce new volumes of serviced urban land.

As described in Chapter 2, the land and taxation reforms that preceded the economic take-offs of Japan, Korea and Taiwan at different times had major structural benefits that significantly facilitated industrial development and urban investments, and directly contributed to rapid growth. Such reforms, which have rarely been successful in other countries, created favorable initial conditions to the EA growth take-offs.

These land reforms had multiple benefits. They achieved a major improvement of the initial distribution of income and wealth across income groups. They resulted in the easier and faster spread of innovations, because land owners had incentives to improve their assets, and clarified property rights now permitted the pledging of land for credit as a last resort. The clarification of property rights and titles also limited the development of informal settlements in East Asian cities. These never reached the massive scale that can still be observed in other parts of the developing world, where the eventual restructuring of rights and the provision of local infrastructure services has been found, in countries like Mexico, to be seven to ten times more costly that the organized supply of new housing would have been.

The coverage of the entire national territory also facilitated national and urban land use policies and, in particular, the implementation of national infrastructure plans. Operational land registries, and the refinement of valuation and brokerage laws and regulations during the growth take-offs, improved the efficiency and speed of a multiplicity of real estate transactions in rapidly growing cities. Problems in the acquisition of serviced land, which is a major recurring cause of delays in new industrial investments around the emerging world, were either avoided or significantly lessened.

The combined influences of high rural population density, and of the strong East Asian social perspective on land ownership, resulted in rigid rural-urban land conversion policies, motivated by food security concerns and socio-political reasons in China, Japan, and South Korea and, to a more moderate extent, in Taiwan. The result has been a very inelastic urban land supply, a high share of land costs in urban housing prices, and rapidly rising real urban house prices compared with urban incomes, as national densities kept increasing.

A common issue that marked the years of peak rates of growth toward the end of the East Asian economic take-offs were extremely high rates of land price appreciation in every type of land use, be it industrial, commercial or residential. China was no exception, and land prices appreciated very rapidly during its great housing boom of 1998–2012, in spite of the significant difference between Chinese land institutions and the land market institutions of the other EA economies. These periods were marked by increasing public interventions to correct land use trends that were considered socially inacceptable, economically inefficient or ecologically dangerous.

To achieve these objectives, public interventions had two dimensions: a physical dimension and a financial one. Physical public interventions aimed to organize the development of urban space with a degree of coherence and rationality that might not be achieved by market forces operating alone. These land use planning and zoning rules aimed to insure sound synergetic interactions across the diversity of urban activities. Financially, government interventions aimed to correct the perverse redistributive consequences of market forces, given the unique characteristics of land as an economic good. A central issue was the unearned capital gains accruing to land owners benefitting passively from public infrastructure investments. In practice, these financial issues led to the proliferation of fiscal laws and regulations, often characterized more by their frequency and instability than their effectiveness, their equity or the solidity of their conceptual foundations.

Policies and instrument for the public recapture of land betterments values during the growth take-off have rested on very different institutional foundations across the six EA societies. In China, the Land Reform Law of June 1950 abolished land markets through the collectivization of agricultural land and the nationalization of urban land. In 1988, amendments to two articles of the fourth Chinese Constitution of 1982 created tradable private urban land use rights, based on leasehold contracts, while land remains under the ownership of local governments, which aimed to maximize land betterment values during the great housing boom in order to maximize their revenues.

In Japan, private property rights are protected by the constitution. National laws were passed to recapture land betterment values, but they were ineffectively applied by autonomous elected local governments. As discussed further, in Chapter 5, major economic inconsistencies in the various laws affecting land use played an important part in the massive Japanese asset price bubbles of 1985–1990.

Unique in the region, continuing rapid land appreciation, and corporate as well as individual land speculation, triggered an intense national debate in South Korea during the second half of the 1980s. This debate focused on the concept of "public ownership of land" or *Gongkaenyum*. Eventually, building on Section 122 of the Constitution, the Korean government drafted three major new laws to be added to the existing 1972 system of public land administration and its framework of land use and urban laws. These three laws, passed in 1988, have had a major impact on the dynamics of Korean urban development ever since, in three ways: the regulation of land and housing ownership; land taxation and the public recapture of capital gains; and the regulation of land use and new private real estate development projects, subject to prior approval by the government (Son, 1994, 2014). As will be discussed in Chapter 10, the micro-management of the sector through government interventions remains a feature of Korean housing policies today.

In Taiwan, the 1946 Constitution promoted by the Kuomintang Party explicitly included the principle of land value recapture developed by Henry George (1879) and strongly endorsed by Sun Yat-Sen, first president of the

Chinese Republic and founder of the Kuomintang. A law immediately followed the completion of the land reforms to set the operational parameters of land use and land taxation (Lam and Tsui, 1998). Together with the exceptional macroeconomic framework of interest rate policies, exchange policies and fiscal policies also adopted by Taiwan (Scitovsky, 1986) that shaped choices of development policies, these land laws contributed to making Taiwan a unique case of *improving* income equality during its very rapid growth take-off (Kuo *et al.*, 1981). In contrast, in recent years, Taiwanese housing markets have gradually become a channel of wealth inequality, in which investments from China appear to play an increasing role since the Economic Cooperation Framework Agreement (ECFA) of 2009.

In Hong Kong, the government has owned most of the land since the origin of the colony in 1841[5]. The Hong Kong land market operates under a system of private tradable leases, initially auctioned off by the government with land use regulatory conditions attached. Land for public housing is directly allocated by the government to the Hong Kong Housing Authority for large-scale integrated new town projects, as part of the spatial development plan of the SAR. Financially, the land market has been a major source of fiscal revenue for the government which, by law, must maintain a balanced budget no larger than 20% of GDP. Some private studies have estimated that no less than 45% of government revenue comes from land, including land premiums from the auction of land use rights, property rates and taxes on property developers' profits, originating in part from rents that are the highest in the world. Income inequality has been rising rapidly, but the likely distorting impacts of the land system, as it operates currently in Hong Kong, have not been systematically investigated (Pilling, 2011).

Singapore is the most unambiguously successful case of land value capture and wealth equality through housing. "A home-owning society" has been a core national goal since independence in 1965. Singapore's housing system became a public system through the control of land, construction and finance. Its three pillars have been the Land Acquisition Law of 1966, the Housing Development Board (HDB), originally created in 1960, which has played a central role in housing supply, and the Central Provident Fund, which has played an equally central role in housing finance since 1968.

A review of the 50-year record of Singapore since independence shows that the share of public land has risen from 50% in 1965, to around 90% of the territory in 2015. As in most other major cities, land and real estate

---

[5] The Hong Kong land leasing system developed stepwise. Britain took over Victoria Island in 1841, after the First Opium War, through the Treaty of Nanking. Then, at the end of the Second Opium War in 1860, Britain gained a perpetual lease over the Kowloon peninsula. In 1898, after yet another armed conflict with China, Britain gained a 99-year lease over the "New Territories". It is this 99-year lease that triggered the return of all of Hong Kong to China in 1997 as a special administrative region (SAR).

prices have increased more rapidly than incomes in Singapore. Unlike most other cities, however, the land rents captured through state land acquisition have been distributed to more than 90% of households through subsidized access to home ownership, which is achievable to 90% of Singapore households. In 2014, the share of Singapore gross housing wealth owned by the bottom 50% of the population was 25% while, in Europe, it was estimated at 5% in 2010 (Phang, 2015). A critical factor in this achievement, has been the sustained high quality of governance, in defining pragmatic housing policies and implementing them over 50 years.

3.4.2 East Asian financial policies and special housing finance circuits

Across the five East Asian market economies, before the 1980s, policy views of housing as a social issue and as a "basic good" tended to dominate over alternative views of housing as a tradable asset financeable through long-term loans. Intra-family transfers, consistent with prevailing East Asian social values, played a major role in financing access to private home ownership during the take-off and its rapid urbanization years. There was a strong preference for cash transactions, and intra-family transfers were often based on the sale of suburban rural land assets, which eventually made urban housing a channel for wealth inequality across East Asia. Household aversion to credit was prevalent and, different from Western markets, mortgage loan curtailment remained the dominant form of pre-payment in East Asian housing finance markets (Chinloy, 1993; Lin and Yang 2005; Lin *et al.*, 2005). An important factor has been the frequently lower cost of equity financing, compared with mortgage financing, in East Asian financial markets. However, there is also an element of circularity between observed household behavior and prevailing financial policies, as shown by the rapid rise of consumer credit including mortgage borrowing.

The financial systems of East Asia have been bank-based rather than market-based like Anglo-Saxon financial systems, and the mobilization of savings and the funding of economic activity have been channeled through banks. Stock exchanges have played a more limited resource allocation role, and bond trading has been dominated by government bonds. It should be noted that bank-based financial systems are a typical feature of financial systems at early stages of economic development[6]. Strong central governments controlled the financial system and made financial capital subordinate to industrial capital.

---

[6] For a comparative analysis of bank-based versus market-based financial systems, see Allen and Gale (2000). For the first global survey of the evolution of financial systems during economic development, see Demirguc-Kunt and Levine (2001).

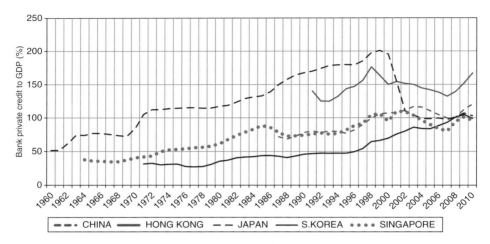

Figure 3.2   East Asia: financial depth and ratio of bank private credit to GDP, 1960–2010.
Source: World Bank Database on Financial Development and Structure, 2013.

At comparable income levels, the ratio of bank *private* credit to GDP has been low in South Korea and Singapore, as well as in China, over the period 1960–2010, as shown by Figure 3.2. This private bank lending ratio is significantly higher in Hong Kong, and is related to its role as a regional financial center. The time path of Japanese bank private credit in Figure 3.2 reflects in part the creation of private specialist housing finance lenders, known as *Jusen*, in 1970, their rapid growth during the real estate boom of 1985, and their closure when the bubble burst in 1991, followed by a protracted banking crisis until 2000 (Kanaya and Woo, 2000; Sheng, 2009).

During their growth take-off decades, Japan, South Korea, and Singapore adopted what is technically known as "financial repression" policies, which have had a deep impact on their housing finance systems, as did China, as it transited from a central-planning financial system to today's financial system (Lardy, 1998). During the take-off stage, these countries financed high rates of domestic investment through indirect resource transfers from the household sector in favor of the corporate sector, SOEs and government investments in three ways:

a) systematic undervaluation of the currency;
b) rate of growth of wages kept slower than the rate of growth of labor productivity;
c) credit allocation directed by the government, and with central regulation of deposit and lending rates significantly below the opportunity cost of capital and its equilibrium level in the economy.

Of the three policies, financial repression causes the largest transfers from households. Depending on the gap between the true costs of capital and the repressed low interest rates on household bank deposits, these resource transfers can be quite large[7].

Financial repression policies have had multiple consequences for housing. Housing became the "asset of refuge" for households aiming to escape the very large implicit taxes on their bank savings. Households were not offered any alternative investment vehicle. Fortunately, the real rates on returns on housing were quite high. However, achieving homeownership was constrained by the need for large amounts of prior equity, and the housing sector became a significant channel of wealth redistribution between households who could achieve home ownership and those who could not, which led to further government regulations.

The large gap between regulated deposit rates and the true cost of capital led to the growth of large, unregulated financial markets. In Korea, the rapid growth of the "curb market" led to a crisis of 1972, which was resolved by forcing the losses unto savers/lenders. In China, the "shadow banking system" has grown extremely rapidly since 2009, and finances a very significant volume of real estate developer loans. In both cases, the unregulated market remained closely intertwined with the banking system, as funds raised in the informal markets pass through the banking system.

Governments created special housing finance circuits, which were state-owned financial institutions. They operated under restrictive lending conditions and made low-LTV, low-interest loans to upper middle-class households (D5–D7), who had to complement the loan with other funds. In Japan, this state lender was the Government Housing Loan Corporation. In Korea, it was the Korea Housing Bank. In Singapore it still is the Central Provident Fund. In China, these lenders are the local housing provident funds, which now combines their inadequate loans with mortgage loans from the state banks, who now originate hybrid loans combining individual provident fund accounts with the bank's own funds.

New private, informal housing finance instruments emerged outside the regulated banking system. In Korea, the *jeonse* rental deposit contract system emerged as a major instrument to actually finance housing investments by landlords in the absence of access to bank loans. In the market-based, non-interventionist housing system of Taiwan, the absence of bank lending during the take-off decades led to *pre-sales* as the dominant source of funding real estate development projects, which continues to this day after the full liberalization of the financial system and the growth of the residential mortgage market, because *pre-sales* contracts are tradable and have advantages for both developers and households. On the other hand, in Korea, the *jeonse* system has become problematic in the aftermath of the post-1997

---

[7] In China, an IMF analysis estimated the value of the resource transfer from households to be at least 4% of GDP toward the end of China's investment-led growth model in the early 2010s (Lee *et al.*, 2012).

financial liberalization; a rising percentage of *jeonse* renters are borrowing to finance their *jeonse* deposits, as they do not have enough savings. Such borrowing by renters is a financial perversion of the initial savings-based *jeonse* system, and monthly rentals can be expected to spread.

From the viewpoint of a tenure-balanced housing system, it is important to note that, under financial repression, EA housing policies have *focused exclusively on homeownership* for the population mainstream. Social rental housing policies have been minimal. In China, after the 1998 housing privatization reforms, a much reduced public rental housing stock remains.

Taiwan has developed a distinctive market-based housing system thanks to a unique combination of macroeconomic policies and housing policies. In its macroeconomic policies, in 1960the Taiwan government adopted price-neutral monetary policies and exchange rate policies, as recommended by economist Sho-Chieh Tsiang (蔣碩傑), which were considered iconoclastic by other development economists at the time. The government also maintained a policy of non-intervention in the housing sector.

A significant restriction was on the provision of bank credit for housing, which later became part of overall liberalization during the 1980s. In Taiwan, banks were partially or wholly state-owned, and were not permitted to issue residential mortgages until 1975, except for a very small volume of social housing loans made by the state-owned Taiwan Land Bank, originally created for farmers. In spite of low inflation, in Taiwan, informal housing finance became dominant in new housing supply, and the financing of new units through *pre-sales* remains a major component of the Taiwanese housing finance system today.

Because regulated interest rates actually reflected the true high cost of scarce capital, industrialization in Taiwan was labor-intensive. Thanks to its unique combination of macroeconomic, industrial, infrastructure, and land policies tailored to its resource endowments, Taiwan is the only EA country where household income inequality *decreased* during the growth take-off stage, which made the non-interventionist housing policy easier to sustain. Taiwan is also the only EA country with a vigorous SME sector, because the banking sector did not discriminate against small enterprises. The indirect benefit of this growth pattern for housing was that Taiwanese households had a wider choice of assets to invest in than in the other EA economies, which also lowered pressure on speculative investment in housing during the take-off years.

Hong Kong, as a British Crown Colony, followed the financial policies of the UK and developed a sound and well-regulated banking system, which laid the foundations for Hong Kong's role today as a global financial center. There is no special housing finance circuit, yet retail mortgage lending is dominated by a small number of local banks.

3.4.3 Housing taxation and subsidies: East Asian approaches

Taxation can have a very large impact on the performance of the entire housing system, because the structure of the housing system is so closely intertwined with the rest of the economy and because housing is one of the longest-lasting assets in the entire economy. Forms of taxation seemingly unrelated to housing can exert a powerful impact on the housing sector. Two conspicuous examples are the destabilizing roles of taxation in both the Japanese asset price bubbles of 1985–1991, and the US housing bubble that burst in 2006–2007.

The taxation of housing, and that of real estate more generally, is central to investment and resource allocation across sectors of the national economy. Taxation can also have a highly differentiated impact across cities[8]. Because taxation affects both new housing investment and the user-cost of existing housing, we expect it to play a very significant role in housing sector performance and volatility. The importance of housing taxation in the national economy also grows steadily over time, as the housing stock keeps growing larger in absolute value and as a share of GDP. As the share of housing assets in national wealth expands as the level of urbanization rise, housing taxation takes an increasing place in national debates about economy efficiency and fairness. Administratively, housing taxation is also an important component of national public finance systems, because local governments have significant direct and indirect impacts on local land and housing markets.

In comparative analyses, few aspects of national housing systems are as challenging to document and analyzes as taxation. There are three main reasons. First, housing taxes are shaped by the complex characteristics of the housing stock. Physically, housing is not exceedingly complex to produce but, as an economic good, housing is highly heterogeneous and fixed in space, with a very long expected life. It is also exposed to a high level of national and local government interventions. The value of housing is also affected by the characteristics of the neighborhood in which it is located. Because of these economic characteristics, taxes on housing and their impacts are not easy to describe accurately, nor their impact appraised across cities of one country – even less so, across countries.

Second, a housing market has two simultaneous dimensions subject to different incentives: the market for the use of housing services; and the market for housing assets, as shown by the DiPasquale-Wheaton conceptual framework of real estate systems. Therefore, both the taxation of housing units and their financing matter.

---

[8] Gyourko and Sinai (2003) show that the distribution of housing tax benefits is highly skewed in the US, and primarily benefits the high-income, high-housing-price cities in California and in the Boston-New York corridor.

Third, the administrative structure of a housing tax system results from the cumulative process of incremental changes in response to shifting socio-political issues over time, influenced by local conditions. Comprehensive reviews of national housing taxation systems are, therefore, rare[9]. Most analyses of housing taxation examine the marginal impact of one tax, and take others as given.

Because land costs form such a high proportion of total housing costs in East Asia, much of housing taxation and subsidies has been related to land, in particular through the differential taxation of land held in agricultural use, compared with land held in various types of urban uses. From the view-point of households and businesses, the taxonomy of a property taxation system can always be broken down into three stages over time: taxation at the time of acquisition; taxation while the property is being held; and then when it is transferred to another party. Along these three stages, the systems of housing taxation and subsidies differ very significantly across the six EA economies. They continue to reflect today the very different national housing strategies adopted during the post-WWII period of 1950–1980, as outlined in Section 3.

In matters of housing taxation, we can again distinguish four EA groups: the repressed housing systems of Japan and South Korea; the market-oriented system of Taiwan; the land taxation solutions adopted by the small and open city economies of Hong Kong and Singapore; and, finally, large and locally diverse China.

In Japan, land is subject to three kinds of taxes at each of the three stages of property ownership. Upon acquisition there are: an inheritance tax (national tax); a registration and license tax (national tax); and a real estate acquisition tax (prefectural tax). While the land is being held by its owner there are: a fixed property tax (municipal tax); an urban planning tax (municipal tax); and a special land-holding tax (municipal tax created during the 1980s boom and later suspended in 1993). Finally, when a property is transferred, there are taxes imposed on capital gains: a corporation tax; an income tax (national tax); and an inhabitant tax (local tax).

The level of the fixed property tax, which is the main tax imposed on the holding of land, has been kept low in Japan, because it is a benefit tax to cover the costs of public services received by local residents. There is a widespread view among Japanese economists that economic inconsistencies in the design of these different land and property taxes were major contributors to the massive bubble of the 1980s, by making urban land supply highly inelastic and preventing a reasonably efficient allocation of

---

[9] For a significant, yet not comprehensive, review of a national real estate taxation system, covering both housing and commercial real estate during the 1985 Reagan tax reforms in the USA, see Follain (1986).

land (Ito and Iwaisako, 1995; Morinobu, 2006). The other major and more usual factor behind Japan's property bubble was the inadequate regulation and supervision of Japan's banking system during its liberalization.

In Korea, the land and housing taxation system was significantly influenced by the Japanese experience, but the Korean taxation system rapidly became more complex and more rigid, and remains subject to very frequent changes. In contrast to Japan, Korea did not experience a destabilizing property bubble. Now that Korea is a fully urban, high-income economy, there are public debates regarding the fact that, "*South Korea has one of the most complex tax codes among advanced countries, with 11 codes for the central government and 14 for municipalities*", and that "*the tax code created to curb bubbles in property transactions now hinders economic recovery*" (Kyongje, 2013).

In Taiwan, the taxation of land and housing is shaped by the Constitution, which sets as a national principle the recapture of the "unearned income" from private land speculation by the state for the benefit of society. The Constitution stipulates measures to regulate land use and ownership rights along market principles, and also measures to collect and share capital gains from the sale of land (Lam and Tsui, 1998). The Taiwanese land value tax is a variant of the property tax that imposes a higher tax rate on land than on improvements, or taxes only the land value in order to improve fairness and economic efficiency.

In practice, land and building value assessments, tax rates and tax administration are major issues. Homeowners are required to pay land value and building taxes while they occupy their house. When they sell, they also pay a tax on the appreciation of the assessed value of land during the period when the property was held. However, the nominal land value tax on housing is one-fifth of the rates that applies to other types of land use. The effective real estate tax rate for owner-occupied houses is low, and was recently estimated at 0.11%, taking into account both land and building taxes. Similarly, the land value increment tax rate for housing at the time of sale was only 10%, compared to 40, 50 or 60% for other land uses. The effective tax rates were actually lower, because the land value assessments for tax purposes tend to be a fraction of market value (Bourassa and Peng, 2011).

In Hong Kong almost all land is under public ownership. This has been central to the functioning of the economy and is a major source of revenue, as outlined earlier. It is estimated that about 40% of the increased in land value was recaptured during the take-off era of 1970–1991. Land-related revenues accounted for about 80% of annual infrastructure investments during the same period (Hong and Lam, 1998). These land-related revenues have several sources. First, there is the large "land premium" collected from lessees at initial land auctions. The initial auction sale contracts also include an annual land rent. In later years, when lessees want to improve or redevelop their properties, and need to modify the land-use restrictions included in the original land lease contract, an additional premium will be charged by the Lands Department, based on the potential increase in land value. Once properties have been developed and sold, owner-occupied properties pay "rates" based on the annual market rental value of the property. Owners of commercial real estate properties pay a "property tax" that is actually based on the income earned from their buildings.

However, the Hong Kong government's monopoly over land sales has had several unintended negative and distorting effects over time. This institutional arrangement has led to the development of a real estate industry dominated by a small oligopoly of very large real estate companies who are able to bid in the auctions of large parcels and to develop profit-maximizing strategies based on land reserves. Because government revenues are significantly dependent on land-based revenues, there has been an administrative incentive to release public land slowly, to maintain and, preferably, raise its value. Research also shows that land supply restrictions have caused much higher private housing prices (Peng and Wheaton, 1994; Lai and Wang, 1999; Tse *et al.*, 2001; Leung *et al.*, 2008; Craig and Hua, 2011).

The organization of Hong Kong's housing system and high housing prices explain why almost half of the population still lives in small public rental housing units. There is no capital gains tax in Hong Kong, which facilitates speculative behavior and contributes to rising inequality and economic volatility (IMF, 2012c). The politically determined timing and scale of land sales by the government can also be problematic, as was the case when large land releases occurred after 1997 when the real estate bubble had already burst. This had the effect of deepening the fall of housing prices and contributed to a large negative housing wealth effect for almost a decade. While institutional arrangements are significantly different in Chinese cities, Hong Kong's experience suggests that local government land monopolies in China's cities are also likely to produce significant distortions and high housing prices.

Singapore's territory is only 60% of the land area of Hong Kong, and land scarcity has been even more pronounced. However, in contrast with Hong Kong's land system, which is a legacy of British rule and aimed to make the colony self-financing, Singapore's land policies have been an integral part of national housing policies. As explained earlier, policies aim to maximize home ownership, and have directed the capture of land price appreciation through public land acquisition to expanding rapidly the supply of affordable housing. Fiscally, land sales have been a much smaller and variable percentage of government revenues in Singapore than in Hong Kong. In Singapore, the mix of public-private land ownership structure has evolved steadily, since 1965, toward public ownership under a land use planning process that is closely integrated with national economic policies. By now, the dual public/private Singapore land market is dominated by public ownership, and the residual private land market is closely regulated. Since 1994, both public sales, and also the collective sales of private land needed for land redevelopment, are conducted by sealed auctions to private developers.

Ever since the beginning of the reforms in 1978, **China** has had to contend with multiple transitions (Naughton, 2007). The fact that China is not a market economy in the Western sense has even led to the authorized expression "socialist market economy" to reflect the political and economic legacies of the Maoist central planning era (Wu, 1992). Regarding the taxation of housing, the legacies of the provision of housing by the state have led to a fragmented tax structure and a very low level of housing taxation. Very low taxation has made the carrying cost of housing investments low through a lower user cost of housing, which has significantly contributed to the Chinese housing boom (See Chapter 9).

Regarding housing subsidies, across East Asia, during the economic take-offs, there was a clear preference for supply-side subsidies channeled through construction processes and builders, for two pragmatic reasons. First, there was the need to expand the urban housing supply rapidly. Second, in real estate markets where public information systems were not well developed, supply-side subsidies were much easier to administer and could include subsidies in-kind through land zoning and infrastructure provision. A similar preference for supply-side subsidies prevailed in Europe during post-war reconstruction, when housing needs, together with continuing urban expansion, also placed great pressures on the existing housing stock. Since then, European housing policies have shifted to demand-side subsidies, with considerable variations from country to country.

3.4.4   Direct provision of public housing: contrasting national choices

The direct provision of housing by the public sector has ranged widely, from very little in Taiwan, to the total supply by the state and severe chronic shortages in China until the experimental reforms after 1978 culminated in the historical housing privatization of 1998–2003.

Managing the interface between public housing and rapidly growing organized urban housing markets has been a recurring policy issue across East Asia. The place given to local government autonomy has been an important factor in the scale and diversity of affordable housing solutions. By the 1980s, the origins of the housing stock varied greatly across East Asia, as seen in Table 3.1. In Japan, a wide range of public housing supply outcomes occurred across the 47 prefectures, their cities (*Shi*) and towns (*cho* or *machi*), who all have elected governments and councils. Large public housing programs emerged in the six major metropolitan regions, where land prices were high and rising rapidly.

Table 3.1   Public and private provision of housing in
East Asia during the 1980s.

	Public	**Private**
China PRC (1980)	100%	0%
Hong Kong, SAR, China (1986)	44.1%	55.9%
Japan (1977, funding)	28.5%	71.5%
Republic of Korea (1980–85)	5.4%	94.6%
Singapore (1985)	85.0%	15.0%
Taiwan, China (1988)	5.0%	95.0%

Source: Li (1998), Table 5, p. 30, and national statistics from Ministries of
Construction.

In Korea, where local government autonomy was minimal and unelected local government officials were directly appointed by the Ministry of Home Affairs until 1985, the centralized government was very reluctant to enter into the public provision of rental housing. As a result, local public housing initiatives were small. The limited social housing stock that was built was designed by policy to be sold to private individuals after five years.

In Taiwan, the public policy has been to rely on private housing market supply. This reliance on market mechanisms, and the strong land taxation incentives provided to private ownership, have led to the marginalization of the private rental market. In the early take-off years, the public provision of rental housing was mostly aimed at the military, civil servants and teachers. Subsidized housing loans were the main form of social housing support because, at that time, access to market housing loans was quite limited by financial policies. The first national programs for the supply of public rental housing for low-income housing started on a limited scale in 1975, after the first oil crisis of 1974. Small public housing programs developed, mostly in the two major cities of Taipei and Kaohsiung, only after the enactment of a "Public Housing Act" in 1975. The design of these projects was influenced by the Singapore experience with low-income housing. Since then, Taiwanese public rental housing programs have been countercyclical and have remained limited in scale (Li, 2011).

In contrast, the public provision of new housing has played and continues to play a central role in Hong Kong, where public rental housing peaked at about 50% of the total housing stock, and in Singapore where about 85% of the total stock was originally produced by HDB, but over 90% of the resident population own their units. In Hong Kong, a significant number of middle-income households who do not qualify for public housing and cannot afford private housing became known as the "sandwich class", and this unsatisfied demand led to new home ownership schemes (Wong, 1998).

In Singapore, a similar issue has also arisen, but on a much smaller scale than in Hong Kong, and was addressed through the market liberalization of housing policies.

3.5 Transition from the take-off stage to sustained long-term economic growth

The growth rates of output *per capita* and household incomes across East Asia during the take-off stage have been truly remarkable by world standards. The transition to sustained long-term economic growth is a critical period, with two dimensions, combining difficult economic adjustments with the major political transitions needed to restructure economic institutions. Each in its own way, and at different times, the first five East Asian economies avoided being caught into the "middle-income trap" and continued to rise to a high-income level. EA transitions have typically occurred not only under considerable domestic, but also under major external uncertainties.

The last of the six EA societies, China, is currently facing this transition during the decade of leadership of the Xi, Jinping and Li, Keqiang administration that started its term in 2013, with a far-reaching program of economic and social reforms. These aim to achieve a transition from the investment-led and export-led growth model of the past to a domestically-oriented consumer-driven growth, with significant implications for furthering the growth of the Chinese urban economy and the housing sector.

Economically, by the end of their growth take-offs, the EA economies had outgrown the initial coordinating benefits of the developmental state for infrastructure investments and labor-intensive manufacturing. The share of the total labor force employed in manufacturing had reached its peak, and industries were migrating to new products, with greater value-added inputs. One after the other, each EA economy needed to deeply restructure their economic policies in order to achieve a type of growth different from the take-off era. Policy instruments had to change, from direct interventions into what had been a small manufacturing economy to the indirect regulation of a much larger more diversified and complex, higher value-added growth, with important services components, which also implied a considerable expansion of the services sector in cities, and of their middle class.

The political difficulty of this economic transition was high, because it significantly affected the interests of the initial elites that had emerged during the take-off, and whose incentives had been aligned with the needs of the country to achieve rapid growth. These new elites had often benefitted in important ways from the organization of the repressed financial system and/ or other incentives. These public policies now needed to be liberalized, in order to serve efficiently the needs of new post-transition economy with new competing elites[10]. Rent-seeking had become a factor.

In the case of housing, the restructuring of the political economy involved the way consumer savings were mobilized and allocated throughout the economy by the financial system, and also the development of a better mortgage finance system to support a much larger real estate sector. It was also necessary to make political space for the rapidly growing and affluent new urban middle class, whose values and preferences were considerable more diverse than were those of the traditional society at the start of the growth take-off. The improved, more diversified structures of the deepening of housing systems that resulted from the transition reforms are presented in the country chapters.

There often were major political markers of the transitions in East Asian societies, which underlines the fact that escaping the "middle-income trap" was far from being a foregone conclusion *ex-ante*, as the difficult transition problems of other middle-income countries, such as Brazil, Mexico or Turkey reminds us. China's present transition challenges have already been alluded to.

In Japan, the political side of the transition was smooth, because the country's democratic structure had long been set by the post-war constitution imposed by the Allied Forces in 1947. The administrative transition between the take-off phase and the phase of sustained growth occurred in response to the rapid build-up of pressures for industrial readjustment during the 1960s. The rebalancing of economic policy-making between MITI, the monetary authorities and the political system occurred in the early 1970s. By the early 1980s, Japan had become a dominant force in the global economy, and the threat of "Japan as Number One" became part of public US debates (Vogel, 1978). Japan's housing system was then very large and very deep. Unfortunately, the mismanaged financial liberalization that was part of the transition became a major contributor to the Japanese real estate bubble in the mid-1980s.

In Taiwan, the transition to democracy began with the lifting of martial law by President Chiang Ching-Kuo in 1987. Democratic consolidation progressed, with amendments to the Taiwanese constitution and the competitive direct presidential election of Lee Teng-hui in 1996, which was

---

[10] Financial development economists have identified six main ways in which governments often repress their financial system: imposing interest rate ceilings on deposits; imposing high reserve requirements on banks; preferential lending to industry and directing bank credit; owning some banks and micromanaging the private ones through regulations; restricting entry into the financial industry, especially by foreigners; and restricting international capital inflows and outflows. See Beim and Calomiris (2001).

a first for any Chinese society. Incremental economic reforms, including financial liberalization and the emergence of a modern housing finance system, progressed in parallel.

In Hong Kong, in addition to the colonial administration responses to the 1976–77 riots, the technocratic impetus for greater political space for the expanding middle class came from the Sino-British Joint Declaration of 1984, about the status of Hong Kong after 1997, when Hong Kong's Basic Law would come into force under the principle of "one country, two systems". This transition led to adjustments in economic and financial policy-making, and new policies to privatize the public housing stock. However, the positive expectations associated with the Joint Declaration combined with the accelerating growth caused by the reconnection of the Hong Kong economy with its Pearl River hinterland, and then the very low interest rates of the US monetary policies transmitted through the Hong Kong dollar link to the US dollar, to convert a housing boom into a bubble that burst in 1997, with depressing price effects that lasted almost a decade.

In Singapore, large structural economic adjustments in response to the end of the economic take-off were triggered by the recession of 1985, which marked the end of the take-off. That recession marked the end of a significant period of over-investment by SOEs taking advantage of their preferential access to state control credit under financial repression. One of these adjustments consisted in much greater flexibility in private savings policy decisions in the operations of the Central Provident Fund, which expanded the decision-making autonomy of individuals. A major consequence, which is discussed in Chapter 6, was the large-scale privatization of the dominant HDB-built housing stock.

Finally, the case of South Korea can illustrate the place of the transition between the high-growth take-off years and the years of sustained long-term development toward becoming an advanced high-income economy that is also fully urbanized. The entire development record of Korea over 60 years is rather representative of the growth experiences of the other four EA economies, even after accounting for the specific political shocks that occurred during the Korean growth transition. Figure 3.3 presents consistently estimated annual growth rates of the South Korean National Income over the entire period 1953–2010. At the end of the Korean War, in 1953, South Korea's *per capita* GDP was $89 in current dollars, and among the lowest in the world. By 2010, its *per capita* GDP in current dollars was $22,150. By 2014, its *per capita* GDP in current dollars was $28,100. In PPP dollars, South Korea's *per capita* GDP of $35,277 was comparable to Japan's *per capita* GDP of $37.289 in PPP dollars.

Figure 3.3 shows that Korea experienced extremely high growth rates, between 10% and more than 15%, during 16 years out 57 (or 28%), with ten of these years occurring before the growth transition, and the peak rate of

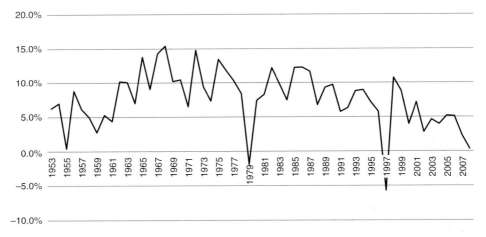

Figure 3.3   South Korea's GDP growth rates, 1953–2010, at 2005 constant prices, percent.

growth being 15.4%, in 1969. Korea also suffered four years of either null or negative growth rates. The recession of 1954 was linked to the instability of the immediate post-Korean war era. Next, the sharp recession of 1980 occurred just prior to the growth transition. This recession followed the assassination of President Park Chung-Hee in October, 1979. The new government engaged in major market-oriented reforms that restarted years of very high growth, above 10%, in the 1980s.

The third recession, in 1998, was caused by the Asia Financial Crisis in Korea, and was followed by a sharp V-shaped recovery. The fourth recession, in 2009, was caused by the Global Financial Crisis, and Korea recovered quickly again. Meanwhile, South Korea's political transition to democracy was marked by the "6.29 Declaration" under Rho Tae-Woo in 1987, which was immediately followed by the 1988 Seoul Olympics, which contributed to crystallizing this political transition. The steady democratic consolidation and decentralization of South Korean society and of the economy continued during the 1990s, which also led to significant adjustments in housing policies and housing finance.

After the growth transition of the early 1980s, the steady mean-reversion of Korea's growth rates over time, toward the slower growth rates of high-income, advanced economies is clear in Figure 3.3. Comparable compressed, high-growth stories can be told for the four other East Asian economies. These five past EA growth experiences are suggestive comparators when considering China's current growth transition challenges.

Part II
Current East Asian Housing Systems

4

East Asian Housing Systems Today: A Regional Overview

Our qualitative understanding of the institutional structure of East Asian modern housing systems that emerged during the growth take-off now needs to be improved with a quantitative perspective on the similarities and differences across the six East Asian economies today. This chapter looks at the six economies in a regional context. It provides evidence on the volatility of housing output across the six economies over the past four decades. Then it examines the impacts on East Asian housing of, first, the Asia Financial Crisis of 1997, then of the Global Financial Crisis and the associated Great Recession of 2008–2009.

This regional overview will then be expanded with profiles of the housing systems of Japan and Taiwan, where local governments play a significant role in the quality of housing supply (Chapter 5), and then in the city states of Hong Kong and Singapore, where external macroeconomic forces feed more directly into housing supply in the absence of the buffer of local governments (Chapter 6). Having laid these foundations, the implications of the econometric analyses of Part 3 will gain clearer meaning. To avoid repetition, we shall discuss China and Korea only once, in Part 4, where we analyze the interactions between housing and the wider economy in a third way, by investigating the distinct behavioral incentives of the six key players that shape housing cycles in these economies: the central bank; the central government; local governments; households; banks; and developers.

Dynamics of Housing in East Asia, First Edition. Bertrand Renaud, Kyung-Hwan Kim and Man Cho.
© 2016 John Wiley & Sons, Ltd. Published 2016 by John Wiley & Sons, Ltd.

4.1 Basic quantitative East Asian comparisons

4.1.1 Main demographic and macroeconomic differences

The country indicators provided in Table 4.1 map important differences and similarities across the six EA economies. The dates of these indicators vary, but all are very close to the year 2010. First, the demographic indicators show the extreme range of population scale between China, with its 1.37 billion people in 2012, and Singapore, with only 5.4 million. They also show that China is the only economy that is still in the middle of its urban transition, while all five others are now fully urbanized. Japan has been the world leader in terms of population aging, but Table 4.1 shows that all six EA economies now face serious population aging prospects.

Table 4.1 also gives the number of cities in each economy, in order to suggest the degree of housing policy decentralization to local government levels and the resulting differences in housing outcomes in each country. This number reflects the national administrative structure more than the actual number of functional urban areas. However, it suggests caution, when looking at housing cycles, not to generalize from cyclical conditions in a few major cities where the media and other opinion makers are concentrated, to the rest of the national system of cities.

The macroeconomic indicators of Table 4.1 show that, together, the six EA economies are a major force in the global economy and represented more than 24% of global GDP by 2012. This EA share of global GDP will continue to rise as long as China's growth remains considerably faster than the growth rate of global GDP, given that China already represented 61.25 % of EA GDP in 2010. Except for China, EA economies are now high-income economies.

To mitigate the impact of currency volatility, GDP *per capita* levels are measured in PPP dollars in Table 4.1. They show that China's income level remains far behind the other five economies. Japan and South Korea are now very close, while Taiwan has pulled slightly ahead of both countries. The city economy economies of Hong Kong and Singapore enjoy the highest income levels, with Singapore now the richest of the six EA economies. Japan's 1990s "lost decade" of deflation and stagnation, following the burst of its bubble in 1991, shows up in the data with negative CPI inflation and minimal GDP growth rate, which contrast with the performances of the five other economies during the same period.

4.1.2 Defensive EA strategies: current account surpluses and foreign exchange reserves

Following the 1997 Asia Financial Crisis, EA countries have aimed to protect themselves against external capital market shocks, and the consequence of their policy reforms are quite visible in Table 4.1. All six economies have

Table 4.1 Comparative country indicators.

	China	Japan	S. Korea	Taiwan	Hong Kong	Singapore
Demographic indicators						
Total Population (million, 2012)	1 367.50	127.1	50.5	23.3	7.3	5.4
Percent urban	52%	90%	83%	83%	100%	100%
Number of cities (市, shi)	665	102	60	25	1	1
Household size	3.2	2.6	2.8	3.1	3.1	4.4
Number of households (million)	427	49	18	8	2	1.2
Population 65 or over (percent, 2009)	8.2	22.7	11.1	10.7	9	10.7
Macroeconomic indicators 2012 (IMF, WEO database)						
GDP current US dollars (billions)	8221	5 960	1 130	474	263	277
Share of world GDP in PPP	14.7	5.5	1.9	1.1	0.4	0.4
GDP per capita current dollars	6071	46 707	22 589	20 336	36 676	52 052
GDP per capita in PPP dollars	9055	35 855	31 950	38 357	50 936	60 799
GDP real growth rate 2000–2010	11.3	1	5.1	4.5	4.9	6.7
Average CPI inflation 2000–2010	2.2	−0.3	3.4	1.1	0.1	1.8
General government budget balance	−0.909	−9.203	2.234	−4.253	−1.613	7.272
Gross national savings rate (%)	51.2	21.6	31.4	30.0	28.8	45.6
Current account surplus	2.349	1.014	3.819	10.529	2.718	18.602
Foreign Reserves 2013 (billion USD)	3557	1275	343	417	309	272
Forex reserves to GDP	43%	21%	30%	88%	117%	98%
Housing and mortgage markets						
Housing Units (million)	n.a.	57.6	17.7	8.1	2.17	1.23
Housing tenure (year)	2010 (urban)	2008	2010	2008	2012	2009
Owner occupied ratio	84.3	61.2	54.2	87.4	58.1	93.9
public (HDB) housing stock	n.a.	n.a.	n.a.	n.a.		74.4
private housing stock	n.a.	n.a.	n.a.	n.a.		19.5
Rental ratio	15.7	38.8	45.8	12.6	41.9	6.1
private	6.5	29.9		7.3	6.9	2.2
public	5.8	5.9		5.3	35	3.9
other	3.4	3				
MDO to GDP ratio (2009)	28%	37%	33%	28%	39%	71%

Source: National statistics.

been running significant current accounts surpluses, and have built up extremely large foreign exchange reserves during the decade following the AFC (Aizenman *et al.*, 2010).

In fact, the prevailing view is that the large global financial imbalances associated with East Asian external policies, matched by years of US and other Western current account deficits, have been a major factor in the GFC (Wolf, 2008). It can be seen that, except for Japan, the ratio of foreign reserves to GDP is now considerably higher than the 20% ratio, which international research suggests is likely to be the threshold value sufficient to insure against external financial shocks.

Research also shows that countries that run persistent current account deficits experience significant real estate price booms, because of the increased levels of domestic liquidity associated with these sustained current account deficits (Aizenman and Jinjarak, 2008).

After the defensive reforms triggered by the AFC, external factors were not likely to have a strong impact on EA housing prices, which now leaves domestic factors as the most likely sources of shocks. In each country, defensive macroeconomic policies have also encouraged domestic currency, as opposed to foreign exchange, borrowing. However, across East Asia, the development of domestic residential mortgage bonds remains small, because banks prefer to securitize non-residential loans and want to keep quality housing loans on their balance sheets.

4.1.3   Housing and depth of mortgage markets

A few points can be made about EA housing and mortgage markets before the econometric analyses of East Asian cycles in Part III. First, the level of home ownership varies significantly across East Asia. As already noted, in the case of Hong Kong and Singapore, care must be taken, when examining ownership-based housing prices cycles, not to confuse the proportion of the publicly *built* housing stock with the very different present ratio of public renters. In both cases, a significant part of the publicly built housing stock has been privatized over the past two decades to mitigate the well-known socio-economic inefficiencies of public rental housing.[1] By now, in Hong Kong, about 52% of the privately owned housing stock was publicly built. In Singapore, about 80% of the housing stock that is now in private owner-ship was originally built by the public Housing and Development Board.

---

[1] In the case of Hong Kong, one of the most thorough argumentation in favor of the privatiza-tion of public housing has been by Wong (1998). In Singapore, the privatization of the HDB housing stock was the intended consequence of the reform of the Central Provident Fund, and of national savings policies induced by the recession of 1985. In both countries, the privatiza-tion of public housing was seen as an integral part of the economic and political transitions to sustained high income growth.

Seen from a privatization perspective, 95% of the HDB-built housing stock has now been privatized in Singapore.

A basic indicator of the depth of a housing finance system and of its evolution over time is the ratio of the residential mortgage debt outstanding at the end of the year to GDP (MDO/GDP). The depth of a housing finance system typically grows as household incomes and housing prices rise. All six EA economies have followed conservative financial policies, especially regarding the development and liberalization of residential mortgage finance (see Chapter 3). As a result, East Asian MDO/GDP ratios are also conservative, compared with those of many Western economies. As Figure 4.1 shows, every East Asian ratio remained well below the 50% mark when the MDO/GDP ratio approached or even passed the 100% mark (Netherlands, Denmark) during the global housing boom. Note that neither Table 4.1 nor Figure 4.1 report this debt ratio for Singapore, where the bank-based part of the housing finance system is co-mingled with the part funded through the public Central Provident Fund.

Also, illustrating the path dependency of housing systems, the number of housing units in China is still not available at the national level for Table 4.1, because China continues to measure annual housing output and the size of its existing housing stock in square meters instead of numbers of units, reflecting the statistical concepts of its central planning past. This difference between China's housing indicators and indicators of housing output in market economies is also a reminder that China's economy has not

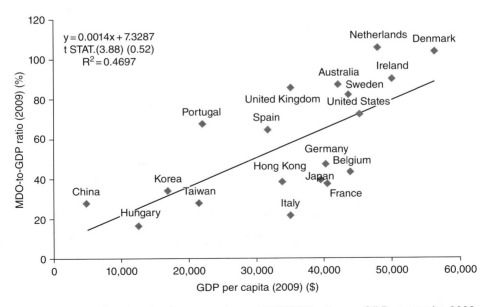

Figure 4.1 Depth of housing finance systems: MDO/GDP ratios vs. GDP *per capita*, 2009. *Source*: Cho *et al.* (2012).

completed its multiple transitions from a centrally planned economy to a market economy.

4.1.4   Government structure and quality of East Asian governance

As emphasized in Chapter 1, East Asia has had strong, development-oriented central governments. All four countries that are not city-states like Hong Kong and Singapore have unitary systems of governments, in which local governments have played very different roles in the local supply of housing – from being passive executant of central government policies in South Korea, to being important regulators of local housing supply in Taiwan. As will be discussed in Chapter 9, China's local governments have, unusually, played a leading role in the over-investment in housing, especially after 2005. In Japan, where all levels of government are elected, local governments have played an increasing role in innovative social housing policies after the Japanese bubble.

Regarding governance, the indicators of Table 4.2 report the *perceived* quality of governance and are subjective rankings, not quantitative scores. These rankings are based on more than 30 periodic international opinion surveys, by English-speaking analysts only. They show that East Asian societies rank high, and are in the top quintile of 200 countries or territories in 2013, with the exception of China. Variations across the six dimensions of governance tracked by the data suggest that democratic processes, and the quality of governance, may be working somewhat differently in East Asian societies than in Western societies.

Hong Kong and Singapore, whose long-term economic performance is heavily dependent on international factors, rank especially high in terms of governance, raising positive expectations for the management effectiveness of their housing systems. Both Singapore and Hong Kong rank very high in the quality of their governance. Both have long had high levels of transparency

Table 4.2   Quality of institutions and governance across East Asia.

	China	Japan	South Korea	Taiwan	Hong Kong	Singapore
	Unitary	Unitary	Unitary	Unitary	Unitary	Unitary
Governance perception indicators, World Bank (Percentile rankings out of 200 countries, 2013)						
Voice and accountability	5	83	66	**72**	66	54
Political stability, no violence	30	78	53	**74**	80	96
Government effectiveness	58	88	84	**84**	96	99
Regulatory quality	42	84	77	**86**	99	100
Rule of law	40	87	80	**83**	90	96
Control of corruption	40	92	70	**74**	93	97

Source: http://info.worldbank.org/governance/wgi/index.aspx#faq.

and quality of financial market regulation and supervision, because these qualities are seen as essential to the long-term competitiveness of these open economies.

4.2   Volatility of housing output across East Asia

The share of urban population has now reached the saturation level for every EA economy except China. Levels of urbanization are higher in East Asia than in Western economies, and range between 80% and 90% for Japan, Korea, and Taiwan, reaching 100% for Hong Kong and Singapore. On the other hand, China just passed the 50% mark in 2011, and its urban population is expected to grow continuously by about 230 million more people for the next two decades (see Figure 2.3 in Chapter 2). Accordingly, we no longer expect EA countries to initiate large-scale, government-led housing development projects, such as the "two million housing units" drive of Korea during the early 1990s. In contrast, such projects are currently being implemented in China. Under the 12th Plan, 2011–2016, the Economic and Comfortable Housing (ECH) program is under way, with 3.6 million low-income housing units.[2]

The long-term evolution of the share of residential investment in GDP over the four decades between 1970 and 2010 is presented in Figure 4.2. This share is higher and much more volatile in the city economies of Hong Kong and Singapore, than in the other EA countries. Due to government-directed funding, the housing investment ratio surged in Singapore during the 1980s, to over 16% in 1985, which contributed to the severe 1985 recession. The Singapore housing investment ratio climbed again to a second peak during the 1990s until the Asia Financial Crisis (AFC).

In Hong Kong, the housing investment ratio has also been strongly cyclical, and has hovered between 10–15% most of the time. The Hong Kong investment ratio reached very high values, above 20%, in the years following the colonial government response to the Hong Kong riots of the late 1970s, but then it fell sharply during the years of growing uncertainty that preceded the Joint Sino-British Declaration of 1984. Housing investment in Hong Kong then climbed back to a second peak rate above 15% during the years leading up to the 1997-1998 AFC. Housing investment in Hong Kong declined sharply and continuously after the AFC, and turned around only in very recent years. The much higher housing investment ratios in the two

---

[2] There are debates in the Chinese and the international media about relying on urbanization to maintain China's high GDP growth rates over the next two decades. Unfortunately, such proposals often confuse the causes and effects of urbanization. Attempts to stimulate China's national economy through excess credit expansion to the real estate sector would be disastrous as the examples of Japan in the 1980s and of the US in the 2000s show.

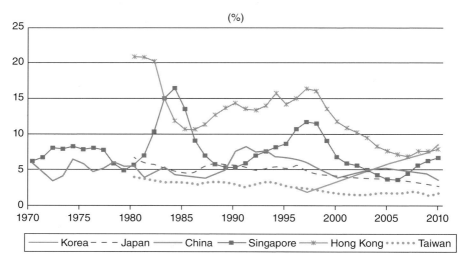

Figure 4.2   East Asian annual housing investment as a share of GDP.
Source: Cho *et al.* (2012).

city-states than in the large East Asian economies result in part from the absence of rural-based investment.

Annual housing investment ratios were lower and less volatile in Japan, Korea and Taiwan. They fluctuated around 5% of GDP, and then have trended downward since the mid-1980s, reflecting the end of rural-urban migration and lesser demographic pressures on the housing stock, with housing demand being driven by rising incomes, intra-urban labor mobility and shifts in household formation. In Korea, the ratio jumped in the late 1980s to about 8% of GDP during the national housing construction drive, but it has been declining gradually ever since. In Japan, the housing investment ratio data shows a surprisingly modest impact of the severe price bubble between 1985 and 1991, and it has also trended downward.

For the last three decades, Taiwan has had the lowest EA housing investment ratio, which has fluctuated within a 2–4% range. Taiwan's investment ratios do not provide clear clues to the strong housing price cycles that are Taiwan's experience. In China, the housing investment ratio shot up sharply following the Zhu Rongji housing privatization reforms of 1998, from about 2% prior to these reforms, to 8% by the end of 2010.

From the perspective of macroeconomic stability, it is important to keep in mind that Figure 4.2 does not include non-residential real estate investment, which typically is more volatile than new housing output. As noted in Chapter 1, in the stylized magnitudes of the total real estate industry, housing represents about 80% of total real estate assets, commercial real estate about 15% and the remaining types of real estate about 5%.

4.3   The 1997 Asian Financial Crisis triggered important structural reforms

When the Asian Financial Crisis (AFC) occurred in 1997, the globalization of both trade and finance had already progressed considerably. The rapid growth of financial systems has been driven by deregulation and financial innovation, with a lag in East Asia compared to Anglo-Saxon economies. Trade integration has also been progressing rapidly, with major innovations in transport and communications, combined with improving trade rules under GATT, which grew into the World Trade Organization in 1995.

The AFC is also linked to the sharp fall in global interest rates (led by Japan after the 1985 Plaza Accord) that stimulated capital inflows into other rapidly growing Asian economies. The crisis started on July 2, 1997, with the collapse of the exchange rate in Thailand. Through financial market contagion, the crisis spread rapidly across Asia and acquired global dimensions. Thailand, Indonesia and Korea were most severely affected and, to a lesser degree, so were Malaysia and the Philippines. In addition to the early lessons of Japan's bubble burst of 1991, the 1997–1998 AFC left the East Asian governments determined to address the structural and systemic weaknesses of their national economies.

Among the six EA economies, Korea was the most severely affected by the AFC. Only Korea experienced a costly dual currency and banking crisis, with the won losing 50% of its value, the stock market losing 70% of its capitalization and GDP contracting by 6.9% in 1998. However, Korea's real estate sector itself played only a passive role, and suffered a sharp price and output contraction during 1998 (Kim, 2000). The immediate factor behind the Korean crisis was that repressed and undercapitalized banks, and the recently deregulated finance companies, had been under constant pressure to lend by their leveraged *chaebol* clients. Both financial institutions and corporations were exposed to currency mismatches, and their foreign currency liabilities exceeded their foreign assets (Cho, 2002).

Hong Kong's own experience was influential across the East Asia region, because Hong Kong became the ultimate real estate speculative play during the AFC. Due to the HK dollar peg to the US dollar, the low US interest rates were inappropriate for Hong Kong's buoyant economy, which was reconnecting to the booming Guangdong Province hinterland. Rising local inflation turned interest rates negative in real terms. The result was growing asset price bubbles in real estate and in the stock market, where about 40% of shares were real estate-related at the time, and the real estate sector made up almost 27% of GDP. Soon after the Thai Baht devaluation of July 1997, the Hong Kong dollar and the fixed Taiwan dollar were subject to speculative currency attacks.

In spite of its sound economy and the existence of exchange controls, Taiwan decided to float its NT dollar in mid-October 1997, but this was not an option for Hong Kong, given the fundamental role of the currency peg in its economy. The Taiwanese floating decision shifted more currency attacks to Hong Kong, which led to a first crisis at the end of October 1997, when the sudden short-term demand for US dollars created liquidity problems for banks and raised local interest rates sharply. This, in turn, caused a precipitous fall of property values and related stocks, yet the peg continued to hold, as the HK dollar was backed by 800% currency reserves.

The most severe speculative attack on Hong Kong occurred in August, 1998. Because Hong Kong had a large foreign exchange market as well as a well-developed futures market for its stocks, it was a very attractive target for speculative attacks by hedge funds. These could borrow HK dollars to short the HK stock market, at the same time that they were shorting the HK dollar in hope of breaking the currency board peg, in a manner similar to the successful attack on the British sterling pound of 1992. This speculative move against Hong Kong became known as the "double play".

During the weeks of late August, 1998, when most futures contracts were expiring, the Hong Kong government successfully defended against this double play by using its own fiscal reserves to make massive purchases in the stock and futures markets for the stocks constituting the Hang Seng Index, thereby imposing large losses on speculators[3]. Hong Kong suffered a real estate crisis as property prices bottomed out in September 1998 at 50% below their 1997 peak. Given the large wealth losses, the cost of the crisis was a contraction of 5.5% in Hong Kong's GDP in 1998, and a sharp increase in unemployment to 4.7% that year. However, because of the high quality of its well-capitalized banking system, and because of the low level of indebtedness of its corporate sector, Hong Kong avoided a very costly dual real estate and banking crisis, as had occurred in Japan after 1991 and has been occurring again a decade later in the USA after 2009.

Meanwhile, Singapore had already been reining in its private real estate market, in which foreign real estate investors played a modest role in 1997. The economy suffered a contraction of 1.4 of GDP in 1998, mainly caused by the sharp fall of trade with Indonesia and Thailand. Taiwan's economy remained unaffected by the AFC, and its GDP even grew by 4.5% in 1998 after the NT dollar started floating.

---

[3] For an analysis by one of the senior officials responsible for Hong Kong's defense against speculative attacks during the AFC, see "Hong Kong: Unusual Times Need Unusual Action" (Chapter 10 in Sheng, 2009). Note that the August 1998 Hong Kong defense was initially severely criticized by US economists, including Milton Friedman. The immediate cost of this defense for Hong Kong is estimated to have been US15 billion. The losses incurred by failing attackers were proportional. Hong Kong's long-term gains are much larger.

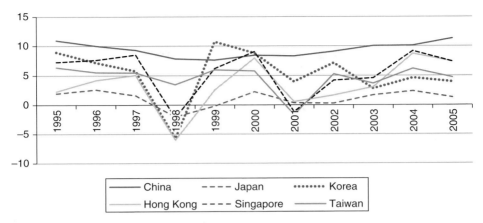

Figure 4.3   Impact of the 1997–98 AFC, East Asian GDP growth rates, 1995–2005.
Source: IMF, World Economic Outlook database, October 2013.

China, whose GDP was still about 35% *smaller* than the other five East Asian countries combined, was left unaffected by the AFC because its capital account was closed, and China had maintained prudent external financial policies. China is also credited for contributing to Asian stability by maintaining a stable Renminbi, and not engaging in a competitive devaluation against the other sharply falling Asian currencies (Zhu, 2013, Document 54).

As Figure 4.3 shows, the EA economies recovered rapidly from the effects of the AFC. Even South Korea, which experienced a V-shaped recovery, built on its strong real economy[4]. Unrelated to the AFC, the economies of Hong Kong, Singapore and Taiwan contracted again in 2001, due to the burst of the dot-com bubble in the US and the fall in electronics exports. The AFC was another blow to the Japanese economy, which had been already sluggish since 1991, when land prices had begun to fall in 1991, and would keep falling continuously until 2013. Adding to recovery pressures across Asia, Japan, a leading trading partner and FDI investor for many Asian countries, saw its GDP contract by –2.8% in 1998.

The years following the AFC saw East Asian countries work on correcting the systemic weaknesses of their real estate systems and reorganizing their macroeconomic management. For Korea, the AFC meant the rapid implementation of long-delayed reforms to modernize the real estate sector, including equal treatment of foreigners in owning land and other types of property (Renaud, 2003).

The most momentous of all EA real estate reforms occurred in China in 1998, when Prime Minister Zhu Rongji launched the historical housing privatization reforms that have now transformed urban China. The short-term

[4] Sheng (2009), Chapter 7 "South Korea: Strong Body, Weak Heart".

objective of the Chinese housing reforms was stabilizing China's economy when Asia was in recession. Their long-term objective was to change household and enterprise behavior, which permanently transformed China's urban economy, as will be discussed in Chapter 9.

Macroeconomic management across East Asia also changed very significantly, in two ways. Internally, Asian financial authorities developed stronger banking regulations and supervision, and more refined micro-prudential policies, in order to mitigate the impact of asset price volatility on individual financial institutions. In Hong Kong, Singapore and Korea, these policies aimed at lowering housing price volatility through the regulation of loan-to-value ratios on housing loans and household debt-to-income ratios.

The most important macroeconomic changes across East Asia relate to external policies. After the 1997–98 AFC, East Asian decision-makers were determined to make their economy as resilient as possible to international financial shocks. They avoided current account deficits, which had played a large negative role during the AFC and also contribute to real estate price inflation (Aizenman and Jinjarak, 2008; Bernanke, 2010; Geerolf and Grjebin, 2013).

East Asian financial authorities also raised very significantly the level of their international reserves, well above 20% of GDP, which improved the stability of their exchange rate and, at the same time, mitigated the GDP volatility that could be caused by this greater exchange rate stability (see Table 4.1). High East Asian international reserves were, for the largest part, a self-insurance mechanism, but they also had a smaller "mercantilist" dimension. A side-effect of these policies was to lower aggregate investment-to-GDP ratios significantly below their pre-AFC trend levels, including lower investment rates in housing and real estate, as is shown by the data of Figure 4.4 (Aizenman *et al.*, 2010; Reinhart and Tashiro, 2013).

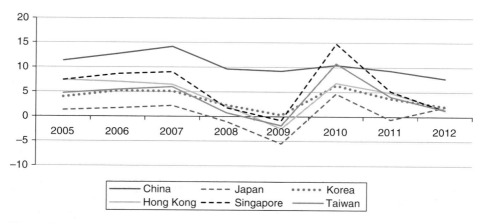

Figure 4.4   Impact of the 2008–2009 GFC, East Asian GDP growth rates, 2005–2012.
Source: IMF, World Economic Outlook database, October 2013.

4.4   Limited impact of the 2008 global financial crisis on East Asian housing

The decade following the AFC was marked globally by the accelerated growth of cross-border capital flows, from an estimated $1.6 trillion (or 6% of global GDP) in 1995, to $11.2 trillion (or 20.5% of global GDP) in 2007 (McKinsey Global Institute, 2008; Atkins and Fray, 2013). Housing finance for high-income economies became global, rather than merely national. Housing prices in high-income economies, which are the only economies where such data had been more or less adequately measured since the early 1970s, had been growing through successive cycles of greater amplitude.

With the massive expansion of global finance and cross-border capital flows, housing prices began to rise extremely fast across OECD countries from the mid-1990s through 2007. National housing cycles among OECD economies also became increasingly synchronized (Renaud and Kim, 2007). East Asian housing prices rose much more moderately during the period 2000–2007 than those of OECD countries, as shown by Figure 4.5a, which is based on a database of 54 countries used by IMF. The exception were Chinese housing prices as China was going through its peak rate of urban concentration, as shown in Chapter 2.

The initial trigger for the global financial crisis of 2008–09, which might be better described as the "Atlantic" financial crisis, was the collapse of the "subprime" mortgage market in the USA in the fall of 2006, soon followed by a freeze of short-term money markets in mid-2007. Then, the bankruptcy of the Lehman Brothers investment bank, on 15 September, 2008, froze liquidity across all financial markets and triggered the Great Recession, which spread almost instantly throughout Asia via financial and trade channels.

Every East Asian economy contracted in 2009, as manufacturing exports shrunk sharply, affecting supply chains everywhere. Japan's GDP contracted by 1.0% in 2008 and 5.5% in 2009. Also directly hit was small and fully open Singapore, whose GDP shrunk sharply, by 8.9% during the first quarter of 2009 and by 1.8% for the full year (see Figure 4.4). However, by 2010, EA economies were growing again, including Singapore, which rebounded at a remarkable annual GDP rate of 14.5%. An important contributor to Asian regional stability was China's very large, credit-driven stimulus package of 2009, funded by state banks and channeled through SOE investments, which has had some destabilizing consequences for China's financial system in later years (See Chapter 9).

The shock to the global financial system caused by the Lehman bankruptcy has been called a "Minsky moment", to reflect the fact that the time path of financial instability across the US financial system, and in particular

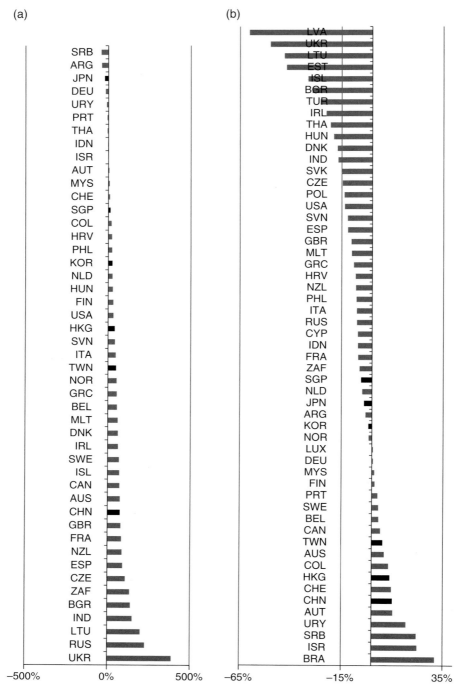

Figure 4.5 **a**. Global housing boom, 2000–2007. Real house prices change in percent. **b**. Global housing bust, 2007–2009. Real house prices change in percent.

Source: Deniz Igan, Macro-Financial Linkages Unit, Western Hemisphere, IMF (database of 54 countries).

across its mortgage finance system, has followed remarkably well the three-stage dynamics of borrowing and increasing financial instability analyzed by Hyman Minsky (1986, 1992) and revisited by Yellen (2009).

The scale and intensity of the US housing crisis were due to the convergence of three factors that were not present in EA housing systems. First, the unregulated US "shadow banking system", which had become larger than the regulated banking system, provided easy credit on a very large scale, while such massive volumes of easy credit to real estate had not occurred in East Asian economies (except earlier in Japan, during its own real estate bubble between 1985 and 1991). Second, loan underwriting standards were steadily loosened during the long US housing boom, which eventually added up to a regulatory debacle. In contrast, underwriting standards had been improved and were better supervised across East Asia after the 1997–98 AFC. Third, there were legal, fiscal and regulatory factors that made the US housing system particularly prone to high leverage and instability, as has been detailed by Ellis (2008) and Jaffee and Quigley (2008).

East Asian housing prices have been among the more stable during the global housing boom of 2000–2007 and during the Great Depression of 2007–2009 that followed, as shown in Figures 4.5a and 4.5b, which includes the OECD group of countries. EA real housing price volatilities were in the more stable range of the volatility during the boom years spectrum, compared with other countries. Housing prices did not fall sharply during the period 2007–2009, even in Singapore, which was seriously affected by the global contagion. Real housing prices continued to rise in China, and even rose in Hong Kong and Taiwan, where they might have been boosted by a new "China effect" created by overseas investors from China.

In addition to the improvements that they had made to the regulation and supervision of their housing systems and of their banking systems, EA governments found that the macroeconomic policy reforms they had implemented over the decade following the AFC had worked. They had followed conservative fiscal and financial policies; they had increased their reliance on borrowing in their domestic currencies; their central banks had adopted inflation-targeting policies; they had maintained stable exchange rates; and they had avoided current account deficits and protected themselves against external capital shocks under the umbrella of very large international reserves. Coincidentally, these reserves had gone to finance the current account deficits of the USA and other Atlantic countries, such as Spain and Ireland, who were now suffering the very high costs and prolonged effects of twin real estate and banking crises.

Since the GFC, the most visible adjustment made in East Asia has been the expansion of financial stability policies, from *micro*-prudential policies focusing on the safety and soundness of individual financial institutions, to system-wide *macro*-prudential policies. Given the lessons of the GFC, the behavior of asset prices has now become an accepted concern of central bankers. The new macro-prudential policies focus explicitly on housing which is, after all, the largest class of leveraged assets in high income economies. Rising housing prices have important impacts on the wider economy through consumption, investment and banking channels, which we investigate in Chapters 5 and 6.

By 2013, at least 46 countries were testing sectoral macro-prudential tools to mitigate sector imbalances and prevent risk from building up in housing (IMF, 2013b). In East Asia, South Korea, Hong Kong and Singapore are already applying macro-prudential tools on mortgage loan underwriting by lenders, which consist of limits on loan-to-value ratios and caps on borrowers' debt-to-income ratios. South Korea and Hong Kong also apply sectoral capital requirements on the residential mortgage loan portfolios of lenders. In addition, Japan, South Korea, Hong Kong and Singapore have been using taxes such as stamp duties and capital gains taxes on housing transactions to cool down price booms. China has also started to experiment with transaction taxes in selected cities, for specific housing market segments, since 2010.

The effectiveness of these macro-prudential tools and their incidence appear to vary significantly according to design and enforcement, as well as the institutional features of the housing markets to which they apply. Taiwan has even embedded the principle of land value recapture in article 142 of its Constitution, and implemented land value taxation in its 1954 Equalization of Land Rights Law. However, the price stability benefits of the land value tax have not been realized, because of the way this taxation has been implemented – in particular, with significant exemptions for home-owners.

4.5   Six economies, six different housing system behaviors

The two leading questions of the study are whether housing volatility in East Asia has differed from Western experiences in recent decades and how the structure of the incentives embedded in each of these housing systems shapes the dynamics of the sector and affects the stability of the economy. In spite of shared foundations and similarities in macroeconomic policies, the structure of each of the six East Asian housing systems still differs significantly from the others.

Financial crises very frequently, if not consistently, have undesirable redistributive impacts in favor of high-income groups. It is, therefore, important to note that this study of housing volatility could not address in detail distributive issues that are usually central to the conduct of public housing policy. These issues are: the degree of access to housing by different income groups – in particular, the poorest and the most vulnerable; financial inclusion and access to housing finance by different income groups; the balance between different forms of housing tenure, and whether the fluidity and stability of rental markets support social and geographical mobility; the efficiency and environmental sustainability of urban land use; and the soundness and responsiveness of the real estate industry in developing appropriate types of housing products, consistent with the changing social structure.

The individual analyses of the first four EA housing systems of Japan and Taiwan, and then Hong Kong and Singapore, that follow the present chapter immediately are not detailed systemic analyses on a monographic scale. They only highlight major structural facts and institutional features, in order to provide the reader with a better understanding of the dynamic factors present in each individual East Asian system, and complement the quantitative analyses of housing cycles of Part III.

Housing cycles can be driven by external or domestic shocks. This present chapter has shown why external shocks are not very likely in the larger EA economies, given the systemic defenses they have raised against such external shocks after the 1997 AFC. Domestic shocks are more likely, and can travel through different channels of interaction between the housing system and the rest of the economy. In Western market economies, these channels typically are: the residential construction channel; the housing wealth and housing consumption channel; and the banking channel (Muellbauer, 2011, 2012). The case studies of China (Chapter 9) and South Korea (Chapter 10) will take the alternative route of investigating the behavior of the six domestic key actors driving housing cycles, to find the significance of these transmission channels in these two East Asian economies.

5

Housing Volatility in Japan and Taiwan: A Study in Contrasts

This chapter examines the dynamics of the housing systems of Japan and of Taiwan. These two East Asian housing systems are a study in contrasts. On one side, we have Japan, which has been the East Asian pioneer of central government policies of household demand redirection and under-investment in housing during its decades of most rapid urbanization. On the other, we have Taiwan, which laid important principles of land use and urbanization in its 1946 Constitution and then, alone in East Asia, eased into non-interventionist central government policies regarding housing. Taiwan did not have a national housing ministry, but only a relatively modest housing unit in its Executive Yuan. Coordinated infrastructure investment remained a national responsibility and priority, but the Taiwanese central government left its decentralized local governments to be the daily regulators of housing in their cities.

If one were to assemble criteria to rank the six East Asian housing systems by their degree of government intervention, the likely result would be that the most interventionist system is Singapore[1]. Second would be China, followed by South Korea, and then Japan, with these last two systems still relatively high on the interventionist scale. The dual public-private housing system of Hong Kong would be harder to characterize, because the spatial dimension of the Hong Kong housing system is subject to direct government control through the land auction system, while the government has long aimed to be

---

[1] In an exercise limited to housing finance, the IMF produced the following rough indices of government intervention, from the most interventionist to the least: Singapore (0.75), South Korea (0.44), Japan (0.38) China (0.38) and Taiwan (0.31) with, by comparison, the US (0.56), Germany (0.19) and the UK (0.13) (Table 3.5, IMF, 2011).

Dynamics of Housing in East Asia, First Edition. Bertrand Renaud,
Kyung-Hwan Kim and Man Cho.
© 2016 John Wiley & Sons, Ltd. Published 2016 by John Wiley & Sons, Ltd.

non-interventionist in the financial system, with its well-known mantra of "positive non-intervention". Taiwan would be found on the least interventionist and least idiosyncratic end of the East Asian housing spectrum.

The contrasts between Japan and Taiwan in the interactions between housing and the wider economy are equally sharp. After suppressing market-based housing cycles through regulations during its decades of rapid urban growth, Japan eventually experienced one of the most massive bubbles on record in 1985–1991. Once it had burst, this bubble was followed by two decades of low deflation and very slow growth (see Table 4.1). Meanwhile, Taiwan experienced four significant market-based housing cycles, but these did not destabilize the wider economy. As seen in Chapter 4, Taiwan went through both the AFC and the GFC unscathed, thanks to conservatively managed institutions, moderately leveraged conditions in the housing market and timely macroeconomic decisions. This is not to say that all is well in Taiwan housing markets today, because the amplitude of housing price movements has increased, and housing affordability and high levels of household debts are now leading policy issues, together with the rapidly aging population.

The overall organization and performance of the Japanese and Taiwanese housing systems has been documented recently by national experts. (See Chapters 16 and 18 in Bardhan *et al.*, 2011). Therefore, the two present country profiles can focus on the drivers and impacts of housing volatility in each economy.

5.1   Japan: housing underinvestment followed by multiple asset bubbles

5.1.1   Introduction: the challenge of giving an account of the Japanese experience

Major financial and economic crises always have a multiplicity of causes, and the challenge is to provide a concise, yet complete, account of Japan's experience that is consistent with the goals of our study.

Japan's massive asset bubbles of 1985–1991 has been a major event in global economic history for a multiplicity of reasons:

- Japan's dominant place in the global economy as the second largest economy when the boom occurred;
- the exceptional role of land prices in the Japanese bubble;
- the structural and systemic weaknesses of Japan's economy that created channels of diffusion of high land prices throughout the economy, different from the usual channels for housing booms;

- the intensity of the asset price bubbles, both in real estate prices and corporate stocks;
- the steepness of the bubble burst after 1991;
- the reliance on the very large domestic bond market and domestic public debt to finance the restructuring of the banking system; and
- the very long period of GDP growth stagnation and price deflation for almost two decades since the 1990s.

The asset price bubble was triggered by two economic shocks. One shock was domestic, with the sectoral concentration and accelerated growth of bank lending to real estate during financial liberalization, when Japan's government decided to boost the flagging economy through infrastructure and real estate investments. The second shock was external, resulting from the abrupt shift of Japanese monetary policies to low interest rates after 1985 that was triggered by major international trade and US dollar-yen issues, leading to a very large revaluation of the yen. But through what channels were these shocks amplified throughout the economy?

By now, Japan's bubble has been extensively documented and analyzed[2]. As usual, with major financial and economic crises, there remain differences of judgments about the impacts of different policy decisions and institutional reforms, especially regarding Japan's very slow growth and its "lost decades" of the 1990s and 2000s. However, there is broad agreement on the causes of the land and equities price bubbles, and on the most important factors in the intensity of the bust that followed after 1991.Where most of the debates lie is on the choice of policies to manage the lengthy duration of the recovery.

We shall discuss Japan's experience with asset bubbles in four parts. First, we shall review the long-term historical antecedents of the persistent underinvestment in housing in Japan. Second, we describe the domestic and external triggers of the asset booms. Third, we examine the cooling measures at the peak of the boom in 1989–1990. Finally, we outline Japan's present housing system during the protracted economic recovery decades.

The primary focus is on the housing price bubble and the list of specific factors that contributed to Japan's high housing prices is long. This list includes: restrictive and distortive land use laws; rigid urban planning laws; economically inconsistent taxes across the three stages of property owner-ship: acquisition, current use, and transfer; and excessive protection of

---

[2] Seven volumes of analysis and evaluation were published by Keio University Press in 2009. Three history volumes, plus one volume of oral history, were published under the sponsorship of the Japanese Cabinet Office in 2010 (see Ishikawa (2011)). The research literature in English is also very extensive.

tenant rights[3]. Regulatory and fiscal inconsistencies were compounded by the lack of coordination, or even competition, across ministerial bureaus and their respective clienteles, and also between central and local governments.

Before proceeding, it may be helpful to assemble in one place a list of structural flaws exposed by the land and equities bubbles. These flaws reappear in different ways during the three stages of the Japanese boom-bust. Issues on this list became part of the reform agenda for housing and the wider Japanese economy:

- A highly inelastic urban land supply, especially in major cities, with land markets permeated by myopic and persistent backward-looking land price expectations, now described as *toshi shinwa* (literally "the land fairy tale", also known as the myth of ever-rising land prices).
- Economically inefficient and mutually inconsistent taxes that prevented a rational allocation of land and other resources.
- Accounting practices and corporate valuations that were distorted by real estate holdings.
- Japan's "main bank" system, inherited from the wartime years, which encouraged banks to own shares in the companies they also financed.
- A financial deregulation that ran into multiple problems, including:
  o Recently deregulated banking institutions moving into second-tier borrower markets and also into commercial real estate lending, after losing an increasing share of their blue-chip corporate clients to the financial markets.
  o Outdated bank loan underwriting policies, dominated by land as collateral.
  o Misleading bank capitalization ratios, including corporate shares of the business groups (*keiretsu*) to which banks have been lending under the "main bank" system.
  o Japanese bank supervision operating on the principle of "no bank failures".
  o Weak banking supervision, replete with moral hazard, under the so-called "convoy system" of sound banks rescuing problem banks.
  o Weak supervision of eight new non-bank, non-deposit-taking housing finance institutions (*jusen*).
  o A government structure and administrative behavior inherited from the "developmental state" era and the take-off decades, which had become unsuited to a complex, advanced, and now very large economy.

---

[3] A discussion of the various factors that contributed to a highly inelastic land and housing supply in Japan is beyond the limits of this country profile. For an effective overview of these factors, see Ito (1992), Chapter 14, and Morinobu (2006).

○ The collusive *"amakudari"* practice of senior officials retiring into senior positions with national and provincial institutions that they had previously been regulating and supervising, which often led to weakly enforced regulations, late decisions and postponed reforms.

○ Bureaucratic fragmentation and competition, which led to a low level of transparency and weakened or prevented timely decision-making.

• Last, yet a major part of the Japanese story, there is the massive role of Japan's postal savings system (PSS). Throughout the 20th Century, the PSS has mobilized a very high share of household savings, and then redirected these savings to political priority investments under the control of the Trust Fund Bureau of the Ministry of Finance. The presence of the PSS remains a partly unresolved structural issue, despite of reorganization in 2003 into a public corporation the Japan Post Bank

5.1.2 Physical and historical perspectives on the Japanese supply of urban housing

A combination of physical and institutional factors explains why the supply of urban land has been so inelastic in Japan. The country's physical and demographic features, institutions and economic history throw considerable light on the interactions between the housing sector and the rest of the economy. Japan is, by far, the largest among the countries with comparable population densities. South Korea and Taiwan have even higher gross densities, but their populations are respectively 40% and 18% that of Japan. Because about 25% of Japan's land has a slope of less than 10%, its cities and farms are concentrated on the remaining small amount of land that is relatively flat. Japanese cities occupy about 25% of the usable land area of the Japanese archipelago. This scarcity of land has made it more complex in private, commercial and public investment decisions than the tradable commodity it is in North America.

The housing supply, and the structure of the residential real estate industry of Japan, is unique in East Asia. It differ greatly from the five other East Asian countries, including South Korea and Taiwan. In addition to the scarcity of land, and the fragmentation of land holdings, Japan's housing supply is exposed to the risk of earthquakes, and has long been dominated by wooden construction.

In terms of housing types, the Japanese housing stock consists of about 60% of (mostly wooden) single-family homes and 40% of low-rise multi-story condominium apartments, found predominantly in the largest cities. In most other cities, owner-built and rebuilt units remain an important share of the stock. Residential mobility is rather low, and the purchase of second-hand dwellings is a very small percentage of all transactions in any given year. Only a third of new units are purchased ready built. "Trading-up" is more likely to be achieved by rebuilding on the same land site (Forrest *et al.*, 2000).

The share of land in housing costs is often very high. It went above 80% in the Tokyo region, and even climbed to 98.5 % in central Tokyo during the bubble (Noguchi, 1994). The unusual use of land price indices, and not house prices, in Japan's housing policy signals this very high share of land costs. Land may be scarce in Japan, but comparisons with East Asian and other countries show that the actual causes of very high housing prices have been social and institutional. The land and housing problem in Japan has been mostly man-made.

The stringent land reforms of 1946–1950 pushed by the US Occupation forces had a similar impact on the share of tenant farmers as the South Korean and Taiwanese land reforms, and the share of tenant farmers fell from 45.9% in 1946 to 10.1% in 1950 (Nakamura, 1981). Together with infrastructure improvements and new rice varieties, food supply improved significantly. However, from an urban development point of view, Japanese cities were now facing a more fragmented supply of land parcels, with a very large number of small owners. The land reforms also left Japan with a powerful rural lobby, represented by the Liberal Democratic Party (LDP), which promoted strong agricultural land protection laws and regulation at a time when Japan's population was still 60% rural. These rigid land conversion rules fell in place just prior to Japan's profound urban transformation, when the urban population ratio climbed fast from 37.5% in 1950, past 75% in 1975.

The great Kanto earthquake and fire of 1923 had a lasting impact on Japanese urban planning rules, which now restricted new buildings to low heights. These planning rules limited the substitution between land and buildings during the years of fastest urban growth, despite significant Japanese construction engineering innovations. Paradoxically, land use in Japanese cities has been characterized by low densities (low floor-area ratios or FAR) and a high degree of parcel fragmentation, which made land consolidation for multi-family housing units and commercial real estate development time-consuming and costly. The inelasticity of urban land supply was particularly severe in the six major Japanese metropolitan regions, where industrialization was concentrating and the overall land price level was high and still rising.

There are significant regional differences in the share of land costs in the total cost of a housing unit. During the asset bubble, this share became exceptionally high in major cities. In the Tokyo and Osaka metropolitan regions it was nearly 90% even in suburbs. In central districts of Tokyo, this share went as high as 98.5% (Noguchi, 1994).

The Japanese real estate industry is dualistic, between very large national firms operating in large metropolitan regions that have a global reach, and many small builder developers. One regulatory factor behind the slow emergence of large real estate firms during the rapid urban growth decades 1950–1970 was the late loosening of the urban planning rules, in force since the 1920s, at the time of the 1964 Olympic Games.

One notable aspect of the Japanese housing system is the sustained supply of new housing throughout the three-part boom-bust-recovery cycle. As discussed by Seko *et al.* (2011), Japan has maintained a high level of housing construction since World War II, even after the bubble burst. Specifically, the total housing starts between 1985–1995 was about 1.5 million units, which is higher than the long-term mean in the USA (which is slightly over one million per year). Even during the depressed period between 1995–2007, housing output exceeded one million units.

5.1.3 Lasting impact of wartime controls and catch-up industrialization on Japanese housing

Since Japan plunged into war with China in the 1930s, historical accounts of the Japanese economy distinguish four periods: the wartime; the post-war; and the rapid growth periods until 1991; followed by the fourth period of low deflation and low growth after the burst of the great bubble. This fourth period of little growth is accentuated by the most rapidly aging population in the world. The rapid urbanization of the 1920s and the 1930s was reversed during WWII, and the urban population ratio had fallen to 37.5% in 1945. After 1945, urbanization resumed at a much faster rate than at any time during the pre-war period (see Figure 2.3).

What explains much of Japan's centralized administrative structure and the suppressed status of housing in Japanese economic policies for decades is that the reforms implemented after WWII were "carried out atop a foundation of institutions and technology handed down from pre-war days" (Nakamura, 1981, p. xiii). Then, between 1950 and 1980, housing underinvestment was the rule, under the single-minded Japanese pursuit of rapid industrialization in order to catch up with the West: "Until the 1960s, the political realities of postwar Japan were shaped, in a very fundamental sense, by Japan's pursuit of industrialization. [...] The broadly shared desire to catch up with the West was the underlying political force majeure [...] providing the nation with a political stability unmatched by any other major industrial nation" (Yamamura and Yasuba, 1987, p. 5).

Japan did not achieve a basic quantitative balance between the number of housing units and the number of households until 1973[4]. In fact, in Japan, housing conditions remained poor, with respect to higher housing costs,

---

[4] This basic indicator is asymmetrical; when the ratio is below 1, it certainly indicates that housing conditions are quite poor, but when it is higher than 1, it does not imply that housing conditions are necessarily good.

both in terms of high rents and high housing prices, with much smaller floor space per household and basic services than in other countries with comparable income levels. The industrialization catch-up era itself ended successfully in the early 1980s, when the Japanese *per capita* GDP overtook the US and Japan's share of global GDP reached its peak. Unfortunately, that remarkable achievement was quickly followed by the asset bubbles of 1985–2001.

The administrative urban structure of Japan is complex. It reflects bureaucratic characteristics once described by a foreign observer as "flexible rigidities" (Dore, 1986). Japan has had 47 prefectures since the Meiji reforms of the 1870s. On the other hand, its urban administrative structure has been constantly adjusting. Table 4.1 showed that Japan has 102 "designated", "special" or "core" cities, but the official count is more than six times larger, at 684 cities, because Japan recognizes as cities population concentrations that would be classified as "townships" elsewhere in East Asia. For instance, China has about 20 000 townships.

Operationally, "centralization and bureaucracy rather than local autonomy were the prevailing principles of local government in pre-war Japan [...] During the American occupation period, a decentralized system, which emphasized home rule, was *superimposed* on the high centralized and bureaucratic ruling heritage of Japan. [...] However, no precise functions and powers are enunciated in the constitution" (Glickman, 1979, p. 292). Thus, local governments have continued to implement directives issued by central government ministries, except for a few major metropolitan governments such as Tokyo.

5.1.4   Financial repression and Japan's special housing finance circuit during the take-off years

During the catch-up, high-growth years, the Japanese financial system was closely regulated by the Ministry of Finance and the Bank of Japan, which was not an independent institution. Regulations were not uniform, but were specific to financial institutions serving different sectors of the economy. The city banks served the financial needs of large private corporations under the "main bank" system of one corporation working preferentially with one bank. The regional banks, as well as mutual savings banks (*sogo* banks) and credit cooperatives (*shinkin* banks), served the needs of medium-and small-size firms. There were also specialized state-owned banks focusing on industry, infrastructure, agriculture and municipal governments, the largest one being the Japan Development Bank (Susuki, 1987). Only a small proportion of these financial institutions was interested in retail deposits by households and in residential mortgage lending. A high percentage of the housing loans these institutions made went to preferred business customers.

This financial system of tightly directed credit had its roots in the war effort, and had carried through into peacetime without many modifications. Under the new post-war constitution, Japan was not allowed to re-arm, and only a small percentage of GDP went into the self-defense program, under the security umbrella of the US. This meant that almost all Japanese investment went into directly productive activities to generate very high GDP growth rates and rapidly rising incomes. The average household savings ratio rose from 9.3% in 1955, to 23% in 1975 (Yamamura and Yasuba, 1997, Chapter 2). Given the rapid rise in household incomes, the flow of retail savings expanded massively. Most of these retail savings were collected by Japan's postal savings system.

Japan's postal savings system (PSS) has changed its name, but it remains a cornerstone of the Japanese savings system to this day, as attempts to privatize failed repeatedly. The PSS was created in 1875 and has grown massively in size. With almost 25000 branches, the PSS has been collecting savings from every area of the country. Favorably regulated, the PSS has grown massively as it was usually able to offer better deposit products than private financial institutions (Hagan-Kuwayama, 2000). As of 2005, the PSS size had grown to ¥330 trillion – equivalent to about 65% of Japan's GDP. Deposits into this postal savings system are transferred to the Ministry of Finance's Deposit Bureau, later renamed the Trust Fund Bureau, which then redirects the funds to the priority areas of the government (Cargill and Scott, 2005; Lincoln, 2013).

In the case of housing finance, the Trust Fund Bureau of MOF funded the Government Housing Loan Corporation (GHLC), created in 1950 to finance initially the construction of owner-occupied and rental housing. Loan conditions were eased into long-term, low-interest loans for a wider variety of housing purposes. The Pension Welfare Services Public Corporation (PWSPC) was later created, to provide subsidized loans for company housing for employees. Later, a small proportion of local government bodies initiated housing loans programs, with partial funding from the MOF Trust Fund Bureau. Until the late 1960s, about 70% of housing loans came from public lenders, and only 30% from private lenders. This public housing finance special circuit remained small, compared to the needs of the Japanese population. Equity financing of housing purchases was dominant, and the main sources of funding to achieve home ownership were private savings, intra-family transfers and, for well-located farm families, the recycling of capital gains from land sales.

The first private housing finance company, or *jusen*, jointly capitalized by six city banks, was created only in 1971. The shortage of housing finance had become very severe, as Japan had, by then, become a highly urbanized country with an urban ratio of more than 72%. Soon afterwards, the 1973 oil crisis slowed the economy sharply. Land prices fell sharply at first, then followed years of minimal rates of land price appreciation. To revive the economy and improve bank profits, other *jusen* were created by other financial groups. The annual rate of increase of housing finance loans rose very sharply, and was the prelude to the asset bubbles of 1985–1991.

5.1.5   Japan's land price dynamics over time and "the land problem"

The rates of increase in industrial, commercial and residential land prices have reflected the pattern of industrialization and urbanization of Japan during its era of high growth. During the early growth years of the 1950s, industrial land price increases outpaced the rise of land prices in other uses. Then, residential land prices grew the fastest in the 1970s. Eventually, in a third stage, commercial land prices reflecting domestic and global corporate interests increased fastest during the second half of the 1980s and the Japanese (Figure 5.1). There is abundant evidence that the boom in domestic Japanese commercial real estate spilled over into the global markets, and was one of the major triggers of the first global real estate boom of 1985–1994, which was a boom in *commercial real estate*, unlike the global *housing* boom of 1996–2006 with its US-led components (Renaud, 1997).

During the initial phase of rapid manufacturing growth, land prices in the six major cities of Japan rose faster than the national average in the early 1960s, then moved back close to the national average[5]. They reached a second peak in 1973, during the period when Japan's industrial capacity doubled in five years. This is consistent with export-oriented industrialization, which encourages urban concentration in the largest cities that can provide the economies of scale, the urban externalities, the physical infrastructure and the services necessary to the rapid growth of exports.

Nationally, Japan's ratio of aggregate land value to GDP was under 1.4 in 1955 at the start of the high growth era. It reached a first local peak around 2.0 in 1963, and then a value of 3.0 during the real estate boom of 1973 at the end of the growth take-off. Then, when Japan was already fully urbanized and high income, misguided government policies aimed to stimulate economic growth through real estate, which led to the great bubble and a peak ratio of land value to GDP of 5.0 in 1988 (Noguchi, 1994, Figure 1.1).

High and rapidly rising land prices became a cause of deep public concern in Japan, as the share of land costs in total housing costs rose to levels never

---

[5] The land price statistics of the "six major metropolitan cities" refer to Tokyo, Yokohama, Osaka, Nagoya, Kyoto and Kobe. However, functionally, the three metropolitan regions where major urban concentration occurred during the high growth take-off were the Tokyo, Osaka and Nagoya metropolitan regions. Together, these three regions' share of Japan's population rose from 32% in 1950 to 44.5% in 1975, and then marginally more, to 45.4%, by 1985. The Tokyo region grew from 15.5% of Japan's population in 1950 to 24.2% (or 27.1 million persons) in 1975.

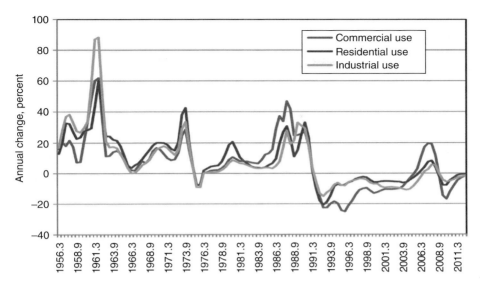

Figure 5.1   Japan: annual rates of change in land prices, 1956–2013.
Source: Watanabe and Shimizu (2012). (Note: more recent versions 2013–2014 of the paper no longer contains this graph).

experienced in Western economies. The share of land in the total cost of housing rose so high in major cities that the housing problem became "the land problem." in public debates[6]. For the majority of Japanese, the way that land was used and priced became the most important social and economic problem facing the country.

As Figure 5.1 shows, there were three peaks of land price inflation. The highest peak occurred in the late 1950s, during the growth take-off. The second peak coincided with the doubling of the capital capacity of Japan in five years, just before the first oil crisis of October 1973, which snapped Japan's export-led growth and kept land price inflation low until the third peak of the great asset bubbles. The fourth peak, around 2007, is misleading, since it is only a local blip in rising land prices during two decades of falling land price levels, as shown by Figure 5.2.

Public demands for land price restraints became increasingly intense during the 1980s. Various government councils and commissions raised three main concerns:

1. The land market had become a major engine of wealth inequality, and rapidly rising land prices widened the wealth gap between those who owned land and those who did not.

[6] Yukio Noguchi shows that the share of land in the total cost of a housing unit in different districts of Tokyo ranged from 82% to 98.5% during the bubble in 1989. In other major Japanese cities, the land share ranged between 61.4% and 87.2%. It was only in small local cities that the share would range between 31.3% and 40.6% (See Noguchi and Poterba, 1994).

2. Home ownership was rapidly becoming beyond the reach of ordinary households.
3. Earned income was becoming insignificant, compared to unearned income, which had a negative effect on labor force motivation.

5.1.6   Why did Japanese land prices rise for so long and so high? The financial domestic shock

The seeds of the housing and commercial land price bubbles were planted by government policies during the 1970s. Because the first oil crisis of 1973 had drastically slowed Japan's export-driven economy, Prime Minister Kakuei Tanaka launched a nationwide program of infrastructure and real estate development, accompanied by a rapid expansion of the money supply to revive the economy. A major structural change was the creation of the eight housing finance companies known as *Jusen*. The Tanaka program was the beginning of the massive real estate boom that fuelled "the myth of ever rising land prices". Land prices rose by 215% in nominal terms (85% in inflation-corrected terms) in the six biggest cities in the 1970s, and by 180% nationally (23% in real terms) until 1980. But why did Japanese land prices rise for so long and so high?

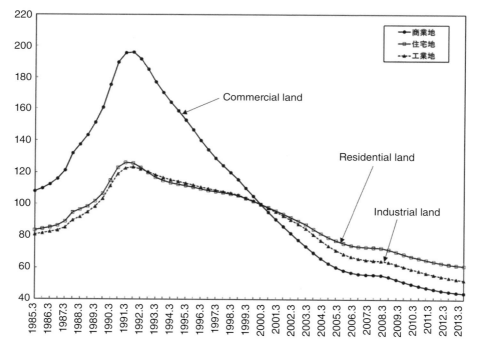

Figure 5.2   Japan long-term evolution of land prices by type, 1985–2013.
Source: Japan Real Estate Institute.

On the demand side, a major driver of the land and housing boom of the 1980s and 1990s was the transformation of the housing finance system. During the era of suppressed consumption in the 1960s, Japan's housing finance system was small, subsidized, and dominated by the two public lenders – GHLC (Government Housing Loan Corporation) and PWSPC (Pension Welfare Service Public Corp.). Together, these two state institutions provided about 70% of all housing credit finance. The limited access to housing credit was an important driver of the very high Japanese household savings rates. Starting with the Tanaka boom, this public-private funding structure was reversed as private city banks, regional banks, and the eight newly authorized *jusen* now provided two-thirds of housing credit finance. The volume of new housing loans rose 24-fold, from ¥1200 billion in 1970 to ¥28 990 billion in 1989.

On the supply side, in addition to physical constraints, the Japanese urban land supply had been made even more inelastic by the various policies preventing rural-urban land conversion and the efficient reallocation of scarce urban land. First, there was the strict law protecting agricultural land. A second, and equally potent, force was the highly favorable tax treatment of agricultural land through low appraisals and low tax rates, which made the long-term hoarding of land parcels well located within urban areas of major cities easy and attractive to small and large landowners[7].

Third, the inheritance laws further encouraged land withholding. As described two decades later by a Japanese economist: "If people invested in land using borrowed funds, interest on the borrowing was deducted from their income. If a building was constructed on land, depreciation was accounted for as an annual loss. For the purpose of inheritance tax, land values were appraised advantageously lower than cash and shares. Therefore investments in one-room apartments rose as a means of avoiding inheritance and income tax (given that the interest on the loan and depreciation of the building were deductible from income)" (Morinobu, 2006).

Figure 5.2 shows the evolution of the land price indices for residential, commercial and industrial land in Japan between 1985, and 2013, with 2000 taken as the base year and dates referring to the start of the Japanese fiscal year. Figure 5.2 shows the much sharper rise of commercial land prices than residential land prices during the bubble, and their much steeper fall since the bubble burst in 1991 for at least 22 years. Industrial land prices rose at rates close to, but slower than, housing prices during the boom, and declined at a similar during the first decade after the bust. They then began to fall

---

[7] In Tokyo, in 1982, 30 261 hectares (or about 74 800 acres) of agricultural lots were located inside residential or commercial zones, and 90% of these lots were exempted from taxes (Ito, 1992, Table 14.10, p. 425).

more rapidly than housing prices after the year 2000. By the mid-2010s, the overall Japanese land price level remains lower than what it was three decades earlier in the 1980s.

5.1.7   The direct trigger of the multiple asset bubbles: the external currency shock of 1985

By 1980, the rapidly growing Japanese economy had become the second largest in the world after the US, with a share of 8.8% of world GDP, and Japan's *per capita* GDP equaled that of the US. With one-tenth of China's population and one-third that of the US, Japan's economy was four times larger than China's and made up 70% of the six EA economies. Given the high household savings rate of 15% of rapidly rising incomes, Japan's domestic financial market grew very rapidly to become the second largest in the world.

The success of the economy caused widespread pride and euphoria across Japan. By 1985, Japan's economy had grown so large that it raised fears in the US of Japan becoming No.1 in the world (Vogel, 1978). At the top of the price bubbles in 1991, Japan's share had become 10.1% of global GDP. During the boom, Japanese investments overseas were the catalyst for the first global commercial real estate boom (Werner, 1994; Renaud, 1997).

The leading edge of the land price bubble in the 1980s were commercial real estate prices in Tokyo, but they rose against a background of rapidly rising residential land prices since the 1970s. As part of the financial liberalization program, membership in the Tokyo Stock Exchange had been opened up to foreigners. Given general expectations of continued economic growth and currency appreciation, the capitalization of firms listed on the TSE rose dramatically. Every major global financial institution, and other types of corporations, set up offices in Tokyo. Office vacancy rates dropped very low. Developers of new offices facing the extreme fragmentation of land in central Tokyo had to offer exceedingly high prices to residential land owners to induce them to sell. These home owners reinvested their windfalls into preferred housing locations, which created chains of high-priced moves (Mera and Heikkila, 1999). This was the direct channel of transmission of price increases between commercial and residential land prices, but a more diffuse potent effect was to strengthen expectations of rapid housing price increases. Spatially, the Tokyo commercial land price boom spread to the six major cities within two years, and from there across the Japanese urban system.

Then, to the domestic shock of rapid rising commercial land prices, was added the international shock of the Plaza Accord of 1985. The 1985 Plaza Accord was an agreement to realign the Yen-dollar exchange rate, but the yen appreciated more strongly than expected, from 260 to 150 per dollar over 18 months, which triggered a recession that was met with a succession of interest rate cuts, until Japan's interest rate reached a post-war low of

2.5%. The 1987 Louvre Accord was then concluded to redress the excessive dollar depreciation caused by the Plaza Accord. Soon, however, this second accord was followed by Black Monday on the US stock market (October 1987), and Bank of Japan dollar-buying interventions convinced the business sector that it was politically unfeasible for the Bank of Japan to raise interest rates, given the conflict that Japan faced between international policy coordination with the US and domestic policy needs.

In the commercial real estate sector, the perception of permanently low interest rates encouraged banks and real estate companies to invest in land, which fueled further land price increases. The intensity of the price bubble was extreme, and land values that had already been rising rapidly before the bubble increased six- to seven-fold in major cities between 1985 and 1989. Between 1980 and 1990, nominal land prices in the six biggest cities rose by 250% (180% in real terms) while, nationwide, land prices climbed 120% (44% in real terms). As can be seen in Figure 5.2, the rates of increase of commercial land prices were significantly higher than the rates of increase of residential land prices[8]. Compared to the domestic picture in Figure 5.2, Figure 5.3 provides an international

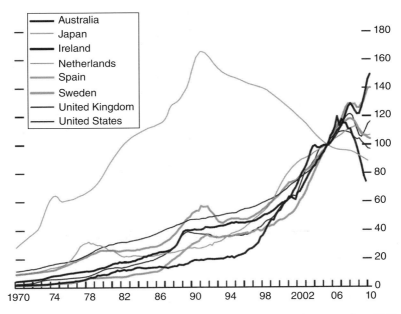

Figure 5.3 Japan's housing price boom and bust in international perspective, 1970–2010. *Source:* IMF, Global Financial Stability Report (2011), Chapter 3, Figure 3.1.

[8] The magnitude of the land price bubble was such that, by 1990, "the total land value of Japan (1637 trillion yen = 2.6 trillion, at 130 yen/dollar) is considered to be three times that of the United States. Since the total area of Japan is about 1/25 that of the United States, the average unit cost of land is about 60–75 times as much in Japan as in the United States" (Ito, 1992, p. 408).

perspective on the massive scale of Japan's housing price boom, compared to the housing booms of other OECD countries.

Concurrently, under the combined domestic shock of financial liberalization and the Tanaka infrastructure and real estate stimulus plan, the sectoral allocation of bank loans was also playing a major role in Japan's real estate bubble (Yoshitomi, 1996). As seen earlier, the eight housing finance companies, or *jusen*, had been created to meet the rapidly rising household demand for housing loans. Seven *jusen* were established by major banks (city, long-term credit, and trust banks), with several of these major banks investing in each *jusen*. The remaining one had been established by agricultural finance cooperatives, which were also depository institutions.

As Japan's financial system became liberalized and internationalized, banks began to lose their blue chip customers, who could now finance themselves more cheaply on the liberalized domestic bond market or on euro-yen capital markets. Looking for new business, the major banks turned to the *jusen's* housing loan business. In turn, feeling squeezed, the *jusen* began to extend loans beyond households to the real estate developers themselves, but one source of *jusen* funding remained their shareholding banks. By now, both banks and *jusen* had moved to high-return, high risk real estate lending. Moreover, both banks and *jusen* relied heavily on rapidly appreciating land as collateral to secure these new loans, which created an accelerator effect.

Nationally, the volume of housing loans more than doubled from ¥12,800 billion to ¥28,990 billion over the short period 1985 to 1989. The land price bubble caused such high housing prices that it led to the creation of multi-generation housing loans, of 40 or 50 years, with repayments made by a parent and his/her child in turn. A factor contributing to the creation of such unique mortgages was a very favorable feature of inheritance law, but the result was highly leveraged households.

5.1.8 Channels between the land price bubble and the stock market bubble

Stock prices also began increasing in 1983 and, from 1986, their price rise accelerated rapidly. Conceptually, the stock price of a company reflects its valuation by investors who consider the liquidation value of the company. Land being an important part of a company's assets, as land prices went up, so did stock prices. Like the price-to-rent ratios of land, the price-earnings ratios of Japanese stocks soared between 1986 and 1989. Japanese PER had been close to, but lower than, US values until the mid-1970s. By 1989, they were 6.5 times US values. Stock prices closed at their historic peak in the final days of year 1989. The downturns in land prices occurred in most metropolitan areas in 1991, but in 1989 in Tokyo.

Japanese research on why and how the two kinds of asset prices influence each other concluded that the initial seed of the two bubbles was the sharp increase in bank lending to real estate, and that a considerable co-movement of stocks and land prices was consistent with the significance of the collateral value of land for cash flow constrained firms (Ito and Iwaisako, 1995). Given the statistical difficulty of identifying the fundamentals of these two classes of asset prices in any period of time, determining the year when the two Japanese bubbles started was more difficult than determining when the bubble burst, as the price fall was sharp for both types of assets.

Compounding macroeconomic instability, bank stock valuations also accelerated rapidly because, under the "main bank" system, banks owned shares of the corporations they were financing, and these share were rapidly appreciating.

5.1.9   Cooling measures and collapse of asset prices

From 1987, the government, led by the Ministry of Finance, adopted a series of cooling measures of four different kinds that were implemented through different agencies:

1. direct controls of land prices during land transactions when the government judged that the proposed land transaction price was excessive;
2. higher interest rates;
3. quantitative restrictions on the extension of real-estate related loans;
4. higher land related taxes through both higher tax assessments and higher tax rates, and also the introduction of a new Land Value Tax law.

In the Japanese context, controls of land price transactions proved ineffective, since their implementation had to be left to the judgment of local officials. Tax instruments work along a longer time horizon.

In retrospect, Japanese officials of the time consider that the quantitative restrictions on real estate-related lending implemented in March 1990 were particularly potent, and had a much more powerful effect than the Bank of Japan's monetary tightening (Ishikawa, 2011). At first sight, such an evaluation seems plausible, since lending restrictions were specific to real estate, while monetary tightening applied to the entire economy. However, it is more likely that it is the *combination* of lending restrictions that conspicuously disrupted ongoing real estate operations, with the rapid increases in the discount rate that shifted expectations, which led to the very sharp fall of land prices that caught everyone by surprise.

Japanese officials and policy analysts did not seem to have the tools to appreciate how deeply negative user-cost of capital values (UC values) during real estate bubbles become a major source of price instability. Low or negative UC values have a potent accelerator effect that fuels demand during a housing boom, but they also accelerate housing price falls as soon as UC values swing to a positive value (as is shown in the section on household behavior in the China chapter). The increases in interest rates by the Bank of Japan (BOJ) between 1989 and 1990 were very rapid and high by Japanese historical standards. Instead of moving the discount rate by traditional 0.25% increments, the BOJ raised it from 2.5% to 3.25% in May 1989 and, from there, raised it over 14 months to 6% in August 1990.

By 1990, not one but three major elements of the Japanese user costs of capital for housing (and for commercial real estate) had swung into strongly deflationary effects. First, the interest rate increased sharply. Second, expectations of future land price appreciation shrunk rapidly, as the number of land fire sales by real estate companies shot up under the quantitative restrictions on real estate loans. Third, land taxes increased sharply as tax assessments rose from a small fraction of about 15%, to 70% of market value, while the land holding tax rate on commercial land increased from 0.2% to 1.3% (Mera and Heikkila, 1999).

Land prices at the national level began to fall very rapidly in 1991 and have been falling continuously for two decades (see Figures 3.6 and 3.7). By most estimates, housing owners saw the value of their houses drop by 60% in real terms, but not their debts while Japan is a recourse-lending country. The impact on Japan's banking system was severe. First to go into bankruptcy were all the housing loan companies. The residential and commercial property crash had a massive effect on the entire banking system, as three-quarters of local banks' lending was to small businesses using property as collateral. Underestimated and under-reported, the volume of bad loans mushroomed at one time to almost one trillion US dollars, when the world's entire GDP was estimated at just over USD 22 trillion in 1990. The banking crisis came into the open only in 1997, when decisions had to be made regarding the allocation of losses, in particular the losses of the *jusen*.

During the "lost decade" of the 1990s, the Japanese economy underwent major structural adjustments under its "balance-sheet recession" and economic deflation, as highly leveraged households, corporations and banks were all deleveraging at the same time (Koo, 2009). The monetary policy of zero interest rates could do little against this kind of balance-sheet recession without properly designed complementary actions, which were not identified or implemented (see Koo, 2009). Moreover, this zero interest rate policy favored the deposit banks and penalized households, whose savings were earning near-zero returns, and this depressed consumer demand. The negative wealth effect on consumption of falling land prices has been present in Japan for two decades.

5.1.10   Changed features of Japan's present housing system

The two-way channels of transmission of housing volatility on macroeconomic stability that are familiar in Western economies were structured and operated differently in Japan. Housing and mortgage markets, consumer spending[9], bank governance and their balance-sheets[10], other asset prices like stocks, credit spreads, and even investor behavior differed.

Changes in the legal and regulatory micro-incentives, both on the urban side and on the financial markets side, have been made in response to the large losses experienced by households, businesses, banks, local governments and other institutions. There are also major changes in the organization and regulation of the financial system, but the reform of the Postal Savings System, with its direct bearing on Japan's very large savings market and on the funding of housing, eventually did not occur. Reflecting Japan's very large number of cities, with their elected governments, land use and urban reforms have been more decentralized than financial reforms.

The multiple Japanese bubbles revealed that the housing system, financial system and economic governance structure inherited from the post-war era and the catch-up decades had become woefully inconsistent with the needs of the very large, advanced, high-income economy that Japan had become by the early 1980s.

Substantial adjustments have occurred in the structure and behavior of major components of the Japanese economy, especially in the financial sector in the years following the 1997 political and economic crisis, regarding the restructuring of the banking sector and the allocation of financial sector losses. This 1997 restructuring transition is often described as the *"jusen* crisis", but it reached far beyond Japan's housing finance system and affected the entire banking sector.

Within the housing system itself, numerous incremental adjustments have been made to existing laws, regulations and practices, but the Japanese housing system is proving heavily path-dependent in the well-known sense that the path of the law shapes the law. The change of

[9] Muellbauer and Murata (2010) find that opposite to the UK and US cases, "in Japan, credit market liberalization for households appears to have been largely absent. Controlling for income growth expectations using a separate income forecasting equation, no evidence is found of any parameter shifts. Consistent with this absence of credit market liberalization, the housing wealth or collateral effect is *negative* for Japan, in contrast to the UK and US. Also, given the preponderance of liquid assets held by Japanese households, the aggregate of a rise in short-term interest rates is *positive*, again differing from the UK and US" (emphasis in the original).

[10] Under the umbrella of the "no-bank failure policy" and the "main-bank system", priorities in corporate governance directed by major banks were as follows: "the order of priority in which the stakeholders in a Japanese company have been placed starts with employees, followed by a main bank, then by the company's managers, and finally by stockholders. This priority order is exactly the opposite of that in the US" (Yoshitomi, 1996).

generations is proving to be a significant factor for the organization, performance and dynamics of Japan's housing system.

The most important structural feature of Japan's present housing system is probably the dramatic change in expectations regarding the attractiveness of housing as an asset. The protracted collapse of property values for two decades has led to a profound change in expectations regarding asset accumulation, especially among young adults, as a number of surveys show. The previously unquestioned superiority of housing as a means of asset accumulation has been seriously undermined.

In addition, the rapid aging of Japan's population may already be playing a major role in compounding the drop in consumer confidence caused by large losses in household balance sheets when land prices and stock prices fell steeply after 1991. It is noteworthy that both the 1970 boom and the 1990 peak of the housing boom had coincided with local peaks in the working population as percentage of Japan's total population (Akihiko, 2006). The absolute peak of Japan's working-age population was 78 million people in 1995. Since that year, the working-age population has been shrinking rapidly. If current trends persist, it will have shrunk by 20 million between 2010 and 2030. The structure of housing demand is therefore changing very significantly, as only Japan's old population (over 65) is expanding. The role of housing assets in funding retirement needs, compared to alternatives domestic and international assets, is now an issue in Japan.

A notable effect of the fall of land prices is the spatial restructuring of major cities, with the return to central locations of a significant proportion of households that were driven out into distant suburbs during the land price bubble and are experiencing extremely long journeys to work. This return to city centers is consistent with the changing demographic structure of Japan and the increase in single-individual households, young and old. Given the daily savings in commuting times, this spatial change is likely to be sustained.

The impact of the AFC on Japanese housing appears to have been muted. In contrast, during the GFC, Japanese housing production dropped sharply in 2009, to about 800 000, while Japan's GDP contracted by 5.5%. In this case, the causal ordering was more from the global contraction in trade and financial markets to the contraction of new housing than in the other direction. In the six largest cities, land prices had finally began to level off in the early 2000s, and were rising again by 2004. They rose by about 3% in both nominal and real terms in 2006, and by about 8% in nominal and real terms in 2007, driven in part by the booming REITs commercial real estate industry (Watanabe and Shimizu 2012). Unfortunately, the global financial crisis led to another fall in nominal and real property prices in 2009. The main channel of transmission of the US subprime shock was the collapse in the demand for Japanese REITs. The losses experienced by Japanese securities firms and major banks from the purchase of "toxic"

US securities, such as MBSs and CDOs, were estimated at around ¥6 billion, and were considered manageable (Seko *et al.*, 2011).

5.2   Taiwan: a housing market with little government intervention

5.2.1   *A market-based housing system under balanced macroeconomic policies*

Taiwan's housing system, its performance and the conduct of its housing policy contrast greatly with those of Japan. "Housing has been a low priority in Taiwan's development agenda" (Chang and Chen, 2012) and, "for a long time the Taiwanese government had no specific policy. Compared to other governments, the Taiwanese government intervened relatively little in the housing market" (Chang and Chen, 2011). What made it possible for the government to maintain such a distant role in housing over decades of very rapid growth and urbanization? After all, with 640 people per square kilometer, Taiwan has the highest gross density in East Asia. Moreover, almost 52% of the land is mountainous and inhabitable. How is the Taiwanese housing system performing? And why did Taiwan wait until 2012 to pass its first Housing Law?

Taiwan's housing system is market-based. Its performance rests on land use foundations that were laid in the 1950s, and on critical macroeconomic policy decisions that launched Taiwan on its successful development path as a small, open economy (Vogel, 1991). A look back at the period of the economic take-off, 1950–1975, helps in clarifying important features of Taiwan's housing system and its interactions with the wider economy.

5.2.1.1   *Land policy foundations*
First, the 1946 Taiwanese Constitution affirmed the central role of private property rights in land markets. To protect the rights of the community, Section 142 of the Constitution set out the principle of land value recapture (Henry George's land value tax), by which the unearned value of a land price increase originating from the activities of the growing urban community, and not from the specific improvements of its private owner, should be shared with, if not entirely returned, to the community. Separately from the Constitution, the land reforms completed in 1953 led to a high degree of initial wealth equality across the country (Cheng, 1961).

The 1954 Law on the Equalization of Land Rights set out the operational dimensions of land use and land taxation. This law covered four operational aspects of land taxation:

- the valuation of land;
- taxation according to declared value;

- the conditions under which the government can exercise its option to buy the land at that price; and
- the public recapture of future land value increments.

Amendments were made and other laws were passed in later decades. Land taxation has shaped the structure of Taiwan's housing demand in important ways, as shall be seen later (Bourassa and Peng, 2011), and is also a major source of revenue for Taiwanese local governments (Lam and Tsui, 1998).

5.2.1.2   *Macroeconomic foundations*

The dynamics of urban development and housing markets in Taiwan was shaped by early macroeconomic policy decisions. In a market economy, the three key prices are the interest rate, the wage rate and the exchange rate, and Taiwan adopted very unconventional policies for the times. To control destabilizing inflation rates of 70% per year in the early 1950s, the Executive Yuan adopted the recommendation by economist Sho-Chieh Tsiang (蔣碩傑) to adopt a high interest rate policy in 1961, which proved decisive. High interest rates now reflected the opportunity cost of capital in the then under-developed Taiwanese economy. Together with conservative fiscal policies, this unsubsidized interest rate policy was successful in stopping inflation, and the policy was sustained over time. This monetary policy had major developmental impacts. By encouraging labor-intensive, rather than capital-intensive, activities it did not discriminate against household savings or SMEs in favor of large corporations such as *keiretsus* in Japan, *Chaebols* in Korea, SOEs in Singapore and in China (Scitovsky, 1986).

Equally innovative, given the conventional wisdom of development economics at the time, was Tsiang's success in persuading the Taiwanese government to abandon its multiple exchange rate. A unitary exchange rate was set in 1961 at market-level, while adopting an export-led strategy[11]. 1961 was the demarcation line for the economy, and the rate of industrialization accelerated after that date. "At the close of World War II, *per capita* income in Taiwan was about US$70. Such a low *per capita* income increased rapidly to reach $2,280 by 1980 (or 8,650 in 2014 dollars). During this period, population grew at a high rate of 3.5% percent until the 1960s and at about 2% thereafter. Real GNP, however, grew at the much higher rate of 9.2% on the average over three decades [...]. Due to the acceleration of growth, real

---

[11] While adopting a neutral policy, the Taiwanese government retained control over the exchange rate, like many other countries at the time. It was only decades later, during the AFC, that Taiwan floated its exchange to fend off possible speculative attacks against the NT dollar, which moved to attack the Hong Kong dollar. In 1998, Taiwan still grew at 4.5% in 1998. See Sheng (2009), Chapter 10.

GNP doubled every seven years after 1963. As a result, real GNP was eleven times the real GNP of 1952" (Kuo *et al.*, 1981).

Manufacturing grew from 14.9% of total employment in 1952, to 32.4% in 1979. Taiwan's economy reached the "turning point" in 1968, and achieved full employment by 1971, and manufacturing exports were about 42% of total manufacturing in 1976 (Kuo *et al.*, 1981, p. 17). Manufacturing employment in Taiwan's five major cities more than tripled in the 1970s alone. Since the urban population expanded 5.2 times and GNP *per capita* rose by about 4.6 times between 1950 and 1980, the size of Taiwan's urban economy expanded by about 24 times in NT dollar terms.

The SME's full exposure to global markets, together with their ability to diversify risks through joint contracting, have been major factors in Taiwan's resilience to international shocks. One side-effect of the dominance of SMEs, and of the universal awareness that Taiwan is a small, open economy, is that Taiwanese household housing investment decisions appear to be strongly influenced by inflation expectations and macroeconomic conditions, which they closely watch (Chen and Patel, 1998). Also, the collateral value of property is playing a significant role in small businesses investment (Chen and Wang, 2003).

Until 1975, there was no government effort to develop a national housing policy in Taiwan. This may have been due to the outlook of economists at the time, who usually considered housing merely as a social issue and a consumption, not an investment issue. The organization of the Taiwan government could also have been a factor. More pragmatically, social conditions in Taiwan were not only stable, but improving remarkably. Because initial exports were farm products, processed foods and labor-intensive assembly industrial goods, the (intended) initial spatial impact on Taiwan was rural industrialization in this very densely populated country. Such a decentralized urban development mitigated initial pressures on urban housing for a while (Ho, 1978).

A major economic outcome that played a role in the long absence of national housing policies is that the Taiwanese income distribution actually improved during the high growth years of the economic take-off, between 1952 and the mid-1970s. The national Gini coefficient declined from 32.75 in 1964 to 28.53 in 1978 (Kuo *et al.*, 1981, p. 140). Taiwan is a very rare case of rapid growth with improving equity. High growth rates, together with improved income equality, is certainly not the case for mainland China today. Except for a few emergency social housing programs from the center, whatever public housing activities occurred in Taiwan were carried out by local governments. Taiwan's first, and limited, national housing policy program was triggered by the widespread impact of 1973 oil crisis, and was developed in association with the Six-Year Economic Plan of 1975–1981.

5.2.2   *Taiwan's four market-driven housing price cycles in four decades*

Alone among the six EA housing systems, Taiwan has experienced four market-driven housing price cycles since the early 1970s (Chang and Chen, 2012). Contrary to western housing cycles, which typically have a long build-up of prices, followed by a short period of sharply falling prices, Taiwanese housing price cycles have been marked by a few years of rapid price increases, followed by a much longer period of slowing declining prices.

As already noted, inflationary expectations have been an important factor in Taiwan's housing price cycles. Reflecting the small, open economy of Taiwan, external shocks have often played a leading role in these cycles. The 1972–74 cycle reflected the 1973 oil crisis and the oil embargo that caused very high inflation, and led the government to apply stabilization measures that deflated housing and real estate prices. The second price boom, in 1978–1980, was caused by the inflation of the second oil crisis. Its longer contraction phase reflected the more stringent policies applied to the construction sector than during the first boom.

In contrast, the third price boom of 1987–89 was due to the internal shock of excessive monetary expansion caused by financial liberalization. The long period of housing price declines after 1989 was caused by the rise of cross-strait tensions, the contraction of Asian economies during the AFC, and the outflow of capital from the region. As noted, Taiwan's economy was not strongly affected by the Asia Financial Crisis of 1997–1998, because of conservative and realistically priced government policies that matched the conservative financial policies of the banks and SME enterprises, which were averse to excessive leverage. As a defensive measure against currency speculators, Taiwan floated its NT dollar, which permitted it to maintain export growth as the NT dollar devalued. The fourth price boom was related to the significant improvements in cross-strait relations with China, and expectations of a higher level of foreign investment in Taiwan.

Reflecting the secular trend of rapidly rising incomes, increasing scarcity of land and the concentration of population in large metropolitan regions, there has been a ratcheting upwards of prices in Taiwan from boom to boom. After each price dip, Taiwanese housing prices eventually settled at a new and higher level after each boom, as can be seen in Figure 5.4. In Taiwan, as in the rest of East Asia, fundamental prices are not static, but can have a steeply rising secular trend. Such secularly rising prices add to the difficulty of identifying housing price bubbles as irrational deviations from fundamental prices (Pavlidis *et al.*, 2013).

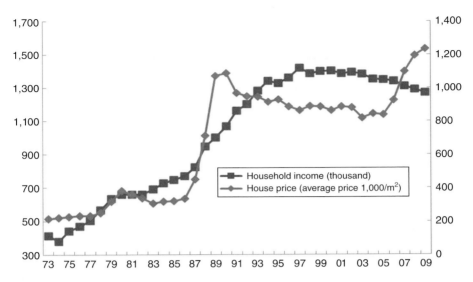

Figure 5.4 Taiwan: housing price cycles versus the rise of incomes, 1972–2010.
Source: Chang and Chen (2011).

5.2.3 Development of the housing finance system under financial deregulation

During Taiwan's economic take-off decades, most banks were state-owned. Bank interest rates may have been priced closer to the true economic cost of capital than anywhere else in East Asia, but they were set by the central bank. Banks were not allowed to issue residential mortgage loans, nor were they interested in this potential line of business. It is in that context that presale contracts became a core tool of residential construction finance.

Residential mortgage lending emerged during the deregulation of the financial system, which proceeded in an orthodox and risk-focused way during the 1980s. Interest rates were controlled until 1975. Then, in 1985, the "basic lending rate", which had been initially set by designated leading banks, was extended to all banks. Financial liberalization was accelerated by the Asian Financial Crisis in 1997, when the NT dollar was floated, and all foreign exchange controls abolished. Like Hong Kong, Taiwan's financial system became fully integrated into global finance.

Then, in 1991. free entry into the banking system was permitted, and 16 new private banks were created. Today, residential mortgage lending services are competitively offered by private banks, and Taiwan's housing finance system has deepened considerably, with an MDO to GDP ratio of 28% by 2009. Typical mortgage loans are variable rate mortgages, of usually

20-year maturities, but sometimes shorter. The interest rate is administered by the lenders and is not directly indexed. In contrast to US mortgage loans, the Taiwanese borrower is not offered a mortgage menu of choices; it is the Taiwanese lender that offers the maturity of the loan to clients, based on the bank's internal risk management evaluations. Down payments are usually large, as Taiwanese households share the East Asian aversion to long-term debt, and loan curtailment is frequent (See Chapter 3, Section 5). However, the rapid rise of household debt is now a public policy concern, which seems to be related both to socio-economic changes and to the issue of the non-linear dynamics of housing prices in high-density, high-income economies, about which we know so little (see Chapter 1).

Given the high PIR ratios across Taiwanese cities and the strong preference for housing assets, the total Taiwanese household debt level is among the highest in East Asia. Socioeconomic changes, and the erosion of intra-family transfers, may also be a rising factor. Total household debt is high, and rising close to 84% of annual GDP. More than 70% is related to the purchase of real estate. Most of the balance is linked to business investment. The debt-servicing ratio has been rising for the past decade, and was 38% in 2012. Only South Korea has comparable ratio of debt to GDP, but the Korean debt is growing at a faster rate than Taiwan's. Both countries have a household debt level higher than the USA and Japan, where households are deleveraging and the debt level is declining.

5.2.4   Core role of presale contracts in Taiwan's residential construction market

Taiwan's financial development policies have had a lasting impact on the relationship between construction price cycles and housing price cycles, and have led to the early development of informal construction finance contracts. Today's transactions within the existing housing stock may be funded through the residential mortgage market. However, new construction is still significantly funded through presales (or "sales before completion") contracts. For that reason, the residential construction market of Taiwan is referred to as the *presales market* (Hua *et al.*, 2001) .

For policy monitoring, the housing market is separated in Taiwan into two components, each with its own price index and its own type of financing: the *existing housing stock*, which is tracked by the *Sinyi* price index, and *new housing construction*, which is tracked by the *Cathay* price index (See Figure 5.5). One expects the price of new construction and of existing housing eventually to converge according to supply-demand conditions. One also expects the new construction (*pre-sales*) housing prices to adjust faster to supply-demand imbalances, since new housing construction is only a small fraction of the existing housing stock.

Presale contracts emerged as an informal financing mechanism during the pre-1980s decades of little or no residential mortgage lending. Such contracts remain very important in the residential construction market today, because they have significant benefits and risks are manageable for both households and developers (Chang and Ward, 1993).

Because most new housing in Taiwan consists of large multiple-unit projects, there is a significant time lag before the decision to build and the delivery of completed units. Presales contracts are extensively used by developers, even if they have access to financing from other sources, for three strategic reasons. First, presales lower their project bankruptcy risks. Second, presales permit developers to judge changing demand conditions during construction, and what the optimum pricing of their units should be. Third, a developer's reputation and size are critical to the success of a presales program, as presales contracts are traded in most local real estate markets. Where presales are prevalent, oligopolistic markets are dominated by large developers.

For a buyer, the advantages of presales contracts are: to face small periodic payments, a high degree of leverage; the avoidance of transaction tax before construction of the unit is completed; and the possibility of trading the contract. Some important disadvantages are: the lack of security for the deposit; the risk of delay in completion; the risk of default by the developer; and discrepancies between the design contracted and the unit actually delivered. Under the presale system, a significant amount of overpricing might take place, and a "market for lemons" is also a potential issue. For all these

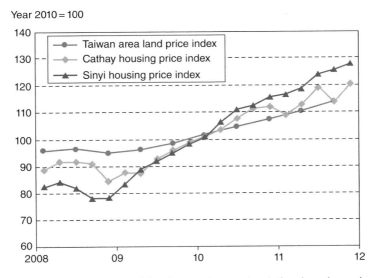

Figure 5.5 Taiwan: movement of land, presales and existing housing price indices, 2008–2012.
Source: Central Bank of the Republic of China, Financial Stability Report #7, May 2013, Chart 2.37.

reasons, the structure of presales contracts and their resale terms must be regulated for transparency, stability and secure trading[12].

The role of lenders who might partially finance the developer should not be ignored. Some lenders may require that a high percentage of the units in a project must be pre-sold to insulate the lender from the risk that the project cannot be completed. East Asian research also shows that the trading of presale contracts tends to increase housing price volatility (Wang *et al.*, 2000). There is little or no comparison between the widespread use of presale contracts across East Asian residential markets, and their trivial use in Western markets, where little trading of contracts occurs.

5.2.5   Worsening affordability issues in a system tilted toward home-ownership

For a market-based system, Taiwan has a very high level of home ownership that fluctuates around 85% and peaked at 88% in 2007. This ownership ratio is way above median values in high-income housing markets, which usually range between 50% and 60%, depending on the national structure of housing investment incentives. This tax structure also explains the very high housing vacancy rate in Taiwan,

The unusual tenure structure in Taiwan has been traced back by Bourassa and Peng (2011) to the very low user cost of housing ownership for almost three decades. The very high ownership rate comes from the highly preferential taxation of land in home ownership, compared to the taxation of land in other uses, among which is rental housing. A reinforcing factor that is endogenous to this distortion is the low quality of the private rental stock. Like private rental units, public rental units are of much lower quality than privately owned housing units, which is also the case in Japan.

Together with the very high rate of vacant housing, the very high percentage of home-owners results from a strong and persistent bias, in favor of homeownership, of housing policy measures taken over several decades. This has two consequences: first, housing has become the asset of choice, with rising inflation expectations having a rapid positive impact on ownership demand. Second, Taiwan's rental housing stock is a residual stock of lower quality, which encourages young adults to seek housing ownership as early as possible. The Taiwanese public housing sector has remained very small by East Asian and international standards. Today, the stock of public housing units represents slightly more than 5% of the total housing stock. The 2012 Housing Law addresses issues of sector efficiency and social welfare.

---

[12] The regulation of presales contract varies from country to country, and sometimes from market to market. Hong Kong has one of the most developed regulatory frameworks to handle the range of information asymmetries and risks present in a presale market (see Leung *et al.*, 2007).

Looking ahead, two megatrends are changing the dynamics of Taiwan's housing sector. The first is the wage stagnation resulting from the migration of Taiwan's manufacturing to China over the past two decades, which has been "hollowing out" Taiwan's manufacturing sector differentially across cities (Liu and Shih, 2013). This wage stagnation may be playing a significant role in city price-income ratios and in the difference between other cities and Taipei County, which includes Taipei City and is now a metropolis of almost 10 million people, with 40% of Taiwan's population. Taipei could be the beneficiary of the Memorandum of Understanding and the Economic Cooperation Framework Agreement of 2010 in developing industry-related services and higher value added technologies. The second megatrend is population aging.

5.2.6   Main features of Taiwan's present housing system: a summary

Taking as given the familiar anatomy of a market-base housing system, the profile of Taiwan's housing system is easier to draw than that of the other EA housing systems, where the complexities and volatility of government interventions can be difficult to interpret correctly and to communicate concisely on time. Major features that distinguish Taiwan's housing system from other EA housing systems are:

- The cyclical growth of the sector with four housing price cycles since the early 1970s.
- A very high level of home ownership, of the order of 85%, accompanied by a significant degree of mobility across the housing stock – the opposite of Japan, where housing mobility is low.
- A very high housing vacancy rate in the existing stock, which was 20.0% according to the 2010 Census and is considerably above the natural vacancy rate consistent with housing market conditions in various Taiwanese cities (Wang and Chang, 2007).
- Distinct price cycles for new housing construction and for the existing housing stock caused by expectations, investment lags that are also related to the different financing tools for new construction, and for the existing housing stock with *presales* contracts for new construction, and residential mortgage contracts for the existing stock.
- Land taxation and land use regulations that play a very significant role in housing investments decisions.
- The strong secular trend of rising – and possible accelerating – housing prices, around which housing cycles are occurring, together with important socio-economic changes such as the decline of intra-family transfers, as in South Korea.

- A high and rising level household indebtedness, that was almost 84% of GDP in 2012 and is related to the high and rising housing price-to-income ratios in major urban centers.
- Since the Global Financial Crisis, the Central Bank of the Republic of China (Taiwan), or CBC, has implemented macro-prudential policies to cool housing prices. One notable feature of the macro-prudential policies of the Central Bank is that its regulation of mortgages is not uniform across the country, but is spatially differentiated. More restrictive lending conditions apply to Taipei City, where the PIR ratio had risen above 13.1 in 2012 (based on CBC estimates), while it was also quite high, at 8.3, in the six metropolitan areas. The mortgage debt-income ratio is also significantly higher in Taipei, at 47.6%, while it is lower, but still high, at 32.0% in the six metro areas.
- The passage of the Housing Law in 2012 reflects national concerns with persistent housing affordability and access problems for lower-income groups.
- There are now anecdotal reports of a "China effect" on housing demand and prices in the highest quality segment of the housing markets.

6

Housing Volatility in East Asian City States: Hong Kong and Singapore

Studying the dynamics of the housing systems of Hong Kong and Singapore can deepen our understanding of the relationship between macroeconomic conditions and housing sector performance. In these two economies, it is impossible for macroeconomists to ignore the impact of housing conditions on aggregate economic performance, as was happening in the USA before 2007. In a symmetrical way, urban decision-makers can readily see the need to understand the impact of macroeconomic conditions on housing. The reason is that local governments in these two economies are absent from the housing cycle dynamics, and do not obscure or buffer the impacts of national and international changes.

In Hong Kong and Singapore, channels of interactions between housing and the macroeconomy are uniquely transparent, which does not mean that they are identical. These channels of interactions, are statistically, among the best documented in the world. Elsewhere, for reasons of market failure, too many housing systems are weakly documented in several ways – in terms of spatial coverage and housing detail, statistical accuracy and comparability, frequency and timeliness, as well as scope (Goodman, 1992). This is not the case for Hong Kong and Singapore, where housing conditions are well documented, with the highest reporting frequencies of any country, especially in the case of Hong Kong. At the other end of the quality spectrum in East Asia, we have China's "socialist economy with Chinese characteristics" where housing cyclical conditions across its very large number of dissimilar cities are not monitored well yet, and remain difficult to compare, beyond a small percentage of major cities.

Dynamics of Housing in East Asia, First Edition. Bertrand Renaud,
Kyung-Hwan Kim and Man Cho.
© 2016 John Wiley & Sons, Ltd. Published 2016 by John Wiley & Sons, Ltd.

In spite of their similarities as small open economies, there are important structural differences between Hong Kong and Singapore in three critical areas: national governance; the management of the exchange rate and interest rates; and the structure and behavior of the housing system itself, with different interactions between private and public housing.

Looking ahead, the two city economies face several challenges: minimizing the volatility of housing prices; managing the increasingly scarce government-controlled land supply; dealing with rising income and wealth inequality among residents; and managing the impact on the top tier of the private housing market of the wealthiest residents of the surrounding region, who see luxury housing in these two economies as safe, financially attractive and fashionable investments. Like every other East Asian economy, Hong Kong and Singapore also have to manage a population aging problem.

6.1   Hong Kong: volatility in an open economy with a dual housing system

6.1.1   Basic structure of the Hong Kong economy

Hong Kong is a small, highly open, high-density urban economy, where the relationship between housing price volatility and the stability of the economy is closely monitored by policymakers and residents. After becoming one of the Asian NICs (newly industrialized countries) during the post-WWII decades of its insulation from China, Hong Kong reconnected to its hinterland and played an influential direct and indirect role in the real estate reforms of China, especially after the famous South China trip of Deng Xiaoping in 1982, and his visit to Shenzhen, directly across the Hong Kong border[1]. Since then, most of Hong Kong's industrial base has migrated to the Pearl River Delta and beyond, in Guangdong province (Vogel, 1990).

Hong Kong has become an information-intensive economy, and its four key industries are financial services, trade and logistics, tourism and professional services. Well over 80% of the labor force works in the service sector, and lives on a territory of around 1090 km², with a population of 7.2 million people in 2013. In spite of its small GDP on a global scale, Hong Kong has a financial sector that ranks among the top 20 in importance for the systemic stability of the global financial system, both in terms of scale and interconnectedness[2]. On a PPP basis, Hong Kong's *per capita* income is now among the top ten in the world, and was higher

---

[1] For the contrast in industrialization strategies between Hong Kong and Singapore, see Vogel (1993).
[2] In its surveillance of the global financial system, the IMF ranked Hong Kong among the 20 most important financial sectors in terms of size and of global interconnectedness. In 2010, Hong Kong ranked third in Asia after Japan and China, and ahead of South Korea and Singapore (IMF, 2010).

than that of the US, at \$52,000 in 2012 prices – but a city economy differs from a continent-sized economy.

6.1.1.1   *Hong Kong's government system since 1997: the Basic Law*

In the late 1970s and early 1980s, Hong Kong's society and its economy were under great stress for a confluence of reasons: an unstable exchange rate; bank failures; capital outflows; and rising anxiety regarding the return of Hong Kong to China in 1997 under unknown conditions. The political and economic disorders of the Cultural Revolution in the PRC next door caused great concern. Not unrelated to the PRC disturbances, the Hong Kong labor riots of the mid-1970s were also fresh in memories.

The historical Sino-British Joint Declaration of 1984 stabilized the domestic environment in Hong Kong, by clarifying the conditions of its return to China. Meanwhile, order was also returning in China under Deng Xiaoping, and the Joint Declaration also had a direct impact on the land system. Annex III of the Declaration redefines and unifies the land lease system until 2047. It also included a clause (Article 4) that restricted new urban land supply to 50 hectares per year from 1985 and until June 1997, except in the case of land to be used for public housing. In effect, this clause expected to make the land supply even more inelastic than it had been and, in the process, stabilize real estate prices[3]. However, as shown later, the short-term dynamic of the Hong Kong land supply is shaped by additional factors to new government land auctions. The timing and scale of Hong Kong government land auctions has also been, and continue to be, problematic.

In accordance with the "one country, two systems" principle, adopted in 1984, Hong Kong operates with the status of Special Administrative Region (SAR) under the rules set in its Basic Law since its handover to China in 1997. As a mini-constitution, the Basic Law guarantees that Hong Kong will continue to operate for 50 years until 2047 under the capitalist system and the common law in force when Hong Kong was a British Crown Colony. This condition is critical to the continued success of Hong Kong as a global financial center of strategic significance to the economy of the PRC. The Basic Law also states that Hong Kong's way of life shall remain unchanged for 50 years[4].

---

[3] The two government parties to the Joint Declaration agreed to this cut in new urban land supply for opposite reasons. The Chinese side was concerned that the colonial British government might accelerate the sales of leases and misuse the sales proceeds. The British side was concerned about the rapidly rising level of uncertainty and growing turmoil regarding the 1997 handover: stabilized real estate prices should have a beneficial impact. Only half of the proceeds of the land grants sales could be used by the British colonial government for infrastructure purposes. The other half would be deposited in a savings account usable only by the HKSAR government after 1997.

[4] The Basic Law of the Hong Kong Special Administrative Region of the People's Republic of China was passed by China's People Congress in April 1990, six years after the signing of the Joint Declaration. It came into force on 1 July 1997 when Hong Kong was handed over to China by the UK government. It will remain in force for 50 years (i.e., until 2047).

A fiscal surplus is mandated by the balance-budget rule of Hong Kong's Basic Law. The government's fiscal surplus has grown quite large, and was of the order of 35% of GDP in 2013. The actual size of this fiscal surplus is driven by additional self-imposed government considerations, including the "golden rule" of keeping public expenditures below 20% of GDP. This very large Hong Kong fiscal surplus has a direct link to the government's monopoly over the supply of new urban land, and its direct and indirect impacts on government revenues, as discussed below.

6.1.1.2   *The Linked Exchange Rate System (LERS)*

The Hong Kong dollar has been pegged to the US dollar since 1983. As a consequence, Hong Kong does not have an independent monetary policy. The functions and objectives of the Hong Kong Monetary Authority (HKMA) created in 1993 are not those of a usual central bank. They are limited to managing the LERS, maintaining the stability of the banking system and increasing the efficiency of the financial system.

Unlike a typical central bank, the HKMA does not issue banknotes and is not a banker to the government. Hong Kong interest rates are determined by US monetary policies and not by local economic conditions – in particular, local inflation. For instance, during the run-up to the crisis of 1997, low US rates were at odd with the accelerating GDP growth rate of Hong Kong, inflation rose rapidly, in part because housing rents are a major component of the Hong Kong CPI, and housing prices were appreciating rapidly. The years of quantitative easing policies by the US Federal Reserve since 2009 are once again a major factor in the accelerating Hong Kong housing price boom after the GFC.

In terms of insurance against external shocks, it is important to differentiate between the Exchange Fund, which safeguards the US/HK dollar exchange peg set at HK$7.8 per US dollar, and the government's own large fiscal surplus. The Exchange Fund has grown very large since the speculative attacks in 1997 and 1998 during the AFC and the "double play" targeting jointly Hong Kong's currency and its stock market with a large percentage of shares issues by real estate corporations. By the end of 2013, the Exchange Fund assets had grown to US$ 388 billion, or six times Hong Kong's annual GDP.

The rebalancing of economic relations between Hong Kong, the US and Mainland China is leading to questions about the continuing validity of the LERS. The 1983 peg to the US dollar was very successful in stabilizing the Hong Kong economy because, in those days, most of Hong Kong's trade was with the US, and China was still a small, closed economy. But is it now necessary to reconsider the LERS three decades later, because those were the period of most rapid economic growth in the entire history of China?

Arguments in favor of a LERS review do not fit the reality of the structure of trade and finance in Hong Kong and, more importantly, they are based on premature views of the role of China renminbi as a global currency, when the RMB is not yet a convertible currency, and China's current account is closed in contrast with the US dollar (Prasad and Ye, 2012).

6.1.1.3 Hong Kong economic cycles and growth trends: trading places between the USA and China

Hong Kong is a gateway for the flow of goods, business and financial services between mainland China and the rest of the world. In such a small urban economy, the external demand for goods and services drives business cycles. Domestic residential and non-residential real estate cycles result – mostly – from the supply responses from the shifts in the growth and composition of this external demand. The LERS reinforces the transmission of economic shocks from the US to Hong Kong. Beyond this structural factor, the integration between the Hong Kong and mainland Chinese economies has steadily raised the degree of co-movement in growth between mainland China and Hong Kong.

In a significant shift over the past decade, 51% of Hong Kong merchandise and services exports went to the mainland in 2012, while 21% went to the US. However, on a valued-added basis the trade picture becomes different: the share of merchandise exports to the mainland in value-added terms was about 22% in 2012. The US share, though having declined from a decade ago, was still around 25% in 2012. In terms of financial services, US demand represented 33% of services exports, while the mainland's share was 4%. Contrary to a frequent perception, it is not China but "overseas investors that have been driving the demand for mainland-related financial products supplied through the Hong Kong platform" (Hong Kong Monetary Authority, 2014). For mainland China, the Hong Kong financial sector is a vital link to interface with global financial markets and for modernizing its own financial system and gradually developing the international role of the Renminbi.

An econometric analysis of how shocks originating from mainland China and the US affected the cyclical output and growth trend of the Hong Kong economy during the period 1985–2013 finds that, domestic shocks originating from Hong Kong contributed the most to its cyclical output and inflation fluctuations over the short-term horizon. However, US shocks have had a much larger impact on Hong Kong business cycles over the longer term than shocks originating from the mainland or internally from Hong Kong. When it comes to growth trends, in contrast with short-term cyclical fluctuations, the long-run impact of mainland shocks on Hong Kong growth trends increased significantly, from about 15% to 65% during the period 2003–2013 (Hong Kong Monetary Authority, 2014).

6.1.2   Hong Kong's dual housing system

Hong Kong has a dual housing system: it has a market-driven private housing system, and it also has one of the largest public rental housing systems in the world that is directly managed by a single government agency – the Hong Kong Housing Authority (HKHA). After rising to an even 50/50 split in the early 1990s, the market share of public housing has moved down to 30% after 1997, through the combined impact of the 64% fall of real private housing prices between 1997 and 2003, and increased housing privatization of the public housing stock through subsidized homeownership programs. Currently, the private housing market serves 70% of the population, and the very large public housing sector serves the remaining 30%. Externally, the demand for housing by potential homeowners and by investors is affected by unrestricted capital flows in and out of this small economy, facing an inelastic housing supply.

The Hong Kong Housing Authority (HKHA) manages the entire stock of public rental housing (PRH). Hong Kong contrasts very significantly with other high-income market countries, where the supply of social rental housing comes from a diversified mix of non-profit suppliers, municipal housing offices and public-private programs (Peppercorn and Taffin, 2013). Managing the public-private housing interface under the single ownership of the HKHA heightens operational risks. Hong Kong does not have the risk-mitigating benefits of a diversified ownership of the public rental housing (PRH) stock like other high-income countries. Time inconsistencies in public housing decisions are structurally built in by this legacy of the colonial era.

By 2012, the private residential stock amounted to about 1.4 million units and the PRH stock to 0.768 million units, for a total housing stock of about 2.2 million units. About 2.09 million people (30% of the population) live in public rental housing flats (PRH). The private rental market services about 15% of the population, but represents less than 10% of the stock. About 520,000 persons aged 60 or over live in PRH flats, which represents 38% of the elderly population.

The private housing stock of Hong Kong is very homogenous by international standards, as it consists almost entirely of apartment units in large integrated projects. The HKSAR is also probably the most transparent housing system in the world. Timely, accurate and detailed performance data for five classes of housing types, on rents, prices and new output, have been publicly available for decades. These data are now posted on the web on a monthly basis, together with a wide range of real estate, economic and demographic indicators. This transparency is part of the resilience of the Hong Kong economy, but, the volume and frequency of information may also contribute to increased individual decision-making volatility (de Bondt and Thaler, 1994).

6.1.3 Financial system and residential mortgage finance

Hong Kong financial sector policies contrasts with the government-controlled land system. The well-known public-relations description of Hong Kong government policy as "positive non-intervention" was coined by a senior official during the colonial era, and applied most easily to the well-regulated and open financial sector, while it was a misrepresentation elsewhere.

Hong Kong has a three-tiered banking system of licensed banks, restricted licensed banks, and deposit-taking companies. Each tier has some institutions participating in the mortgage markets, where licensed banks dominate. However, the actual supply of mortgage loans is oligopolistic, as five licensed banks, out 190 domestic and foreign banks, have a market share of well above 80% (Batchvarov *et al.*, 2003).

The Hong Kong Mortgage Corporation (HKMC) was created in 1997 as a public corporation to diversify the concentration of risks inherent to the structure of Hong Kong's housing market and to improve the funding of mortgages though the sale of mortgage securities on the global market. However, this strategic objective has yet to be achieved on a significant scale, because the HKMC was of limited strategic value to banks that preferred to keep housing loans on their balance sheets, given their risk-adjusted quality.

Hong Kong residential mortgage instruments are floating rate mortgages, where contract maturities of 20 years dominate. These mortgage loans are plain vanilla ARMs without caps. Mortgage rates are typically indexed to the Hong Kong prime rate. In addition to the loan products for the private markets, banks also develop products tailored to the government's home ownership programs. The ratio of non-performing residential loans is low because, in addition to careful loan underwriting, all loans are full recourse loans. Therefore, even during the deep 1997–2003 housing price collapse, most borrowers whose mortgage loans were under water kept making their mortgage payments.

6.1.4 Dynamic features of the Hong Kong housing supply system

The HKSAR government faces challenges in its goal of stabilizing housing prices through land auctions. One is deciding upon the appropriate annual release of new urban land. The other is managing the interface between the very large public rental sector and the private housing sector. In both areas, decisions are inherent bets about market outcomes that are difficult to predict. The outcomes of the auction sales of land grants involve time lags, changing domestic economic conditions, interactions with the real estate oligopoly and the possibility of large and unpredictable external shocks, which might be positive or negative. Every HKSAR government land decision faces the risk of time inconsistency with changing market conditions.

6.1.4.1   *The government monopoly over land supply has fostered an oligopolistic real estate industry*

The supply of new urban land is directly controlled by the HKSAR government through land auctions of usually large parcels of land. Over decades of operation, this land system has fostered the growth of an oligopolistic real estate industry, in which four to six large corporations have long dominated the entire industry (Bristow, 1987; Renaud *et al.*, 1997). The Hong Kong real estate industry is differentiated into five market sectors: offices, retail, industrial and warehousing, residential and hotels. Barriers to entry into every one of these sectors are very high. Among these barriers are: the extremely high level of capital required to bid for land; the prevalence of capital-intensive high-rise technologies, needed to optimize the substitution rate between land and building, whose regulation is flexible in Hong Kong; and, the need to finance large, mixed-use construction projects, in which economies of scale are significant.

The organization of Hong Kong's private real estate development industry is such that its supply of new housing units is relatively insulated from the immediate impact of government supply of new land in two main ways. First, the use of land reserves by the dominant large developers is a major component of their long-term growth strategy, and these reserves insulate them from annual variations in the scale government land sales. Second, and just as important, government land sales are only a fraction of the total land supply of private developers, and have been a diminishing one over time[5].

For Hong Kong private developers, new land comes from three sources: opening up new areas through public auctions, land redevelopment and land reclamation. Land redevelopment already represented more than half of the new apartment supply before 1997 (Tse *et al.*, 2001). The critical factor is the permissible level of residential development intensity on the parcels being redeveloped, which are constantly gaining in importance for private supply over time. During the transition period 1985–97 between the 1984 Joint Declaration and the 1997 handover of Hong Kong to China, the annual supply of private housing units rose 2.75 times. However, 70% of the new private units were produced by the top nine developers and 56% by the top four (Tse *et al.*, 2001; Lai and Wang, 1999). For the top-tier real estate corporations, the economic carrying cost of these land reserves during that period was affordable, given their monopolistic pricing power,

---

[5] For complementary behavioral evidence on Hong Kong's housing supply during the period 1985–1998, see: Lai and Wang (1999); Tse *et al.* (2001); Peng and Wheaton (1994); Wong *et al.* (2006).

large profit margins that provided the cash, declining real interest rates and the high rates of appreciation of housing.

Compared to the dominant, top-tier vertically-integrated developers, Hong Kong's remaining less than 50 developers played only small opportunistic and localized roles. These 50 fringe developers were heavily dependent on the auctions of green land, and could not afford to finance large-scale projects[6]. Note that, by international standards, these fringe developers remain large: small housing projects in Hong Kong are those with 250 units or less. Compared to the US or to Japan, the size distribution of real estate firms in Hong Kong is truncated; a bottom tier of small local firms does not exist. This is also the case in Chinese cities, as discussed in chapter 9.

6.1.4.2   *Land and real estate revenues are central to HKSAR fiscal revenues and reserves*

The use of land auctions to fund government revenues was part of the early British government policy of making the Crown Colony self-financing, so that it would not be any burden on the British Exchequer. Land auctions are technical executive decisions that do not require legislative oversight. The sale of land grants has an immediate direct impact on public revenues, and a much larger recurring one through the property tax, the profits tax on large developers, and rates on landed properties. There is no official estimate of the total share of government revenues that derives from land sales and real estate taxation. Private estimates are that at least 45% of public revenues derives from land (Hong Kong Consumer Council, 1996).

As a monopolist, the Hong Kong government would have an incentive to undersupply land for private use in order to maximize revenue. Such a policy may receive support from the oligopolistic real estate industry if it stabilizes corporate earnings. The main restraint on the maximization of revenues from the land monopoly is the rapid rise of rents, which affects not only housing, but every other form of real estate and, thus, Hong Kong's competitiveness. High rents feed higher private housing prices, lengthen the "ladder of ownership" that public renters hope to climb to achieve private ownership, and increase pressures to expand the public housing sector.

6.1.4.3   *How effective are land auctions in restraining property price increases?*

Restraining property price increases is a major challenge for the HKSAR government when confronted with powerful interest rate shocks triggered by US monetary policy. A recent econometric analysis found that, among

---

[6] During the period 1987–95, the 931 000 m^2 of new auctioned land yielded 2 275 000 m^2 of new housing, using an observed average plot ratio of 2.44 (Tse *et al.*, 2001). Projects on this new land yielded only 19% of total private housing supply.

the policy tools used by the HKSAR authorities, "land supply is the most effective policy instrument for restraining property price increases, but it operates with a significant lag" (Craig and Hua, 2011). Unfortunately, past experience suggests that government land auctions may be the best one inside a toolbox of weak tools against external interest rate shocks, global financial shocks or trade shocks.

The case of the 1984 Joint Declaration provided unexpected answers about housing price stabilization question. The Joint Declaration included the decision to cut back the size of annual land auctions significantly below past long-term trends, and to keep annual land releases below 35 ha per year, with an escape clause for land in public housing. The property price stabilization goal was the opposite of current concerns; it was to prevent a fall in property values during the years leading up to the 1997 handover.

Three findings emerge from the experience during this 12-year period. First, the assumption made by government officials that they could regulate the supply of housing and housing prices through the size of land auctions alone proved incorrect because, in addition to land auctions, private land supply could be expanded through land reclamation and urban land redevelopment, and the release of land reserves of the large real estate corporation also plays a role.

Second, the land auction cutback played, at best, a minor role in the 1997 housing bubble. The main drivers of the housing price boom were two very large external shocks. One was the reconnection of Hong Kong with a now booming Guangdong economy that shifted upwards the GDP growth trend of Hong Kong. The second external shock was the low interest rates of US monetary policies that were passed through by the LERS, and were entirely inconsistent with the accelerating growth of Hong Kong and its rising rate of inflation. Under the LERS currency peg, Hong Kong's Best Lending Rate, adjusted for inflation, fell close to zero, and became negative between 1987–1990, as Hong Kong inflation rose from 3% in 1986 to past 10% in 1991.

When, in 1991, the Federal Reserve lowered its discount rate sharply to stabilize the US economy after the burst of the dot.com bubble, the impact on Hong Kong was to make local interest rates more deeply negative. The demand for new housing by owner-occupiers and by investors rose sharply. The level of monthly housing transactions, which was less than 2500 sales per months at the time of the 1984 Joint Declaration, rose six-fold to a level of 12 500 transactions during the period 1991–1994, with spikes up to 20 000 units (Renaud *et al.*, 1997, Figure 4.10).

Two local financial factors fed the investment fever. First, there was the fiercely competitive and pro-cyclical behavior of local banks (He and Liu, 1998, p. 66). Then the extensive use of pre-sale contracts, which were very easily tradable, interacted with developers' overconfidence to generate an oversupply of new units (Wang *et al.*, 2000). The cooling measures applied to pre-sales and to bank lending implemented in 1994 were beginning to have significant effects on the housing oversupply and on housing prices, as did the announcement effect of the 2.3 times increase in land supply for public housing. Then the 1997 Asian Financial Crisis hit Hong Kong directly.

6.1.4.4 *Impact of the 1997 AFC compared with the 2007–09 GFC*

The impact of the 1997–1998 Asia Financial Crisis on the Hong Kong economy and on its property sector was severe. The "double play" by global hedge funds that combined the currency attack on the Hong Kong currency peg with the shorting of the stock market, dominated by real estate-related companies, was possible because Hong Kong had the largest and most open financial market of all Asia. The successful defense of the peg led to an intense short-term bank liquidity crisis. The HIBOR interbank interest rates shot up, the stock market crashed and the real estate markets froze[7].

The impact of the sharp increase of the HIBOR rate was severe for the balance-sheets of every player in a Hong Kong's real estate cycle: the government, banks, households and developers[8]. These balance-sheet losses explain why housing prices kept falling for seven consecutive years. The fiscal reserves of the HKSAR government were largely depleted by the successful defense against the 1998 "double play" through the purchase of corporate shares on the stock market, where more than 40% of capitalization and a growing stock bubble had mirrored the real estate bubble.

In parallel, the resources of the Exchange Fund were used to maintain the currency peg. Since Hong Kong mortgages were plain vanilla ARMs without caps, the balance sheets of owner-occupiers, as well as those of housing investors, were drastically weakened by sharply expanding liabilities and shrinking housing asset values. Among developers, the small, overextended ones went bankrupt. The large developers were weakened in multiple ways. Housing demand had collapsed, and the overall HPI had initially dropped by 80% from 172.3 to 95.6 in just 12 months. Funding on the stock market was initially closed off, and then became sharply more expensive. The carrying costs of land reserves also rose sharply. Two main reasons why the Hong Kong banking system resisted the shock, and did not face contagious bankruptcy, were that it had a high level of capitalization, and that households made strenuous efforts to maintain mortgage payments, even if their loans were "under water", because housing loans are full recourse.

---

[7] On Hong Kong's "Black Thursday" of 23 October, 1997, "interbank rates shot up, with overnight HIBOR rising from around 9% to 280% for a few hours. Interest rates eased slightly to around 100% at the close of 23 October" (Sheng, 2009, p. 264).

[8] Two out the six usual players in a housing cycle are partially or entirely missing in Hong Kong: discretionary central bank monetary policies are not possible under the LERS, and there are no local governments.

Possibly because of the ongoing US experience, it is finally acknowledged by economists that, in a financial crisis, the household sector usually pays a disproportionate share of total losses directly and indirectly (Furceri and Loungani, 2013; Furceri *et al.*, 2013). The fiscal and financial policies actually followed after bubble crises to restore economic stability tend to increase income inequality, especially in societies where corporate interests dominate. After any financial crisis, "the losses can be allocated through eight general channels to different classes of potential loss-bearers: interest rate (depositors and borrowers), exchange rate (foreigners), tax rate (taxpayers), inflation (consumers – through the inflation tax), asset prices (wealth holders – e.g. holders of shares, securities, land), wages (workers, through unemployment and reduction in real wages), inter-generational transfers (through government debt)" (Sheng, 1998).

It took seven years, until 2003, for all the players in the Hong Kong real estate system to rebuild their balance sheets. The "sandwich middle class" households actually benefitted from the crisis. Those were the potential home-owners who were still renting in the public housing sector, and who had accumulated enough savings. They suddenly found the "ownership ladder" easier to climb, given the sharp fall in housing prices. They also had the needed equity, because their balance sheets had been minimally affected as they had no mortgage debt. The 50/50 tenure ratio between renting in public housing and private housing ownership started its shift to the current 30/70 ratio.

The HMKA has compared the impacts on Hong Kong of the 2008–09 GFC with those during the 1997–98 AFC (Furceri and Loungani, 2013; Furceri *et al.*, 2013). The 2008–09 GFC led to a peak-to-trough decline of 7.3% of GDP that was comparable in magnitude to the contraction of output during the 1997–98 AFC of 8.9%. Otherwise, Hong Kong's economy fared much better during the GFC. One crucial factor was the much better conditions in the residential property market. In addition, the GFC might be called an Atlantic or Western crisis, because Asian economies played little role in it.

After downward price corrections during the second half of 2008, the housing market turned buoyant in 2009 and prices had a yearly gain of 27.6%. This is in complete contrast to the AFC crisis, when the burst of the property bubbles led to price declines for seven consecutive years. Also, compared with the currency attacks during the AFC, there was a strong inflow of funds into the Hong Kong dollar that caused the Hong Kong Interbank rate to decline to almost zero, which was favorable to the quick recovery of the housing market. The fiscal response during the GFC was also better timed. Unfortunately, the zero interest rate policies of the US Federal Reserve were, once again, driving another local property price boom.

6.1.5   Ever-rising cost of housing and worsening income and wealth distribution

Hong Kong is an important East Asian case of urban development at high density, which provides a significant point of comparison with Chinese cities today, and also with Singapore. Hong Kong's very high rent levels are driven by the high opportunity cost of land in competition with alternative uses, high population density and rapidly rising income. The Hong Kong policy quandary of deteriorating income and wealth inequality illustrates the unanswered question raised by David Miles (2012), and reported in the introduction. Will the impact of further rises in *per capita* income and in population in Hong Kong be non-linear and increasingly affect housing prices?

Over the past four decades, Hong Kong's overall housing price index (HPI) has been tracking the rise of *per capita* GDP in a cyclical way. During boom periods, rents and prices have risen at faster rates than *per capita* GDP. Then, in bust periods, the reverse trend has occurred. Hong Kong's economy is resilient to shocks, thanks to its high degree of wage and price flexibility.

Recent research findings confirm that, in Hong Kong, "real GDP *per capita* is the strongest *long-run* influence on property prices, followed by land supply, which works with a significant lag. The real interest rate and construction costs have less strong effects, while real domestic credit has the weakest effect" (Craig and Hua, 2011; Leung *et al.*, 2008). Real interest rates appear to be a key short-term driver of housing prices. One IMF analysis suggests that, if real interest rates were at their 2003–07 average level prior to the GFC, housing prices would be about 30% lower than they actually are under the US quantitative easing by the Federal Reserve (Craig and Hua, 2011).

However, the satisfactory long-term aggregate relationship between economic growth and the overall housing price level hides a deepening policy challenge of growing income and wealth inequality in Hong Kong. In 2011, Hong Kong *per capita* GDP was HK$274 000, but the *median* individual income was HK$144 000. The HKSAR, which has the highest Gini coefficient in Asia, has also experienced one of the largest increases in income inequality in East Asia over the past two decades, second only after China. The 2011 Census results show that the Hong Kong's Gini coefficient of monthly household incomes has risen from 0.525 in 2001, to 0.537 in 2011. Tax benefits and social transfers can improve the social safety net and mitigate the degree of inequality: the post-tax, post social transfer Gini values are 0.470 in 2001 and 0.475 in 2011.

Access to housing ownership in Hong Kong's dual housing system is a policy issue to address, as the housing system is a channel for wealth inequality. A confluence of structural real estate factors contributes to rising inequality. On the demand side, professionals of the large financial sector, and high-income China investors, are bidding up prices in the luxury market segments.

On the supply side, there are three other factors. First, the finite land supply steadily increases the strategic importance of very costly land redevelopment for new private housing supply. Second, the land system is a major instrument of direct and indirect taxation, and the HKSAR government continues to rely on it to maintain its policy of large fiscal surpluses. The profitability of the monopolistic real estate industry favors the supply of high-priced units, and the gap between the luxury and the private mass housing markets is widening. Spatial and locational factors are also creating pressures toward widening the income gap between private housing supply in preferred locations, and public housing supply increasingly driven to peripheral green sites. Renewed attention to the equity and efficiency of private and public rental housing markets is needed.

6.1.5.1   *Structural adjustments in public housing policies*
Hong Kong faces today an important structural and spatial mismatch between the type of public housing it still produces, and the structure of Hong Kong's new service economy. During rapid industrialization and the growth take-off during the 1960s and 1970s, the public housing strategy was for the HKHA to build new towns that were self-sufficient centers, which would combine housing and jobs – mostly manufacturing jobs. As late as 1986, 42% of all employment was in manufacturing. Two decades later, in 1986, manufacturing employment had dropped to only 7%, because most of Hong Kong's manufacturing has relocated to the Pearl River Delta across the border. What remains in Hong Kong are mostly the services that are intermediate inputs into the higher-valued added manufacturing from the Delta – in particular transport, storage, and import/export services. In parallel, jobs in business services and in finance rose from 9% to 20% of total employment between 1986 and 2006 (Tao and Wong, 2002).

The structure of the public housing stock and its spatial distribution contribute to rising income and wealth inequalities in Hong Kong. Spatially, Hong Kong has three main components: Victoria Island, Kowloon and, separated from them by mountains, the New Territories. At the same time that the employment composition was changing fast, the spatial distribution of the population also changed profoundly. In 1981, more than half of the population lived in Kowloon, and less than a quarter lived in the New Territories. Two decades later, the proportions are reversed, with 50% of the population living in the New Territories and 30% living in Kowloon. There is also evidence that residence in the public housing stock is now a factor of higher unemployment, given the changed structure of the economy (Monkkonen, 2014).

Current trends raise the question not of whether, but how, Hong Kong social housing policies can, like other high-income economies, shift from the supply-side subsidies embedded in the new town approach to demand-side subsidies, such as voucher programs. Such a shift would improve spatial and social mobility throughout the entire public and private housing stock, and might mitigate the impact of cyclical stocks by diffusing it more spatially and socially.

6.1.6 *Hong Kong housing price volatility and macroprudential policies*

Housing prices and housing rents have been extremely volatile in Hong Kong. Private housing rents have, historically, exhibited very rapid adjustments to changing market conditions. While volatile, rents have tended to be less volatile than housing prices, which is usually the case[9]. Housing prices are driven by two types of demands: one from owner-occupiers, and the other from investors. All the variables entering the formation of the user-cost of capital, including price expectations, real interest rates and taxation, come into play. Hong Kong has gone through a powerful housing price cycle between 1995 and 2012.

The primary reason why the Hong Monetary Authority (HKMA) is concerned by housing price volatility is the stability of the banking system. Property loans make up 50% of the total outstanding loans of banks in Hong Kong, with additional risk coming from the use of real estate as loan collateral (IMF, 2012c).

Figure 6.1 shows that the gap between the HPI for luxury apartments and the HP for mass market units has been widening since 2003[10]. The HKMA estimated that, after bottoming out at values around 5.5 in 2003, the average price-to-income ratio (PIR) had climbed to 14.7 by mid-2013, which was above the 1997 price peak and made Hong Kong the most expensive housing market in the world. The HKMA has further tightened its prudential tools, which are now catching in their net ordinary home-occupier investors. In addition, to stop the price contagion, the government has to go beyond HKMA banking tools, and doubled to 8.5% the transaction tax on properties costing more than HK$2 million (US$ 258,000). It was already estimated in 2011 that buyers from Mainland China "accounted for nearly 20% of the number of primary market transactions and around 50% in value terms according to market estimates" (IMF, 2012c, Section 7).

---

[9] During the period 1993–2013, the coefficient of variation of the housing price index for all units was 0.376, but only 0.195 for rents.
[10] For periodical reports on market conditions since 2003, see the half-yearly monetary and financial Stability Reports of the HKMA. For a structural description of Hong Kong's private housing system, see Renaud *et al.* (1997).

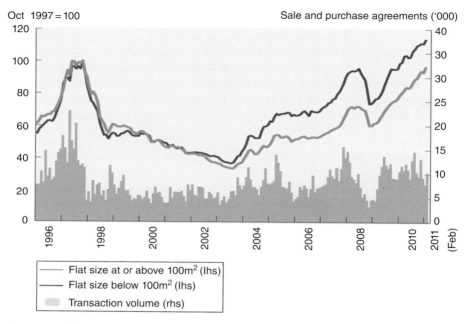

Figure 6.1   Hong Kong: Housing prices and trading volumes, 1996–2011.
Source: HKMA, Monetary and Financial Stability Report, March 2011, Chart 4.2.

Hong Kong's banking sector has long been well supervised. The banking problems of 1981–83, due to the external volatility that preceded the implementation of the LERS, led to the first prudential regulation of LTV and DTI ratios in bank lending, even before the HKMA was created. Today, for macroprudential purposes, the HKMA has been applying various cooling measures on housing demand and prices, such as LTV ratios, debt-to-income ratios and transaction taxes that raise the user-cost of housing. The HKMA is modulating the parameter values of these tools from period to period, according to perceived needs. These parameters are also differentiated between premium and mass housing segments, and according to the residential status of buyers[11].

The prudential strengthening of banks and of the housing finance system, and marginal improvements of the public housing system, as well as more efficient fiscal actions, have mitigated the impact of the 2008–09 GFC. However, Hong Kong interest rates remain exposed to the post-GFC policies of the US Federal Reserve first during the quasi-zero rates of quantitative easing and, later, to the rising rates under the taper. From China, Hong Kong's private housing is increasingly exposed to rising capital flows and to the costs and benefits of using the Renminbi.

---

[11] For a list of the measures used and changes in their parameters from year to year between 2010 and 2012, see IMF (2012c), Table 1.

Asset bubbles detection, especially in the case of housing, has now become an active interest of central banks worldwide (Pavlidis *et al.*, 2013; Phillips *et al.*, 2012). There are new analytical techniques that aim to identify not only the existence, but also the starting and end dates of episodes of irrational bubbles, including the possible occurrence of negative bubbles when price declines overshoot market fundamentals. In Hong Kong, it is difficult to determine whether there is a speculative housing bubble as a deviation from the economic fundamentals, because the fundamentals themselves are not stationary. The latest analyses designed to address this technical issue suggests that episodes of speculative bubbles in Hong Kong can be of short duration, which raises difficult questions of timing for HKMA interventions. The new PSY bubble detection method developed by Phillips *et al.* (2012) has been applied to Hong Kong by Yiu *et al.* (2013). Their results suggest that occurrences of speculative bubbles in the luxury market have differed from the mass market. They find positive bubbles in 1994, 1995 and 1997. They also find negative bubbles in 2000–2001 during the long price contraction.

The efficiency and distributive impacts of macroprudential tools have become a practical challenge. The exclusive focus of macroprudential policies on the stability of Hong Kong's financial system may have to be rethought and rebalanced, because of their negative redistributive effects on household incomes[12]. The current parameters of Hong Kong macroprudential tools are reaching local housing buyers. However, it is far from clear that their design is affecting the influential investment behavior of global high net worth individuals.

6.2   Singapore: where housing is part of macroeconomic policies

6.2.1   *Housing in Singapore versus Hong Kong: contrasting institutional histories*

Singapore is a sovereign city-state with one of the smallest land areas in the world. An island state, Singapore's land area has grown from 581 km², at the time of independence in 1965, to 716 km² by 2013, through land reclamation from the sea. More land reclamation is expected in the coming decades. The estimated total population in mid-2013 was 5.4 million, of which 3.83

---

[12] Beyond present housing-related measures, the HKSAR government can draw from a wide list of potential tools: consumer loan measures; credit limits; capital measures; dynamic provisioning; reserve requirements on deposits in local currency; other liquidity tools, measures to discourage transactions in foreign currency; and residency-based capital flow management measures. See Zhang and Zoli (2014).

million are "residents" (3.3 million citizens and 0.5 million permanent residents), and the balance of 1.55 million "non-residents", with visas of fixed duration, comprise high-income foreign professionals and lower-income foreign workers and students. This residency status plays a key role in housing policies.

Singapore's gross population density of 7540 persons/km² in 2013 is 15% higher than Hong Kong's. A small land area and a high population density preclude land-intensive activities such as agriculture, and there remains only 1.01 km² of actual farmland. A small population means a small domestic market, an open economy and external dependence on global markets. As population increases and incomes rise, the physical constraints of its very small land area is becoming more binding; different from Hong Kong, Singapore activities do not have access to a functional hinterland.

Both Hong Kong and Singapore started off as British colonies and harbors for entrepôt trade serving their surrounding region – in Singapore's case, South Asia and Southeast Asia. Singapore was also a strategically located naval base on the Malacca Strait. However, the post-war political history of Singapore differs fundamentally from that of Hong Kong, and has been a central factor in the development of Singapore housing policies and institutions. Hong Kong remained a Crown Colony, run by the British civil service, until its return to China in 1997, and its local population was almost entirely Chinese, the greatest majority of whom spoke the Cantonese dialect. After World War II, the colonial British administration pursued laissez-faire policies for five decades, and its paradoxically very large public housing program grew unexpectedly out of a government short-term response to a massive fire that destroyed a large squatter settlement of 50 000 people on Christmas Eve, 1953.

In contrast with Hong Kong, Singapore became independent from the UK in 1963, first as a Malay state, and then in 1965 as a tiny and precarious independent state that operates under a British-style parliamentary system. Today, Singapore's parliamentary system contrasts with Hong Kong, where important misalignments between the executive and the legislative branches, inherited from the colonial era, remain in place. The governance structure may prove to be an asset for the resolution of the new housing challenges that Singapore now faces.

At the time of independence, Singapore's population was a heterogeneous mix of Chinese, speaking very different dialects, Malays, and Indian residents, with English as the language of business for everyone[13]. For the majority party, PAP, housing was seen as a fundamental building block toward the

---

[13] In June 2013, the ethnic composition of the citizens and permanent residents of Singapore was: 74% Chinese. 13% Malay, 9% Indian and 3% others. This ethnic breakdown did not cover the 1.55 million population share of foreigners in the entire population of 5.4 million.

creation of a stable national polity in an open international economy[14]. Therefore, housing institution and housing policies were developed systematically, comprehensively and pragmatically, to promote both social integration and the long-term economic development of Singapore. The housing system in operation today results from the fifty-year evolution of these housing institutions and policies during the most rapid industrialization and economic development among the six East Asian economies. Singapore's housing policy challenges have now become those of a very high-income post-industrial society, with an aging resident population.

6.2.2   The three pillars of Singapore's housing strategy

"Singapore's housing strategy is inherently policy-driven and centrally controlled, with major decisions on saving rate, saving allocation, land use, housing production and housing prices being largely determined by the government" – Phang (2007). The Singaporean housing system does not fit at all the neo-classical economist's view of housing markets, where choices are driven by consumer sovereignty on the demand side and there is freedom of entry on the supply side. The exceptional success of Singapore's economic development and the performance of its unusual housing system fit Dani Rodrick's point that in economic development there is only one economics, but there can be many institutional recipes.

Singapore's housing system has been built upon three pillars. Two major institutions and one law passed after independence continue to shape the Singaporean housing system today. First, the Housing and Development Board (HDB), which had been created in 1960 under the British colonial regime, was given an entirely different and comprehensive housing and town planning mission after 1965. In organizing its large scale operations, the HDB studied the lessons in high-density urban development and new towns gained by the Hong Kong Housing Authority over the earlier decade 1953–1963.

Second, the Land Acquisition Act of 1966 abolished eminent domain provisions, and gave power to the government to acquire land for any public, residential, commercial or industrial purpose. During the period 1973–1987,

---

[14] "A competitive, winner-takes-all society, like colonial Hong Kong in the 1960s, would not be acceptable in Singapore. A colonial government did not have to face elections every five years; the Singapore government did. To even out the extreme results of free-market competition, we had to redistribute the national income through subsidies on things that improve the earning power of citizens, such as education. Housing and public health were also obviously desirable. [...] My preoccupation was to give every citizen a stake in the country and its future. I wanted a home-owning society. [...] I believed this sense of ownership was vital for our new society which had no deep roots in a common historical experience [...] Finding the correct solution was not easy. [...] I was determined to avoid placing the burden of the present generation's welfare costs onto the next generation" Lee (2000), Chapter 7.

when public housing expanded very rapidly, the government acquired land at 1973 prices, and not at current market prices. Through the Land Acquisition Act, the share of public land has risen over time from around 40% at independence, to over 80% today.

Third, the Central Provident Fund (CPF), initially created in 1955 as a small compulsory savings scheme for worker retirement, was restructured to become a core instrument of national savings mobilization. The CPF has evolved over five decades into a comprehensive social security scheme encompassing retirement, healthcare, homeownership, family protection, and financial assets enhancement. Contribution rates to the CPF have changed at various times to adjust labor costs for employers as macroeconomic conditions dictated.

Through coordinated public actions in serviced land supply, construction and finance, the Singapore government was able to address, during the 1960s and 1970s, the market failures that it was facing in the provision of low and middle-income housing, as the private sector was unable to finance and produce affordable housing in an adequate way and on an adequate scale[15]. A private contracting industry developed out of the massive HDB housing programs of new towns, ranging in size between 30 000 and 50 000 units each during the 1970s. The share of Singapore's resident population living in HDB flats rose from 9% in 1960, to a peak of 87% in 1990[16]. During the 1970s and 1980s, annual housing construction alone averaged 9% of GDP, without counting the contribution to GDP of construction activities for other types of real estate and for infrastructure.

6.2.3 Restructuring of the housing system during the growth transition

The severe recession of 1985 was a turning point, marking the time when Singapore successfully faced its "middle-income trap" (i.e. the risky transition from its very successful industrial growth take-off to its second stage of sustainable long-term development at a high-income level). By 1985, Singapore was already a middle-income country, with a *per capita* income of US$15,000. The 1985 recession marked the end of two decades of a massive infrastructure investment buildup and the closing of the quantitative housing shortage. The 1985 recession led to a comprehensive rethinking of the ways the Singapore economy was functioning in every sector. The choice made was the long-term rebalancing and liberalization of the economy, toward

[15] For an economic review of the development of Singapore's housing system until 2000, see Phang (2001).
[16] For a comprehensive institutional, technical and social description of Singapore's housing during the economic take-off, see Wong and Yeh (1985). Regarding the contracting industry, see Chapter 6, "Contracts Management."

private sector initiative, supported by an appropriate financial system and financial institutions. The emphasis of the national reforms was on better market signaling, in particular within the housing sector.

Overinvestment and the efficiency of resource allocation across the economy had clearly become issues by the end of the growth take-off (Young, 1992). In 1984, Singapore's national savings rate, of 42% of GNP, was the highest in the world at the time (until China's even higher savings rates in the 2000s). Between 1974 and 1984, the share of Singapore private sector savings had declined from 76% in 1974 to 36% in 1984 and, out of this 36% share of private savings, 31% came from the CPF mandatory savings[17]. The complete dominance of public savings in the economy resulted also from savings by the various public statutory boards, such as HDB, and the government-linked corporations that were commercially run, but usually remained under the strategic control of Temasek Holdings, which is Singapore's strategic public investment corporation, created in 1974.

In response to external shocks like the global oil crises, high growth rates of the construction sector especially during the years preceding the 1985 recession had been used to boost the economy. This had led to an oversupply of every kind of construction – most particularly of HDB housing, funded by the rapidly growing CPF, whose contribution rate had been raised to 50% of the wage base (25% by employers and 25% by workers). One important and lasting structural consequence of the total control of savings by the state is that Singapore does not have a significant SME sector and, in addition, housing could not be a collateral for SME business loans.

Being a small and entirely open economy, Singapore has a very limited domestic market, where any government fiscal stabilization plan faces a high degree of external leakage. Housing wealth effects on domestic consumption from the small private sector were still insignificant around year 2000, but were significant from the very large public housing sector (Phang, 2004; Edelstein and Lum, 2004). Even the construction sector itself has weaker and weaker domestic growth effects, as it has become dependent on foreign labor. What drives Singapore's growth are the export of manufacturing goods (led by global corporations), major logistical services and, increasingly, important financial and other high value added services, in addition to traditional services like tourism. Singapore's GDP can be quite volatile, as the open economy is exposed to the full force of global external shocks.

The government's objective of promoting the ownership of housing has never wavered. Singaporeans have become legal owners of the units they

---

[17] See Chapter 8 "Savings Policy" in Lim and Associates (1988). This book reports the findings of one of the working groups tasked to diagnose the Singapore economy in 2005–06 and make reform proposals after the severe 1985 recession.

occupied through the purchase at subsidized prices of their HDB units, by using their individual mandatory CPF savings accounts[18]. In 1970, a major housing policy transition occurred as public homeowners were given the option to resale their unit at a profit under certain conditions, and the public resale market was born. From 1971 forward, a public housing unit was no longer merely for shelter – it could become an investment vehicle and traded as well. A major objective of the 1971 *public resale policy* was to improve the efficiency of the housing market by allowing greater spatial and social mobility across Singapore's hierarchy of unusually homogenous market segments (Singapore Statistics, 2006). In 1981, mobility not only across the HDB stock but across the entire housing stock was made possible, when CPF members were allowed to use their CPF assets for down payments on purchases of private housing units. Mobility was further improved when CPF members were allowed to use their savings to meet mortgage loan payments for private property purchases. Given the momentum of the system, the share of Singapore's population housed in HDB flats peaked at 87% in 1990. HDB housing supply has been declining since then, in favor of the private housing supply, to 76% in 2013.

6.2.4 Allocation of housing space in Singapore and changing drivers of price formation

The institutional structure born out of the three-pillar housing system of 50 years ago has evolved significantly since the 1990s, together with the fundamentals of the Singapore economy itself. However, the Singapore housing system remains defined by the coexistence of the large and dominant public sector, better described as the HDB sector, and the small private sector, with its higher quality housing in terms of both unit quality and neighborhood amenities.

A detailed analysis of the dynamics of the Singapore housing system of its components is well beyond the scope of a country profile (see Lum, 2012; Phang and Kim, 2013). Tenure forms in Singapore are complex and heterogeneous. Government policies have kept changing the bundles of housing property rights accessible to different kinds of households, through regulations on eligibility conditions for purchase, resale, subletting, housing loans, and even land leases.

Today, there are three different kinds of households who live together in the city but have access to different bundles of housing property rights. First,

---

[18] Singapore has relied on three sources to fund subsidies for HDB public housing prices: (1) expenditure grants from the government current budget; (2) long-term government loans from the Government's Development Fund; and (3) land acquisition below market prices from state land and through the Land Acquisition Act. See Phang (1992).

only citizen households are eligible for public rental housing and the direct purchase of public HDB units. Second, the resale HDB sector, which emerged after incremental deregulation in the 1970s, is open to both citizens and permanent residents, regardless of income. However, there are housing grants available to purchasers on that HDB resale market that are tightly based on citizenship, marital status, and income. Third, the private housing sector, which is of better quality, is open to higher-income Singapore citizens, permanent residents, locally working expatriates and foreign investors. However, even in the private sector, different households have access to different bundles of rights. Landed properties cannot be purchased by foreigners, except by individual ministerial permission, and these "landed properties" are restricted to a specific location. Otherwise, foreign owners are essentially confined to private flats and public-private hybrid condominiums.

The changing demographic shares of these three different types of households is playing a major role in the shifting dynamic of housing prices. In 1970, at the start of the economic take-off, the total Singaporean population was 2,007.4 million (90% citizens, 7% permanent residents, 3% foreigners). In 2000, at the start of the fundamental liberalization of the housing system, the population was 4,027.9 million, with a 74 : 7 : 19 composition. In 2013, towards the end of the global post-GFC recovery, Singapore's population was 5,399.2 million, with a 61 : 10 : 29 composition. The foreign population has now become a major source of housing demand, creating the expectations that housing price diffusion now starts from the private housing sector and no longer from the HDB resale market. Note also the 213% increase in population density between 1970 and 2013, and the seriously rising land scarcity that it implies.

The Singapore rental sector is small, but very important for foreigners, and it is also significant for residents moving through the housing system. About 5% of the total HDB housing stock remains a residual low-income rental stock, confined to one-room and two-room units and subject to strict eligibility requirements. Private rental housing has two sub-markets: one where rents are determined by market forces, and the other where rents are fixed under the Control of Rent Act. The size of the controlled private rental sub-market is shrinking through the process of urban redevelopment. The URA publishes a private-rental price index, whose relationship to housing values can throw light on housing price conditions in the private sector.

The outcome of the complex system of government regulations is a hierarchical pyramid of clear housing segments, where housing units increase in value and the size of the market segment shrinks as one moves toward the top of the pyramid. Figure 6.2 describes the segmented Singapore housing system across the HDB and private sectors in 2009. The shape of Figure 6.2 is not exactly that of a pyramid laid on its side, because the housing stock still includes housing units such as public HDB executive flats, whose

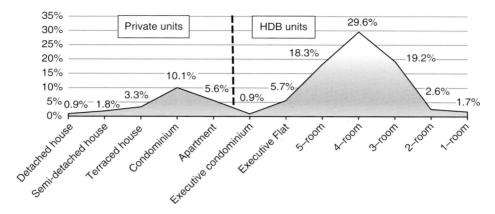

Figure 6.2   Segmentation of Singapore housing across the HDB and private sectors, 2009. *Source*: derived from Table 1 in Lum (2011).

supply was terminated years earlier. Also, given the very high rates of income growth, the rate of economic obsolescence of housing units is high in Singapore. The share of one- to three-room units is steadily declining, through the inevitable and costly process of urban redevelopment in this severely land-constrained island city. The official policy since the 1991 Concept Plan of the Ministry of National Development is to expand the relative size of the private housing stock up to 30% of the total housing stock.

Given Singapore's extremely high economic growth rates, increasingly affluent households want to upgrade their housing and climb at least to the next higher segment of the pyramid, if not better. However, there are also "downgraders", by necessity and, more rarely, by choice. At any time, this household mobility creates co-movements of prices in public and private housing (Sing *et al.*, 2006). The question is always of what sub-market is more influential in short-term price formation. Do bottom-up price movements come from the HDB resale market, or do price increases percolate down from the private market?

The dynamics of interactions between these two unequal housing sub-systems has changed significantly over time. Figure 6.3 provides a long-term perspective on Singapore housing prices between 1975 and 2012. There has been a long-term trend of Singapore housing price appreciation that is consistent with the Belassa-Samuelson effect, which is the widely observed positive correlation between a country's price level and its *per capita* income; and Singapore's *per capita* income rose at the fastest rate in the world.

However, actual rates of price increase for both HDB resale units and private units have been far from smooth over four decades, under the combined impacts of the stepwise deregulation of the public housing system and of external macroeconomic shocks to the economy, which led immediately to recessions, given the open structure of the Singapore economy without effective automatic domestic stabilizers (Phang, 2007).

6.2.5 From suppressed to open housing price cycles after deregulation

Between 1970 and 1981, Singapore government policies had entirely sup-pressed housing price cycles by keeping the dominant HDB-CPF public housing system functionally closed. The trading of (subsidized) HDB units, financed with CPF loans, could only occur within the HDB stock, leaving negligible room for interactions with the much smaller private housing sector. The overall housing price level remained exceptionally low by world standards, as price/income ratios for the sale prices of new HDB units were kept very low, such as PIRs of 1.9 for three-room, 2.1 for four-room and 2.3 for five-room units in 1972[19]. The first significant system deregulation linking the HDB resale market and the private market occurred in 1981, when CPF savings became usable for private housing mortgage payments (for approved properties).

Singapore's first major housing price cycle occurred between 1989 and 1997, as can be seen in Figure 6.3. It was the result of structural changes within the housing sector, while the macroeconomy kept growing at very high rates. The large amplitude of this first housing price cycle probably reflects the release of pent-up forces that had accumulated when housing price adjustments within the HDB stock were suppressed, but Singapore household incomes continued to rise at the fastest rate in the world. For Singapore citizens, the potential windfall capital gains to be made on HDB units, bought at heavily subsidized prices, could now be realized under the new mobility policies. Unsurprisingly, the rapidly rising HDB resale prices led also to the rapid rise of private housing prices during this first cycle.

The deregulatory steps toward greater household mobility and an improved use of the housing stock across the two-part housing system included: the use of CPF housing finance for the purchase of private housing units; the permission granted to permanent residents and to owners of private housing to purchase HDB resale units; and the removal of the income ceiling on buy-ers of HDB resale units. Ownership of several housing units had also become possible, as HDB owner-occupants were also allowed to invest in private units. As in housing booms elsewhere, HDB resale transactions, which had been a small 3% of total HDB transactions in 1979, soon rose past 40% and continue to rise above 60% by 1996, when the public resale HPI reached a

---

[19] In fact, the low PIR values selected for the sale of new HDB units even followed a declining trend between 1972 and 1989, as household incomes kept rising rapidly; see Table 4.7, p.88, in Phang (1992).

peak at 3.5 times the 1990 level. The first macroprudential policies to cool the boom were implemented in 1996, but the boom turned into a sharp bust in 1997, under the impact of the 1997 Asia Financial Crisis, which coincided with a short-term oversupply of HBD units.

Financial liberalization proceeded further during the recession caused by the US dot-com burst of 2001, soon followed by the SARS health crisis. In 2002, domestic banks were not only permitted to compete for a share of the HDB loans market, but were given priority over HDB lending in providing credit for the purchase of both private housing units and HDB resale, and even new HDB units. Reflecting all of these cumulative structural changes, almost 40% of the non-resident foreigners had become home owners by 2004. Singapore's housing finance system was deepening rapidly, and the total value of HDB and bank housing loans outstanding reached 70% of GDP by 2000. Today, Singapore still has the deepest East Asian housing finance system, based on the ratio of total mortgage debt outstanding to GDP (MDO/GDP).

6.2.6   External shocks and demand from high net-worth housing investors

Since the peak of HDB resale prices in 1996, Singapore housing prices have been subjected to repeated external shocks. The external shock of the 1997 AFC was soon followed by the burst of the US dot.com bubble in 2001,

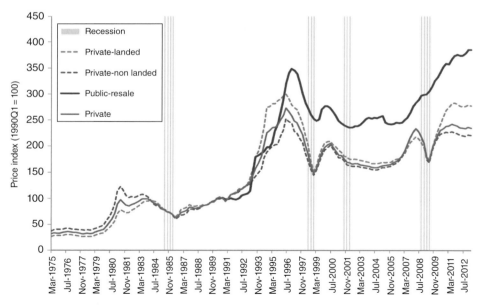

Figure 6.3 Long-term evolution of Singapore housing prices, 1975–2012.
Source: Figure 7, page 59, IMF, Singapore Financial System Stability Assessment, October 2013.

then by the SARS epidemic of 2003, and eventually the 2007–2008 GFC, followed by the slow global recovery from the Great Recession of 2009. HDB resale prices did not reach their 1996 level again until 2010[20]. Meanwhile, private housing prices have been under rising external and domestic pressures. On the demand side, the increasingly affluent foreign non-resident population had risen to 29% of the total population by 2013. Mortgage affordability was also at its best, under the very low mortgage lending rates driven by the capital inflows triggered by the US monetary policies of quantitative easing and zero real interest rates, which only began to taper in late 2013.

Furthermore, Singapore's unique monetary policies, that work through the nominal effective exchange rate (NEEF) and aim to keep inflation low, are leading to the gradual appreciation of the Singapore dollar, which is making Singapore private housing even more attractive to foreign investors. On the supply side, the increasingly acute shortage of land is leading to ever-rising land redevelopment costs. In addition, government land releases for new private housing development have shown difficulties in timing the market properly (Lum, 2011).

6.2.7 Macroprudential policies in Singapore: focus on housing and use of diversity of instruments

The stability of the housing market is a major macroeconomic policy objective for Singapore, given the very high ownership rate the importance of housing wealth, its impact on retirement cash flows, and the absence of instruments and markets that would allow households to hedge their housing investment risks. In fact, household wealth in Singapore remains entirely dominated by housing assets and, except for the highest income groups, Singaporean household balance sheets remain remarkably undiversified into other asset classes, compared with those of other mature high-income economies, including East Asian ones.

The macroprudential policies (MaP) of Singapore target the systemic links between the housing market, the financial system and the real economy. They focus on two main channels of risk: the asset-price inflation risk

---

[20] In an HPI graph, only the price level and rates of change along the same HPI line are visually comparable when the base year is changed. For instance, re-basing every HPI series from the base 1991Q1 = 100 to a new base of 2001Q4 = 100, to better reflect the more recent years, gives a different picture of the relative levels of the different HPIs, because the largest price gains of HSB resale units occurred before 1997. Under the more recent base of 2001Q4, both the URA Private Resale index and the NUS Residential Price Index now lie above the HDB Resale Price index.

channel and the credit/leverage risk channel[21]. In particular, proactive MaP measures aim to ensure that credit supplied at very low interest rates by banks does not drive housing prices above levels consistent with underlying income growth.

Of special concern to the Singapore authorities is the estimated 5–10% of households who are currently over-leveraged on their property purchases, and face total debt service payments in excess of 60% of income. Given that all mortgage loans are ARMs in Singapore, lower-income households with smaller savings, and other households with multiple mortgages of long loan tenor, are particularly at risk, as global and domestic interest rates rise again as US Federal Reserve monetary policy shifts. These households at risk may not necessarily default, because all bank mortgage loans are recourse loans in Singapore, but their asset position and long-term economic security could be seriously impaired. During the period of slow global recovery in 2009–2014, myopic consumer borrowing occurred, as banks' mortgage-lending rates fell below the HDB policy loan rates, in a manner reminiscent of the rates on policy loans from the Government Housing Loan Corporation of Japan after the 1991 burst of Japan's bubble.

Singapore MaP instruments are targeted microeconomic measures on the demand side and on the supply side of the property market. Between 2009 and 2013, successive rounds of proactive measures have been implemented pragmatically, in view of the uncertainty regarding their transmission effects. They appear to have achieved a degree of success in cooling prices and lowering the volume of transactions in the booming housing market segments, especially in the private market segments open to foreign investors.

The proactive rates on these tools are cyclical, and are modified as new housing market conditions seem to dictate. However, one MaP tool that is expected to remain a permanent feature of Singapore's financial regulatory system is the Total Debt Servicing Ratio (TDSR), resulting from all the loans granted by financial institutions to individual households – property loans, car loans and credit card loans. This TDSR framework was introduced in 2013, and is one response to the rapidly rising level of aggregate Singaporean household debt since financial liberalization.

---

[21] For a conceptual summary of Singapore's MaP policies, see Box 1, "Macroprudential Policy Instruments in the Singapore Context" in MAS (2011). Every Financial Stability Review by MAS contains detailed information updates on the performance of the housing system and the risks this performance generates for the banking system and for the macroeconomy. Each FSR report also provides the latest information on MaP measures taken during the year. For third party comments on Singapore's macroprudential oversight of the housing market, see IMF (2013c).

Singapore's variety of MaP instruments applied to housing is one of the most extensive in the world[22]. Regulations regarding residential mortgage lending and price stabilization include:

- Limits on LTV ratios applicable to both private housing and HDB housing loans made by banks.
- A maximum loan tenor, capped at 35 years, applies to all residential loans (new loans and loan refinancing) for the purchase of private housing, with a 25-year cap when it is for a HDB unit.
- The prohibition of interest-only mortgages, of loans with teaser rates, and of the negative amortization of principal.
- The regulation of total debt-to-income ratios within the TDSR framework. Borrowers who do not meet the 60% cap on the TDSR ratio must bring formal loan guarantors.
- Tighter regulations on the multiple ownership of housing units include larger minimum cash down-payments.
- An additional transaction tax on property sellers, on top of the existing recording tax, named the Seller's Stamp Duty (SSD), penalizes property "flipping" during the first three years of ownership, with the highest rate applied to first-year resale.
- Some measures are also targeted to specific market segments, including bank loans financing the purchase of HDB housing, and a new maximum floor size of 160 square meters for public-private executive condominiums.
- The public supply of land for HDB housing and of land sold to private developers was increased after 2009.
- Regulations applied to land supply by residential developers and also on competing land use by industrial property developers were changed incrementally.

6.2.8 Another long-term transition for the Singaporean housing system

In Singapore, incremental macroprudential measures have a short-term cyclical focus, with the dual purpose of strengthening the stability of the financial system and of protecting the socioeconomic achievements of earlier decades. However, Singapore's unique blend of government-led and, increasingly, market-based housing system, appears to have entered yet another long-term transition. This time, there is little international precedent on the new constraints that Singapore now faces. Domestic policy

---

[22] See Box 3, "Singapore Macroprudential Measures on Housing. A Historical Perspective" in IMF (2013c).

debates aim to chart a suitable growth path to meet the perennial goals of macroeconomic efficiency, social equity and environmental sustainability for the housing system of a high-income society with diversifying values and preferences.

The issues that the Singaporean housing system faces issues are not new, but they appear to be deepening, as stabilizing housing prices have become a growing challenge. On the supply side, the pressures on land supply are more acute, as the total population living in Singapore has risen by 34% in a decade, from 4.03 million in 2000 to 5.4 million in 2013. The successful high-density urban development model of previous decades has to be refined further, in a systemic way, to meet the demand for quality space at very high income levels in a socially and environmentally sustainable manner. The cost of land is rising in a non-linear fashion, as more and more housing has to be built on very expensive redeveloped urban land, as economic activities compete with residential land use.

The close relationship between housing and the evolving economic growth base of Singapore is raising important questions about what mutually con-sistent objectives of housing policy might be in the medium and the long term. The long-standing HDB goal has been to achieve integrated neighbor-hoods from social, income and racial perspectives. Another implicit goal of government policy has been housing asset appreciation as a major source of retirement funding. A third goal is housing price affordability.

How resilient are these goals to the rapid aging of the population, the increasing reliance on foreign immigration and increasing mobility across the housing stock, which tends to induce spontaneous social segregation, as shown by Schelling (1978)? What is the impact of illiquid housing assets and undiversified household asset portfolios for the retirement of most income deciles, except for the highest ones? Can the various CHF accounts compen-sate for such illiquidity and limited diversification? Is a larger rental market not necessary in order to accommodate more foreign (skilled) labor, and improve housing liquidity across the income distribution? Is the present way of accommodating the foreign demand for Singapore real estate consistent with other housing goals, especially price stability? Or, as in the UK, will rich foreigners make homeownership less and less affordable to the general population?

Part III

Drivers of East Asian Housing Cycles: Evidence and Analysis

7

East Asian Housing Price Cycles: The Evidence

7.1 An overview of East Asian housing cycles

7.1.1 Observed East Asian housing price cycles

Most of our international knowledge of housing price cycles so far has been based on US and European experiences, where asset price cycles almost always follow two phases: a run-up phase of several years, followed by a declining phase that is usually steeper and of shorter length. Some of these housing price cycles have been amplified into large boom-busts, driven by various market and institutional factors, which have had a contagious effect on the broader economy. The usual amplifying factors include overbuilding by builders, pro-cyclical lending by banks, and increasingly frenzied trading by home buyers during the run-up phase, as was observed in the US and Europe during the recent financial crisis. East Asian (EA) countries have also exhibited significant cyclical housing price movements during the last three decades, which we now investigate, empirically in this chapter and conceptually, as well as econometrically in the next chapter.

Within an urban system, local housing markets typically differ. This is why housing prices aggregated at the national level through housing price indices tend to be less informative than housing price cycles at the city level, especially in very large, spatially differentiated economies. In investigating the interactions between housing and the wider economy, an important operational factor therefore becomes the share of national GDP that originated in the cities whose price cycles can be investigated. Due to all too common data limitations, our analysis of East Asian cycles focuses

Dynamics of Housing in East Asia, First Edition. Bertrand Renaud,
Kyung-Hwan Kim and Man Cho.
© 2016 John Wiley & Sons, Ltd. Published 2016 by John Wiley & Sons, Ltd.

primarily on capital regions and major cities where, fortunately for our analyses, a major share of national GDP originates, including in the very large Chinese economy so far. In contrast with comparisons of housing price volatility, direct cross-country comparisons of housing price *levels* across Western economies and across East Asian economies, or between these two groups of economies, face significant problems of heterogeneity in measurement and are not included. These price level issues are addressed indirectly through the use of important ratios, such as price-to-income ratios and price-to-rent ratios.

Over the past four decades, large-scale housing price cycles have occurred in the major cities of the six East Asian countries, as shown by Figure 7.1. Seoul, Taipei, and Tokyo have experienced large cycles in the mid-to-late 1980s. In Singapore and Hong Kong, cycles were identified in the mid-to-late 1990s. In China, the first market-based, demand-driven housing cycle occurred only after the massive urban housing privatization of 1998–2003. In China, therefore, housing price indices (HPI hereafter) are available only since 1998. This HPI shows that housing prices have been increasing steadily and rapidly in major cities, especially after the very large, bank-financed stimulus of 2009. Recent empirical studies show soaring housing prices in China's eastern coastal cities, such as Beijing, Shanghai, and Shenzhen, with housing prices becoming heavily overvalued relative to market fundamentals (Kim and Cho, 2013).

The amplitude of housing price movements in the six East Asian capital cities, measured in terms of the mean and the standard deviation of annual changes in real housing price indexes, are presented in Table 7.1. These price movements are presented separately for the 1990s and the 2000s, except for Beijing, for which the housing price index is available only from 1998, as just noted. Across East Asia, the average rate of increase in housing price was larger, but its standard deviation was smaller in the 2000s than in the 1990s. There is also a wide variation in both the mean and the dispersion of housing price appreciation across the six cities. Tokyo is exceptional in the region, as its inflation-adjusted housing prices have kept falling throughout the 1990s and 2000s, in the aftermath of the burst of Japan's multiple asset bubbles by 1991. Beijing stands out among the six cities, with a much larger average rate of housing price appreciation during the 2000s that is more than double the price increases in the other EA cities. Seoul's rate of housing price increase in the 2000s was close to the average of the six countries, but its volatility was one of the two smallest, next to Tokyo.

Reinhart and Rogoff (2009) identify the collapse of the Japanese real estate bubble, and subsequent financial market instability, as one of the five major financial crises in the world since World War II. However, it is notable that there have been several instances of East Asian primate cities where rates of

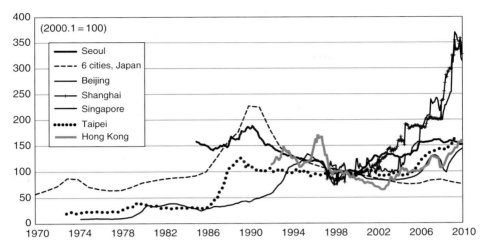

Figure 7.1   Housing price dynamics in major East Asian cities.
Source: Kim and Cho (2014).

Table 7.1   Basic descriptive statistics of real housing prices in six EA cities.

	1990s		2000s	
	Average	Standard deviation	Average	Standard deviation
Seoul	−5.1	8.1	4.6	7
Tokyo	−11	6.6	−2.3	4.3
Beijing	−	−	8.7	16.1
Hong Kong	0.4	24.8	2.4	14.8
Singapore	9.1	18.9	1.6	13.5
Taipei	−1.3	6.8	3.8	9.2
Average	−1.6	13.0	3.1	10.8

Notes:
1. The data for Tokyo and Hong Kong start in the second quarter of 1994.
2. The ending points were the first quarter of 2012 for Seoul, the fourth quarter of 2010 for Tokyo, Beijing, and Hong Kong, and the first quarter of 2010 for Taipei.
Source: Kim and Cho (2014).

increase in housing prices have *exceeded* those of Japan in the mid-to-late 1980s. The difference with Japan is that the unwinding of these other housing price booms has not had a large negative impact on the wider economy. The rates of housing price appreciation in Taipei (1986–90), Singapore (1993–96), Beijing and Shanghai (2008–2011) were all higher than the 21.8% appreciation rate registered in Tokyo between 1986 and 1990. In Seoul, by contrast, the annual average rates of house price appreciation during the two cycles of 1987–91 and 2001–08 were 7.2% and 6.8%, respectively, which were quite moderate, compared to other East Asian cities.

7.1.2   *Price changes and their duration in East Asian housing cycles*

There is no established consensus on how to define an asset price cycle statistically, and identify its peak and trough. Depending on the particular statistical method applied, one can come up with a highly variable number of cycles for a given city and time period. For example, among several tested approaches, we have replicated for East Asia the statistical analysis carried out by Igan *et al.* (2011), who uses the identification algorithm for peaks and troughs in time-series data developed by Harding and Pagan (2002). However, this algorithm generates too many cycles of very short durations for East Asian economies.

This statistical outcome of a very large number of cycles is similar to the results for OECD countries, reported by Igan *et al.* In Korea, for example, 11 peaks and troughs were identified for the relatively short five-year period between 1986 and 2011. These statistical artifacts of a succession of many short cycles are not consistent with the long-term pronounced price swings observed in the country. In our main analysis, we therefore took a more heuristic approach, in which we identified inflection points for both troughs and peaks – namely, those points at which a sustained upturn or downturn were observed. We then validated the identified upturns and downturns in each country-based available data and published research. Finally, we measured the duration and the average price increase during the *upturn* for each cycle[1].

Most of the identified EA housing price booms coincide with a strong macroeconomic performance of each respective economy, which is identified as one likely cause of the cycle. In addition to a strong macroeconomic performance, there are three other important underlying forces that the EA housing price upturns tend to share.

First, the demand-supply imbalance caused by rapid demographic urbanization interacting with chronic shortages of urban land and affordable housing is also a likely cause of some of the price booms – for example, in the case of Seoul, 1987–91, and the recent price booms in Chinese cities between 1998 and 2013.

Second, an influx of liquidity into the real estate sector either as a result of financial liberalization or monetary and exchange rate policy shifts appear to be a coincidental factor in Seoul, 2001–08, Tokyo, 1986–90, Singapore, 1993–96, Taipei, 1986–90, and in the recent price rises in China's major cities.

Third, increases in the supply of construction financing, in combination with other market and institutional factors, are also likely causes of the

---

[1] The duration and average price changes during the *downturn* were more idiosyncratic and hard to measure, because some of them showed either flat or fluctuating price movements. We describe the patterns of post-peak price changes in Table 7.2.

Table 7.2 Comparison of housing price cycles in Major East Asian cities.

	Period of increase	Average annual rate of increase	Cumulated rate of increase	Subsequent price trend	Cause of rise and policy response
Seoul (1)	Jun 1987–Apr 1991	7.27	28.3	Stable (before foreign exchange crisis)	• Cause: ①, ② • Response: ⓐ, ⓑ, ⓓ
Seoul (2)	Jan 2001–Apr 2008	6.89	50.3	Decline (esp. in greater Seoul area)	• Cause: ①, ③, ④ • Response: ⓑ, ⓒ, ⓓ
Tokyo	Oct 1986–Dec 1990	21.84	91.7	Long-term recession	• Cause: ①, ②, ③, ⑤ • Response: ⓒ, ⓔ, ⓗ
Singapore (1)	Feb 1993–Jun 1996	28.22	93.1	Rapid decline between 1996 and 1998	• Cause: ①, ③, ⑧ • Response: ⓑ, ⓒ, ⓖ
Singapore (2)	Dec 2006–Dec 2010	12.47	49.9	Sustained increase through present	• Cause: ⑤, ⑦ • Response: ⓒ, ⓖ
Taipei (1)	Aug 1986–Feb 1990	50.39	181.4	Small decline, stable	• Cause: ①, ③, ④, ⑥ • Response: ⓑ, ⓒ
Taipei (2)	Jan 2006–Jan 2010	13.1	53.7	Sustained increase through present	• Cause: ③, ⑤ • Response: ⓐ, ⓒ
Hong Kong (1)	Oct 1995–May 1997	32.02	51.2	Sharp decline during AFC period	• Cause: ①, ⑤, ⑦ • Response: ⓕ
Hong Kong (2)	Dec 2008–Nov 2010	24.2	46	Sustained increase through present	• Cause: ⑤, ⑦ • Response: ⓒ
Beijing	Oct 2008–Sep 2011	29.82	86.5	Sustained increase through present	• Cause: ①, ②, ③ • Response: ⓐ, ⓑ, ⓒ
Shanghai	Oct 2008–2011	28.55	82.8	Sustained increase through present	• Cause: ①, ②, ③ • Response: ⓐ, ⓑ, ⓒ

Price increase factors and policy responses outlined as follows.

Likely causes:
① strong macroeconomic performance; ② shortage of land/housing supply due to urbanization; ③ increased housing loans (deregulation, interest/exchange rate fluctuations, etc.); ④ increased construction financing (project finance loans, etc.); ⑤ influx of international liquidity; ⑥ increased liquidity due to payments of compensation for land owners; ⑦ increased population (due to foreign migration, etc.); and ⑧ increased availability of public housing to different segments.

Policy responses:
ⓐ large increase in housing supply; ⓑ heavier real estate taxation (acquisition/ownership/ transfer taxes, taxes on non-business real estate); ⓒ mortgage regulations (DTI, LTV, etc.); ⓓ price regulations on housing; ⓔ monetary policy (interest rates); ⓕ foreign exchange policy response to "currency attack"; ⓖ regulations on property purchases by foreigners; and ⓗ other financial market policy responses to long-term recessions (e.g., increased use of REITs).
Source: Kim and Cho (2014).

price booms. Price upturns in Seoul, 2001–08 and in Taipei, 1986–90 coincide with the expansion of construction financing. The Taipei price upturn of 1986–90 also coincides with large-scale land compensation payments for the public acquisition of private land under eminent domain procedures. The two booms in Singapore of 1993–96 and 2006–10 coincide with relaxed eligibility qualifications for the purchase of public housing and changes in migration policy.

Policy responses to these price booms have varied widely across EA countries. Policy measures have included a supply response such as the two million units construction drive in Korea during 1989–92; or, more frequently, policies focusing on the demand side such, as changes in tax policy for purchasing, holding, reselling housing units, and lending restrictions mostly in the form of a Loan-to-Value (LTV) Ratio cap.

Based on this heuristic analysis, we have identified a total of 11 continuous and large-scale cycles in housing prices in seven cities of the six EA econo-mies since 1980. The average duration of the upturns identified was 3.6 years, and the average annual price increase during those periods was 23%. The post-peak price movements were more idiosyncratic across the cycles and showed less uniform patterns. Note that the upturns observed for the Chinese cities were still in progress as our data analysis took place. We summarize in Table 7.2 the key features of each of these 11 cycles, in terms of the period of housing price increase, the average annual and total price changes, and the price pattern after the period of increase. Based on published studies on each country's housing market[2], we also summarize the main causes of, and policy responses to, the identified price upturns.

7.1.3   East Asian housing cycles compared to Western cycles

How do East Asian housing price cycles compare with Western cycles? Following the same heuristic approach used for East Asia, we have identi-fied the housing price cycles of selected countries and cities from North America and Europe that experienced price boom-busts in the 2000s. The comparative results are mapped-out in Figure 7.2, which combines the amplitude of the cycles and their duration in both groups of countries. Overall, the cycles of the EA countries tend to exhibit similar magnitudes in terms of average price appreciation during the boom, but we also find a much shorter average duration of the booms, relative to Western cities. Notably, the average annual growth rates observed for two Chinese cities far exceed those of the US cities during the 2000s boom-bust. The average annual growth rates during the Chinese booms were 28.3% for Shanghai and 29.8% for Beijing, compared with 15.7% for Los Angeles and 14.9% for

---

[2] Various chapters from Bardhan *et al.* (2012) in particular.

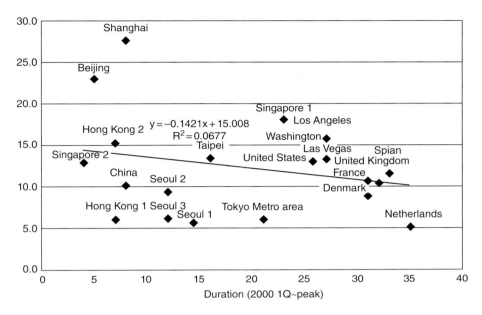

Figure 7.2 Average annual rates of price increases versus cycle durations, Western and East Asian cities and countries.
Source: Cho *et al*. (2012).

Washington, DC. Overall, the longer the duration of the boom, the smaller the average growth rate during that period. There is a statistically weak negative correlation between the duration of cycles and their amplitude.

We will provide further evidence on the difference in volatility between the 1990s and the 2000s across nine East Asian capitals or major cities, as well as that between East Asian cities and selected Western cities, in chapter 8. The analytical work there confirms that basic volatility was greater in China than in the rest of East Asia during the 2000s (see Table 8.1).

Comparing unconditional volatility (before de-trending the data by applying the Hodrick-Prescott filtering method) across 15 Western economies and four EA economies, as well as selected East Asian and US cities, shows that volatility was higher in East Asia than in Western economies, and also that volatility was higher in the 1990s than in the 2000s in East Asia (Table 8.1). We also confirm our intuition that city level data is more informative that aggregate national data.

7.2   Country-specific housing price dynamics

The goal of this section is to provide comparative insights into the individuality of each East Asian capital city's price cycles. The description of key events and institutional factors driven by these cycles are kept to a minimum, because detailed analyses of the structure of each EA housing system are provided in the country chapters of Part II and Part IV.

The specific dynamics of housing prices differ significantly across the six capital cities of East Asia, namely Seoul, Taipei, Singapore, Hong Kong, Tokyo and Beijing. For each capital city, we present a graph showing the behavior of the housing price cycles over several decades, ranging from less than two decades in Beijing to more than four decades in Tokyo. In order to separate the intrinsic dynamics of housing prices in each of these cities from the overall dynamics of the relevant macroeconomy, we have decomposed the original housing price index of the city into its trend and its cyclical component, using the Hodrick-Prescott filter method.

The graphical contents of each of the six capital city graphs are similar. Each has three price lines. First, the heaviest line represents the evolution of the official housing price index (HPI), measured along the left axis, with 1998Q1 = 100 for each city. Second, the rather volatile dotted line represents the cyclical component of housing prices after applying the Hodrick-Prescott filter, measured along the right axis. Third, the smooth long-term trend in light grey tells a very different price story for each capital city. Like the HPI, the price trend line is measured against the left axis.

To illustrate the insights provided by the grey price trend line, the comparison of Seoul in Figure 7.3 and Taiwan in Figure 7.4 shows how very different the cyclical behavior of these two markets has been. Seoul's price trend has been truly cyclical over time, with a significant amount of mean reversion and limited net gains by the end of three decades. In contrast, the price trend in Taipei has been stepwise, with major gains between 1980 and 2010. The short-term cyclical component of housing prices also differs greatly across the six cities. The two vertical shaded areas in every one of the six graphs mark the period of impact of the Asian Financial Crisis around 1997–1998, and a decade later, that of the Global Financial Crisis of 2007–2009.

7.2.1   Seoul, South Korea

Due to the strong economic performance of the Korean economy since the mid-1960s and the highest tempos of urbanization in East Asia, the prices of land and housing in Seoul and other major Korean cities have been high and have risen rapidly. A statistical analysis for the entire period 1960–2010 is not feasible, because a consistent time series of the housing price index (HPI) starts only from 1986. Prior to that year, less reliable price evidence suggests that Korean real estate prices were highly volatile throughout the 1970s and the 1980s. As will be detailed in Chapter 10, the Korean government has been intervening into the real estate sector with a high frequency, using a wide range of policy instruments. Between 1967 and 2007, the central government introduced 60 major housing policy packages, which is more than one every year for such a long-lasting asset class as housing.

The first pronounced housing price cycle since the publication of the official HPI occurred in the late 1980s, is seen in the sharply rising cyclical component of HPI, which is the dotted line in Figure 7.3. The cause of the surge in housing prices was a strong increase in demand, spurred by unusually favorable macroeconomic conditions and the resulting high GDP growth, which ran against a very inelastic housing supply response. The sharp housing price hike led to a severe affordability problem in both owner-occupied and rental housing markets in major Korean cities. The government responded by initiating a two-million housing construction drive, which was successfully carried out over the short period 1989–92. This milestone event increased the urban housing stock on a very large scale, resulted in a sharp drop in housing price-to-income ratios in major cities and helped to stabilize housing prices from 1991 until the outbreak of the 1997 Asian Financial Crisis (AFC), as shown by the downward path in the housing price trend in Figure 7.3. The increase in cyclical volatility observed after 1995 (dotted line) reflects the mismanaged financial liberalization that contributed to the severe impact of the Asian Financial Crisis in Korea (See Sheng, 2009, Chapter 7).

The Asian Financial Crisis was the first severe macroeconomic shock to the South Korean economy and to its real estate sector. As seen in Figure 7.3, the HPI dropped sharply, and it took several years for prices to recover to their pre-crisis level. The crisis served as a catalyst for implementing

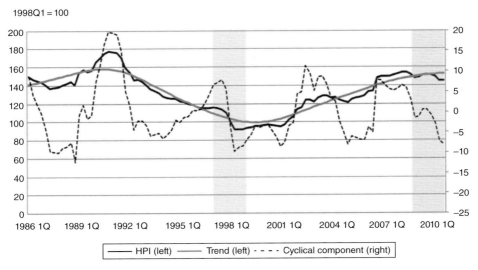

Figure 7.3 Seoul, South Korea: housing price dynamics, 1986Q1 to 2010Q1.
Source: Cho et al. (2012).

appropriate financial reforms and the long-delayed liberalization of the real estate sector, as a part of the recovery effort. These financial and real sector reforms resulted in the rapid expansion of a market-oriented mortgage finance system for Korea. The ratio between the mortgage debt outstanding (MDO) to GDP rose from about 10% before the AFC, to over 30% in about a decade. A secondary mortgage market was also established after the AFC, with the creation of the Korea Mortgage Corporation (Komoko) in 1999 as a joint venture between public and private investors. In 2004, Komoko was transformed into today's Korea Housing Finance Corporation (KHFC) in 2004, which is a wholly government-owned entity with the mission to fund private mortgage lenders via MBS issuance.

In terms of housing price dynamics, two peaks are observed in the 2000s. The first, in 2001–2003, reflected the fast recovery from the AFC. The other in 2006–2007, was propelled by low interest rates and the boom in new construction for residential and non-residential properties. Mindful of the growing importance of the housing finance sector after the AFC, the government adopted restrictions on home mortgage lending: first, on the loan-to-value (LTV) ratio in 2003–2004, with the maximums set as 60% for commercial banks and 70% for KHFC; and second, on debt-service to income (DTI) ratio in 2006–2007, which varies between 40–65%, depending on the geographic location of collateral and mortgage product type (this is discussed again in more detail later in Chapter 10).

Concurrent with the economic upturn of 2006–07, there was a construction boom-bust in Korea, caused by the confluence of rising real estate prices, low interest rates, and a surge in financial market liquidity, facilitated by the rise of international short-term borrowing by commercial banks. The DTI/LTV restrictions on residential mortgage lending sector appear to have had an indirect effect on construction lending. Given the restrictions on mortgage lending, the growing liquidity caused by international borrowing in 2005–07 flew into construction lending, in the form of what is known in Korea as "project financing" or PF loans, causing a large construction cycle in the mid-to-late 2000s. There was a surge in construction lending and construction activity in 2005–07, which turned into a credit crunch with the outbreak of the Global Financial Crisis (GFC), causing rising non-performing loans (NPLs) among PF loans and bankruptcy among construction companies (Son, 2014). Note that the conditional housing cyclicality (dotted line) has followed a downward trend since the GFC.

In South Korea, the risks resulting from housing price cycles have not spilled over into the wider economy, and the dominant causal direction has been the other way, from the macroeconomy to housing. Overall housing conditions have improved, but the structural changes in the housing sector caused by demographic shifts and slower economic growth create new challenges for housing and macroeconomic policies, as will be discussed in Chapters 10 and 11.

7.2.2   Taipei, Taiwan

Taiwan and South Korea may have followed remarkably similar overall economic development strategies (Lau, 1986), but Taiwan's housing price path during the last three decades shows a very different pattern from that of Korea. A distinctive feature of Taiwanese housing price behavior is the dramatic upturn in 1987–91, with its four-fold increase in housing prices. After a short cyclical downturn, the housing price path has followed a long flat trend until turning up again since the mid-2000s, as seen in Figure 7.4.

Three particular factors have been the main causes of the very sharp housing price rise in the late 1980s (Chang and Chen, 2011). The first factor is financial liberalization. The Taiwanese government started interest rate liberalization in 1980, by giving banks more flexibility in setting lending and deposit rates. The process of deregulation accelerated in 1985, and ten leading banks in Taiwan were allowed to set their own prime rates. Credit restrictions were fully relaxed in 1987, causing the expansion of the volume of lending to the housing sector.

The second factor was the shift of the exchange-rate policy from a fixed rate regime to a floating rate one in 1987. The New Taiwan Dollar had been under strong upward pressure due to the huge export surplus from the early 1980s, and the move to a floating rate resulted in a rapid currency appreciation (Sheng, 2009, Chapter 10). The lifting of restrictions on capital flows resulted in a surge in capital inflows, which induced higher speculative activities toward both equity and real estate markets.

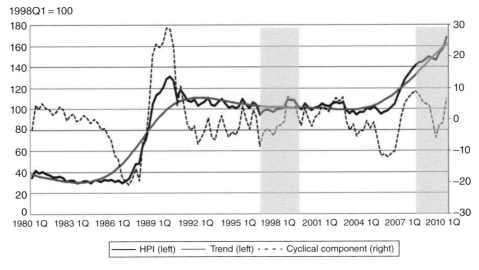

Figure 7.4   Taipei, Taiwan: housing price dynamics, 1980Q1 to 2010Q1.
Source: Cho *et al.* (2012).

Third, the long-planned expropriation of reserved land for public facilities caused large sums of compensatory payments to private land owners, and these funds went into the asset markets. The government had reserved large amounts of land for public facilities in the early 1970s, for which a budget was finally secured in 1989. In response to the housing boom, Taiwan's central bank adopted lending restrictions, including the prohibition of uncollateralized loans for land, restrictions on construction loans, and LTV caps for residential mortgages at 50%.

The second pronounced housing price boom, which started in 2006, has been sustained much longer than the first boom. The price inflation, which is more concentrated in Taipei, was caused initially by the record low interest rate environment, and the ample liquidity in the global financial system in the mid-2000s. In addition, the latest boom has been driven also by expectations about Mainland China investments into Taiwan, after the Memorandums of Understanding (MOUs) on financial supervisory cooperation was signed by Taiwan and China in 2010, together with the Economic Cooperation Framework Agreement (ECFA) that widened market openings for both economies. This new China spillover effect on housing price movements appears also to be present in Hong Kong and Singapore (Kim and Park, 2014).

Responding to the second price boom, the Central Bank has adopted targeted credit tightening measures in specific areas (including the city of Taipei, and ten cities in Taipei County). Under these measures, if those who are already homeowners want to apply for mortgages for newly acquired residential properties in the specified areas, three restrictions in lending apply:

1. maximum 70% LTV;
2. no grace period (or amortization of principal from beginning of loan term);
3. no second loan to be allowed against the same collateral.

7.2.3   Singapore

Since independence in 1965, the Singaporean government has placed a high policy priority on promoting home ownership as an integral component of nation building. Singapore is the East Asian economy where macroeconomic policies and housing policies have been the most tightly coordinated through the close regulation of land supply, real estate development and housing finance. Over the past three decades, housing price movements in Singapore have reflected both the gradual deregulation and privatization of the housing system, in response to the recession of 1985–86, and to the large if transient external shocks of the AFC and GFC on the small, entirely open economy (see Chapter 6).

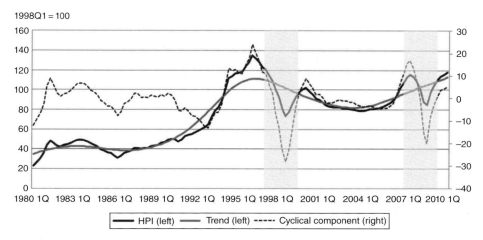

Figure 7.5 Singapore: housing price dynamics, 1980Q1 to 2010Q1.
Source: Cho *et al.* (2012).

The HPI in Singapore started to rise gradually after 1986, and then rather sharply after 1993 in response both to domestic institutional factors and international macroeconomic factors, as can be seen from the housing price trend line (solid grey line) in Figure 7.5. The reasons behind a strong demand for both public and private housing were: the very high rate of economic growth of Singapore, which was the highest among EA economies; rapid household formation; and the favorable housing finance environment. Sentiment for speculation was also heightened by the spectacular bull-run in the Singapore stock market during the early 1990s, and by the inflow of external hot money, as Singapore has long been an island of stability in the middle of a more unstable neighborhood (for the domestic deregulation details, see Chapter 6).

To dampen the powerful housing price boom, the government introduced a set of policy measures in May 1996, just prior to the AFC. These measures included: the capital gains taxes and stamp duties for housing re-sales within three years from initial purchase; an LTV limit of 80% of the purchase price or assessed value, whichever was lower; and restrictions on home purchases by non-residents and non-Singaporean companies. These anti-speculation measures are deemed to have had an impact, as both transaction volume dropped and the prices softened in the private residential market.

Singapore's housing prices declined sharply during the AFC, but they bounced back quickly in a V-shaped pattern, as seen in Figure 7.5. In 2001, however, housing prices turned to a mild declining path again, due to international factors such as a global electronics slump, and the slowdown of the US economy in the aftermath of the burst of the dot-com bubble. To combat the downturn, the government announced in July 2005 a package of measures to stimulate the market, including:

- Raising the maximum LTV ratio of housing loans from 80% to 90% and reducing the cash down payment from 10% to 5%.
- Lowering the minimum lease period of properties that could be purchased with CPF savings from 60 to 30 years.
- Allowing non-related CPF members to use their CPF savings to purchase private housing units jointly.
- Relaxing restrictions on foreign ownership of units in low-rise apartments.
- Reinstating private residential properties, as allowable investments under the state's Global Investor Program, for a foreigner seeking to qualify for permanent residence (Lum, 2011).

The HPI rose again after 2006, due in large part to foreign capital inflows. Two other demand-side drivers for the housing boom were record job creation and the rapid influx of foreigners, as a direct consequence of Singapore's liberalized immigration policies, to attract a highly skilled workforce. However, the external shocks from the US subprime mortgage crisis and the Global Financial Crisis and global economic slowdown followed, but the effect of the GFC on the price dynamics in Singapore has been short-lived. The HPI once again showed a strong and sustained V-shaped upturn after 2009. Since that date, the Singapore government has been implementing an increasingly comprehensive set of macro-prudential regulations, in order to stabilize housing prices and mitigate financial sector risks (see Chapter 6).

7.2.4   Hong Kong

Over the past five decades, Hong Kong has risen to become a high-income, advanced economy, right behind Singapore, with a strong service sector and a well-regulated global financial center, with offices and branches of 80 of the world's top 100 banks already by 1997. Given scarce land resources, the continued economic and population growth has led to a strong housing demand, as well as expectations of high housing price appreciation in the private housing market.

In spite of significant similarities as two small, completely open city economies, the long-term cycle of Hong Kong's HPI has been driven by structural factors very different from those of Singapore (See Chapter 6). In particular, the year 1997 is a historical watershed that permanently divides Hong Kong's housing price record into two separate periods. That year marked the return of the British Crown Colony of Hong Kong to China, with a new 50-year status as the Hong Kong Special Administrative Region (SAR) and a new Basic Law with important real estate clauses. The year 1997 was also the year when the Hong Kong real estate sector boom was turned into a costly bust by international currency attacks associated with the Asian Financial Crisis. The shock to the housing system was severe, and it took a full decade for Hong Kong housing prices to recover to their 1994 levels.

A critical factor in the dynamics of Hong Kong's private housing and other asset prices is the Linked Exchange Rate Regime between the Hong Kong dollar and the US dollar that has been in force since 1983, and fixed the exchange rate at HKD 7.76 per USD. The market consequence of this currency board arrangement is that interest rates in Hong Kong are dictated by US Federal Reserve monetary policies, and are not driven by domestic Hong Kong economy, as would be the case for an economy with its own central bank.

The Hong Kong's HPI cycle before 1997 is directly linked to major shifts in expectations regarding the future of Hong Kong after the 1997 handover to China. The Hong Kong economy had been unstable and inflation-prone until the 1983 adoption of the currency board that linked Hong Kong to the interest rates, and inflation rates, of the USA. Rising anxieties about the future of Hong Kong were stabilized with the Sino-British Joint Declaration of 1984, which specified the terms of the handover and the future of the Hong Kong SAR after 1997.

Hong Kong's housing prices turned around in 1995 when its economy was booming, as Hong Kong become a major provider of services for the rapid industrialization of the Pearl River Delta, as part of the Deng Xiaoping market reforms. Capital inflows and the financial sector grew rapidly following the clarification of Hong Kong's future status by the Joint Declaration, and given the strategic role that Hong Kong's financial sector would be playing in the development of Asia, including China. The real estate sector (construction and real estate service industries) also grew and, by 1997, had become the largest sector in the Hong Kong economy, contributing about 30% to GDP (trade 20.7%, finance 10.3%) (Sheng, 2009). The rapid rise of housing demand collided with the limited housing supply. The clause of the 1984 Joint Declaration that reduced the supply of new land leases by the government to only 50% of past trends until the 1997 handover to China also fed rising price expectations. The housing price-to-rent ratio became very high and began to look like a bubble's ratio (Renaud *et al.*, 1997).

Going into the AFC, the overall market fundamentals of Hong Kong were sound, and there was no obvious reason for Hong Kong to be a victim of the crisis, which had started in Thailand in July 1997 with speculative attacks that quickly led to the Thai triple currency, real estate and banking crisis. Nonetheless, Hong Kong was also subjected to speculative attacks from global hedge funds in what became known as the "double play", whereby these speculators shorted both Hong Kong's currency peg, under the expectation that the scale of its financial backing would prove too small. The Hong Kong stock markets were also shorted, because a very high percentage of the market's total capitalization consisted of real estate stocks and would, therefore, be damaged by the interest rate effects of the attack. Moreover, shorting the market was technically possible in Hong Kong, which already had the most developed financial markets in Asia.

The government and the Hong Kong Monetary Authority responded jointly, quickly and successfully. The government used its large fiscal reserves to support the stock market, while the HKMA used its own reserve fund to defend the peg[3]. However, during the currency attack launched on Hong Kong on "Black Thursday" in October 1997, the HIBOR rate shot up from 9% to 280% for a few hours, which lead to a dramatic fall in both stocks and real estate values. This, in turn, triggered a deep recession, with a 4.5% drop in real GDP in 1998.

Housing prices fell 66% in total over five quarters, and remained depressed for seven more years. However, despite the collapse of property prices, Hong Kong did not suffer a triple crisis like Thailand, nor even a costly and lasting twin banking and real estate crisis like the US, after the subprime debacle and other crises, as analyzed by Reinhart and Rogoff (2010). Hong Kong's dollar peg did not collapse, and Hong Kong's banking system suffered bearable damages because its banks were well regulated and well capitalized. As a result, there was no massive non-performing loan issue, and no banking crisis. One major region-wide lesson of the Hong Kong crisis (and of the Korean crisis) is that every one of the six EA governments decided to build up very large defensive reserves against future external financial shocks. When the GFC erupted, a decade later, East Asian economies were better prepared to face financial shocks, and the main channel of transmission of the GFC proved to be trade supply chains.

As Figure 7.6 shows, The Hong Kong HPI has exhibited a stable upward path since 2003, with only a short but sharp drop during the GFC, followed by a quick recovery since early 2009. Currently, Hong Kong tops the list of global cities in terms of the house price-to-income ratio (PIR) (*Demographia,* 2014). The record low interest rates driven by the US Federal Reserve policies through the currency peg, very tight housing supply conditions, and strong expectations about housing price appreciation are contributory factors to the latest housing price inflation. As in Taiwan and Singapore, the strong economic growth of China appears to be a spill-over factor contributing to the strong housing price performance since 2009 (Kim and Park, 2014).

---

[3] See Sheng (2009), Chapter 10: "Hong Kong; Unusual Times Need Unusual Action". As chair of the Securities and Futures Commission at the time, Andrew Sheng was part of the senior team that led Hong Kong's defense against the "double play" attack.

1998Q1 = 100

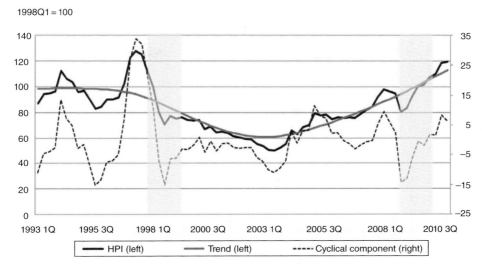

Figure 7.6   Hong Kong: housing price dynamics, 1993Q1 to 2010Q3.
Source: Cho *et al*. (2012).

Hong Kong has been implementing macroprudential policies since 1995 to prevent bank credit from fueling property price bubbles, and to contain excessive leverage by households. The Hong Kong Monetary Authority (HKMA) has introduced six rounds of macroprudential measures between October 2009 and February 2013, lowering caps on LTV and the Debt Service Ratio (DSR). To counteract speculative property flipping, the government has also introduced a special stamp duty to control property transactions (He, 2013, 2014).

7.2.5   Tokyo, Japan

The Japanese asset price bubbles for land and stocks during the period 1985–1991 are detailed in chapter 5. Here, we provide the information needed to understand the dynamics of land and housing prices in Tokyo. Early in the 1970s, the total number of housing units had finally exceeded the number of households. From 1977, however, the Land Price Index, which is used in Japan in preference to an HPI, started on a long run growth path, fuelled by the massive infrastructure and real estate development projects launched by successive Japanese governments since the early 1970s.

Land prices rose by 215% in nominal terms (85% in inflation corrected terms) in the six biggest Japanese cities in the 1970s, and by 180% nationally (23% in real terms) until 1980. Then, the monetary policy of extremely low interest rates adopted after the 1985 Plaza Accord on the Yen-dollar exchange rates, which had dramatically increased the value of the Yen, turned the powerful domestic real estate boom into one of the biggest

1998Q1 = 100

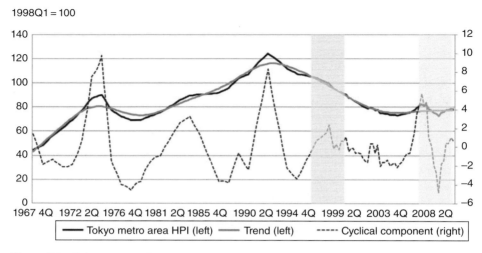

Figure 7.7 Tokyo metropolitan region: land and housing price dynamics: 1967Q4 to 2008Q2. *Source*: Cho *et al.* (2012).

bubbles in world history. Stock prices also began to rise in 1983. The rise in land prices moved in tandem with stock prices, and spread from Tokyo to major cities such as Osaka and Nagoya, then to other cities. The particular period of 1986–91 exhibits an extremely strong LPI growth, with 20% per annum in real terms (a 170% rise in total). Figure 7.7 illustrates the behavior of the residential land price index in the Tokyo metropolitan area.

On the demand side, strong income growth and ample liquidity for mortgage lending were the major driving forces. Rising corporate earnings in the 1970s and the 1980s increased liquidity in the residential mortgage market, leading to high-LTV lending (up to 120%), with 40–50 years multi-generational maturities. The volume of housing loans more than doubled over the short period 1985–1989. On the supply side, access to land for urban development was highly inelastic due, in particular, to two policies: the strict law protecting agricultural land, and the highly favorable tax treatment of agricultural land (see Chapters 2 and 5).

In the early 1990s, the Bank of Japan raised interest rates sharply, which eventually led to the bust of the long-lasting housing boom. The consequence was a crash of residential and commercial property values, and the bankruptcies of the seven housing loan companies, with massive spillover effects on the ineffectively liberalized and regulated banking system. The volume of bad loans mushroomed to almost one trillion US dollars, when the world's entire GDP was estimated at just over USD 22 trillion in 1990. By most estimates, Japanese homeowners saw the value of their houses drop by 60% in real terms between 1991 and 2005. Japan's very rapid population aging has also been a factor (see Chapter 11).

In Japan's six largest cities, land prices finally began to level off in the early 2000s, and then to rise mildly again by 2004. Land prices rose by about 3% in both nominal and real terms in 2006, and by about 8% in nominal and real terms in 2007, driven in part by the booming REITs industry (Watanabe and Shimizu, 2012). Unfortunately, the global financial crisis led to another fall in nominal and real property prices in 2009. The main channel of transmission of the US subprime shock was the collapse of the demand for Japanese REITs. On the other hand, the losses of Japanese securities firms and major banks from the purchase of "toxic" US securities, like MBSs and CDOs, were estimated at around ¥6 billion, and considered manageable (Seko *et al.*, 2011).

A very unusual aspect of the Japanese housing price boom-bust is the sustained large housing supply, even during the price bust. The cause lies in the unique structure of housing supply in Japan, which consists of a large percentage of rapid rebuilding of (wooden) housing units by individual owners on the same land plot (Chapter 5). As a result, Japan maintained a very high level of housing construction for a long time, even after the bubble burst. Total housing starts between 1985 and 1995 were about 1.5 million units, which is higher than the average long-term housing supply in the US, which is slightly over one million units per year, yet the US has a population that is more than 50% larger than that of Japan. Even during the period of depressed prices, between 1995 and 2007, housing supply exceeded one million. Housing supply dropped sharply only in 2009, to about 800,000 (Seko *et al.*, 2011).

7.2.6   Beijing, China

The history of a market-based housing price dynamics is short in China. Until 1998, the traditional state housing regime continued to prevail (see Chapter 9), so the emerging new real estate developers had limited incentives to build residential housing, the private housing market was small and rates of return were low. The shortage of residential dwelling remained an acute issue in Shanghai and other large cities, as urban housing demand was very strong, due to rapidly rising household incomes and rapid urbanization since the early 1980s.

The historic housing privatization of 1998, soon followed by the complete liberalization of re-sales in 2003, gave rise to the first demand-driven housing price boom in China (See Chapter 9). Through a series of reforms, the residential real estate industry was completely liberalized in a few years after 1998, and quickly became one of the most profitable business activities in China. By 2003, the majority of residential dwellings were supplied through the market, and the percentage of public welfare housing supply had become quite small. For instance, public housing supply had become less than 7% of total new construction space in Shanghai. Over the three decades of market-oriented reforms, the living space *per capita* more than tripled, from five square meters in 1982 to 17.2 square meters by the end of 2009. The mortgage lending business was also liberalized in 1998, with the promulgation of "management provisions on resident housing loan". Residential mortgage loans in China are almost all adjustable-rate mortgages (ARMs), with a maximum LTV of 80%, a maximum DTI 70%, and loan maturities up to 30 years, with amortizing principal.

Housing prices have been rising since 1998 in Beijing and many other first- and second-tier cities, as can be seen from Figure 7.8 for Beijing. The GFC led to a short-term decline in the HPI in 2008. A major driver of the nation-wide housing price boom after 2009 was the very large stimulus package of 2009, primarily funded by the five large state-owned banks. Then, in order to cool the housing price boom, the government promulgated various anti-speculative regulations in 2010, including lowering the maximum LTV from 80% to 70% for resident owners and to 50% for second homes, with additional lending restrictions for third or additional homes. Experimental holding taxes have also been levied by some local governments. Like Singapore and Korea, the central Chinese government intervenes frequently in the housing market, and so do large local governments.

There is evidence of very strong housing price appreciation, and worsening housing affordability across major cities. The price-to-rent ratios (P/R) in large Chinese cities rose from 26 in 2007 to 46 in 2010, implying user cost for owning being lowered to very low values compared to the P/R values observed in Korean and US cities. Also, the constant quality land price index (CQLPI) has risen eight-fold between 2003–2007 (Wu *et al.*, 2010). The dynamics of

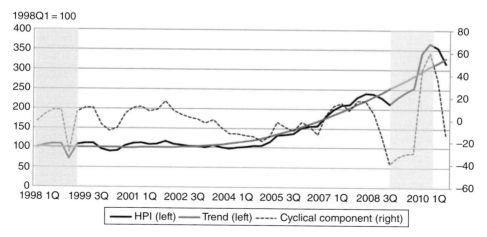

Figure 7.8   Beijing: housing price dynamics, 1998Q3 to 2010Q1.
Source: Cho *et al.* (2012).

housing prices has varied considerably across cities. For example, while there was a pronounced housing price boom-bust in Shanghai in the mid-2000s, Beijing and inland cities did not follow a similar cyclical pattern. The housing correction that started in late 2013 has been affecting primarily lower tier cities, where housing production had been supply driven[4].

7.3   Institutions and regulations shaping East Asian housing cycles

The role of government varies across countries, depending on the unitary or federal structure of government, social policy mandates, and the political landscape. A common policy objective is to promote home ownership, but the extent and modality of intervention differs from country to country. Among the six East Asian countries, Singapore has the most active program of supporting home ownership, through its unique regulatory system, which integrates housing supply, financing and saving through the Central Provident Fund, its mandatory national pension fund. In China, local government plays a key role in housing supply, as the local government units manage land sales, which provide a major source of revenue. Both Korea and Hong Kong have tight land use regulations. The differences in housing supply elasticity caused by physical and institutional constraints are crucial in explaining the volatility of housing across countries, as well as across cities within a country.

7.3.1   Channels of interactions in open economies and key players in their housing cycles

To investigate key institutional characteristics of relevance in the East Asian countries, we look into the behavior of the key players in amplifying any housing cycle. These are the households, lenders, and developer-builders. The usual supporting cast of the central bank and national and local governments are shown in Figure 7.9, which was initially presented in Chapter 1 to highlight the focus of this study on two-way interactions between housing and the macroeconomy.

Households are (potential) homebuyers, to whom housing is both a durable consumption good and the most important asset in their portfolio. In their decisions to purchase a house, households are driven by housing price (P) and

---

[4] Housing indicators have been varying widely in quality across Chinese cities after 1998. However, constant quality land price indices for 35 cities are now published by a consortium of Tsinghua University, NUS of Singapore and the Wharton School. It was also announced in early 2015 that Tsinghua University would be publishing a nationwide HPI across major cities, using a methodology similar to the Case-Shiller housing price index used in the US.

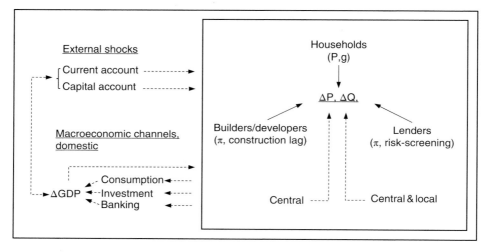

Figure 7.9   Channels of interactions in open economies and key players of housing cycles.
Source: Cho *et al.* (2012).

expectations about its future course (g). They are conditioned by their current and expected income, as well as the degree of ease of access to credit and the terms of mortgage loans.

Lenders provide residential mortgage loans to homebuyers and development finance to developers to facilitate the production and exchange of houses. They apply underwriting criteria such as loan-to-value ratio (LTV) and debt service to income ratio (DTI) to screen borrowers. Bank lending tends to be pro-cyclical, increasing in a boom and decreasing in a downturn, which amplifies real estate cycles. Lenders often exhibit a myopic behavior and are also constrained by information asymmetries. The availability of various loan products and the volume of credit are important in affecting the volatility of housing cycles. Mortgage systems also affect the extent to which the housing wealth effect influences private consumption, especially when home-equity loans are available.

Developers and builders maximize profits from housing development, given the demand for new housing by households. They need to make development decisions several years ahead, in multi-unit projects, since housing development entails a lag, which requires them to anticipate market conditions when the project will be completed and the output is placed on the market. Many behavioral studies suggest that developers tend to be myopic, due in part to the length of construction periods. Interactions among competing developers in the local market are also an important aspect of new housing supply. The local institutional structure, including access to development finance and pre-sale schemes, also affects the behavior of developers. Pre-sales contracts are widely used in East Asian housing markets, except in Japan.

7.3.2 *Financial sector stability and macro-prudential regulations*

The influence of the central bank on housing markets has become more important in recent years. Although there is controversy over whether the central banks should consider asset prices in addition to targeting inflation in conducting monetary policy, the central banks are monitoring the housing market very closely. Central banks and financial supervisory authorities are also involved in regulating the LTV and DTI ceilings, in order to pre-empt systemic risks.

Mortgage market represents the major driver of housing demand and, hence, housing price. Table 7.3 summaries key features of mortgage markets and government intervention in mortgage markets in the six East Asian countries.

The two financial factors that influence the magnitude of housing price appreciation and its volatility are the rate of increase in outstanding mortgage debt and the share of adjustable rate mortgages (ARM), as a percentage of total mortgage lending. The larger the rate of increase in mortgage lending, the larger the shift in housing demand and, hence, the larger the magnitude of housing price appreciation. Regarding the relationship between the composition of mortgage debt and the volatility of housing prices, IMF (2004) was the first to suggest that housing prices are more volatile the larger the share of ARM loans, in a study of 18 developed countries. Kim and Cho (2014) analyzed the data of 32 countries and classified them into those with predominantly FRM loan products, ARM loan products, or a mix of both types of products. They found that the volatility of housing prices is the smallest in housing systems dominated by FRMs, and the largest in countries dominated by ARMs.

As Figure 7.10 shows, the difference between the housing finance systems of Western and East Asian countries at the start of the 21st Century is significant. There is a wide spectrum of Western experiences, ranging from housing finance systems relying primarily on FRM loans, to housing finance systems that rely mostly on ARM loans, with a significant number of Western systems using a mix of loan products. These Western systems rely significantly on capital market funding, through the use of either residential MBS or covered bonds. In contrast, EA housing finance systems are heavily reliant on ARM products. In terms of funding, these EA housing finance systems are either dominated by depository institutions that are "portfolio lenders", and/or rely in a major way on government-controlled savings channels, such as the Postal Savings System of Japan or the Central Provident Fund of Singapore. Together with the inelastic supply of housing, this type of mortgage lending contributes to the widespread EA housing price volatility.

With financial liberalization since the 1990s, retail banks have become the dominant lenders in all six EA countries. As just seen, ARMs are the

Table 7.3 Key features of mortgage markets in East Asian countries.

	Lenders	Maximum loan term (years)	LTV (%)	Pre-payment penalty	Share of ARMs (%)	Capital market funding (%)	IMF index government intervention	MDO/GDP (%)
Korea	Banks	10–30	60(70)	Yes	85	5 (MBS)	0.44	31.5
Japan	Banks	20–30	70–80	No	36	10 (MBS)	0.38	35.6
China	Banks	30	70– 2nd home 40	n.a.	99	n.a.	0.38	14.4
Singapore	Banks	35	80(90)	Yes	99	n.a.	0.75	48.5
Hong Kong	Banks	10–29	50–75	n.a.	99	n.a.	n.a.	42.3
Taiwan	Banks	20–30	70– 2nd home 50	n.a.	Floating hybrid loans	5 (MBS)	0.31	40.0

Source: Kim and Cho (2014).

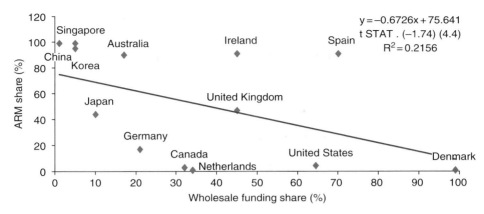

Figure 7.10 Spectrum of housing finance systems: East Asian reliance on ARM loans vs. wholesale funding.
Source: Cho *et al.* (2012).

dominant loan products of these banks, except in Japan, where the share of ARMs is currently around 40%, due to access to long-term postal savings funding, at attractive rates that reduced the interest risks of FRM loans. Capital market funding of residential mortgages is very limited in East Asian countries. Japan, Korea and Taiwan have small MBS markets. This very limited reliance on capital market funding is reflected in the very small market for fixed rate mortgages (FRMs) in East Asia. East Asian banks are mostly portfolio lenders, who value the attractive risk-adjusted returns on their mortgage loan portfolio and are not keen to package them into MBS securities for sale on capital markets.

The regulations of mortgage lending in East Asia have a dual purpose. One purpose is prudential, and aims to mitigate lending risks and to improve the stability of the banking system. The other purpose is social, and aims to dampen housing price cycles, thereby marginally improving access to housing ownership in societies where housing is the primary channel of wealth accumulation, and inequalities are rising. Ceilings on loan-to value ratios (LTV) and debt-to-income ratios (DTI) have been adjusted in response to housing price booms in East Asian countries, as a preemptive measure with the aim of promoting financial stability and stabilizing housing prices. Presently, LTV ceilings are more stringent in Korea and Hong Kong than in Japan and Singapore. China and Taiwan apply lower LTV ceilings on second homes.

Empirical research on the impact of such macro-prudential regulation of mortgage loans on housing markets is still small and exploratory. He (2014) reports that there is no evidence that tightening LTV caps dampens housing prices in Hong Kong, although these caps are likely to have reduced mortgage default risk. He also suggests that additional stamp duties might be effective in restraining housing price appreciation. On the other hand, Igan and Kang (2011) find that lowering LTV and DTI limits reduces housing transactions and house price appreciation, as well as dampening expectations in Korea.

7.3.3   *Range of government interventions in EA housing markets*

East Asian governments differ in their use of housing regulations, taxation and the direct provision of public housing. To convey these differences, Table 7.4 offers quantitative and qualitative indicators of the degree of government intervention in six areas across the six EA economies. The first column reports quantitative index scores of the intensity of government real estate regulations across the six housing systems, which are presented in more detail in Section 7.3.4 below. These scores suggest that Korea has the most intense degree of government intervention into real estate, and Hong Kong the least. The second column consists of point estimates of the supply price elasticity of housing in the capital city of each country, which plays a direct role in the housing supply response and price volatility. These supply elasticity estimates appear to be inversely related to the indicators of government regulations: Korea that has the highest score in terms of the government regulation of real estate, also has the smallest housing supply elasticity. The third column simply asks whether or not the supply of new housing units is subject to government regulations. The next two columns report the existence and intensity of capital gains taxes and property taxes across the six EA economies. Finally, public housing being one of the most significant form of government intervention, the sixth column provides the share of public housing in the total housing stock around 2010.

Capital gains taxes are levied in four EA countries, but not in Singapore and Hong Kong. In Japan, China, and Korea, capital gains taxation applies to residential housing, with exemptions in Korea restricted to owners of units priced below a ceiling, and if the owner has owned and resided in the house for a certain period. Until 2014, Korea also used to be the only country that taxed the owners of two or more houses at higher rates. A property tax is levied on home owners in five countries, but not China, the tax base being the assessed asset value (Japan and Korea) or the market rental value (Hong Kong and Singapore).

The property taxation systems in East Asia are fundamentally different from that of the USA, where property taxes are local taxes in the pure sense of the word, with rates and standards determined by local governments to finance a very high share of their budgets. Korea has both a local property tax and a national comprehensive real estate tax, which is a

Table 7.4 Government interventions in housing markets in East Asia.

	Comprehensive index of real estate regulation	Supply elasticity	Regulation on the price of new housing	Capital gains tax (heavier tax on owners of two or more houses)	Property tax (rate)	Share of public housing out of total housing stock
Korea	16	0.04	O (public/private)	O (O)	O (<0.5%)	5%
Japan	8	0.99	x	O (X)	O (1–1.5%)	n/a
China	8	−0.45	x	O (X)	X	<10%
Singapore	11	0.37	O (public)	X	O (<0.5%)	83%
Hong Kong	2	1.1	x	X	O (<0.5%)	29%
Taiwan	8	1.3	x	O (X)	O (0.5–1%)	1%

Note: housing transaction taxes applied in all cities (acquisition/registration or stamp tax).

Source: Kim and Cho (2014).

strongly redistributive tax with a progressive rate structure applied on an ability-to-pay basis. Finally, transaction taxes can take the form of acquisition taxes or stamp duties, which have been used in Singapore and Hong Kong as a method of cooling an overheated housing market.

The share of public housing as a percentage of total housing stock varies across countries. Singapore is unique, because more than 80% of its housing stock has been publicly produced but is now under private ownership (see Chapter 6). Hong Kong also has a sizable share of public housing, which is mostly rental units. The six countries have different regulations on the supply of new housing units: Korea and Singapore regulate the prices of new housing units sold. In Korea, there is a price ceiling on new apartments and the developers are required to reveal their costs broken down into major categories.

7.3.4   Real estate regulations, supply elasticity and price volatility across East Asia

The two relationships between government regulations and the supply elasticity of housing, on the one hand, and that between the supply elasticity and housing price volatility in response to a demand shift on the other, are the main supply side factors in the volatility of East Asian housing prices. Conceptually, it would be easy to show using a simple demand and supply diagram that a demand shock of a given magnitude will generate a larger (smaller) variation in housing price (housing quantity), the less elastic housing supply is (Malpezzi and Wachter, 2002). The supply elasticity of housing is influenced by natural constraints that have determined the physical availability of developable land, and by man-made constraints in the form of land use regulations, and other regulations affecting the economic characteristics of new housing supply.

To compare the intensity of the government regulation of housing supply across countries, Kim *et al.* (2008) conducted an international survey of experts knowledgeable about specific cities around the world, including capitals or major cities of each of the six East Asian economies. The survey consisted in 19 questions on the presence of major types of government interventions in land use regulations, and the supply of new housing in each of the 16 cities. A summary of the contents of the 19 questions to which the experts provided detailed answers is presented in Table 7.5. These expert answers were scored, and the scores were aggregated into a composite index of the intensity of government regulation in each of the 16 cities. The values of the composite housing regulatory index for the six EA cities are presented in the first column of Table 7.4. The larger the value of the composite index, the heavier is the regulatory environment in that city.

Table 7.5 An international survey of real estate property rights and regulatory interventions.

Index	Coverage of the regulatory survey	Scoring values
I-1	Is there a national or local limit on the amount of residential land that an individual or a household can own?	Yes: 1, No: 0
I-2	Is there a limit on the amount of agricultural land that an individual or a household can own?	Yes: 1, No: 0
I-3	Is there a law or regulation that requires a permit to purchase land?	Yes: 1, No: 0
I-4	Are foreigners allowed to buy and sell land/homes?	Yes: 1, No: 0
I-5	Amount of compensation relative to market value	Over 10%: 1, Under 10%: 0
I-6	Can the national or local government reserve a site for public facilities without compensation for an extended period of time?	Yes: 1, No: 0
I-7	Is there a zoning mechanism or other institutional mechanism intended to enable government to acquire land at below the market price?	Yes: 1, No: 0
I-8	Is there an official land development agency that can acquire land at below the market price?	Yes: 1, No: 0
I-9	Who finally decides on the development of residential, commercial or industrial areas in the largest city?	Central Gov't: 1, Local Gov't: 0
I-10	Is there a green belt or urban growth boundary around the largest city of the country?	Yes: 1, No: 0
I-11	Is there a regulation on land use conversion from agricultural to urban use?	Yes: 1, No: 0
I-12	What best describes the locational opportunities of private land developers?	Strict: 1, Regular: 0
I-13	How long does it take to obtain the permits and permission necessary for a typical midsized (e.g. 100 unit) residential subdivision?	Over 1 Year: 1, Under 1 Year: 0
I-14	Are rent controls being enforced?	Yes: 1, No: 0
I-15	Does government intervene in the allocation of new houses produced by the private sector?	Yes: 1, No: 0
I-16	Are there price controls on new houses?	Yes: 1, No: 0
I-17	What is the approximate share of the total supply of housing owned by the public sector?	Over 10%: 1, Under 10%: 0
I-18	Do different capital gains tax rates apply depending on the number of houses owned?	Yes: 1, No: 0
I-19	Who sets the rate of recurrent taxes on property holding?	Central Gov't: 1, Local Gov't: 0

Source: Kim *et al*. (2008).

Across East Asia, the value of the composite regulatory index is the highest for Seoul, and the lowest for Hong Kong.

The comprehensive regulatory scores for individual cities can be compared with estimates of the price elasticity of housing supply available from various sources. The negative correlation between the value of the composite regulatory index and estimates of the price elasticity of housing supply in each city is illustrated in Figure 7.11. The match-up between the regulatory index values

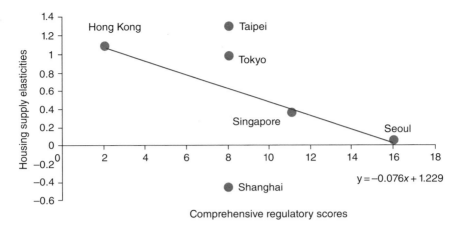

Figure 7.11 Extent of supply regulation and housing supply elasticity for major EA cities. *Source*: Kim and Cho (2014).

and the housing supply elasticity estimates is reasonable, but is not perfect. Seoul has the heaviest regulatory score, and also a very low estimate of housing supply elasticity. Next comes Singapore, with a slightly lower regulatory score and a slightly higher, but still very low, supply elasticity.

Three cities then receive similar scores regarding the intensity of their housing regulation: Taipei in Taiwan, Tokyo in Japan, and Shanghai in China. However, these three major cities have very different estimates of housing supply elasticity. This can be readily explained, and qualitatively matches the institutional analyses of these three countries. Of the three housing systems with comparable degrees of regulation, Taipei has the most elastic housing supply, and we would expect higher housing elasticity estimates for the other cities of Taiwan than for Taipei. The unexpected negative supply elasticity estimate for Shanghai can be attributed to the non-market nature of real estate development processes, which are the legacy of central planning in China, with a land supply entirely monopolized by local governments and housing production decisions determined by political processes until 1998. Among the six EA housing systems, the least heavily regulated market is Hong Kong, which also has the most elastic supply estimate that is still relatively low.

A direct linkage between housing supply elasticity and housing price volatility is harder to establish, because actual housing price outcomes are influenced by both demand and supply factors, while demand conditions are likely to have varied across cities during the period of study. For example, the standard deviation of housing price appreciation during the first decade of the 21st century was largest in Beijing, followed by Hong Kong and Singapore, whereas that of Seoul was the smallest next to Japan.

Last, but not least, changing expectations are a major force in shaping the demand behavior of participants in markets for long-term assets like housing markets and their price volatility. Structurally, China, Japan, Korea, Singapore, Hong Kong and Taiwan are all faced with comparable problems of low fertility, population growth slowdown, and aging. Japan has been the Asian leader of demographic aging and population decline. Changes in the structure of demand, and the impact on Japanese housing prices, are already quantifiable (see Chapter 11).

In addition, housing prices have been temporarily weak across Asia in the aftermath of the shock caused created by the Global Financial Crisis. In Korea, for instance, there are debates about whether the shrinking demand for housing is now driven by pessimistic expectations in the light of demographic changes, and whether a pessimistic shift in expectations may have been crystallized by the shock of the GFC. Only in China would we expect the negative impact of population aging on urban housing demand and housing prices to be mitigated by significant rises in incomes and an additional large volume of urbanization.

Thus, it seems premature to conclude that our case studies lend firm support to theoretical predictions about the linkage between supply responsiveness and house price volatility. Further analyses should consider both demand and supply factors, as well as expectations, and the regulatory policies that have been recently introduced. This is a demanding task.

8

Drivers of East Asian Housing Price Cycles: An Analysis

In Chapter 7, we provided evidence suggesting that East Asian housing prices tend to be more volatile, and that their cycles tend to be of shorter duration than in Western housing markets. In the present chapter, the goal is to understand better the drivers of cyclical housing price changes, by quantifying East Asian volatility and price cycles through the application of established time series econometric measurements of cycles to the best available housing price data on primate cities of the six countries. Can we quantify and distinguish the relative importance of several fundamental drivers of these cycles?

Chapter 8 is divided into three main parts. First, we review the conceptual foundations of what makes housing prices cycles and what existing research has to say about the fundamental drivers of price cycles and the existence of bubbles. Then, we compare quantitatively housing price volatility in East Asian and Western markets, through alternative metrics applied to both city and national data. We shall look at the degree of dispersion of the cyclical components of housing price cycles in two different decades. We shall also specify a suitable housing price model that will permit us to compare, across selected East Asian cities, the quantitative impacts of usual demand-side and supply-side fundamental drivers of housing prices, namely: household income; demographic factors; the user cost of capital in housing; land prices; and construction costs. We shall also make a similar comparison between the capital region of Korea and the rest of the housing system, taking advantage of our access to appropriate data.

Dynamics of Housing in East Asia, First Edition. Bertrand Renaud, Kyung-Hwan Kim and Man Cho.
© 2016 John Wiley & Sons, Ltd. Published 2016 by John Wiley & Sons, Ltd.

Throughout our entire study, we have emphasized that, at the high levels of urbanization which characterize East Asia today, the interactions between the large housing sector and the wider economy go two ways. The third part of Chapter 8 is devoted to quantifying these endogenous two-way interactions. First, relying on the Granger causality test, we shall aim to identify the causal directions of these interactions for four drivers of housing price cycles in each of the six EA economies, which are: the GDP growth rate of the economy as a proxy for incomes; the rate of expansion of credit; the level of long-term interest rates; and the past behavior of real housing prices.

These tests are based on quarterly time series that differ significantly in length across the six countries. Are these interactions bi-directional or one-way? Are they always statistically significant? Are these interactions uniform across the six economies, or do they differ? If they are different, do our previous institutional analyses of the six economies provide insights into these differences among countries? Finally, because East Asian economies have been exceptionally dynamic by world standards, we apply Johansen co-integration tests to find out how important housing has been for the long-term relationships among the three macroeconomic variables of GDP growth rates, the growth of credit, and long-term interest rates. Are the dynamic relationships between the three macro-economic variables seemingly unstable if housing price behavior is ignored? Is there a stable long-term relationship among them when the dynamics of housing prices is taken into account? Do the results of the Johansen test differ across countries?

Finally, we shall discuss very briefly the evidence available on the causal role of housing in the AFC and the GFC. What was the causal direction? Did housing play an active role in any EA country during these two crises, as real estate did for Thailand during the AFC or as the subprime sector did in the US during the GFC? Alternatively, was housing at the receiving end of these two crises across the six economies?

8.1   What makes housing prices cyclical? An analytical overview

8.1.1   Conceptual foundations

Cyclical housing price movements are caused either by changes in market fundamentals (abrupt or faster-than-expected ones) or by a bubble (that is, a deviation of asset price from the level that demand- and supply-side market fundamentals indicate). To elaborate this point, and to provide a base for conceptual discussion, realized housing price at a given point in time, P_t, is specified as a sum of its fundamental value, $P_t^\star$, and a residual component, b_t:

$$P_t = P_t^\star + b_t \tag{8.1}$$

$P_t^\star$ is, in turn, a sum of two discounted cash flow streams – expected future rental income during asset holding, and expected resale price at terminal point. Assuming a constant discount rate, r, a constant expected rent growth rate, g^e, and the transversality condition[1], the fundamental price is trans-formed as:

$$\frac{R_t}{P_t^\star} = r - E_t\left[g^e \setminus \Omega_t\right] \tag{8.2}$$

This states that, for a marginal investor, the revenue for holding the asset (rental yield, $\dfrac{R_t}{P_t^\star}$) should be equal to the net expected cost, the latter of which consists of the market determined discount rate, r, minus the expected rent growth rate assessed on the basis of on all available information at current time point, Ω_t (i.e., $E_t[g^e\setminus\Omega_t]$, where $E[\cdot]$ is an expectation operator). Assuming a perpetual holding, g^e, is equivalent to expected capital gain as a ratio to the asset price, $P_t^\star$.

The bubble component in Equation 8.1, representing a part of asset price movement that is not captured by market fundamentals, has its own dynamic process:

$$b_t = \sum_{j=1}^{J} \delta_j b_{t-j} + \varepsilon_t \tag{8.3}$$

where δ and ε are regression coefficient and white noise (that is, error term with zero mean and a constant variance), respectively.

8.1.2   Drivers of price cycles and existence of bubbles

Using Equations 1–3 as a conceptual basis, several drivers of cyclical housing price changes can be identified. First, a large swing in market fundamental will influence the realized housing price (P_t) through two channels – via current rent (R_t), if they are current (and realized) ones, and via expected capital gain (g^e), if they are future (and expected) ones. For example, a fast output growth expected next year can work as a demand-side fundamental, pushing g^e and, hence, P_t, upward. As a slow-moving market fundamental, population aging expected in future years can lower labor force participation and output, pushing both g^e and P_t downward. On this point, Nishimura (2012) elaborates linkages of the declining inverse dependency ratios

---

[1] That is, $\lim_{T \to \infty} E_t\left[\sum_{\tau=1}^{T-t} \dfrac{1}{(1+r)^\tau} P_{t+T}\right] = 0$, the present value of resale price goes to zero as holding period approaches infinity (assuming a constant discount rate, r).

(non-labor force population divided by working age, 15–64 years old, population) with macroeconomic and housing market outcomes in Japan and other EA countries. Other demand- and supply-side market fundamentals, such as changes in urbanization rate and in construction cost, will impact the asset price through the same channels.

Second, the existence of a bubble, b_t in Equation 8.1 can be another driver of the housing cycle, as it makes an asset price movement non-linear (or regime-switching), in that an explosive price path during a run-up phase is usually followed by a sudden and sustained price decline in a crisis phase[2]. As an illustration, the Minsky's narrative of the five phases in financial bubble (as summarized by Kindleberger (1978)) sums up the underlying mechanics of this structural break in the price process:

1. *displacement*, with expectations of increased profits and economic growth (due to a new technology or financial innovation);
2. *boom*, with low volatility, credit expansion, increases in investment, and rising asset prices that start exceeding fundamentals;
3. *euphoria*, with investors trading the over-valued assets in a frenzy, resulting in a high trading volume, explosive asset price path, and a suspicious sense about bubble, but confident for selling the asset to a greater fool;
4. *profit-taking*, with investors starting to reduce their positions, but still strong demand from less sophisticated investors; and
5. *panic*, with prices starting falling rapidly, resulting in fire sales, constrained lending criteria and margin calls (by lenders), and weakened balance sheets (of investors).

Economic analyses until now have generally failed to explain how a bubble starts in the first place. It is also difficult to measure its magnitude empirically, due to the nature of joint statistical tests of bubble existence and model specification for market fundamentals, through the proper decomposition of P_t^* and b_t in Equation 8.1 quantitatively)[3]. Nonetheless, a rational bubble, and the resulting explosive price path, can be tested statistically, based on the residual process in Equation 8.3, as done by recent studies. That is, a rational investor will still be willing to invest, even if b_t is positive (that is, the asset being over-valued), as long as s/he expects it will grow

---

[2] The role of bubble in asset price dynamics has long been a topic of economic analysis: Samuelson (1958), Tirole (1985), Englund and Ioannides (1997), Malpezzi (1999), Ortalo-Magné and Rady (2001), among others. See Brunnermeier and Ohemke (2012) for a survey of studies on financial bubbles and systemic risk in financial markets, and Guykaynak (2008) for a survey of papers on testing bubbles in stock markets.
[3] Refer to Brunnermeier and Ohemke (2012) and Gurkaynak (2006) on these points.

bigger next period, so as to offset discounting[4]. In the context of housing market, Lai and Van Order (2010, 2014) have tested the explosiveness of the housing price processes in US metropolitan areas over the period 1980–2012, by imposing a particular condition on the sum of the regression coefficients in Equation 8.3[5]. Although no US metropolitan area was found to exhibit the explosive price path that satisfies their condition, they did report that the sum of the coefficients was larger for time periods after 1999 than before, and for "bubble-MSAs" than for non-bubble ones.

The likelihood of a bubble is correlated with market fundamental variables. For example, Glaeser *et al.* (2006) demonstrate that the chance of a bubble in housing prices has a negative correlation with housing supply elasticity: the higher the supply elasticity in a given location, the lower the chance of a bubble. Restrictive land use controls can contribute to lowering supply elasticity and can heighten the chance of forming a "frothy" price path.

A leverage cycle caused by the pro-cyclical lending behavior by mortgage lenders is another driver, which has been examined by a number of researchers after the Global Financial Crisis[6]. In particular, Geanakoplos (2010) elaborates the stages in the leverage cycle during the subprime mortgage debacle in the USA. There was a large-scale relaxation of lending standards during the boom, especially during the subprime lending frenzy between 2003 and 2006. The bad news of the housing price decline and rising mortgage delinquency led to a sudden tightening of lending standards in 2007 which, in turn, reduced new mortgage issuance as well as the rollover of existing mortgage contracts. The result was a "liquidity trap" and a vicious cycle of asset price decline, fire sales, margin calls, further decline in asset prices, further fire sales, and so on.

Several recent studies examine the impact of lending activity on housing prices based on the market fundamental equation (Equation 8.2). Their results show that the leverage rate, measured by the average loan-to-value (LTV) ratio has a positive correlation with the housing price-to-rent ratio (the inverse of (R/P) in Equation 8.2. The higher the LTV ratio (or the more relaxed the lending standard), the higher the P/R (and, hence, the lower the R/P), which will raise the asset value P_t. In particular, one percentage point increase in average LTV for first-time home buyers is shown to raise P/R by 0.82% in the US (Duca *et al.*, 2011), and a similar result has also been documented in Korea (Cho *et al.*, 2013). Nonetheless, a leverage boom also

---

[4] That is, $E_t[b_{t+1}] = \hat{\delta} \cdot b_t > (1 + r) \cdot b_t$, assuming one-lag dependent variable in Equation 3.

[5] That is, a price path is defined as explosive if $\sum_{j=1}^{J} \delta_j > 1$.

[6] Geanakoplos (2010), Mian and Sufi (2011) and Pavlov and Wachter (2011), among others.

influences consumer expectation of future asset price appreciation which is, in turn, likely to increase the share of optimistic buyers in the market place willing to bid up asset prices, as theorized by Geanakoplos (2008, 2010). As long as that effect is not captured in the fundamental equation (Equation 8.2), a surge in leverage during the boom can make the price path more explosive.

The construction sector can be another source of housing price cyclicality, due in large part to the inherent structure of the real estate development process: construction lags behind initial demand, and myopia on the part of developers[7]. There is evidence of the amplifying effect of new construction cycles on real estate price volatility both in Western economies, such as the recent housing price boom-bust in the US, and among EA countries, with Japan's price boom in the 1980s. Yet, compared to the leverage cycle, the impact of overbuilding on real estate price boom-bust has received less attention from academic economists. However, central bank economist Ellis (2008) provides empirical evidence that the magnitudes of over-building in the housing markets of the USA and Spain were larger than those of other European countries, which later contributed to the deeper price downturns in those countries. The cyclical nature of construction financing can also contribute to volatility in new housing supply, as shown by the "Project Financing" loan crisis in Korea after the 2008 global financial crisis.

What are appropriate policy responses to regulate these different sources of housing price cycles? In the aftermath of the global financial crisis, there has been a strong focus on regulating the demand-side through lending regulations. Caps on LTV and DTI ratios gained popularity among around the world as effective macro-prudential instruments (Crowe *et al.*, 2011; Kuttner and Shim, 2013). However, the relative effectiveness of these ratios, compared to other available policy tools, such as supply-side controls (loss reserve, capital requirements, and exposure limits), as well as conventional housing market stability measures (holding and transfer taxes on housing), still remains unproven.

Also, how to balance between two competing policy goals of ensuring housing market and macroeconomic stability, and of extending financial service to the marginal (low-income and less creditworthy) borrowers, is a relevant research topic to be further explored. In subsequent chapters, we will attempt to shed light on these issues by comparing market forces and institutional attributes relevant to taming housing market cycles across the six EA countries (including Sections 8.3 and 8.4 in this chapter), and by offering detailed case studies on two countries – China and Korea (Chapters 9 and 10).

---

[7] Grenadier (1996) and Wheaton (1999) theorize this construction-driven real estate cycle.

8.2   Quantifying the role of market fundamentals in EA price cycles

To assess quantitatively the dynamics of East Asian housing markets, we proceed in two steps. First, we compare alternative measures of home price volatility across selected cities of the six EA countries with selected Western countries, to determine if there are distinctive features in the EA countries' housing price dynamics that differentiate them from those of Western countries. Second, we estimate quantitatively the relationships over time between housing prices and a selected set of market fundamentals, by specifying and estimating suitable housing price models. Constrained by data availability across the six countries, these housing price models consider only three major variables reflecting market fundamentals: real GDP; the user cost (UC) of capital for owning; and residential investment[8]. We estimate two econometric models – one for housing prices, and the other for price-to-rent ratios. Based on the results, we explore whether these market fundamentals influence housing prices across East Asia as expected, and whether there are similarities with the Western economies.

8.2.1   Comparing housing price volatility between East Asian and Western countries

To make international comparisons of price volatility, we have compiled two volatility indicators. First, the standard deviation of annual real housing price changes, both at the city and the national level, provides an unconditional estimate of volatility. Then, to reveal cyclical components, we calculate the standard deviation of de-trended housing price changes, extracted by applying the Hodrick-Prescott (HP)-filtering method, which provides us with estimates of conditional volatility.

The measures of unconditional volatility are presented in Table 8.1. The results show that, while Singapore and Hong Kong exhibit very large dispersions in the 1990s, these city states, and the Chinese cities of Shanghai and Beijing, are top of the list in terms of both mean and volatility during the 2000s. Some of the primate cities of the East Asian countries exhibit a large volatility in the 2000s, compared with other cities in the sample: the standard deviation is 16.1% for Beijing, 14.8% for Hong Kong, 13.5% for Singapore, 12.7% for Shanghai, and 9.2% for Taipei. These figures are significantly greater than those of European and North American cities: 10.5% for Las Vegas, 4.9% for Los Angeles, and 2.7% for Washington, DC (in the 2000s). While Beijing and Shanghai are characterized as high-risk high-return cities

---

[8] An additional variable, mortgage lending activity, is considered only for the analysis of Korean cities.

Table 8.1 Means and volatility of real house price growth rates in the 1990s and 2000s.

Country	1990s		2000s	
	Mean	Std. Dev.	Mean	Std. Dev.
China	−3.73	4.27	7.25	6.26
Beijing	−	−	8.65	16.08
Chongqing	−4.7	9.47	−1.4	4.92
Shanghai	−3.23	7.92	13.67	12.72
Korea	−5.92	6.97	1.85	5.24
Seoul	−5.09	8.09	4.56	6.98
Busan	−14.95	7.98	10.87	10.03
Hong Kong	0.4	24.76	2.37	14.77
Tokyo Metro area	−10.97	6.59	−2.27	4.33
Singapore	9.12	18.93	1.63	13.46
Taipei	−1.27	6.77	3.79	9.15
Australia	2.27	3.86	4.01	8.74
Austria	0.96	7.8	1.57	4.27
Belgium	2.97	2.33	4.69	3.47
Denmark	6.05	5.17	3.13	9.18
France	2.01	3.48	5.94	6.06
Finland	−	−	2.36	5.19
Germany	−	−	−0.54	1.56
Ireland	−	−	−4.84	10.26
Italy	0.8	4.85	2.71	3.02
Netherlands	10.41	2.98	2.48	4.94
Norway	7.05	4.97	5.42	6.36
Spain	1.95	3.39	5.03	7.43
Sweden	−0.41	8.43	6.3	3.99
United Kingdom	0.62	6.78	6.03	8.47
United States	−0.7	4.93	2.8	11.3
Los Angeles	−2	3.82	0.84	4.86
Washington	−1.18	2.28	1.17	2.7
Las Vegas	0.62	4.51	−3.68	10.45
Canada	−2.29	3.45	1.99	3.02

Source: Cho *et al.* (2012).

in the 2000s, Seoul can be labeled as low-return, low-risk. Both mean and volatility are shown to be unstable between the two sub-periods.

Country-level comparisons yield different outcome from city-level analyses. In the 2000s, some of the North American and European countries have higher standard deviations than EA countries, with the standard deviation of Ireland being 10.26%, followed by Denmark with 9.2%, and Australia with 8.7%, compared to 6.3% for China and 5.2% for Korea. The two city-states of Singapore and Hong Kong are highly volatile in the 2000s, with 13.5% and 14.8%[9]. This outcome confirms our intuition that more granular city-level housing price indexes are better in depicting housing market

[9] The standard deviation of the US is quite high in the 2000s, at 11.3%, which we think is biased as it is based on the composite housing price index of the 20 largest cities.

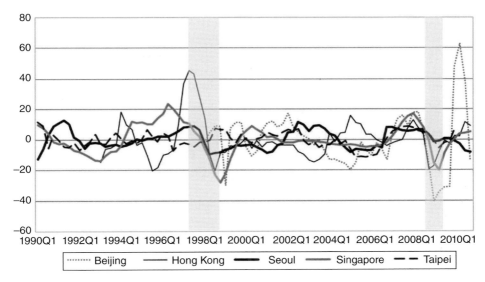

Figure 8.1 Cyclical components in the housing price dynamics.
Source: Cho *et al.* (2012).

Table 8.2 Dispersion of the cyclical components.

	1990s	2000s
Seoul	5.4	6.1
Busan	10.1	8.9
Beijing	–	19.9
Shanghai	–	16.6
Chong Qing	–	4.1
Hong Kong	18.9	8.0
Singapore	14.0	7.0
Taipei	3.9	5.8
Tokyo Metro area	6.6	2.4

Source: Cho *et al.* (2012).

conditions in a given country and, hence, are more appropriate for international comparative analysis like ours.

Next, the conditional volatility measures extracted from the de-trended housing price changes via HP filtering are presented graphically in Figure 8.1 and numerically in Table 8.2. The results are fairly similar to those observed from unconditional volatility measures. During the 1990s, Hong Kong and Singapore exhibited a much larger conditional volatility, with standard deviations of the cyclical component of 18.8% for Hong Kong and 14.0% for Singapore, compared with 6.6% for Tokyo, 5.4% for Seoul, and 3.9% for Taipei. However, during the 2000s, Beijing and Shanghai had much larger conditional volatilities than other cities: 19.9 % for Beijing, 16.6% for Shanghai, compared with 8.0% for Hong Kong, 7.0% for Singapore, 6.1% for Seoul, 5.8% for Taipei, and 2.4% for Tokyo.

During the two financial crises, the AFC in the late 1997 and the GFC in 2007–09, which are represented by the shaded areas in Figure 8.1, the cyclical components in the real housing price growth took a downturn in most East Asian countries, implying that the EA countries' housing prices react to the economy-wide adverse shocks with a sustained downturn and a low level of serial dispersion, which is essentially what the cyclical component extracted represents).

Just before and during the Asian Financial Crisis (AFC), Hong Kong's housing price shows a very large swing, much more so than in Singapore and other countries, indicating that Hong Kong's housing prices were influenced more by the shock than other countries. A comparable large volatility is observed from Beijing during and immediately after the Global Financial Crisis (GFC). In the post-GFC period, the housing prices of Hong Kong and Singapore show upward movements (or positive cyclical components) similar to those of the Chinese cities, while that of Korea is in a downward pattern (negative cyclical component), which suggests that those city states benefit from the strong macroeconomic performance of their neighboring country, China, more so than Korea.

8.2.2   Specification of the housing price model

Many variables qualify as demand- and supply-side fundamentals of housing market. The usual ones are household income, various demographic factors, the user-cost of capital, land prices, and construction costs. In our econometric analysis, we focus on three major variables – real GDP as a country-level proxy for aggregate income, residential investment to reflect the housing quantity supplied (HQ), and the user cost of capital (UC). The housing price model specified below, is similar to one used in a recent study (Muellbauer, 2011) and represents a housing demand function as an inverse demand function with the price variable in the left hand side and the quantity variable in the right hand side:

$$Log(P_t) = \beta_1 \cdot Log(GDP_t) + \beta_2 \hat{Q}_t + \beta_3 UC_t + \varepsilon_t \tag{8.4}$$

This particular model is attractive because all the parameters estimated have readily feasible economic interpretations, thus permitting the derivation of the income and price elasticities of housing demand. In this model, a quantity variable is included as an explanatory factor. However, to implement this model, we have to properly control the simultaneity between the price and quantity variables. Hence, we adopt a two-stage estimation process where we estimate an HQ equation first, and include the predicted value for Q when estimating Equation 8.4.

The expected sign of the quantity variable in Equation 8.4 depends on housing market conditions in each urban market. If a market is in reasonable equilibrium, the market price clears any gap between quantity demanded and quantity supplied, and a positive shock in supply function lowers the equilibrium price. However, if a housing market is in disequilibrium – say, with a large and sustained excess demand, as is the case for the EA cities during the phase of rapid urbanization – or if price and quantity variables are affected by common factors (e.g., macroeconomic conditions), then the two variables may actually exhibit a positive relationship.

The user cost (UC) is compiled for each city, as the after-tax net holding cost of housing asset (the right-hand side of Equation 8.2). Specific factors incorporated are similar to the ones used by recent studies (Harding and Pagan, 2006; Himmelberg *et al.*, 2005; Muellbauer, 2011, in particular), as shown below:

$$UC_{i,t} = \left(1-t_I\right) \cdot r_t + \delta_i - \left(1-t_c\right) \cdot \left(g_{i,t}^e\right) \tag{8.5}$$

where r is the real mortgage interest rate, δ is sum of property tax (1.5%, as in Harding and Pagan, 2006), depreciation rate (2.5%, as in Harding and Pagan, 2006) and maintenance cost (assumed to be 1%) ($\delta = 1.5\% + 2.5\% + 1\% = 5\%$ in our empirical analysis). $g_{i,t}^e$ represents expected rate of real housing price appreciation which, as done by Himmelberg *et al.* and Muellbauer, is proxied by lagged housing price changes at each time point (in particular, average annual real housing price growth rate during two lagged years)[10].

Figure 8.2 shows that the user cost variables for the EA counties rose sharply during the AFC and the GFC, which largely reflect the downturns in housing price growth rates (g^e in Equation 8.5), indicating that consumer expectations of future price appreciation declines during these economic crises. In the Korean case, the market interest rate also sharply increased, which should shift UC further upwards. UC becomes negative when the expected price appreciation becomes large, which is a common problem in empirically measuring UC, as discussed in length by Muellbauer (2011).

The price equation (Equation 8.4) is implemented for five cities – Seoul, Hong Kong, Tokyo, Taipei, and Los Angeles (as a comparator city), by regressing log real HPI on log real GDP, UC (in a non-logarithm form, due to the negative values in some time periods), and logarithm of the ratio between residential investment ratio and GDP as a proxy for the quantity variable. The third variable is estimated via a two-stage process to deal with the simultaneity problem, and the predicted values are included.

---

[10] Two tax rates in Equation 8.5 are assumed to be non-time varying and the same across locations, which is a strong assumption, to be relaxed if we can compile appropriate data. We will also assume that the income tax deduction of mortgage interest does not exist in the EA countries, and the capital gains tax rate is zero.

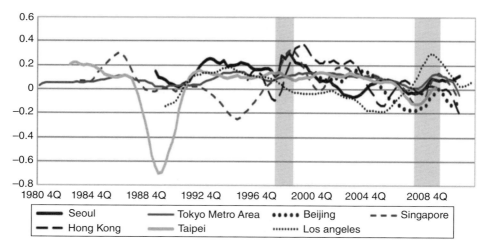

Figure 8.2 User cost of housing ownership.
Source: Cho *et al*. (2012).

Observations are quarterly, and different cities cover different time spans. We perform the Johansen co-integration test to verify that there exists at least one long-term relationship among the included variables.

Next, we estimate the price-to-rent equation, but only for Korea, due to data availability. The specification is similar to that used by Duca *et al*. (2011), as shown below:

$$Log\left(\frac{P_t}{R_t}\right) = \delta_1 \cdot Log\left(UC_t\right) + \delta_2 \cdot M_t + v_t \qquad (8.6)$$

where (P/R) represents average selling price divided by average rental price of a same quality housing unit (in each of the eight large metropolitan areas), UC is the same variable used in Equation 8.5, and M represents a set of variables for mortgage lending activities. In particular, three variables being used – the yearly growth rate of mortgage debt outstanding, the average loan-to-income ratio, LIR, and the average loan-to-value, LVR. LIR and LVR, compiled from micro household panel data sets, reflect the extent of market penetration by the mortgage lending sector, and are described more in detail below. Due to data availability, the price-rent equation is estimated for only two geographical areas in Korea – the capital region (including Seoul and metropolitan areas in its vicinity) and non-capital region (including six major cities not in the capital region).

8.2.3 Estimating results

As shown in Table 8.3, the three variables representing market fundamentals exhibit the expected signs and are statistically significant. The GDP variable, used as a proxy of household income, is positive and significant in all five cities. The user cost (UC) is negative for all five cities, but is

Table 8.3   Estimates of the housing price equations with residential investment.

	Seoul	Hong Kong	Tokyo	Taipei	Los Angeles
Ln (residential. investment ratio); fitted	0.698***	0.004***	56.599***	−1.910*	−27.435***
	(0.001)	(7.461)	(12.280)	(−1.716)	(−31.143)
Ln (GDP)	2.158***	0.690***	0.297***	0.332***	0.666***
	(0.001)	(66.379)	(90.964)	(−30.344)	(66.966)
UC	−0.003	−0.826***	−0.107	−0.961***	−2.197***
	(0.241)	(−5.002)	(−0.344)	(−5.893)	(−6.363)
Observations	51	60	68	108	90
R-squared	0.541	0.539	0.687	0.538	0.180

Note: t-Statistic in parentheses.
***$p < 0.01$
**$p < 0.05$
*$p < 0.1$.
Source: Cho *et al*. (2012).

significant only for Hong Kong, Taipei, and Los Angeles. The ratio of residential investment is positive and significant for Seoul, Hong Kong, and Tokyo, but negative and significant for Los Angeles (at the 1% significance level) and for Taipei (at the 10% significance level).

The variable of particular interest is the residential investment ratio. The result indicates that, while the typical price-quantity interaction holds for Los Angeles, housing price and housing supply tend to co-move in the EA cities, possibly being affected by common economic factors. It is worth mentioning that housing prices in Korea have responded much more keenly to changes in the GDP growth rate than those of other East Asian countries. For example, the average rate of housing price volatility for one percentage point change in real GDP was 2.16% for Seoul, compared to 0.69% for Hong Kong, 0.33% for Taipei and 0.29% for Tokyo.

The results for the price-to-rent equations that could be estimated only for Korea are reported in Table 8.4. They show that, overall, the capital and non-capital regions show very different determinants of the price-to-rent ratios. The user cost UC exhibits a significant negative effect in the capital region (as expected), which is robust across alternative models tested, while its sign and statistical significance change across the models for the non-capital region.

In addition, three mortgage lending variables, compiled separately for the capital and non-capital region and included in the (P/R) equation, are:

1. annual growth rate of the residential MDO (mortgage debt outstanding);
2. the share of households with total consumer loan to income ratios (LIR) exceeding 2.5 (LIR ≥ 2.5) among young and low-/moderate-income families (as an indicator of affordable mortgage lending); and
3. the share of households with loan payment to income ratios (LPR) exceeding 40% (LPR ≥ 0.4) within the same household cohort.

Table 8.4   Estimates of the price-rent ratio equation for two regions of Korea.

	Capital region				
	(1)	(2)	(3)	(4)	(5)
ln (UC Metro)	−0.066***	−0.086***	−0.072***	−0.074***	−0.076***
	(−4.846)	(−5.381)	(−6.127)	(−5.248)	(−5.343)
LIR Metro		0.070***		0.004	−0.001
		(4.100)		(0.215)	(−0.029)
LVR Metro			0.012***	0.012***	0.012***
			(6.486)	(4.394)	(4.340)
Mortgage outstanding growth rate	1.127***				0.384
	(3.744)				(0.962)
Constant	2.823***	0.993**	2.488***	2.376***	2.473***
	(58.935)	(2.027)	(29.761)	(4.500)	(4.597)
Observations	79	58	58	58	58
R-squared	0.307	0.357	0.527	0.527	0.535
Non-capital region					
	(6)	(7)	(8)	(9)	(10)
ln (UC local)	−0.121***	0.081**	0.033	0.032	0.161**
	(−6.335)	(2.035)	(0.740)	(0.675)	(2.005)
LIR local		−0.007		0.001	0.008
		(−0.945)		(0.076)	(1.616)
LVR local			0.030**	0.030*	0.010
			(2.041)	(1.798)	(0.919)
Mortgage outstanding growth rate	0.308				−0.198
	(0.839)				(−0.494)
Constant	2.209***	2.762***	1.156	1.112	2.300***
	(30.427)	(15.344)	(1.597)	(1.191)	(3.372)
Observations	97	113	113	113	76
R-squared	0.328	0.042	0.070	0.070	0.155

Note: t-Statistic in parentheses.
***$p < 0.01$
**$p < 0.05$
*$p < 0.1$.
UC is replaced by 0.0001 when UC is less than zero.
Source: Cho *et al.* (2012).

Both LIR and LVR, developed using household-level micro data, and the cut-offs, are similar levels to those used by Fernandez-Corugedo and Muellbauer (2006). The last two variables show the extent of market penetration by the mortgage lending sector to highly-levered marginal borrowers in Korea. While the estimated coefficients of the two lending variables carry a significant positive sign for the capital region, implying that increase in leverage raises the price-rent ratio, they do not exhibit consistent effects in the non-capital region. Similar results and regional differences are found for the mortgage lending volume variable.

Based on these empirical findings, we conclude that the role of market fundamentals is fairly comparable between the six EA cities and Los Angeles in the US. The GDP or household income, the user cost of capital for owning home, and the terms of residential mortgage are important determinants of the housing price dynamics. However, the quantity variable (the residential investment ratio) exhibited the opposite sign for four out of six East Asian cities, which warrants further investigation.

8.3   Two-way interactions between housing and the macroeconomy

Up to now, we have treated the macroeconomy (represented by GDP as a proxy) as exogenous – that is, we have assumed that it influences, but is not influenced by, the housing market. The relationship, however, is two-directional, in that the macroeconomy and housing markets are endogenously linked. This relationship has been drawing growing attention from both macroeconomists and housing/real estate economists. Three main transmission channels have been identified in the literature – private consumption, investment, and banking (or credit) channels. To illustrate the linkages between housing and the macroeconomy, consider a sequence of events that begins with a downturn in housing price, caused either by poor performance of market fundamentals or by turnaround of consumer expectations.

Suppose housing prices start falling. First, due to the negative wealth effect and the collateral effect, private consumption will decline. Second, due to a drop in the level of new residential construction, total investment will also be depressed. Third, faced with rising defaults and delinquencies following the decline in housing prices, and consequently impaired capital positions, mortgage lenders will reduce new lending and tighten their origination standards, which can eventually lead to a credit crunch. Fourth, aggregate demand will shrink, as a result of all the developments described above following the housing price downturn. Finally, the downturn in macroeconomy will set in which, in turn, will exert a secondary negative effect on housing price. A new cycle of the endogenous interactions between housing and the macroeconomy will thus begin. These linkages are described in Figure 8.3.

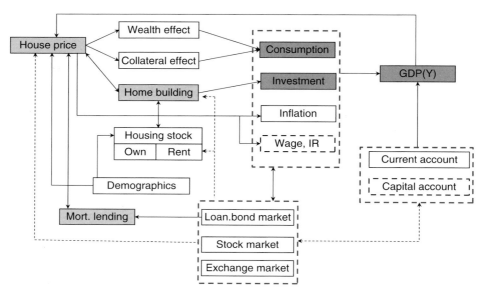

Figure 8.3   Endogenous interactions between housing and the macroeconomy.
Source: Wachter *et al.* (2014).

8.3.1   *Direction of interactions in East Asia and Granger causality tests*

To investigate two-way interactions between housing and the macroeconomy in EA economies, we conducted a Granger causality test. Granger causality is a statistical concept of causality that is based on prediction. If a time series variable X "Granger-causes" another variable Y, then past values of X should contain information that helps predict Y, above and beyond the information contained in past values of Y alone. We check Granger causality among four variables from each East Asian country – log real GDP (GDP), log real private credit (Credit), long-term interest rate (IR), and log real housing price (HP), all measured on a quarterly basis. As shown in Table 8.5, there exists a wide variation in causality test results across countries. Nonetheless, several common patterns emerge: HP and GDP Granger-cause each other (except in Korea and Taiwan); IR Granger-causes credit, obviously, but not in Japan and Hong Kong; and HP Granger-causes credit for three countries (China, Hong Kong and Singapore).

8.3.2   *Long-term dynamics of EA interactions and Johansen co-integration tests*

Because EA economies have been very dynamic, we also conducted a test for a co-integrating relationship among the same four variables, to test the dynamic effects of housing on the macroeconomy. Co-integration is an

Table 8.5   Granger causality test of EA interactions between housing and the macroeconomy.

Null hypothesis	Korea	China	Japan	Hong Kong	Taipei	Singapore
GDP ↛ Credit	4.00*	2.60*	0.65	1.61	3.40**	4.43**
Credit ↛ GDP	0.03	4.23***	0.70	0.99	0.98	0.56
Hp ↛ Credit	2.21	2.93**	0.39	5.54***	0.87	2.95*
Credit ↛ HP	0.01	1.71	3.00**	0.32	4.75	3.68**
IR ↛ Credit	4.52**	7.72***	0.79	0.19	5.88***	5.34***
Credit ↛ IR	0.13	0.37	2.91**	1.84	0.07	0.24
HP ↛ GDP	0.00	4.07***	4.93***	5.56***	0.68	2.55*
GDP ↛ HP	0.26	2.15**	3.65**	2.73*	6.18	5.61***
IR ↛ GDP	2.20	7.16***	0.30	2.48	5.81***	1.38
GDP ↛ IR	0.01	0.43	1.88	0.09	0.57	0.85
IR ↛ HP	0.92	0.88	1.16	0.37	0.93	0.50
HP ↛ IR	0.01	0.30	0.42	0.09	4.67**	0.70

***$p < 0.01$
**$p < 0.05$
*$p < 0.1$.
Source: Cho et al. (2012).

Table 8.6   Results of co-integration tests without housing price.

Country (lags)	Johansen trace test			Long-run relationship				
				HP + Y + R + Constant = 0				
	$r = 0$	$r = 1$	$r = 2$	HP	Y	R	C	Constant
Korea (1)	16.24	4.05	0.28	no co-integration				
Japan (4)	59.63	26.32	3.86	no co-integration				
China (4)	41.63	20.55	7.18	no co-integration				
Singapore (2)	23.98	12.22	3.25	no co-integration				
Hong Kong (2)	24.03	6.08	1.7	no co-integration				
Taiwan (2)	24.22	5.7	0.04	no co-integration				

econometric technique for testing the correlation between non-stationary time series variables. If two or more series are themselves non-stationary (i.e., the characteristics of the stochastic process change over time), but a linear combination of them is stationary (i.e., the stochastic process is fixed in time), then the series are said to be co-integrated.

Goodhart and Hofmann (2007) carried out the Johansen test of co-integration for 16 OECD economies using the same four variables we used in the Ganger causality test. They found that, while only five of the OECD countries exhibit long-run relationships among the four macroeconomic variables when house price variable is not included, all 16 countries exhibit long-run relationships when the housing price variable is included. We obtained similar results to those of Goodhart and Hofmann from our analysis of the data on East Asian countries. No long-run relationship among the four variables is found without the housing price variable HP (Table 8.6), but four East Asian countries – China, Japan, Singapore, and Taiwan – exhibit co-integrating relationships when HP is included (Table 8.7).

Table 8.7   Results of co-integration tests when housing price is included.

Country (lags)	Johansen trace test				Long-run relationship HP + Y + R + Constant = 0					Loading
	$r = 0$	$r = 1$	$r = 2$	$r = 3$	HP	Y	R	C	Con.	
Korea (1)	42.27	10.65	3.68	0.40	no co-integration					
Japan (2)	52.63*	23.04	8.73	2.20	1.00	1.87	−0.28	−0.03	−28.4	0.05
						0.56	0.02	0.09		0.02
China (4)	50.01*	21.62	8.37	0.25	1.00	−0.31	−0.21	−0.64	4.6	0.10
						0.30	0.04	0.33	−16.9	0.17
Singapore (2)	55.78*	22.43	11.34	2.98	1.00	2.09	−0.04	−2.48		−0.03
						0.63	0.05	0.60		0.02
Hong Kong (3)	88.04	13.39	5.04	1.29	no co-integration					
Taiwan (2)	50.88*	21.84	3.06	0.41	1.00	−11.88	−0.50	9.96	77.1	0.00
						2.09	0.10	2.18		0.01

Source: Cho *et al*. (2012).

The quantitative investigation of the drivers of housing prices cycles across East Asia has been constrained by the availability of consistently measured data of good quality. This a recurring challenge for quantitative comparative analyses of housing and other real estate cycles across countries. Nevertheless, we have obtained useful findings regarding the role of market fundamentals. as well as the linkages between housing and the wider economy across East Asia. These quantitative results have added important insights to our understanding of the dynamics of East Asian housing cycles.

8.3.3   *Comparing the effects of the Asian Financial Crisis and the Global Financial Crisis*

In accounting for the pattern of housing price dynamics in the six East Asian countries since the 1980s, we need to consider the effects of the two major economic shocks: the 1997–98 Asian Financial Crisis (AFC) and the 2008–2009 Global Financial Crisis (GFC). These economic crises are important to our understanding of East Asian housing systems for at least two important reasons. First, the housing sector could have contributed to the outbreak of the crises, or suffered from the crises. However, in all six EA countries, the causal direction was the opposite: these two crises influenced the property markets, not *vice versa*. Second, government responses to large economic crises often lead to institutional changes that may have a lasting impact on the dynamics of housing markets. It appears that East Asian government stimulus packages, and policy reforms in response to these two crises, have had a lasting impact on the housing sector.

The six East Asian economies countries have been affected differently by the AFC and the GFC on their economies and housing markets, as was seen in Section 8.2, describing the dynamics of housing prices over several decades. Korea, Hong Kong, and Singapore were impacted by both shocks on house prices and GDP trends, while China and Taiwan were essentially not affected, even though China's house prices and GDP experienced a small dip after the GFC. Japan is a special case, because its property prices were already in secular decline when these two shocks occurred. For the first group of economies, the AFC caused more severe damage to housing prices than the GFC, in terms both of housing price indexes and of their cyclical components, as well as in GDP and private credit trends. Taiwan is the only country that came out virtually unaffected by both crises.

An appropriate methodology to compare the effects of these two economic crises would be an event study that traces the behavior of the housing price and the key macroeconomic and policy variables after specific amounts of time have passed since the outbreak of the crises[11].

Peak-trough duration of housing price cycles.

	Starting Period	Peak	Trough	Average annual growth rate (starting period to peak)	Average annual growth rate (peak-trough)	Duration (starting period to peak)
United States	2000Q1	2006Q2	2009Q1	13.0	−13.6	26
Los Angeles	2000Q1	2006Q3	2009Q1	15.7	−19.2	27
Washington	2000Q1	2006Q2	2009Q1	14.9	−14.0	26
Las Vegas	2000Q1	2006Q3	2010Q4	13.3	−18.3	27
Denmark	2000Q1	2007Q3	2009Q1	8.8	−11.9	31
France	2000Q1	2007Q4	2009Q2	10.4	−6.6	32
Spain	2000Q1	2008Q1	2010Q4	11.5	−5.0	33
United Kingdom	2000Q1	2007Q3	2009Q1	10.7	−9.3	31
Netherlands	2000Q1	2008Q3	2010Q4	5.1	−3.1	35
Average				11.5	−11.2	29.8
Seoul	1988Q1	1991Q3	1997Q2	5.6	−6.62	14
	2001Q2	2004Q2	2005Q3	9.4	−0.66	12
	2005Q4	2008Q4	n/a	6.1	n/a	12
Tokyo Metro area	1986Q3	1991Q4	2005Q1	6.0	−3.94	21
Singapore	1991Q1	1996Q4	1999Q3	18.1	−10.97	23
	2009Q4	2010Q4	n/a	13.0	n/a	4
Hong Kong	1996Q2	1998Q1	1999Q3	6.0	−18.21	7
	2009Q2	2010Q4	n/a	15.3	n/a	7
Taipei	2006Q1	2010Q1	n/a	13.5	n/a	16
China	2008Q4	2010Q4	n/a	10.1	n/a	8
Beijing	2009Q3	2010Q4	n/a	23.2	n/a	5
Shanghai	2008Q4	2010Q4	n/a	27.7	n/a	8
Average				12.8	−8.1	11.4

Source: Cho *et al.* (2012).

[11] See Leung and Tang (2012) and K.H. Kim and M. Cho for an event study of Hong Kong and Korea, respectively.

Part IV

The Six Actors of Housing Cycles in China and in Korea

9

Housing During China's Growth Transition

The urban economy of China has grown extremely rapidly and massively during the period 1998–2013. Looking back, the first decade of the 21st Century in China will be remembered as one the most profound periods of peacetime economic transformation in China's very long history. Accounting for the institutional and economic changes that occur during a country's rapid growth take-off can be a challenge for any economy. This is particularly so for China, given the many institutional and economic transitions that the country has been experiencing since it embarked upon market-oriented reforms in 1978. For instance, analysis shows that seemingly unrelated reforms, such as the privatization of state-owned enterprises, have played a major role in the housing boom by changing the structure of housing demand.

Because China's multiple transitions to a market economy are incomplete, there remains considerable merit in the characterization of the economy, as a "socialist market economy with Chinese characteristics", after three decades of reforms and rapid growth (Wu, 1992). In the case of housing and urban development, three major challenges that remain to be fully and successfully met are: the creation of unified land markets around cities by ending the duality of land property rights between rural and urban areas; the elimination of the discriminatory impacts of the *hukou* household registration system on rural residents of China; and the correction of the destabilizing behavior of local governments through systemic financial and fiscal reforms. One constraint on the implementation of these national reforms is the great diversity of social, economic and geographical conditions across China's rapidly expanding urban system.

Dynamics of Housing in East Asia, First Edition. Bertrand Renaud,
Kyung-Hwan Kim and Man Cho.
© 2016 John Wiley & Sons, Ltd. Published 2016 by John Wiley & Sons, Ltd.

The present analysis of housing conditions in China has four parts. First, we examine the multiple impact on households, and on housing, of funding the investment-led growth model that has just come to an end as China is now entering its growth transition. Second, we examine the pattern of over-investment in housing that has occurred during the very rapid growth take-off stage, particularly between 1998 and 2012, and especially after the 2009 stimulus in response to the Global Financial Crisis. We compare that period in China with earlier East Asian experiences.

The central part of the chapter then focuses on the incentives and behavior of the six groups of players that drive housing cycles everywhere, and we show how these incentives have differed in China from other East Asian market economies. The goal is to complement, in China's case, the econometric analysis of housing cycles presented earlier, in Part III. The fourth section is forward-looking, and examines how the real and financial channels of interaction between the real estate sector and other sectors of China's economy have expanded over the past decade, and how the housing correction that started in late 2013 might work its way through the Chinese economy, which is moving toward a second-stage steady state growth at higher levels of urbanization.

9.1   Impact of investment-led growth policies on households

9.1.1   *Similarities with earlier East Asian growth take-off stages*

During the six East Asian take-offs, strong central governments controlled the financial system, and made financial capital subordinate to industrial capital. East Asian financial systems have been bank-based, which is typical of financial systems at early stages of economic development, rather than based on capital markets, like high-income Anglo-Saxon financial systems (see Chapter 3, Part 5).

To fund industrialization during their growth take-off stage, Japan, South Korea, and Singapore adopted "financial repression" policies, which had a deep impact on the flow of household savings and the development of the housing finance system. Latecomer China also did this, with the added complexity of transforming from a central planning system, where all investment decisions had been made by the state, into a market economy. Under central planning, the financial system had been reduced to a mono-banking system, with a small number of public accounting institutions. After 1978, a genuine financial system had to be entirely recreated, starting with a new central bank at the core of what remains, today, an unfinished financial sector transformation (Lardy, 1998). In practice, this has meant that the Chinese government has had even greater control over investment patterns than in the other East Asian market economies, where the investment decisions of large private business groups, such as keiretsus in Japan and *chaebols* in Korea, also played an influential distinct role in investment patterns.

Familiar with earlier East Asian experiences, Chinese policy makers chose to finance very high rates of domestic investment in indirect ways, through resource transfers from the household sector in favor of the corporate sector, SOEs and government investments. These resource transfers operate through three macroeconomic policies:

a) A systematic undervaluation of the currency, which favors corporate exporters at the expense of domestic household consumers.
b) A rate of growth of wages kept slower than the rate of growth of labor productivity, which was facilitated by the fact that China was operating in a labor surplus economy, and had not reached its Lewis turning point.
c) "Financial repression policies", with credit allocation directed by the government, and with central regulation of deposit and lending rates significantly below the true opportunity cost of capital and its equilibrium level in the economy.

Of these three macroeconomic policies, financial repression causes the largest transfers from households. The actual size of these transfers has varied from year to year. Their magnitude depends on the gap between the changing true cost of capital in the economy and the repressed low interest rates on household bank deposits. These resource transfers can be quite large, and range between 4–8% of GDP, depending on current growth and inflation conditions.

One reason why these transfer policies were politically sustainable was that the real growth rate of household incomes remained quite high by international standards, given the even higher rates of growth of the Chinese economy, with rates of real household income growth of the order of 7–9% per year when the GDP growth rates was 11% or better, during the growth take-off. Between 1998, which was the year of the housing privatization reforms, and until 2007, when the global financial crisis begun, the average rate of growth of real wages was very high, at 9% per year, but lower than the 11.2% average GDP growth rate. The real urban unemployment rate was also improving.

Financial repression policies had consequences for housing that have been rather similar across the East Asian growth take-offs of Japan, Korea, Singapore, and now China. Housing became the "asset of refuge" for households aiming to escape the very large implicit taxes on their bank savings. Households were not yet offered reliable alternative investment financial assets, such as stocks and bonds, during that stage of growth.

However, because GDP growth rates were extremely high, real urban house-hold incomes also grew rapidly, and household savings rates as well. The pool of domestic savings available to finance further domestic investments grew larger and larger in absolute scale.

The real rates on returns on housing were quite high during the take-off, as the population in major East Asian cities grew at annual rates above 7% per year, often much more in the new industrial core of the economy. These rate of return to housing ownership were consistently higher than GDP growth rates. In contrast, one would normally expect housing prices to rise at a pace similar to GDP growth rates under steady state growth. However, with access to housing finance services limited by financial policies, achieving homeownership was constrained by the need for large amounts of prior equity. The housing sector became a significant channel of wealth redistribution, which led to increasing public pressures for more detailed financial, fiscal and planning government regulations. A very active role of government in housing and frequent short-term public interventions became a shared feature of the East Asian economies with formerly repressed financial systems, with Singapore and Korea having the most interventionist government role until today.

9.1.2   Distinguishing features of the Chinese model of investment-led growth

Contrary to the experiences of Japan and Korea, which had *under-invested* in housing in favor of industrial investments under financial repression policies, China has *overinvested* in housing and real estate during its peak growth decade, in spite of its own financial repression policies. However, it would be wrong to compare China's great housing boom with Japan's boom and bust of the last 1980s, or the US subprime debacle of the 2000s. The fundamental difference with China is that both the Japanese and US bubbles occurred after the two countries were already fully urbanized, and their populations much more than 70% urban. In contrast, China's overinvestment in housing during the first decade of the 21st century occurred when the country had not yet passed the 50% urban marker, and the demand from an additional 230 million of urban residents over the next two decades is likely to soak up much of the housing and urban overinvestment. China's great housing boom is better compared to the state-led overinvestment in housing by Singapore, prior to its severe recession of 1985, which triggered the structural reforms during Singapore's successful transition to high-income steady state growth.

An exceptional feature of the great housing boom that distinguishes China from the other five East Asian urbanization experiences, and other countries, is the impact that the massive housing privatization of 1998–2003 has had on the Chinese transition to markets, and on the overall evolution of China's economic reforms. This was by far the largest housing privatization in history, and it is a unique example of how far the interactions between housing and the macroeconomy can go. The depth and reach of the impact of the housing privatization on the transformation of China's economy can be compared in importance to the de-collectivization of agriculture between 1978 and 1983. The dynamic effects of China's housing privatization have interacted closely with several other major domestic structural reforms that have occurred during the same time period, and also with the global boom.

Local experiments and extensive internal government debates on housing privatization had started after the 1988 land property rights reforms. Alternative ways of relieving employers from the burden of directly supplying their workers with housing had been tested. The actual strategic decision to privatize the greater part of the urban housing stock was made by then Vice-Premier Zhu Rongji, in response to the recession caused by the 1997 Asian Financial Crisis (Zhu, 2013, Documents 47, 48, 53, 54).

A massive housing privatization was expected to have multiple long-term benefits:

- It would relieve SOEs from their social burdens and prepare them for more intensive international competition, as China was negotiating its entry into the WTO, which occurred in 2001.
- It would facilitate a massive industrial restructuring and the privatization of the large number of non-strategic SOEs, which also began in 1998.
- It would also facilitate labor mobility and the restructuring of the labor system.
- It would improve the autonomy and economic security of households through the wealth transfer from SOEs and other public employers (*danwei*).

Finally, housing privatization should be consistent with the deepening of financial reforms. These were not ordinary incremental housing reforms. Their immediate macroeconomic impact was quite large and, like rural reforms, they are a major transformative shift in the development trajectory of China.

The massive housing privatization of 1998–2003 was done at an artificially low price, because there was no choice, as administered cash labor wages were still quite low and there was no mortgage market. This privatization had the unintended consequence of fueling a housing boom after 2003, following the lifting of the temporary restrictions of the 3–5 year resale restrictions. Millions of households who had gained significant housing equity through the massive housing wealth transfer from the state could now use that equity to upgrade their housing units or to buy additional properties. The mortgage finance system, dominated by the five large state-owned banks, grew very rapidly and further fueled the housing boom.

The structural changes that took place simultaneously in China during the period 1995–2014 have had a direct bearing on the speed and location of urbanization, and on overinvestment in housing and real estate. Externally, China's share of global trade grew extremely rapidly after its entry into the World Trade Organization in 2001. Internally, the privatization reforms of housing had a large stimulating impact on the development and growth of the mortgage finance system, which furthered the growth of the housing sector. The accelerated privatization of SOEs after1998 also had large indirect impacts on the level and composition of housing demand, in favor of the highest household income deciles.

By the end of the 2000s, China had become the second largest economy in the world, and its internal dynamics now had a systemic impact on the global economy. The housing and real estate sector became a major part of the economy, and was drawing close attention from global financial markets. These structural changes occurred in the context of internal and external imbalances, which kept growing until the Global Financial Crisis (GFC) of 2007–2009, to which they contributed (Wolf, 2008, 2014). These structural changes, distortions and imbalances are reasons why financial repression policies in China did not lead to underinvestment in housing, as they did in Japan and Korea (as detailed in Section 9.2.1).

The rapid integration of China into the global economy opened the linkages between domestic activities and the international flow of goods and capital. The national savings rate soared to the extraordinary level of 53.2% of GDP in 2008, at the time of the GFC. The investment rate rose from 35% of GDP in 2000, to 44% in 2008. The gap between aggregate savings and investments was reflected in the current account surplus, which exceeded 9% of GDP that same year, rising from USD 1.6 billion in 1995, to USD 436.1 billion in 2008. Foreign exchange reserves passed USD 3 trillion by 2011, which was almost three times the reserves held by Japan. At the start of the decade, in 2001, China was still a low-income economy, with a limited share of global trade. By the end of the decade, China had become the second largest economy in the world, and was the first or second largest trading partner with 78 countries, representing 55% of World GDP, compared to just 13 countries, amounting to 15% of world GDP in 2000.

In one decade, China's net foreign asset position swung from a debtor position of 6.2% of GDP in 2000, to 30.5% of GDP in 2010, when real GDP itself expanded 2.7 times and real *per capita* GDP grew 2.56 times. These financial assets played a major role in funding the housing and real estate booms and bubbles of Western economies, with current account deficits, notably in the US, Spain and Ireland. Chinese imbalances were feeding Western imbalances in an increasingly integrated global economy. The three major sources of the rapid rise in aggregate until the GFC were: a sharp rise in the disposable income of the corporate sector dominated by SOEs; an increase in household savings rates; and a rise of the rate of government savings. SOE and government savings fed the overinvestment (Yang, 2012).

China's housing boom was not driven only by domestic factors, but also coincided with the global housing boom of 1995–2012. In China's case, the cyclical synchronization did not occur through the effects of global financial liquidity, because China's capital account was closed and its financial system was liberalized very cautiously. The synchronization channel was the export sector: China's rapid domestic growth was amplified by the massive export growth that occurred with its entry in the WTO in 2001 – precisely when the global housing boom was stimulating economic growth across OECD countries.

Meanwhile, financial repression varied significantly during the market transition and the development of the new banking system. Household deposit rates in banks received low, but positive, real interest rates during the1990s, but fell below inflation during the real estate boom decade. Negative real deposit rates drove Chinese households, with their rapidly rising real incomes and very high and rising saving rates, to invest most of their funds into housing, because it was one of the rare assets available to them that offered positive and rising returns. The volatile and inadequately regulated stock markets of Shanghai and Shenzhen suffered from insider trading, and provided an investment alternative to housing, mostly to the highest household income deciles, who were also actively investing in housing, especially in eastern provinces.

9.2   The great housing boom during a unique decade

The transformation of housing in China has happened with a speed and intensity, and on a scale, that is unique in the annals of world economic development. The first decade of the 21st Century is the decade when the real estate sector became a major component of China's national economy. Chinese housing was driven, for the first time, by household choices, as a result of the housing ownership reforms of 1998 and the generalized use of market wages. This followed the prohibition of direct provision of housing by work units as part of the total compensation of their employees. It is an irreversible transformation, but China remains a middle-income economy in transition, with an urban sector burdened by important distortions that are legacies of the Maoist central planning era. China also has to deal with the consequences of having used the real estate sector and urban investment as major channels to stimulate the economy in 2009, in response to the Global Financial Crisis.

Because the discussion of the structural drivers of the housing boom in Section 9.2.1 below focuses primarily on investor behavior, prices, rates of returns, and expectations for urban housing, it is important to keep in mind the magnitude of the real estate transformation that was taking place (Man, 2011). Extremely rapid growth was profoundly changing China's urban housing markets. China became the world's largest construction market, and was adding more than two billion square meters of new floor area every year, which was about half of the global real estate supply. About half of that new floor space was for residential use, which was almost evenly divided between urban and rural housing. Part of this new residential supply was needed to meet demographic growth and urbanization, but a larger part reflected the dramatic rise in housing standards in terms of residential space *per capita*.

China's total population had increased by about a third, from 1.0 billion in 2002, to 1.33 billion in 2010, when China was crossing the 50% urbanization marker. At the same time, residential space *per capita* in cities had quadrupled, from 6.7 m² in 1978, to 28.3 m² by 2007. Over the same period, residential space tripled in rural areas, from 9.4 m² to about 29 m². China's average *per capita* floor space now exceeds European averages, as well as those of Japan and most of East Asia. This space average is not expected to rise much further, as increasing housing quality standards are now becoming the leading dimension of new supply in response to rising incomes.

9.2.1   Structural drivers of the great housing boom of 1998–2012

As occurred decades earlier, in the earlier growth take-offs of Japan, Korea and Taiwan, China's urban housing boom was driven by a structurally massive labor reallocation and rapid industrialization. In addition, the housing privatization reforms of 1998, and the aggressive restructuring of the SOEs through privatization since 1997, had a major impact in changing the composition of housing demand across income deciles.

During the boom, housing prices rose faster that household incomes in most Chinese cities. In major cities like Beijing and Shanghai, housing prices rose 2–3 times faster than the average real growth rate of disposable income, which was itself growing at 9% per year between 1998 and 2007. The gap between the real rate of growth of housing prices and the real rate of growth of wages was more than seven percentage points. Therefore, housing price to income ratios kept rising, and affordability kept deteriorating for the average population, as housing prices were determined as the margin by the highest income groups, which included a substantial share of the new private entrepreneurs, who benefited from the large labor reallocation that was taking place.

The housing price indices (HPI) of the National Bureau of Statistics are under revision, because they had a widely known downward bias in reporting housing price movements during the boom. The best HPI is the Tsinghua University HPI (TU-HPI), based on the sale of newly built housing units in

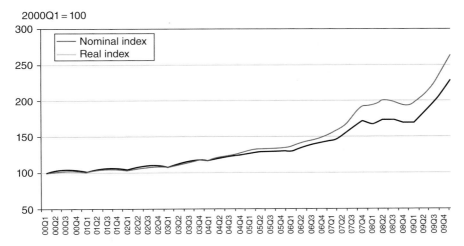

Figure 9.1 China: Trend in constant quality housing prices in 35 major cities, 2000–2010.
Source: Institute of Real Estate Studies, Tsinghua University, Beijing (Wu *et al.*, 2012).

35 major Chinese cities over the period 2006–2010 (Wu *et al.*, 2014). The national TU-HPI reports a price increase rate of 17% per year between 2006-Q1 and 2010-Q4. If the negative impact of the 2008 financial crisis is removed, the average rate of housing price inflation was more than 20% during the period.

The main driver of housing price inflation was the rapid rise of land values. Nationwide, real constant quality land values increased by more than 16% per year between 2000Q1 and 2013Q2. Land price increased were much higher in major eastern cities. The average share of land in total housing costs rose from 37%, before 2008, to over 60% after 2010 in Beijing (Wu *et al.*, 2012). The national TU-HDI data clearly records the temporary drop in housing prices in 2008 caused by the Global Financial Crisis followed by the acceleration in nominal and real housing prices that resulted from the 2009 financial stimulus, as can be seen in Figure 9.1 for the period 2000–2010.

An important feature of China's housing boom are the continuously rising and extremely high vacancy rates in major cities. As Chen and Wen (2014) show, "*According to China Household Finance Survey (2014), in 2013 the average vacancy rate in the first-, second- and third-tier cities in China was 21.2%, 21.8% and 23.2%, respectively[1]. Among different groups of households, 35.1% of entrepreneurial households own vacant houses (or 29.9% of*

[1] There is no yet a uniformly accepted tier composition of Chinese cities. In the Household Finance Survey, the first tier consists of the four major cities of Beijing, Shanghai, Guangzhou and Shenzhen. Second-tier cites include provincial capitals and the special cities directly under the central government. The third tier includes all other cities. A major private provider of real estate market information like *Soufun* uses a different tier breakdown. Other analysts use again different tier breakdowns, according to their research objectives.

them have multiple apartments), compared with 22.6% among non-entrepreneurial households. Furthermore, the proportion of households with vacant housing increases with household income. In the top 10th percentile income group, for example, 39.7% of households have vacant (multiple) houses, which is about 22% percentage points higher than that of households in the bottom income quartile."

Throughout the exceptional first decade of the 21st Century, the real rate of return to capital in China remained, *"on average, 20% between 1998 and 2102. In particular, it increased steadily from 18% in 2001 to 26% before the financial crisis year of 2008."* (Chen and Wen, 2014). The cause of these exceptional returns to capital was the massive reallocation of labor from SOEs to new private firms that benefitted from the associated low wage rates and high productivity, especially after 1997, when the government kept pressing for a faster privatization of SOEs. The share of private employment in total urban employment rose sharply, from 16% in 1998, to 65% in 2008[2].

As China has now entered its growth transition, and labor markets have reached their Lewis turning point, the large-scale reallocation of labor to higher productivity jobs is slowing down significantly. Wage rates are rising rapidly, and a mean-reversion of rates of return to capital has been taking place. This process is similar to the structural transition that occurred decades earlier in Japan, Taiwan and Korea. The end of the massive labor reallocation also marked the end of their very high GDP growth rates during their take-off.

There is an apparent behavioral inconsistency between three economic facts: a decade of very rapidly rising housing prices at rates even faster than already rapidly rising household incomes; exceptionally high housing vacancy rates; and the unprecedented high rates of returns to capital during the decade. Why do high income households, especially entrepreneurial households (who play the determining role in the formation of housing prices), choose to maintain such high rates of vacant housing, when the rate of return on capital invested in private enterprises is so high? Why is empty housing perceived as such a high store of value by economically more sophisticated households? What are their expectations?

Chen and Wen (2014) argue that the very productive entrepreneurs who run financially constrained new firms have been speculating that the high capital returns of the boom decade have been driven by labor resource reallocation that is not sustainable in the long run, and will come to an end. These entrepreneurial households are speculating on housing as long as the resource reallocation lasts, which creates a self-fulfilling bubble.

---

[2] This private employment ratio is specific to China. It is the sum of employment in domestic private enterprises and foreign enterprises, divided by total employment in these types of firms, plus employment in state-owned enterprises and collectively-owned enterprises. See Chen and Wen (2014), Figure 3, Panel B.

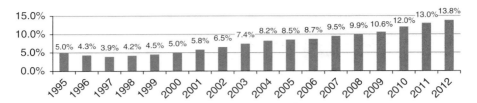

Figure 9.2 China: moral hazard by local governments leading to real estate overinvestment.
Source: Statistical Yearbooks 2010, 2012, NBS China, Tables 2.1 and 5.2.

They develop a quantitative model that is capable of accounting for the growth dynamics of housing prices during the boom decade, and for the eventual transition to a steady state growth at lower GDP growth rates, as urbanization continues to rise at a slower pace.

During the great housing boom, the share of real estate investment (including non-residential real estate), which was 4.2% of GDP in the year of housing privatization, had doubled, to 8.2% of GDP, in 2004, and had almost tripled, to 12.0%, by 2010 (Figure 9.2). With the 2009 credit stimulus, the weight of real estate rose further, to 13% of GDP in 2011 and 13.8% in 2012. Such ratios were higher than the peak ratios to GDP observed in Spain during its real estate bubble. Within total real estate investment, the share of housing also rose from 65% at the start of the decade, to above 70% by 2012.

9.2.2   Spatial dimensions of the housing boom

If China appears to have overinvested in housing during the period 1998–2012 on an aggregate basis, the relationship between housing investment and city economies has varied considerably across China. The Chinese economy is of a continental scale, very diverse, and its spatial integration through massive infrastructure investments only occurred during that same period. China illustrates, by itself, the Burns and Grebler cross-country hypothesis that the ratio of housing investment to GDP follows an inverted U-shaped pattern that is linked to the stage of economic development (Burns and Grebler, 1978). At low levels of economic development, the ratio of housing investment to GDP is low. This ratio rises and reaches a peak during the economic take-off, when the economy reaches a middle-income stage, and then it tends to taper off as the economy matures. The size of the real estate sector itself keeps growing in the national economy beyond this peak so, even at the high income stage, when an economy is fully urban, a lower ratio of housing investment to GDP still means a large absolute volume of annual housing investment.

When the Chinese economy is divided into its three main regions, the Burns-Grebler hypothesis holds between its lagging western region, its rapidly growing central region and its much richer and more mature eastern region. At the national level, the Granger causality between housing invest-ment and GDP is bidirectional. However, leads and lags between housing investment, non-housing investment and provincial GDPs during the period 1999Q1 and 2007Q4 become strikingly different across the three national regions (Chen and Zhu, 2008). Until 2006–07, national aggregate data do not definitely show China overinvesting in housing, but investment patterns differ across the three regions. A powerful housing price boom and quantita-tive overinvestment occurred primarily in the large high income cities of the eastern region, where a high share of GDP still originates. Meanwhile, the most rapid rates of urban growth were occurring in the medium-sized cities of the country, at least until 2000 (Chan *et al.*, 2008), By 2010, China's network of cities had become economically almost 60 times larger than in 1980, and labor markets are almost fully integrated spatially across regions and provinces.

Recent evidence suggests a housing price diffusion pattern from large to small cities, and from east to west (Guo *et al.*, 2011). Large national develop-ers are playing a significant role in this price diffusion, as they are promoting new types of (higher income) units across still fragmented local housing markets. Among China's top 100 banks, smaller regional banks have been growing at very high rates, and are reporting much higher returns on assets and high profit rates (ROA) than national SOE banks (Cooper, 2011). Given the overheated state of the real estate sector, the actual strength of the balance sheets of these regional banks is a major issue for bank regulators, because this segment of the financial system has become an important factor in the stability of China's new urban economy. Spatially, the beginning of the housing correction is revealing significant excess housing supply in smaller third-tier cities from national and regional developers.

9.3   Incentives and behavior of the six key players in China's housing boom

The existence of the powerful structural drivers of China's great housing boom of 1998–2012 does not mean that housing market demand and supply fundamentals in the housing market of each city have been overridden by these structural changes. Rather, housing market fundamentals operate incre-mentally along the long-term trends generated by these structure changes.

To gain a basic understanding of the organization of Chinese urban housing markets, we should consider the individual risks, decisions and constraints of the players that have been shaping China's first market-based housing boom since 1998. These six players (or groups of them) are always present in any housing cycle. To complement the earlier quantitative analyses of East

Asian housing cycles, the present section examines in turn the role of these six players:

1. the central bank and financial authorities;
2. the central government;
3. local governments;
4. households;
5. banks and other lenders; and, finally
6. developers as suppliers of residential and non-residential real estate.

9.3.1 Central bank, monetary policy and financial regulations affecting housing finance

In every country, the central bank and monetary authorities play a central role in housing cycles, through interest rate policies and the regulation of mortgage markets. In addition, in China, financial authorities have to promote the continuing development of the financial system. However, the degree of autonomy of the People's Bank of China (PBC) is so far limited, and its governor does not have a seat at the highest level of economic decision-making. While China's financial system has expanded rapidly quantitatively, the financial reform process set in motion during the 1980s has been increasingly lagging behind the rapid growth of the real economy, as can be seen in the operations of the central bank, in the undiversified structure of the banking system and financial repression (IMF, 2011d).

Official aggregate data suggest that it is well within the monetary and fiscal capacity of the Chinese economy to manage a housing soft landing. The constraints are elsewhere. In China, the still rudimentary monetary architecture constrains the government's ability to manage both the cyclical and structural challenges that the economy faces. In a market economy, such as the USA, interest rate policy can play a significant role in stabilizing the economy, or in fueling a housing boom and causing bubbles (Taylor, 2010). In China, quantitative monetary tools still play a dominant role in the mid-2010s, because the crude monetary infrastructure, dating back to the early years of financial reforms, has been centered on controlling the exchange rate and sterilizing the massive liquidity caused by the very rapid accumulation of foreign currency reserves. The Reserve Requirements Ratio, or RRR, is a major link between China's external and internal imbalances. Interest rate liberalization has been on the reform agenda for a decade now, but has yet to be achieved.

The controlled interest rate environment is linked to the dominance of the PBC's *reserve requirement ratio* (RRR) as an instrument of monetary policy. Usually, the RRR is a minor tool of monetary policy but, in China, the role of the RRR has become increasingly central. After remaining stable for very long periods of time since the early banking reforms of 1984, the RRR has been subject to frequent adjustments since July, 2006. Because of the increasingly massive accumulation of foreign reserves that had to be sterilized, the RRR had risen to a very high level above 20% of bank deposits by the end of the boom decade.

From the perspective of Chinese housing, the reason for becoming familiar with the RRR is that this monetary instrument has become the link between the sterilization of the ever-growing foreign exchange reserves of China and the taxation of banks, especially after 2006. The higher the RRR rises, the higher is the implicit tax burden on banks, who then pass a major part of this cost onto their customers – mostly on households and business depositors, and especially on SMEs. Therefore, the higher the RRR, the stronger are the incentives for households to move their savings out of banks and to use housing as asset of refuge, and for businesses to place their savings in the informal financial sector. The scale of the reserves controlled by the RRR in China is now very large, and has risen above 30% of GDP, which is exceptional in international experience (Ma *et al.*, 2011). The rising tax burden of the RRR has led to its differentiation in 2008 across different types of banks, to mitigate the pass-through taxation effects from banks onto their customers.

Operationally, the RRR has become a preferred instrument of the PBC, because its frequent fine-tuning is directly under its control, and avoids policy confrontations over interest rate policies with SOEs, local governments and other vested interests within the CPC and the broader economy. An important indirect consequence of the RRR has been the rapid expansion of China's weakly regulated shadow banking system, which has been collecting deposit from "high net worth" individuals, and funding real estate firms at significant risks (see Section 9.3.5 below). However, while Chinese monetary policy have remained dominated by quantity-based tools, monetary cooling measures have also included a series of small incremental increases through the RRR, in the base lending rates and the base deposits rates for banks.

Raising bank lending rates has an immediate and direct impact on the variable rate mortgage loans made by banks to households. At the margin, the impact of increased mortgage lending rates on new housing demand should have the largest effect in those Chinese cities where the user cost of housing is the lowest, and the ratio of prices to rents is the highest, but the net effect depends on the actual structure of the user cost of housing on households (see Section 9.3.4 below). The impact of changing mortgage rates also depends on the effective maturity of mortgage loans, which are of short duration in China and are, therefore, less interest rate-sensitive than in Western economies, where ARM loans tend to dominate. Changes in mortgage loans rate by the central bank have, so far, contained a modest element of interest deregulation as the PBC allowed banks to widen their lending rates.

During the boom decade, PBC policies have been dominated by the necessity to accommodate the enormous volume of foreign exchange reserves held by the PBC, which grew from \$150 billion at the beginning of 2000, to \$3.88 trillion by the end of 2013. As foreign exchange reserves taper off during the growth transition, the PBC will gain more control over domestic monetary policy, and will be able to move away from quantitative regulatory tools, to price-based monetary tools and better interest rates policies. Such changes will have large direct and indirect impacts on the dynamics of the housing sector, by changing household saving and investment behavior, and through the mortgage finance system.

9.3.2 Central government: low debt leverage and available fiscal space for stabilization

The Chinese public debt is somewhat under-reported, as is so common internationally, as shown by Reinhardt and Rogoff (2009). However, excessive debt leverage by China's central government is not an issue, so far, for the stability of the economy. China's central government has pursued balanced macroeconomic policies. After a spike in fiscal expenditures above 20% of GDP, during the global Great Recession of 2008–09, the central government has been moving back towards a balanced budget, as the fiscal stimulus was being withdrawn. Budgetary spending on education, health, and social security are priority issues, and hover around 7% of GDP. Looking forward, however, fiscal policies are rapidly becoming more important for the rebalancing of China's economy and its ecological sustainability.

The impact of the central government on Chinese housing is mostly regulatory. The legacy of previous decades, when the state was responsible for providing housing to workers, is that the taxation of housing ownership is extremely low in China by international standards (see Section 9.3.5). Direct financial contributions to social housing by the central government have, so far, been limited. In fact, support to social housing by the central government declined steadily during the "noughties", and reached a very low budget share by 2010. The 12th Plan has set a goal of building 36 million new social housing units by 2015, with front loading in 2011 and 2012.

Social housing investment has been considered a major component of the housing cooling measures, to improve access to housing and also to stabilize the construction industry. However, the success of this social housing program has been questioned, because it places almost the entire burden on local governments, local social housing companies, and on the end users themselves. For instance, in the financing plan for 2011, the central government's share was RMB 100 billion, out of a total required investment of RMB 1.4 trillion – that is, a small 7% contribution by the central government (World Bank, Beijing Office, 2011). The social housing objectives of the plan are expected to be met on paper, but, concerns are rife about local misreporting, and about the misallocation of the units actually built for higher-income local buyers.

9.3.3   *Chinese local governments: nexus of key structural distortions adding to the boom*

What differentiates China from other East Asian economies, and most other countries, including other transition economies, is the dominant role of local governments in China's housing boom from other booms and busts around the world, including those in other transition economies. Chinese local governments are the nexus that connects together all the main players in the housing boom. They are also at the intersection of three of the most problematic distortions in Chinese society. If there is a risk for a twin asset price bubble and banking crisis in China, local governments will be the primary channel, and falling land prices the likely trigger. Local governments have played a critical role in the emergence of the new real estate industry in the 1990s. In many cities, local governments maintain formal and informal governance links with the new real estate firms (Hsing, 2010). Drawing on the implicit or explicit guarantees of local governments, these new firms have a strong incentive to overinvest in housing.

Local governments connect three fundamental institutional distortions of the Chinese urban economy. First, the duality of property rights between rural and urban areas, embedded in Article 10-iv of the Constitution in 1988, causes an extremely large land price multiplier between rural land and urbanized land, under a contentious land urbanization process that remains poorly managed under the Land Administration Law, despite several revisions of this law. Second, the *Hukou* registration system creates *de facto* two classes of Chinese citizens and is a tool that local governments have used to deprive migrants and their families from the full benefits of industrialization and urbanization. Third, the 1994 intergovernmental fiscal reforms, which initially left local governments with 77% of all public responsibilities and only 46% of public revenues, have driven local governments to become heavily dependent on land transactions over time, giving them a strong incentive to fuel land prices and promote the real estate sector (Man and Hong, 2011).

Since the inter-governmental fiscal reforms of 1994, land transactions have become central to local government finance, and represent 30% or more of local revenues. As noted earlier, in Section 9.2.1, during the great boom, the share of land costs in housing costs rose, until it is at least 40%, and usually 60% or more, depending on the city and the type of housing. The first careful analysis of all land transactions in Beijing between 2003Q1 and 2010Q1 shows that *real*, constant quality land values have increased by more than 750% during these seven years (Wu *et al.*, 2012). Beijing's land price experience is suggestive of how strong urban land price inflation could also be across other cities.

In most housing markets, land prices are structurally much more volatile than housing prices (Phang *et al.*, 2012). Usually, the channel through which falling land prices can destabilize an economy is the real estate sector and, indirectly, the banking sector. In China, rapidly falling land prices are a major risk, not only because of their impact on the housing sector itself but, more importantly, because of their impact on the cash flows and balance-sheets of highly leveraged local governments. Officially, Chinese local governments could not borrow or issue bonds or guarantees until 2014. In practice, local governments have bypassed these regulations, by creating autonomous municipal investment companies, or *Chengtou*, to borrow for infrastructure and other projects[3]. Local government debt increased tenfold between 1998 and 2008, then accelerated sharply, at the extraordinary rate of 62% in 2009, and almost doubled between 2008 and 2010. In 2010, 79% of local government debt was held by banks.

Eventually, during the first quarter of 2012, the regulator CBRC issued guidelines to banks on how to rollover the loans made to local governments. The aim was to avert a wave of defaults that could affect the entire economy, and to forestall larger financial sector problems down the road. It was estimated that about 35% of the loans to local governments were due over the subsequent three years, and some as early as April 2012. However, many of the investments had not yet started to generate revenues. Based on the audit review carried out in 2011, new CBRC guidelines provided a loan classification in five categories of risks, with debt resolution guidelines (Rabinovitch, 2012). In October 2014, a major step was taken towards the resolution of the large volume of local government debt, with the introduction by the State Council of a legal framework allowing cities and provinces to issue debt directly. This step is also supportive of the development of a genuine Chinese municipal bond market (Tu, 2014).

9.3.4 Chinese households: rapid income growth, high saving rates, low leverage, high expectations

Now that China's housing markets have become demand-driven, the parameters of household demand and household expectations have become central elements of a housing market correction. We therefore need to examine in turn the structure of household incomes, the drivers of household savings,

---

[3] These presumably "arms-length" municipal investment companies are variously called "local government financing vehicles" (LGFV), "local government investment vehicles" (LGFIV) or "Local Government Financing Platforms" (LGFP). In practice, these funds are controlled by local governments.

and the likely impact of lower expectations on housing prices during a housing correction.

9.3.4.1   *An increasingly unequal household income distribution is driving up housing prices*

Official NBS statistics report that household incomes are rising at the same pace as housing prices, but prices privately collected by the largest internet real estate portal *SouFun* contradict such favorable NBS findings, and show housing prices rising faster than incomes in the top 100 cities – especially in eastern cities. Interpreting the Household Finance Survey, Chen and Wen (2014) shown how Chinese housing markets have become increasingly dominated since 1998 by the top household deciles, whose speculative holdings of vacant units are facilitated by the exceptionally low holding costs of housing investment in China by international standards (see Section 9.2.1).

Two income distribution surveys, for years 2005 and 2007, by Wang Xiaolu, also show that the official household income distribution data has a very large downward bias caused by unreported grey incomes (Wang and Woo, 2010). This downward bias of incomes could have been welcome news for overall housing affordability if it had benefited every income group, but this is not the case. The two Wang surveys indicate that the large unreported grey income goes entirely to the top four household income deciles (D7–D10), and benefits mostly the top income decile (D10). In addition to being very large, this underreporting bias of top incomes appears to have grown during the boom. The surveys find that the actual income of the D9 decile could be twice as large, and that of the top decile D10 could be three times as large as the incomes reported by the NBS. The composition of housing supply in cities of China appears to be driven by the richest households at the top of the income, especially in the high-income cities of the Eastern region. The problem of housing affordability appears to be worse than officially reported.

If the Wang estimates of grey incomes are close to reality, 80% of this grey income may be going to the top two household income deciles, and the top urban household decile had incomes 26 times higher than the lowest household decile in 2008 (Wang and Woo, 2010, Annex 5). The implications for the composition of effective housing demand in favor of high income buyers, and more difficult access to housing by lower income groups, are direct. Compounding the social problem of inequality of access to housing across incomes, the share of social housing units in the total number of new housing units completed dropped continuously during the entire decade of the boom, from 28.2% in 2000, to 6.6% in 2010.

Given the highly skewed urban household income distribution and the high degree of real estate wealth concentration in the hands of the households at the very top of the income distribution, the use of *average* household values in policy discussions will be quite misleading. The use of *median* values will provide much more realistic policy solutions.

9.3.4.2 How financial repression and precautionary motives have been affecting Chinese household savings

The other side of low aggregate consumption is that, during the housing boom, urban household savings rates have increased from 19% of disposable income in 1996, to 30% in 2009, while incomes themselves were rising at real rates of about 9% annually throughout the period. Three important factors have been driving these high and rising urban household saving rates. The privatization of the urban housing stock in 1998 has created a new homeownership motivation for young households and their families to save[4]. The very rapid rise of urban household incomes, at an annual rate of 10%, has facilitated saving.

A third factor is the strong influence of a precautionary *target saving level*, and of negative real deposit rates during most of the decade (Nabar, 2011) provides robust statistical evidence that the increase in urban savings rate in China is linked, in part, to the decline in real interest rates, particularly after 2003. This leads to the unconventional conclusion (the opposite of the US experience) that raising real interest rates in China should be expected to *lower* household savings at the margin, given the present household incentive structure.

In high-income OECD economies, the ratio of household debt to income soared from an average of 39%, to 138% during the five years leading up to the onset of the global crisis in 2007. This high level of household debt has amplified economic downturns and has weakened recoveries in these economies (IMF, 2012b). In contrast, high and rising levels of household savings in China have been a core source of funds to finance the investment-led growth strategy of China during the take-off decade. As will be seen in section 9.3.5, the degree of housing finance leverage is modest for median households, and average for the entire urban population. However, under the worsening urban income distribution, high rates of housing finance leverage by the top two income deciles probably hides much lower consumption levels for other households. Also, very little is known about the degree of leverage of the richest households, who are relying heavily on shadow banking services.

9.3.4.3 User cost of housing capital and critical role of household expectations in a housing correction

The new Chinese housing system, driven by household demand, is less than 15 years old, and there has been no research, so far, on expectations in residential and non-residential real estate investment. With the market information

---

[4] Wei *et al.* (2012) also show that home ownership is an effective way of signaling wealth and prosperity in the marriage market, and increasing the probability of securing a good partner, especially in areas where the male-female imbalance caused by the one-child policy is particularly pronounced.

available, is it possible to understand what has been the dynamics of expectations during the boom decade? Given the likelihood of a housing market correction, can we gain a sense of what the impact that lower household expectations of future housing price growth might have on housing prices, household wealth and developer profitability?

Two metrics frequently used to reflect overheating housing markets and housing ownership affordability are published for major Chinese cities: the housing price-to-rent ratio (P/R) and the housing price-to-income ratio (PIR). In China, housing P/R values are less affected by measurement problems than PIR values, and provide more meaningful market information. Given the overwhelming dominance of multiple-unit housing in China, the comparison of owner-occupied housing prices with rental units is also more meaningful than in non-East Asian countries, especially in the USA, where the physical characteristics of the two markets are very different. The rapid rise of P/R values after 2007 in most very large Chinese cities suggests that the carrying cost of owning housing R/P has become very low. Table 9.1 reports estimated P/R ratios in cities of China, Korea, and the US, from national sources.

The conceptual framework of the housing tenure choice under competitive equilibrium tells us that the rental price of housing for a renter should be equivalent to the user cost of housing capital (UC) for the owner of a housing unit, whether it is an owner-occupant or an investor. Measurement problems apart, we expect to find R/P = UC in balanced housing markets[5].

Four factors can cause fluctuations in the P/R ratio in China. First, international research shows that changes in rents are the least important driver of P/R fluctuations, because rent levels tend to change only slowly over time. A second factor can be changes in expected future real interest rates. A third factor is the risk premium for owning housing, compared to other assets. A fourth factor is the expected rate of appreciation of housing prices. It is this fourth factor that has the largest impact on the value of the housing P/R ratio and its volatility across cities and housing market segments within these cities.

Given the increased riskiness of high P/R values at the end of the great housing boom, we can ask how severe housing price declines could become if household expectations were to shift to a lower rate of housing price appreciation? Specifically, if in a given city, the user cost UC of owning housing increases by 1%, how large will be the adjustment in the R/P ratio and the housing price?

---

[5] There is a substantial literature on the user-cost of capital for housing and its relation to the housing price-to-rent ratio since the seminal paper by Poterba (1984). For China, four conceptually and empirically relevant papers are: Campbell *et al.* (2006). comparing 23 US cities; Deng *et al.* (2010), comparing eight Chinese cities; Ahuja *et al.* (2010), comparing 35 Chinese cities, and Cho (2011), comparing 10 US cities, seven Korean cities and 22 Chinese cities.

Table 9.1 Range of housing price-to-rent ratios observed in China, Korea and the USA.

	Hangzou	Beijing	Shenzen	Tianjin	Los Angeles	NY City	Houston	USA	Seoul (Gangnam)	Busan	Gwangiu
Max	65.0	46.0	42.0	31.0	101.0	87.6	39.7	55.5	61.3	40.9	36.5
Min	33.0	26.0	26.0	16.0	33.0	30.7	27.3	35.8	7.8	7.1	7.0
Median	n/a	n/a	n/a	n/a	51.3	54.0	32.1	40.3	19.1	17.1	17.8
Std	n/a	n/a	n/a	n/a	15.6	15.1	3.5	4.8	14.7	7.3	6.0
Period and Frequency	Quarterly, 2007Q1–2010Q1				Semi-annual, 1975–2007				Monthly, 1986–2010		
Source	Deng et al., 2010				Campbell et al., 2006; Cho, 2011				Cho, 2011		

Following Poterba for the US case, a common expression of the user cost of capital (UC) per unit of housing value during a given period is:

$$UC = (1-t)(r+p) + m + d + RP - E(HP)$$

Where: t is the owner marginal tax rate
r is the real interest rate at which households can borrow or lend
p is the local property tax rate
m is the maintenance cost
d is the economic depreciation rate
RP is the required premium for investing in housing
E(HP) is the expected rate of appreciation of housing prices in the next period.

This formulation brings out major institutional differences between China and the US as one point of reference. Mortgage interest rates are not tax-deductible in China, so $t = 0$. There is no property tax in China (except in three new experimental sub-market cases), so $p = 0$ also. In the case of China, the formula for the user cost reduces to four main terms:

$$UC = r + (m+d) + RP - E(HP)$$

First, the real interest rates r on deposits have been kept artificially low in China under the policy of financial repression, so the opportunity cost of capital for housing r has been depressed by public policies. Nonetheless, these lending rates have fluctuated.

Second, the term $(m + d)$ is expected to be larger in China than in the US, because the quality of new housing is often questioned and criticized in China. Widespread problems in the quality of construction should be resulting in a larger value for m. Third, changes in household preferences, in terms of floor space and amenities, are rising rapidly by international standards, since *per capita* incomes are growing very fast. Thus, the value of d should also be higher than in mature economies.

Third, under present financial policies, the required premium for holding housing, measured as RP, is low because the majority of Chinese households have very few investment alternatives outside housing. They face negative real rates on their bank deposits, very volatile domestic stock markets plagued by insider trading, and international financial markets remain close. However, the value of RP should be higher and rising for high income households, with the rapid growth of the shadow banking sector where they can invest.

Fourth, the expected rate of housing price appreciation, E(HP), has been very high, given a very strong demand caused by rapidly rising incomes and urban migration interacting with an inelastic housing supply and land prices affected by local governments.

Given the likely estimates of these four factors in China, we expect the user cost of capital in housing to be low in most Chinese cities during the boom. Unfortunately, for public policy, this means that a relatively small increase in the user cost can lead to a large decline in housing prices in the short term, under the relationship UC = P/R and sticky rent levels[6]. This relationship between a rising user cost UC and a declining P/R ratio has been illustrated by Ahuja *et al.* for selected Chinese cities, in a table which is reproduced below as Table 9.2. The increase in user cost could come from rising interest rates or from lower expected price increases. In Table 9.2, user cost values are positive for expository purposes, but it should not be surprising to find, with more precise data, that UC values were actually negative in some major cities during some periods of the boom, especially after 2007.

The riskiness of owning housing in China, in terms of wealth effects, appears to be high in some of the major eastern cities. However, the level of leverage of the balance sheets of Chinese households invested in housing is low, and many of them own housing units debt-free. A large unknown is the degree of leverage of the households at the top of the income distribution, who own multiple vacant units. Overall, China's household sector should be able to absorb a significant volume of nominal wealth losses without causing widespread social problems, in contrast with the USA, Ireland or Spain. Nonetheless, a large nominal wealth loss could have a significant impact on depressing aggregate consumer demand. In the short term, this negative wealth effect on aggregate consumption is mitigated by the fact that household consumption in China, as a share of GDP, was the lowest ever observed in any country, at 34.5% percent of GDP in 2011.

The *investment effect* of a housing price drop on new investment is expected to be much more significant than the *wealth effect* on Chinese private

Table 9.2   China: impact of an increase in user cost on the P/R ratio in selected Chinese cities.

	Current User Cost (percent, approximate)	Decline in P/R ratio (percent, approximate)
Beijing	2.0	33.0
Hangzhou, Guangzhou, Shenzhen	3.0	25.0
Shanghai, Tianjin	3.6	21.0
Nanjing	7.0	11.0

Source: Ahuja *et al.* (2010), Table 3 (2004–2009).

[6] Deng *et al.* (2010), Ahuja *et al.* (2010) and Cho (2011) all find that the coefficient of variation of housing prices are several multiples of the coefficient of variation of rents in every Chinese city they studied.

consumption for the economy. Ahuja *et al.* (2010) estimate that a 10% fall in housing prices could induce a 0.7% decline in private consumption, but could reduce investment by about 4%. The regional impact of a 10% drop in housing prices would differ significantly across cities and regions. For, instance real estate fixed asset investment (FAI) has been fluctuating around 50% of FAI in Beijing, but at less than 30% of total FAI in Guangzhou.

9.3.4.4 Problems in interpreting Chinese housing data: the case of housing space per person

We have already seen with incomes, housing prices and vacancy rates, that the quality of basic official data for the Chinese housing sector has been lagging seriously behind the rapid growth of the sector. Similar problems arise with reported housing quality data. How should we interpret the high "average floor space" *per capita* of 28.3 square meters, and 21.3 square meters of "usable area", as reported for 2010 (Man, 2011)?

Are these housing space ratios really pointing at a stellar achievement of China's growth policies, considering that these ratios are already higher for China than in South Korea, Japan and also Europe? The respective national PPP *per capita* GDP figures of the three East Asian countries were $8382, $31 714 and $34 740 in 2010, which means that China's *per capita* income remains only one-fourth those of Japan and Korea under this more favorable measure. Are these very high Chinese *per capita* housing space ratios unquestionable evidence of overinvestment in housing? Do these high values result from a grossly imbalanced Chinese housing supply, dominated by the 10% richest households? Do they result from the "man made" nature of local statistics produced by ambitious local CCP officials[7]?

Another interpretation could be that these extraordinary housing space consumption numbers are caused by the systemic undercounting of urban residents in urban statistics because of the Hukou system. The floating population of urban migrants who have no urban Hukou registration was enumerated by the 2010 demographic census at 261 million, or 39% of the entire urban population of China. These migrants without a local city Hukou have no legal access to urban housing ownership, they are not covered by most urban official statistics, and they are cut off from administrative services by local governments. But where do these people live? Should China's housing space figures be cut back by 39%, and the true average floor space and usable floor space ratios in China today be taken as 17.2 and 13.0 square meters[8]?

---

[7] Vice-Premier Li Keqiang, 2007, as quoted by Reuters on December 6, 2010. (http://www.reuters.com/article/2010/12/06/us-china-economy-wikileaks-idUSTRE6B527D20101206). Mr. Li became China's Prime Minister in 2013.

[8] Illustrating the pro-cyclical role that the media can play in feeding real estate booms and frenzies, the *Economist Intelligence Unit* recklessly projected in early 2011 that "Residential floor space per head in urban areas will increase from 30 m² (in 2008) to 41 m² by 2020." (*Economist*, 2011).

9.3.5   Banks: exposure to real estate and to local government debt

The Chinese financial sector has expanded very rapidly after the initial 1984 banking reforms (IMF, 2011d; Lardy, 1998, 2012). In 2010, China had 3,640 financial institutions, and total financial assets amounted to 234.2% of GDP, but the financial system is still heavily dominated by commercial banks, which owned 70% of all financial assets that year. The assets of the commercial banking sector almost quadrupled to RMB80 trillion between 2003 and 2010. The asset share of non-bank financial institutions (including long-term institutional investors, such as insurance companies and pension funds) was still quite small, with only 12.4% of GDP, which implies that mortgage lending in China is funded by deposits and held on bank balance sheets. The five state-owned large commercial banks (SOCBs) dominate the commercial banking system proper, with over 60% of banking assets and 45% of the entire financial system[9].

This section focuses on two parts of the financial system: the housing finance system that serves the majority of households and remains the domain of the SOCBs; and, the Chinese-style shadow banking system, which has grown extremely rapidly at the end of the great housing boom. The latter plays a major role in providing financial services to the high net worth Chinese households at the top of the income distribution and to real estate developers, especially second-tier developers.

9.3.5.1   Structure of China's housing finance system

The housing privatization reforms of 1998, and the resulting high rate of urban housing ownership, have transformed China's housing finance system. Until then, China's residential mortgage market was minimal, and the ratio of mortgage loans to GDP was only 2.3% in 1997. Between 1997 and 2007, the growth rate of the housing finance system was an average of 64% per year, which is an exceptionally rapid rate even for a system started from almost nothing (Shen and Yan, 2008). Banks have been attracted to mortgage lending as a profitable new line of business on a risk-adjusted basis. As housing prices rose, so did the rate of mortgage lending, as shown by Figure 9.3. Under the impact of the 2009 stimulus, residential mortgage market depth increased further sharply, from 19% of GDP in 2008, to 28% in 2010. International experience tells us to expect a negative impact on credit quality from such a massive credit expansion.

---

[9] The non-state-owned commercial banks include 12 joint-stock commercial banks (JSBCs), 147 city commercial banks (CCBs), 85 rural commercial banks (RCBs) and 130 foreign banks (FBs). Mutual forms of deposit-taking institutions include 2870 cooperative financial institutions and 2646 new types of rural financial institutions. The rate of growth of regional banks has been much faster than the five large SOEs, and their exposure to the real estate sector has expanded rapidly.

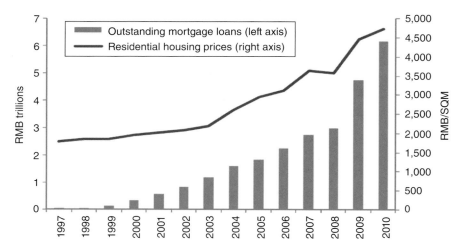

Figure 9.3   China: rise of housing prices and residential mortgage loans outstanding, 1997–2010.
Source: IMF (2011d), Figure 6.

The Chinese housing finance system has two channels of very different sizes: a policy-driven housing finance channel and a market-oriented one[10]. The policy-driven channel consists of the mandatory municipal housing provident funds (HPFs). The first HPF was created in Shanghai in 1991, and they are now operating in the 265 prefecture-level cities. The market-oriented finance system has been provided by commercial banks since the MOF and the PBC jointly issued the first set of mortgage regulations, in May, 2008. This second channel is entirely dominated by the big four SOCBs, especially CCB and ICBC. The commercial bank system held 83.1% of residential loan outstanding by the end of 2007, and HPFs 16.8%, but estimates of market shares vary[11]. While there are regulatory problems with the network of HPF, the largest systemic risks in the housing finance system remain concentrated in the SOCBs. Second-tier banks still play a minor role in housing loans to ordinary households, in contrast to their lending to real estate developers and local governments' LGFVs.

China's HPF system is a mandatory housing savings scheme that exhibits many of the traditional design and management problems of such provident funds, to which China has added new regulatory and supervisory problems

[10] For an overview of the early years of development of China's housing finance system, see Deng and Peng (2008).
[11] Based on a sample of 20 HPFs in the 20 large cities taken by PBC, HPFs provided 11.9% and commercial banks 79.4% of total housing loans (Shen and Yan, 2008). However, the official Chinese response to a global Financial Stability Board survey in November 2010 gives market shares of 95% lending by commercial banks and 5% by HPFs in 2010. The difference between these two Chinese reports may come from the allocation to banks of the share of HPF funding in the now very frequent hybrid bank-HPF loans.

with the decentralization of HPFs at the municipal level. Each local HPF is operated in different ways by autonomous local Housing Provident Fund Management Centers, under the supervision of the municipal government, which sets policies, decides administrative matters and fund use within the policies set by the central government. The national HPF system is under the broad regulation and supervision of the Ministry of Housing and Rural-Urban Development, which is a non-financial ministry. The central government has set the minimum contribution rate at 5% by workers, matched by a 5% contribution by their employers. Some autonomous cities have raised these contribution rates higher (Shanghai 7%, Beijing 8%), and some eastern cities have created supplementary accounts. As is common internationally with such mandatory housing funds, actual coverage through employers is closer to 50% than to 100% (Chiquier and Lea, 2009, Chapter 11). The appropriate long-term role of HPFs in China is still being debated.

Chinese banks are portfolio lenders: they fund housing mortgages from their own funds, and keep these loans on their balance sheets. Except for two pilot securitizations, banks keep their mortgage loans in portfolio and fund them from deposits. Because housing prices have been rising extremely rapidly during the 2000 decade, HFP loans have not been sufficient for most households to purchase a housing unit, and the market share of HPF in the housing finance system has kept declining. The two main types of housing loans are by the now commercial bank loans and "hybrid loans", for which a commercial loan is used to top off an inadequate HPF loan. The HPF part of a hybrid loan lowers the debt-to-income ratio, since the interest rate is lower than for a commercial bank loan, the maturity can be up to 30 years, and the LTV ratio up to 80%. The China Construction Bank, which has 70% of the trustee business for HPFs, also dominates the hybrid loan sub-market.

Pre-payment and default risk behavior in China are quite different from the more familiar US case. All mortgage loans in China are adjustable rate mortgages without cap, and there is no refinance-driven prepayment in the Chinese mortgage market. However, Chinese borrowers are quite sensitive to increases in mortgage rates, and many borrowers chose to pay off mortgage loans before maturity. During the high growth period, NPL ratios have been low, at around 1.5% of total mortgage portfolio.

There have been three main causes of default. Mortgage fraud is the dominant cause of default in China, representing up to 80% of total defaults. Fraud often involves developers who want to take advantage of the preferential treatment of residential mortgage loans. The second cause of default is presales disputes. As noted in Section 9.3.6, presales are the largest source of developer finance. Home buyers refuse to pay their mortgages when there are disputes with real estate developers regarding the quality and the timing of delivery of their housing unit. These households are *de facto* using mortgage loans as a means of sharing their presale risk with a bank (Deng and

Liu, 2009). The third, and quantitatively least important, source of default is a drop in household affordability, due to unexpected unemployment or overestimated ability to repay.

A significant feature of Chinese housing finance during this first period of household-driven housing demand has been the aversion of households to mortgage debt, which coincides with very rapidly rising incomes and extremely high savings rates. Median to high-income borrowers, as well as white-collar workers, are more likely to prepay their mortgage debts. They are the group most influenced by stock market performance as an investment trade-off (Deng and Fei, 2008). A mortgage survey of 20 cities, conducted by the PBC in 2007, found an average maturity of 15.6 years and an average down payment of 37.4% (Shen and Yan, 2008). Most down payments have been above 30% of the value of the housing unit or more. Less than 5% of transactions involved a down payment as low as 20%, and purchases with 40% equity or more are very significant. Chinese borrowers appear to choose low LTV levels, due to the high rates of housing appreciation compared with low or negative real deposit rates at banks[12].

9.3.5.2 *Direct and indirect bank exposure to housing and other types of real estate investments*

The share of housing and non-residential real estate in total bank credit rose in six years from a 13% share of total outstanding bank credit at the start of 2005, to 20% at the start of 2011. That share had dipped temporarily in 2008–2009, because of the decline of household borrowings during the global crisis. It then rose again, and appears to be leveling off in the vicinity of 20% of total bank credit (IMF, 2011a, 2011d). Residential mortgages make up two-thirds of the banks' entire real estate portfolio. Riskier commercial loans to real estate companies have fluctuated in a trendless way between 4.5% and 6% of total bank loans. This is a moderate level of exposure; US prudential standards define 25% or less of total loans as a low exposure to real estate for community banks. The Chinese banks' direct exposure to housing and commercial real estate appears to be quite manageable, but the volume of bank loans to the real estate sector has fluctuated very significantly from year to year. Such strong pro-cyclical lending creates the possibility of different loan quality and risk performance by vintage year.

If the *direct* total exposure to housing and non-residential real estate is moderate, there is greater concern about the much higher *indirect* exposure of the commercial banking sector to real estate, because loans in China, as

---

[12] An investment behavior driven by the sharp rise of housing prices in boom cities has been family members resident in other cities pooling their equity together, to co-finance the purchase of housing by a family member resident in one of these cities. This way, other family members can share in the expected very high returns in boom cities. The quantitative significance of this effect is unknown.

in many developing banking systems, rely heavily on real estate collateral. A strong housing correction can reduce these collateral values and loan recovery value in the case of defaults (loss-given-default). It is estimated that between 30–45% of the loans made by the five largest banks are backed by real estate collateral (IMF, 2011d).

In a separate study of the composition of Chinese bank loans according to their collateral, it was found that, among the loans that were secured by real assets, those that were secured by real estate represented 66% of total secured loans (International Finance Corporation, 2007). The same study found that 35% of the loans were secured by personal guarantees and third party guarantees. Chinese bank regulators are advising the large SOCBs and the other banks to adjust their underwriting practices to the new market-based real estate conditions, and to develop forward-looking valuation practices instead of the present valuation of loans at entry only, because they need to control their risks and the pro-cyclicality of their lending.

A second component of indirect bank exposure to a real estate downturn is related to the credit provided to industries that provide inputs to the real estate sector, such as construction, cement or steel. The third component of indirect bank exposure to a real estate downturn in China is the role played by local governments in support of their LGFVs, through land sales and other guarantees, as seen in Section 9.3.3. The financial authorities' decisive action, reported in March 2012, to restructure the loans to LGFVs and transfer a substantial share of these loans from the banks' balance sheets to state asset management companies, was an important, if costly, step to maintain the stability of the banking system and its ability to continue to lend to the economy.

9.3.5.3   *Shadow banking with Chinese characteristics and exposure to real estate volatility*

One important characteristics of China's economy today is the extraordinarily low share of GDP retained by ordinary households. Those are the households who rely on the regulated housing finance system. For the highest income groups, and high net worth individuals, the shadow banking sector has become a key source of financing and a place of investment. Shadow banking has also become a major source of finance for real estate developers.

The rise of shadow banking has been a major part of the transformation of the Chinese financial system during the high-growth decade of the 21st Century. Shadow banking is a form of non-bank credit, driven by market forces searching to circumvent the effects of financial repression policies, given these policies' deposit rate ceilings and credit directed to SOEs and other government-connected activities.

Cyclically, the rapid growth of shadow banking has been closely associated with the 2009 government stimulus, when SOCBs channeled a massive amount of credit to state-sponsored long-term projects and to the property sector. Precise measurements of the sector are difficult, and estimates are that shadow banking activities surged massively, from less than 10% of GDP in 2008, to more than 40% by 2012 (i.e., from USD 455 billion to USD 3.35 trillion in four years). Shadow banking is now playing the leading role in the rising debt leverage of China's economy, which has passed 200% of GDP and may now be high enough to constrain future growth (Pettis, 2014a).

Given the pro-cyclical nature of shadow banking activities, the mispricing of risks and moral hazard problems in the sector can become a major problem for the stability of the economy during a downturn. These problems were overlooked or ignored during the great housing boom, especially at the end of the high growth decade, when shadow banking grew at very high rates (of the order of 50% per year). These risks are becoming increasingly problematic during the housing correction and the slowdown of the economy (Dang *et al.*, 2014). Success in structural reforms in this segment of the financial system will play a large role in the success of China's growth transition.

Except for a common name, the US shadow banking sector and the Chinese shadow banking system are different, both in the nature and location of risks embedded in each system. Chinese shadow banking could not have grown to its present scale without the active involvement of regulated commercial banks, and differs for that reason from the US shadow banking, which operates in the highly developed US capital markets. In China, unregulated shadow banking funds pass through the banking system in a manner similar to the Korean curb market during the 1970s before financial liberalization. In Korea, a poor understanding and management of risks in the curb market led to the domestic financial crisis of 1972, which was eventually resolved by the government, at the expense of savers, in favor of business interests (Cole and Park, 1983, Chapter 5).

The nature and scale of risks varies throughout the Chinese shadow banking system. China's shadow banking system is defined in China as consisting of three main segments of different size, degree of organization and significance for the stability of the national economy. These three segments could be thought of as a pyramid in terms of the scale of operators, sophistication of financial products and distance from central government financial regulators (Li and Hsu, 2012).

At the bottom of the shadow financial pyramid is unregulated informal finance. It is the largest and least organized component the shadow banking system. It has existed for a long time, and is marked by close familiarity between lenders and borrowers. In the countryside and towns, it takes the form of mutual assistance and informal credit cooperation networks. Most lending is short-term and quasi-seasonal. This segment of shadow banking is very sensitive to credit conditions, and tends to expand faster during credit crunches. The mid-section of the pyramid – its "mezzanine" – consist of small loan companies, investment companies financing guarantees, insurance brokerage firms, and what might be called private equity investment funds and venture capital funds.

The top of the shadow banking pyramid provides non-bank financial services, but is closely associated to the formal banking system. While it is unregulated, this market segment is best known to regulators. It includes off-balance sheet products offered by banks, and otherwise supplements commercial banking activities. Mispricing of risks is rife in this sub-sector, given the misperception that the products offered are implicitly guaranteed by banks.

High net worth households and real estate firms are extensive users of the financial products offered by this segment of the shadow banking system. Among the products offered are so-called Q-REITs. *"Q-REITs is the short name for real estate investment trusts. It is a kind of investment funds issued by companies that own and usually manage income-producing real estate property such as apartments, offices, and industrial space"* (Li and Hsu, 2012). "Entrusted lending", which is also part of shadow banking and consists of lending between large corporations and smaller companies, with banks acting as middlemen, has grown rapidly, and includes also some real estate lending (Hong Kong Monetary Authority, 2014, Box 2).

In addition to a mispricing of risks in shadow banking, another factor of potential instability during a housing and real estate correction is that smaller banks, besides having lower quality and less diversified loan portfolios, have much more unstable funding bases. Their credit decisions are also much more exposed to local government officials, especially regarding the funding of infrastructure investments and real estate.

9.3.6   *Chinese developers: new industry structure, local oligopolies, impact of the housing correction*

Access to land is the critical input to real estate development, but access to funds is equal in importance. In China, the structure and behavior of the real estate industry is closely associated with the monopoly over urban land development held by local governments. Many large real estate companies have their origins in large state holders of "allocated" land in prime urban locations, which dominated Chinese cities before the 1988 land property rights reform. Other firms were created by former land use officials working closely with local governments (Hsing, 2010). During the boom decade, the total number of real estate firms had grown to more than 85 000 in 2010. They were directly employing more than 21 million workers and, indirectly, a much larger number of sub-contractors.

The structure of the Chinese real estate industry has drastically changed during the growth take-off decade. By the end of the boom, the industry is

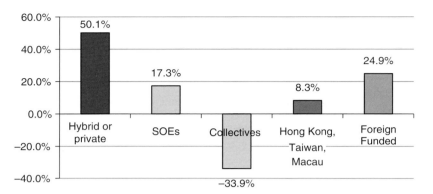

Figure 9.4 China: RE industry transition from SOEs and collectives to competitive firms, 2006–2010.
Source: China, NBS Statistical Yearbooks 2010 and 2011, Table 5.27.

entirely dominated (88%) by a mix of unknown proportions, between hybrid firms, who maintain opaque connections with local governments, and truly private firms. The number of real estate SOEs has declined dramatically, but the 4% of SOE real estate firms that remain have been of strategic significance to the government under the 2009 stimulus program (Deng *et al.*, 2011). There is also a small, but significant percentage, of firms funded from Hong Kong and Taiwan (and, to a minor extent, Macau) that have played a vital role in bringing engineering, construction management and other real estate innovations into China since they were permitted to operate in China in the early 1990s. Despite extensive capital controls, foreign capital inflows into the sector have been significant. Larger real estate firms have been funded by foreign investors making an investment double-play, by seeking direct high returns from the sector and expecting foreign exchange gains from the appreciation of the Yuan.

By 2010, the transition of China's real estate industry, from one dominated by SOEs and urban collectives in the early 1990s, to a competitive industry dominated by hybrid or purely private firms, was essentially completed. Figure 9.4 shows the changing structure of the RE industry, as reflected in employment growth (or decline) by main type of RE firms.

An important new feature of China's RE industry has been the rapid emergence of large national developers, who have been growing through internal growth combined with mergers and acquisitions (M&A), in a process that resembles the consolidation of the US real estate industry since the 1980s. Because a real estate industry differs from other industries, by not having fixed plants and being dependent on location-specific projects, M&A activities are an important growth strategy to gain access to local land and market information of quality at the city level. A second important feature that the Chinese RE industry now shares with the US homebuilding industry is that the largest firms have easier access to more diversified sources of funds (Ambrose and Peek, 2008). Approximately 160 Chinese firms are now listed on the Shanghai, Shenzhen and/or Hong Kong stock exchanges. Thirty of these Chinese firms are rated by Standard & Poor's.

In the USA, the homebuilding industry has three main segments: very large national builders; smaller, but still large, private builders; and a very large number of small local builders. In total, there are approximately 180,000 builders in the US, but the 100 largest builders account for about 50% of new housing production today. In contrast to the US, in China, the third tier, of very small builders, is practically non-existent, given the high transaction costs of gaining access to land under local government monopolies, and the minimum capital requirements and technology needed for large multiple-unit buildings. The absence of this third tier explains why the number of developers in China is only half that in the US.

At the top end of the scale, concentration and an increased market share of the very large firms is an ongoing process that could be speeded up by the housing and real estate correction. The three main factors driving the concentration of market shares into large RE firms are access to land, to finance and greater scale efficiencies. A strong cyclical downturn could be expected to lead to more RE industry concentration in China, with the absorption of developers facing liquidity problems by the largest firms, as happened in past decades to the US real estate industry, which is the best comparator for China in terms of scale, scope and urban diversity (Ambrose, 2009; Melman, 2010). The Japanese real estate industry is not a good comparator, given the physical and institutional idiosyncrasies of housing supply in Japan, as seen in Chapter 5.

The sources of funds for RE firms are diverse in China. A private estimate of the total sources of funds for the real estate sector was RMB 8.3 trillion in 2011. The breakdown is presented in Figure 9.5. The largest source of funds is presales to households (26%), followed by self-financing and own funds (21.2%). Capital financing by various governments and enterprises also appears to very important (19.7%). Bank loans (13.2%) and financing on the capital markets (1.9%) are more important than household mortgage loans. In spite of the sharp increase in retail mortgage lending to households under the 2009 stimulus, this source represents only 10% of total funding (ChinaScope Financial, 2012).

As a whole, the Chinese real estate industry relies on a diversity of financing sources and is not dependent on a single major source. What is also significant is the importance of cash-financing from presale contracts with households and developers' own funds. The monetary breakdown of funding sources is presented in Table 9.3. These aggregate figures do not give any insight into the funding position of individual firms, and the liquidity pressures they faced as the housing correction started in late 2013 and kept widening.

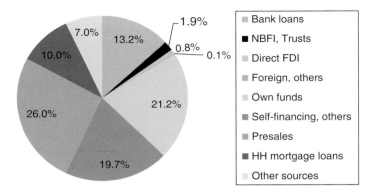

Figure 9.5   China: Dominance of pre-sales and own funds in Chinese real estate firms, 2011.
Source: ChinaScope Financial (2012).

Table 9.3   China: breakdown of real estate industry funding in 2011 (billion CNY).

Domestic loans		
Bank loans	1101.89	13.2%
NBFI, trusts	154.48	1.9%
Foreign funds		
Direct FDI	70.47	0.8%
Others	10.89	0.1%
Self-financing, others		
Own funds	1768.38	21.2%
Others	1640.96	19.7%
Sales funding		
Presales	2161.01	26.0%
Mortgage loans	835.98	10.0%
Other sources of funds		
Others	580.52	7.0%
TOTAL	**8324.58**	100.0%

Source: ChinaScope Financial (2012).

In addition to access to land and access to funding, the strategic role of *presales* is a third factor encouraging local real estate oligopolies in Chinese cities, because presales raise major issues of developer credibility, in terms of promised unit quality at delivery, that large developers are in much better position to meet as their reputation grows stronger, as observed in the housing markets of other East Asian economies. If, at the national level, the best comparator for China is the US, when it comes to the oligopolistic organization, behavior and performance of local real estate markets in Chinese cities, Hong Kong is a valuable comparator (Leung *et al.*, 2006; Choy, 2007).

The liquidity squeeze caused by falling housing sales and prices since the start of the housing downturn is affecting the large- and medium-sized firms that do not have easy access to non-bank funding. As a result, the downturn is likely to lead to an increased concentration of market share into large, listed, national developers, in a manner comparable to the US experience, where weaker developers have been weeded out of the markets.

However, the largest listed developers are not immune from the downturn. Standard and Poor's rates the off-shore bond issued by 30 large Chinese developers, and has issued a warning that liquidity problems, spreading since the year 2012, could lead a major market correction for the industry: "*Developers facing refinancing risks on offshore debt and trust loans are likely to push property sales by cutting prices aggressively or sell assets [...] due to rising inventory and liquidity pressure. [...] When the pinch starts to bite, benign price discounting could turn into a price war [...] indeed, 2012 will test the survival of more than 80 000 property developers in China.*" (Standard and Poor's, 2012). Two years later, S& P was reporting that "*conditions in China's real estate market continue to toughen*" [...] "*We see the credit trend for developers we rate to lean toward negative actions*" (Standard and Poor's, 2012, 2014).

Concerns about a potentially sharp correction in housing markets have been rising. First- and second-tier cities have seen larger price drops than third-tier cities, and transaction volumes have trended downward since the middle of 2011. The increasing tightening of administrative controls, with increasing restrictions on sales and credit tightening since 2010, have been important factors. Large, listed developers that have an increasingly dominant market share are considered to be in good liquidity conditions, due to their strong profitability over several years, and their ability to raise funds on the capital markets and in the large domestic informal financial. However, their current ratio (ratio of current assets to current liabilities) has been eroding since 2010.

9.4   Channels of interaction between housing and other sectors of the economy

During the great housing boom of 1998–2012, the real estate sector has expanded very rapidly, at the same time that the level of urbanization crossed the 50% mark. By every aggregate metric, whether real or financial, the weight of real estate in the economy has grown considerably larger. The share of real estate investment to GDP more than doubled, from 6.5% in 2002, to the extremely high ratio of 13.8% in 2012, as shown in Figure 9.2.

In terms of fixed asset investment (FAI), real estate has consistently accounted for a high ratio, of about 25% of total FAI in the economy. Similarly, the annual value added generated by the stock of housing rose by over 25% from less than 4.5% in 2002, to over 5.8% in 2010.

In financial terms, the share of total property loans in total bank loans from the regulated sector had risen from less than 14% in 2005, to close to 20% in 2010. In addition, the shadow banking exposure to real estate is estimated to have climbed to over 30% of total trust products during the final years of the boom. Sample surveys, and various reports, also suggest that close to 20% of the loans made by the middle-tier financial institutions of the shadow banking pyramid have been made to real estate developers.

What will happen to the national economy as the housing correction that is following the great housing boom of 1998–2012 gets under way? There is a broad consensus that the Chinese government has the incentives, the institutional means, and the financial resources to avoid a hard landing. But what can be said about the magnitude and duration of the housing correction in terms of prices and annual output[13]? Because of the critical role of household expectations discussed in Section 9.3.4.3, it is difficult to evaluate the degree of price and output decline, or the possible overshooting that might occur, because the correction will be city-specific.

Evaluating the specific multiplier effects of housing on the national economy is not possible, due to lack of suitably disaggregated data. However, a study by Zhang et al. (2014) examines the real and financial linkages between the entire real estate sector, plus construction activities and other sectors of the economy. Real linkages are explored through input-output analysis, while financial linkages are more complex to explore. On the real linkages, the study shows that the real estate construction sector has been much more important to China's economy output than suggested by the share of its value added in the economy's total value added. The total direct and indirect contribution of the real estate-construction sector to China's economy is of the order of 32% of total value in the economy, compared to the 12% recorded by national accounts, including construction (Zhang et al., 2014). The study finds that the real linkages between housing, real estate and construction with the other sectors of the economy have become stronger during 2005–2010 – that is, the multiplier effects are larger.

There are least three financial channels through which China's real estate sector is linked with other sectors. First, shocks to the property sector will

[13] Liu et al. (2002) tested the relationship between housing investment and GDP growth nationally over the period 1981–2001, which covers mostly the pre-privatization era. They found that housing investment had a stronger effect than non-housing investment on GDP fluctuations. Chen and Zhu (2008) tested the relationship across 30 provincial-level regions over the period 1999Q1 to 2007Q4, and found the impact of housing on GDP to be cyclically bi-directional in the east, one-way strongest and fastest in the middle region, and weak in the west.

affect the profitability of any sector that is vertically integrated with it, and will thereby weaken its debt service capacity. Second, risk-based lending by banks is not well developed, and real estate collateral to support loans is widely used. The 2011 assessment of China financial systems showed that 35–45% of loans by the big five SOCBs use real estate collateral (IMF, 2011). Any decline in real estate prices will affect collateral values and raise credit risks. Third, a large volume of local government debt is supported by revenues from land sales, so a decline in land values will affect the quality of local government debt. Moreover, land prices are usually more volatile than housing prices.

Corporate credit risks have increased during the end of the boom. Real estate, construction, and industries with severe overcapacity problems, such as cement, aluminum, ship-building, iron and glass, have higher risks than other sectors, reflecting the faster growth in their leverage, as well as weakening profits (Zhang *et al.*, 2014). The study also finds that the real estate sector and the machinery sectors generate the largest risk spillover effects across all sectors. The risk spillovers are both direct and indirect. Credit risks of the real estate sector may spill over directly into construction, chemicals, ship building, and iron industries which, in turn, spread their risks to other industries, including glass, coal, plastic, cement, and so on. Real estate and the machinery industries appear to be the most influential in terms of contemporaneous spillover effects. If spillover effects are taken into account, *"the two industries together might explain nearly 50% of the volatility of other sectors' default likelihood on average"* (Zhang *et al.*, 2014).

10

Korea: Overcoming Housing Shortages and Stabilizing Housing Prices

10.1 An overview

Over the past 50 years or so, South Korea has risen from one of the poorest countries in the world to being the world's 15th largest economy. The *per capita* income of the country rose from \$79 in 1960 to \$22 590 by 2012. During the same period, the country was transformed from an agrarian economy into a major industrial powerhouse. Industrialization and economic development resulted in rapid growth of urban population. Propelled by a continuous influx of population and economic activities into Seoul and other major cities since the 1960s, the share of urban population jumped from 39% in 1960, to 50% in 1970, to 69% in 1980, 82% in 1990, and to 90% in 2012[1]. This confirms a strong correlation

---

[1] There is an issue with the definition of the urbanization rate used by different sources. The currently available data on urbanization rate comes in two definitions. One measure is the share of the nation's population residing in cities and towns with 20 000 inhabitants or more. The other measure is the share of population living in places classified as urban in land use, The former measure is due to the Ministry of Security and Administration (formerly Ministry of Home Affairs), while the latter is due to the Ministry of Land, Infrastructure and Transport. The difference between the data based on the two is very small – around one percentage point, at most. For example, the 2012 figures were 90.2% and 91.0%, respectively. However, some international sources report Korea's urbanization to be much lower than either of these two measures. For example, the UN defines urbanization as the share of the nation's total population residing in Dong (the smallest administrative unit in administrative cities). The UN's World Urbanization Prospects 2014 Update reports that the urban population is 40.8 million, the rural population is 8.7 million and, hence, the urbanization rate is 82.4%. The World Bank and OECD use the UN data of urbanization rate.

Dynamics of Housing in East Asia, First Edition. Bertrand Renaud,
Kyung-Hwan Kim and Man Cho.
© 2016 John Wiley & Sons, Ltd. Published 2016 by John Wiley & Sons, Ltd.

between the level of economic development and the urbanization rate, as well established in the literature[2].

The Korean case differs from those of other East Asian countries in several ways. First of all, Korea was able to resolve urban housing shortages by following a highly interventionist approach. Korea has had to cope with severe housing shortages in its cities since the 1960s, but the government did not allow much resource to be allocated to housing during the early stages of economic development, as it wanted to deploy scarce financial resources to promote industry and infrastructure development. Starting in the early 1980s, the government introduced a new scheme of land development, relying on the public sector developers with the power of compulsory purchase with compensation to facilitate land and housing development. The government then raised the scale of housing supply dramatically through the 1989–1992 drive to build two million new dwelling units. They devised various rules and regulations to steer the location and the size of development projects, to control the size distribution of the housing units produced, and to ensure that houses should be distributed to eligible home buyers to attain the social goal of one house for each household.

In essence, the central government has controlled the whole process of the production and allocation of housing for many years, and this framework remains essentially intact to date. Some public sector institutions played a key role in implementing government housing policy. The Korean system worked to improve the overall housing conditions of its people in terms of both quantity and quality. However, this rigid and convoluted system has made housing supply very inelastic.

Second, housing price stability has been an overarching goal of housing policy in Korea. This has been true regardless of the political inclination of the administration in power. One obvious reason for the obsession with housing price stability is that it has direct implications for housing affordability. Another reason is that this housing price path influences the formation and the distribution of wealth among people. Occasional housing price increases invited ever stronger responses from government to contain speculation. The government has mobilized various policy instruments, including taxes, regulations on transactions, and restrictions on mortgage lending. These instruments have then been used in reverse gear to facilitate recovery when the housing market has gone into a serious recession. Thus, government intervention in the housing market is often described as a "hot-bath-cold-bath" approach.

Third, the nexus between housing and the macroeconomy has drawn more attention in recent years. Housing is by now a major sector of the Korean economy and, as such, its performance is closely linked to that of the wider

---

[2] For recent literature , see Spence *et al.* (2009) and Birch and Wachter (2011).

economy. Korea has experienced two major economic crises over the past two decades – the 1997 Asian Financial Crisis and the 2008 Global Financial Crisis. In both cases, housing and real estate sectors were victims, rather than the causes, of the crises (Kim, 2000; Kim, 2012). The speedy recovery of the housing market as the economy bounced back quickly after the outbreak of the AFC supports this claim. One positive side effect of the AFC was that important reforms were made to the real estate market, and to the real estate finance system in particular. In contrast, the GFC had a smaller initial impact on the housing market, but it triggered a change in the public expectations about the future course of housing price, combined with the realization of the implications of ongoing demographic changes.

Korea now faces a new set of housing policy challenges. These include: addressing the housing welfare needs of low income households and the socially disadvantaged; adjusting to a rapidly aging society on both the housing service provision and unlocking the housing wealth held by the elderly; facilitating the structural change in the rental housing sector; and managing the potential risk to the financial system from large household debt, of which mortgage loans comprise about one half of the total household debt.

This chapter is organized as follows. After this overview section, Section 10.2 presents some indicators of housing conditions and discusses the cycles of new housing construction and housing price. Section 10.3 explains major objectives of housing policy and assesses their achievements. Section 10.4 describes the behavior of the key actors in the housing market and their impact on housing market volatility.

10.2   Housing outcomes and housing cycles

10.2.1   Housing outcomes

Over the past 40 years, housing conditions in Korea improved greatly on both the quantity and the quality side, as can be seen from table 10.1. The Housing stock has expanded from 4.4 million in 1970, to 14.7 million in 2010. Housing units per 1000 persons increased from 138 to 302 during the same period[3]. The housing supply ratio, defined as the ratio between the total number of housing units and the total number of households, is the most popular housing policy indicator in Korea. This is because it is a measure of housing

---

[3] The definition of a housing unit has been changed since 2005. Population and Housing Census, prior to 2005, defined a housing unit by ownership. Therefore, if a building consisted of ten independent units, but was owned by a single person, it was counted as one. The new definition counts it as ten housing units. The figures presented in table 10.1 are based on the old definition. Using the new definition, the housing stock is 17.7 million, and the number of dwellings per 1000 persons is 363.

Table 10.1   Evolution of the housing stock in Korea: 1970–2010.

	1970	1980	1990	2000	2010
Number of housing units (thousand): A	4360	5319	7357	11 472	14 677
Number of households (thousand): B	5576	7470	10 167	11 928	12 995
Housing supply ratio (%): 100 × A/B	78.2	71.2	72.4	96.2	112.9
Total population (million) C	31.5	37.4	43.4	46.1	48.6
Dwellings per 1000 population A/C	138	142	170	249	302

Source: Population and Housing Census, various years

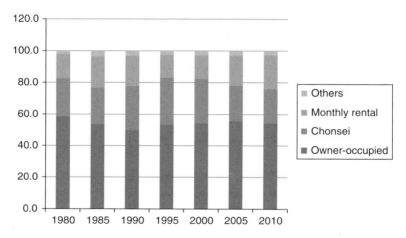

Figure 10.1   Distribution of housing tenure in Korea: 1980–2010.
Source: Korea Population and Housing Census, various years.

shortage (surplus) relative to the number of households, which is considered to be the target for housing supply. The housing supply ratio fell from 78.2% to 71.2% between 1970 and 1980, but it increased steadily since then, and reached the 100% mark in 2002 for the nation as a whole. The 2010 figure was 112.9% for the nation, but it varies across cities. It is much lower in Seoul (77%) and other metropolitan areas, but is rising rapidly (for Seoul, from 77% in 2000, to 97% in 2010). The number of dwellings per 1000 persons is a more widely used indicator for international comparison. The indicator improved dramatically since 1980, but the current level is substantially lower than those of Japan, the UK and France, not to mention the US.

Over the past 30 years, the housing tenure distribution has changed in a gradual manner, as illustrated in Figure 10.1. The owner-occupancy rate fell from 59%, to 50% between 1980 and 1990, and then rose slowly to 54.2% by 2010. It should be noted that there is a sizable discrepancy between the owner-occupancy rate (the share of housing stock that is owner-occupied) and the home ownership rate (the share of households who own at least one house) in Korea. This is because many renters own a house somewhere else, reflecting the widespread separation of ownership and residency in Korea. The home ownership rate was 60.3% in 2005 and 61.3% in 2010. Both the owner occupancy rate and the home ownership rate are lower in the Seoul Capital Region than elsewhere.

A unique feature of the Korean rental market is the dominance of *chonsei* contracts. *Chonsei* is an asset-based rental lease, whereby the tenant leaves a large lump sum deposit to the landlord to occupy a house for a typical period of two years, instead of paying a monthly rent. The deposit is fully refunded to the tenant at the end of the lease. Meanwhile, the landlord invests the deposit to earn a return. *Chonsei* emerged naturally in the post-war era in an environment of severe housing shortages, high interest rates, credit rationing, high inflation and rapidly rising housing prices. However, the share of pure *chonsei* has been falling, and that of the hybrid type, featuring a varying amount of deposit and monthly rents, has been rising fast for the past ten years or so following financial liberalization. By 2010, hybrid contracts (denoted as monthly rental in Figure 10.1) and *chonsei* contracts held about the same share in the rental market. However, pure monthly rental contracts, with a security deposit equivalent to one or two months rent, are still rare in Korea.

Housing conditions in Korea greatly improved inequality as well. Table 10.2 presents some indicators of housing quality during the period 1980–2010. During this period, the number of rooms per household increased from 2.2 to 3.7; housing floor space *per capita* increased from 10 m² to 25 m²; the number of people per room (a measure of crowding) dropped from 2.1 persons to 0.7 person; housing units with flushing toilets from 18% to 97%; and housing units with warm water from 18% to 98%.

Table 10.2 Indicators of housing quality in Korea: 1980–2010.

	1980	1990	2000	2010
Average number of rooms per household	2.2	2.5	3.4	3.7
Average number of persons per room	2.1	1.5	0.9	0.7
Average floor area per person (m²)	10.1	14.3	20.2	25.0
Average floor area per household (m²)	45.8	51.0	63.1	67.4
Percentage of houses with piped water (%)	56.1	74.0	85.0	97.9
Equipped with modern toilet (%)	18.4	51.3	86.9	97.0
Equipped with bathroom (%)	22.1	44.1	89.1	98.4
Equipped with hot bath (%)	9.9	34.1	87.4	96.9

Source: Population and Housing Census, various years

To sum up, the post-1980 policy regime in Korea contributed to a vast improvement in housing conditions within a reasonably short time period, both in terms of quantity and in terms of quality.

10.2.2 Housing cycles

10.2.2.1 Housing construction cycles

As shown in Figure 10.2, new housing construction in Korea has been highly cyclical. Such fluctuations reflect not only the market forces at work, but also changes in government policy. Two features of the housing construction cycle are notable. First, fluctuations are more marked for the units delivered by the private developers than those supplied by the public sector agencies. Second, the volume of new housing construction made a quantum leap as a result of the drive to build two million dwelling units between 1989 and 1992, including the development of five new towns in the Gyeonggi Province surrounding Seoul. There was another peak in housing construction in the early 2000s, due partly to the development of the second-generation new towns in farther-out locations in the Seoul Metropolitan Region.

The drive to build two million units represents a milestone in Korean housing policy. As a result of the drive, the average annual volume of new housing construction more than doubled from the previous level. The drive was a response by government to the skyrocketing housing prices in the late 1980s, caused by cumulated shortage and the brisk demand following very rapid economic growth in the mid-1980s. The housing price hike was con-sidered a serious threat to social stability, and the government responded

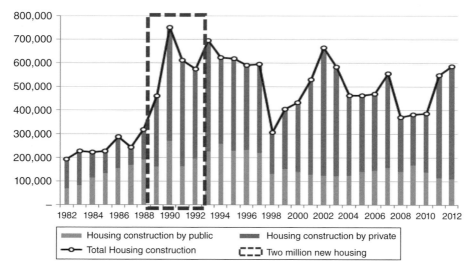

Figure 10.2 Trend of housing construction.
Source: Ministry of Land, Infrastructure and Transport.

with a concerted effort, engaging all relevant ministries and public sector institutions, to increase the housing supply on a massive scale. Outside observers may wonder how such an abrupt increase was possible and sustained in the years to come. The answer lies in the fact that housing supply is constrained primarily by the supply of developable land, and that government controls the supply of developable land, through the conversion of non-urban land into urban use on a large scale. Government also expanded the supply of mortgage loans, through the National Housing Fund, to support the demand for housing.

The goal of the two-million housing drive was reached one year ahead of schedule on a permit base, and nominal housing prices started falling in 1992, when the first batch of new housing units was completed and ready for occupancy.

Some side-effects of the two-million housing program also followed. The sudden rise of the level of construction activity led to excessive demand for construction labor and materials, which resulted in soaring construction wages and compromise in quality in some projects. The sudden construction boom also caused inflationary pressures in the economy, as well as disturbing the allocation of labor between the construction industry and the rest of the economy.

In the long run, the relative size of the construction sector tends to decline, as indicated in Figure 10.3. Total residential and non-residential construction investment as a ratio to GDP has gradually declined in Korea,

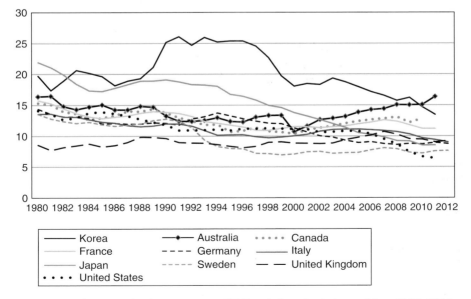

Figure 10.3   Construction investment to GDP ratio in selected countries: 1980–2012.
Data source: OECD.

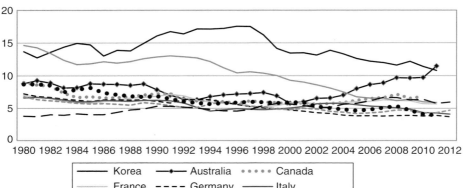

Figure 10.4 Residential investment to GDP ratio in selected countries: 1980–2012. *Data source*: OECD.

to about 13% in 2013, from its peak level of 20% in the early 1990s. Its current level is still higher than most other OECD countries.

The ratio between housing investment and GDP has also been falling in Korea in recent years, and its current level is lower than those in many OECD countries, as seen in Figure 10.4. The long-term average for the figure over the period 1970–2010 was 5.4%, but it fell to around 3% in the aftermath of the Global Financial Crisis. In short, Korea's construction sector remains large, relative to the size of the economy, but housing investment is relatively small[4].

10.2.2.2 *Housing price cycles*

Studying housing price cycles obviously requires time series data on consistently measured housing prices. Unfortunately, the longest available time series data on housing price indices start only from 1986[5]. The Korea Housing Bank started publishing a monthly housing price index in 1986, and Kookmin Bank (KB) took over the index when it merged with KHB. The KB indexes cover both a purchase price index and a *chonsei* deposit index for Seoul and six other metropolitan areas (along with the eight provinces) by using a Laspeyres index method. The KB indices cover both purchase prices and *chonsei* prices from those areas. It should be noted that the KB index is not entirely based on actual transactions, as the raw data come from designated real estate agents, based on the actual number of

---

[4] Kim and Suh (1991) showed that there was an under-investment in housing until the mid-1980s. Despite the large increase in housing investment since the late 1980s, the ratio between housing investment and GDP is not large compared with other advanced economies.

[5] The land price index dates back much longer than the housing price index. Cho (2012) discusses several land price boom-busts in Korea between 1968 through 1985.

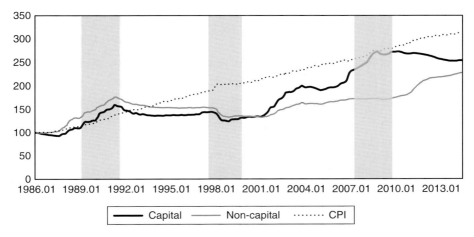

Figure 10.5 Housing price indices for the Capital Region and the Non-Capital Region. *Source*: Cho and Son (2014).

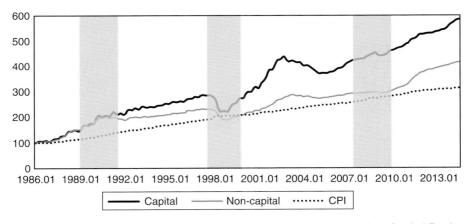

Figure 10.6 *Chonsei* deposit indices for the Capital Region and the Non-Capital Region. *Source*: Cho and Son (2014).

transactions and on their estimates of going prices[6]. In Figures 10.5 and 10.6, we report the long-term price trends for the capital Region (Seoul and its vicinity) and the non-capital Region (six other large cities).

Contrary to a widespread belief, neither the rate of housing price appreciation, nor its volatility, have been very large. As can be seen from Figure 10.5, the growth rates of the purchase prices in both regions during the period 1986–2014 were smaller than that of the Consumer Price Index (CPI).

---

[6] The Korea Appraisal Board started publishing a housing price index using actual transaction price data two decades later, in 2006, as it became mandatory for buyers to report actual transactions data.

Table 10.3   Rate of change in housing prices and their volatility by region.

Region	2000–2014				1987–1999			
	Capital Region		Non-capital Region		Capital Region		Non-Capital Region	
Mean/std. dev.	μ	σ	μ	σ	μ	σ	μ	σ
Housing price	2.6	8.6	2.7	8.8	5.0	7.3	3.6	4.1
Chonsei deposit	7.6	10.7	5.6	10.0	6.0	7.9	5.1	4.9

The average annual rate of appreciation was merely 2.6% and 2.7%, for the capital Region and the non-capital Region, respectively (Table 10.3). A comparison with five other East Asian countries shows that the price volatility, measured as the standard deviation of the rate of change in housing price in Seoul, was smaller than those of other large cities (Cho *et al.*, 2012). However, the volatility of *chonsei* price changes is greater than for purchase prices, especially in the earlier period 1986–99. This outcome contrasts with the usual findings from other countries that housing rents are more stable than housing prices[7].

10.2.2.3   *Three episodes of rapid housing price changes*
There have been three episodes of pronounced housing price dynamics since 1986 for which systematic housing price data is available. These are: the steep price appreciation across the country during the period 1987–1991; the price increases in the early- to mid-2000s, which was much stronger in the Seoul and a few cities in the Capital Region; and the divergent price dynamics after the Global Financial Crisis (GFC), with a sustained price downturn in the Capital Region and an upturn in provincial cities in the rest of the country.

The first price increase resulted from a combination of the accumulated housing shortage with the unusually strong performance of the economy, due to the favorable macroeconomic conditions often referred to as the "three-lows" economic boom: the low local currency value, especially against the Japanese Yen; the low crude oil price; and, the low interest rate in the mid-1980s. The rapid increase in housing price in both the Capital Region and the non-Capital Region caused a housing affordability problem that became so severe that housing moved to the forefront of social issues during the 1987 presidential election campaign. Mr. Noh, the ruling party candidate then, made a campaign pledge to build four million housing units during his presidency. The target was later scaled down to two million units after he was elected, but two million still amounted to one-third of the existing housing stock as of 1985. As a result of the successful completion

---

[7] It should be remembered that the price of a *chonsei* contract is very different from monthly rental leases found in other countries: it is based on the asset value of the units, and also reflects the level of interest rates in addition to local supply and demand conditions.

of this ambitious initiative by the government, housing prices began to fall gradually in nominal terms from 1992, then they dropped sharply at the outbreak of the AFC. However, *chonsei* prices continued to increase, especially in the capital Region.

A second price run-up started in Seoul in late 2001. This was somewhat surprising, given the pessimism about housing markets, that prevailed in the few years following the AFC. The fast recovery of the economy, the low interest rate level, the increase in mortgage lending, and the decrease in new supply in the wake of the AFC, were the main reasons for the rise in housing price, but the pattern of housing price increases differed this time from the first one in the late 1980s. Housing price increases were most pronounced in the sub-market area of Seoul, known as Gangnam, consisting of three autonomous districts located south to the Han River. This more localized housing price increase was due to a mismatch between local demand and supply within Seoul. Housing prices also increased elsewhere in Seoul and in some other submarkets within the Capital Region, but housing price increases were not a national issue.

The government tried to contain the housing price hike in Gangnam early on, because it feared that price increases might spill over to other markets. There was a political pressure to stabilize housing price in the submarkets with the most expensive prices. The government responded with various measures to suppress demand by discouraging speculation, using various instruments. It raised the rate of capital gains tax on the owners of two or more houses; it strengthened the existing property holding tax and introduced a new national tax, called comprehensive real estate tax, targeted on the owners of expensive houses and of two or more houses; the price control on new housing was re-introduced; and new regulations were introduced to make high-density redevelopment of existing apartments in Seoul more difficult. Also, ceilings on the loan-to-value (LTV) ratio and the debt service to income (DTI) ratio were introduced, to control the growth of mortgage lending.

The third episode of rapid housing price changes occurred in 2009, with the outbreak of the Global Financial Crisis of 2008. The magnitude of price declines was much smaller than those that took place in the wake of the AFC. In fact, housing prices kept rising in some provincial cities, while prices were either stagnant or falling in the Capital Region. This pattern was unprecedented and somewhat more difficult to interpret. Regulatory arbitrage can offer one possible explanation – that is, the LTV ceiling in the non-Capital Region was higher than in the Capital Region, and the DTI regulation does not exist in the non-Capital Region. Alternatively, the purchase prices in both regions may simply be reverting to their respective long-term means after several years of boom or bust (See Figure 10.5).

One important feature of this latest phase of housing price cycle is the strong appreciation of *chonsei* deposit price in both the Capital Region and the major cities in the rest of the country since 2011. One major reason for the steady increase in *chonsei* deposit is the decrease in the demand for home purchases, due to pessimistic expectation about housing price appreciation and low domestic interest rates, reflecting quantitative easing by the US Federal Reserve and other western central banks. Many would-be home owners decided not to purchase homes and to remain as renters, imposing pressure on demand.

The government was faced with the challenge of stabilizing the rental market, as well as boosting the demand for home purchases to facilitate economic recovery. They tried to remove the regulations and tax policies that had been introduced by the previous government to contain rising prices, such as LTV and DTI ceilings on mortgages, punitive taxation of capital gains, and the comprehensive real estate tax mentioned above. Some of these efforts were blocked or modified by the National Assembly. The current government follows a similar policy of regulatory reform, and also tries to manage the transition taking place in the private rental housing market.

10.3   Key issues in housing policy

10.3.1   Resolving housing shortages

A housing shortage was prevalent in Korea in the 1960s, even before its economic growth took off. About 18% of the nation's housing stock had been destroyed during the Korean War, while the population boomed in the post-war era – from 20 million in 1949, to 25 million in 1960, which created a large demand for housing. Not surprisingly, housing took the main stage in public policy early on. In September 1953, the government issued a presidential proclamation, pledging to build one million housing units within five years, but this was not realized, due to an unrealistic financing plan. They declared another large-scale housing development plan in 1972, a ten-year plan to construct 2.5 million units. That plan did not materialize either, due to the lack of financial resource and the absence of proper institutions to implement it.

When housing is recognized as a good, and something socially important enough that public sector has to be involved, then governments tend to allocate adequate resources to housing. Such a moment arrived in Korea in the late 1980s. As discussed above, housing prices soared so much that securing a decent shelter in Seoul and other large cities went beyond the reach of most low- and middle-income households. Government responded with the two million unit construction drive – a milestone in housing policy in Korea. Unlike the prior similar plans, the two million unit drive was successful in delivering the promised quantity and, one year ahead of schedule. Although there were concerns about the feasibility of the plan, even within government, the plan was carried out by a concerted effort by all relevant government ministries and public sector institutions, with the backing of the president. The project was financed largely with private sector money, 68% of total cost by prospective buyers (via pre-sales), while 22% of funding came from the National Housing Fund, and 10% from government general budget (Noh, 2011).

On the positive side, the massive government-initiated supply increase was effective in resolving the excess demand for housing space in Seoul and other major cities within a short time period. Considering the magnitude of the accumulated demand for housing space, caused by an extended period of rapid economic growth and urbanization, it is hard to think of alternative ways to deal with the excess demand more efficiently and expediently. Implementing such a large scale supply drive was a real challenge, but the housing institutions established since the 1960s did contribute to the timely implementation of the project. The strong effective demand for new housing built in good locations was the other reason for the success of the drive. An indirect proof is seen in similar, but less successful, projects of developing several new towns in locations farther from Seoul. On the negative side, however, the first project produced several unintended consequences, such as the lack of diversity in building design and poor building quality in some units, inflated costs of building materials and construction wages, and the creation of excess capacity in the construction sector.

10.3.2 Public housing institutions and the dualistic housing supply

The central government, and the Ministry of Construction (MOC) and its descendant ministries in particular, have played a leading role in formulating housing policy in Korea, including the creation, over time, of housing agencies from the early stage of urbanization. The public institutions that have played important roles in the housing delivery system include:

- **The Korea National Housing Corporation (KNHC)** was established in 1962 when the first five-year economic development plan started. KNHC was charged with the mandate to conduct housing development and construction projects with partial government financing.
- **The Korea Housing Bank (KHB)** was created in 1969 to meet the financing needs of home buyers and home builders. It was privatized in 1997 under the new name "Housing and Commercial Bank", and later merged with Kookmin Bank in 2001.

- **The National Housing Fund (NHF)** was established in 1973 as a public sector funding source for affordable housing to construction companies, as well as to target consumers
- **The Korea Land Development Corporation (KLDC)** was created in 1982, to fulfill land expropriation and *development* needs for large-scale housing and urban development projects (both public and private). Its operation was based on the Land Development Promotion Act, which grants it a status of monopoly in large-scale land development and the power of compulsory purchase of land.
- **The Korea Housing Guarantee Corporation (KHGC)** was re-established in 1999 from the former Home Builders Co-op established in 1993. KHGC provides guarantee service to home buyers under presale contracts. It will be renamed as The Korea Housing and Urban Guarantee Corporation to extend guarantee service to urban redevelopment projects, as well as housing development projects.
- **The Korea Housing Finance Corporation** (KHFC) was created in 2004 by absorbing the Korea Mortgage Company (KoMoCo) to issue Mortgage-Backed Securities (MBS), backed by long-term fixed-rate mortgage loans.
- In 2009, the housing corporation KNHC was merged with the Korea Land Development Corporation to form a new institution called the **Korea Land and Housing Corporation (LH)**, to supply most of the nation's public rental housing stock.

These institutions played an important role in building, allocating, and financing affordable housing units for low- and moderate-income households and, as such, in forming a sizable middle class in Korean society within a short time period. Nonetheless, the social missions of some of these institutions waned over time, and they created a risk of crowding out competing private sector institutions in delivering affordable dwelling units and in providing financial services.

The Land and Housing Corporation (LH) is now the dominant public sector player in the supply of new housing. The land and housing development process in Korea, starting from purchasing raw land, all the way to selling completed new units to consumers, is governed by various public rules and regulations stage. To speed up the process, the Korean government changed the land expropriation method in the early 1980s, from the time-consuming and less efficient land re-adjustment scheme, which relies on voluntary agreements among land owners[8], to the public land development method, which granted the power of eminent domain to KLDC and other development agencies, with pre-determined compensation to landowners. The new method enabled the public sector development entities to proceed speedily with the large scale housing and urban development projects. However, as the shortages

[8] See Doebele (1980) for a description of the land readjustment scheme.

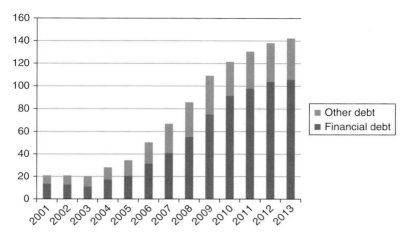

Figure 10.7 Increase indebtedness of the LH Corporation.
Source: LH Corporation.

of housing have been resolved to a great extent, the demand for large develop-ment has decreased. Therefore, the government announced its plan to abolish in 2014 the Land Development Promotion Act, which regulates large scale land development by the LH Corporation.

Another mandate of LH, which has become even more important since the turn of the century, is the construction and management of subsidized public rental housing. LH incurs large losses from public rental housing pro-grams. It has been able to make up the loss from the profits from sales of land and housing in the past, but such cross-subsidization no longer works, because of sluggish markets for developable land and housing in recent years. The corporation now faces serious financial difficulty with its large debt and debt service requirements.

The combined total debt outstanding of KLDC and KNHC has increased five-fold between 2001 and 2009. Then, the total debt outstanding of the LH corporation, which was established in September 2009, increased by about 30% within the following four years, as shown by Figure 10.7. About one-third of the total LH debt outstanding is attributable to the production and management of the public rental housing stock. The case of LH demonstrates the importance of assigning the right mission to housing institutions, and of closely monitoring their operational and financial soundness, as well as re-aligning both the mission and operations as necessary.

10.3.3 Developing a market-oriented housing finance system

The 1997 Asian Financial Crisis became a milestone in the development of a market-based housing finance system in Korea. The Korea Housing Bank and the National Housing Fund (administered for a fee by KHB) had monopolized

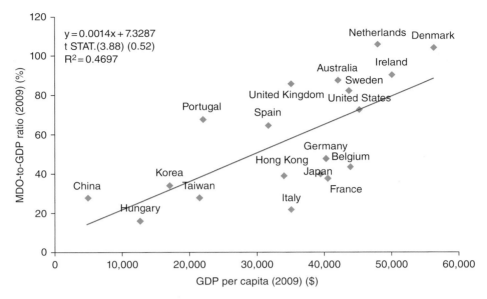

Figure 10.8   MDO to GDP ratio vs. GDP *per capita* in selected countries, 2009.
Source: Cho *et al.* (2012).

the housing finance system in Korea before the AFC, in terms of mortgage funding lending and servicing. These two special-circuit housing finance institutions accounted for 80% of total housing loans outstanding as of 1997, when KHB was privatized. However, they served a very small clientele, with mortgage loans below market interest rates, and low loan-to-value (LTV) ratios typically below 30%. Loan limits and other non-price criteria were applied to ration the limited supply of funds. After the AFC, LTV ratios increased to about 50%, with the maximum LTV of 70% differentiated according to location (the Seoul Capital Region vs. other regions), lender type (commercial banks vs. second-tier financial institutions) and loan types (fixed-rate amortizing mortgages vs. adjustable bullet mortgages). The lending volume also increased dramatically after the AFC, with the MDO-to-GDP ratio currently over 30%.

The current size of the mortgage market appears to be at an average level, considering the size of the economy. As shown in Figure 10.8, the MDO-to-GDP ratio is strongly positively correlated with *per capita* GDP, an increase of $1000 USD in the personal income causing 1.4 of a percentage point increase in the MDO-to-GDP ratio. Korea is on the trend line, implying that the size of its residential mortgage lending is neither too large nor too small.

One peculiar feature of housing finance in Korea is the existence of large claims on *chonsei* deposit. *Chonsei* contracts are a lump sum deposit paid in lieu of monthly rents, and the current level of *chonsei* deposit is around 70%

of the value of the house. However, a *chonsei* contract can also be regarded as an informal loan provided by the tenant to the landlord. Indeed, *chonsei* deposits are sometimes used by would-be landlords to finance the purchase of other houses to be rented out. Although it is debatable as to whether *chonsei* should be regarded as a same financial liability of the home owner as mortgage loans, the financial risks that this widespread type of contract can pose to the financial system needs to be properly monitored[9]. In any case, there is concern that Korean figure for the mortgage debt outstanding to GDP ratio will be around 70% if all *chonsei* claims are counted as mortgage loans.

Since the mortgage market was liberalized after the AFC, the residential mortgage lending sector in Korea has been dominated by the commercial banks. The commercial banks issue short-maturity (very often, three years), non-amortizing, adjustable-rate mortgages, using short-term deposits as the primary funding source. This lending practice by the banks has placed the burden of interest rate risks onto the borrowers. In fact, it was the very reason why the government established the Korea Housing Finance Corporation (KHFC) in 2003, to expand long-term fixed-rate mortgages (FRM) with MBS-based wholesale funding. In 2012, KHFC designed a conforming mortgage loan (CML), to be originated by the participating financial institutions and to be securitized by the corporation. The KHFC conforming mortgage loan is a fixed-rate fully amortizing loan of 10–35 year maturity, with the maximum LTV ratio of 70%. This new CML product is expected to serve as a useful benchmark in safely extending loans to the under-served consumers who are wealth- and/or income-constrained. Important market infrastructure that is needed to promote fixed rate mortgages in Korea includes an industry practice of proper measurement and management for the two competing risks embedded in loan products (i.e., prepayment and default risks), as well as a risk-sharing mechanism among involved parties, such as a mortgage insurance contract.

Further improvement of the Korean housing finance system would require several changes. The first of these is maximizing intermediation efficiency, which is equivalent to minimizing excess yield (EY), defined as $EY = r^m - r^f - RP$ where the three right hand side variables represent mortgage lending rate, risk-free rate (government bond with comparable maturity, and risk premium (Diamond and Lea, 1992). The second is extending market completeness, or maximizing financial inclusion (Mercer Oliver Wyman, 2003; Lea, 2010; Dübel, 2014), and ensuring real estate market and macroeconomic stability via macro-prudential regulations and other policy means (Crowe *et al*, 2011; Muellbauer, 2012).

---

[9] During the 1997 AFC, the funds available in the National Housing Fund and the securitization of the high quality NHF loan portfolio were partially used to rescue failing *chonsei* contracts.

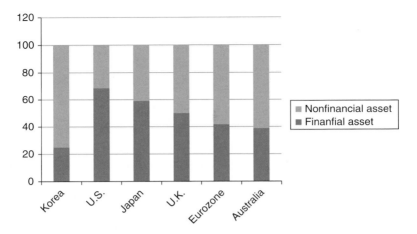

Figure 10.9   Composition of household wealth in selected countries.

10.3.4   *Promoting the stability of housing mortgage market outcomes*

Real estate assets constitute a very large share of national wealth and household wealth in Korea, compared with other OECD countries. For example, the Bank of Korea estimates that the total national wealth in Korea is about 10 000 trillion KRW, as of 2011, out of which 74% is real estate (land, and residential and non-residential buildings)[10]. In the USA, on the other hand, the share computed using a comparable method is only about 30%. At the household level, non-financial assets (mostly real estate) represent 75% of total assets in Korea, which is much larger than US (31.5%), Japan (40.9%) and the Eurozone (58.3%), as can be seen from Figure 10.9.

The impact of the commercial real estate boom-bust in the 1980s, and the recent subprime mortgage crisis in the US, have demonstrated the possibility of contagion of real estate market volatility to the whole economy. Given the sheer size of the real estate asset in Korea, the likelihood of a real estate-driven systemic shock can be relatively high, and the government needs to intervene if and when such real estate driven macroeconomic volatility increase is deemed likely. In fact, government has intervened in the real estate market to cool down speculation ever since the 1960s. The first instrument introduced was the special levy on capital gains from land of 1967, which was developed into the capital gains tax later. After the AFC, the restrictions on residential mortgage lending, with LTV·DTI limits, combined with the designation of certain geographical areas as "speculative watch zones", have been added to the list of policy instruments.

---

[10] Bank of Korea, "The National Wealth in Korea", 2014.

As to the effectiveness of policy instruments, Crowe *et al.* (2011) found that lending restrictions, such as DTI·LTV limits (macro-prudential regulations), are more effective in cooling overheated housing markets than other policy means, such as broadly based monetary policy, and real estate taxes. In a related vein, Kuttner and Shim (2013) emphasize the importance of finding a policy mix that works in a given country among the conventional stabilization measures (e.g., real estate taxes), the demand-side policy instruments in mortgage market (e.g., DTI·LTV limits) and the supply-side policy tools (e.g., exposure limits, risk weights in computing regulatory capital, and loss reserves). Further research needs to be done to explore the "right" policy mix in the Korean context across various economic scenarios.

There are several other issues that should be addressed in dealing with overheated housing markets. First, if the ultimate goal of the policy is to avoid (possibly *ex-ante*) those real estate market outcomes that are likely to inflict a systemic shock, then it will be useful to explicitly define such market outcomes *ex-ante*, based on proper empirical evidences. In that way, policy intervention can become a more rule- and evidence-based decision, rather than being pushed by myopic media relying on unreliable data.

Second, going directly to the source of market volatility (whether it is from households, from lending institutions, or from home builders) will be more effective than broad-based stabilization measures. That is, if the source of risk is speculative borrowers, then restricting their leverage by loan purpose, or by the number of housing units owned, will be more appropriate. If the source is developers taking high risks, then requiring minimum capital or imposing other lending restrictions will be appropriate. If the source is pro-cyclical lenders, then beefing up their loss provisions and raising capital requirements will be appropriate. Finally, ensuring macroeconomic stability via micro-/macro-prudential regulations should also be weighed against expanding financial inclusion to marginal borrowers, whose intents are to purchase affordable homes.

10.3.5 Developing a well-functioning rental housing sector

Each country has its own policy goal of promoting home ownership. The result of such policy influences household choices between owning and renting, as well as the size of the rental housing stock. Figure 10.12 shows that the share of rental housing in the total housing stock and that of public rental housing varies widely among developed economies. This means that there is no golden rule determining the optimal size of the rental housing sector in a given country. The size depends upon the philosophy of housing policy on how to ensure housing affordability by instituting various owner-focused and renter-focused housing programs. Nonetheless, a sizable and well-functioning rental housing sector not only enhances housing affordability for low- and moderate-income families, but also helps to stabilize the whole housing market. As a case in point, Gramlich (2007) argues that lack of affordable rental housing stocks in major metropolitan areas in the US is a main reason for the surge of the subprime mortgage lending during the housing boom in the early- to mid-2000s.

Korea has pursued the goal of one house for one household by encouraging the production of houses for eligible households. Some of the units sold were called rental housing, but they were *de facto* owner-occupied units under rent-to-own contracts, to be of 5–10 years at the outset. The rental sector has relied on individuals who own two or more houses and rent out the units they do not reside in. Formal housing policies targeted at rental housing was very limited. The first program was to build permanent 230,000 public rental housing[11] units, as a component of the drive to build two million dwellings, but the program ended up producing 190,000 units. Greater attention was given to public rental housing from the late 1990s, and the rental stock has increased steadily since 2000. The public rental housing stock available for renting for five years or longer is about one million units as of the 2013 year end, which is about 5% of the entire housing stock.

Korea is a late starter in establishing an efficient and transparent rental housing sector, for which the sizable *chonsei* market works as a stumbling block. The government has recently been attempting to foster the formal rental housing sector through various policy initiatives, including: expanding the public rental housing stock; implementing a housing voucher program (which is currently in a pilot mode); increasing deductions of rental expenditures from personal income taxes; and promoting REITs (Real Estate Investment Trusts) specialized in developing and operating rental housing units. In addition, the government plans to incentivize private sector players, both for-profit and not-for-profit organizations, to develop and operate rental housing units.

10.4 Main players in Korean housing cycles and their behavior

Housing outcomes are determined by the interaction among the participants in the housing market and government interventions in the market. The key players in the housing market are households, developers/builders, mortgage lending institutions, the central bank, and national and local governments. The media may influence consumer perceptions of market conditions and the formation of expectations about the prospect, as well as

---

[11] It was called "permanent" rental housing to differentiate it from conventional rental housing units that were sold to the tenants after 5–10 years of renting.

the political process of housing policy. In recent years, the national assembly has become increasingly important in the making of housing policy in Korea. The complex interplay between these players is governed by a political economy where different players pursue their own objectives, subject to various constraints[12].

10.4.1 Households

Households are a key player in affecting the housing price path and, hence, are a possible contributor to the housing price cycle. They make decisions on the consumption of housing services and the holding of housing assets. They decide whether to own a house or to rent one. They also decide how much to borrow to finance home purchases, and also which type of loan product to take, from which financial institution.

The behavior of potential home buyers is driven by market fundamentals such as current and expected income, the availability and the terms of mortgage loans, as well as their perceptions about the current housing price level and the expectation about the future course of housing prices. Accustomed to rising housing prices, due in large part to the chronic shortage of affordable housing units, Korean households used to believe that housing prices could only go up, not down. This can be understood in the context of the user cost of housing. In its simplified specification presented below (Equation 10.1), the strong expectation of a price appreciation, g^e, works as a negative cost for owning a home, pushing the demand for home ownership upward.[13] Furthermore, the price ceiling imposed on new housing units in Korea contributed to the strong demand for owning as new dwellings were sold at below-market prices, providing a *de facto* subsidy to those who were eligible to purchase.

$$uc = r^m + \delta - g^e \qquad (10.1)$$

One countervailing force to the strong housing demand was the high market interest rates, r^m. As shown in Figure 10.10, the three-year corporate bond rates in Korea were in double digits before the AFC. They had dropped from the early 1990s, to stabilize in the 10–12% range until the outbreak of the AFC. The user cost of housing in Seoul exhibited a downward trend in the late 1980s, reflecting the run-up in housing price then, but sharply increased until 1993, possibly due to the cooling down of price expectations

---

[12] See Kim and Kim (2000) for a discussion of this issue and a few examples of real estate policy, and Cho and Kim (2011) for the explanation of how the reform of regulations on housing supply and that of the housing finance system have been affected by the political economy.
[13] In equation (10.1), δ represents all other factors including depreciation, maintenance cost, property tax, and risk premium.

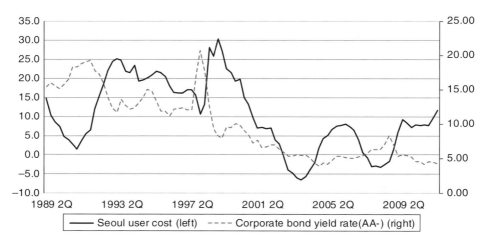

Figure 10.10   User cost of housing (Seoul) and three-year corporate bond rates in Korea. *Sources*: Authors' computation, Bank of Korea.

following the massive increase in new housing supply, through the two million housing units drive, along with the rising interest rates.

Housing market conditions changed vastly in the aftermath of the Asian Financial Crisis. Housing prices collapsed and interest rates soared in 1998, raising the user cost of housing temporarily. However, the housing market started bouncing back in 1999, as a result of the fast recovery of the economy. The interest rate started falling after the AFC, and so did the user cost of housing, with a time lag until 2003, making homeownership less costly and more attractive. Another important factor that boosted the demand for home ownership was the expansion of residential mortgage lending, thanks to the low and stable interest rate environment and the deregulation of real estate lending after the AFC shock, as discussed below.

It is well-established, in both the US and Korea, that the expansion of leverage in the housing market leads to an increase in the number of "natural buyers" (i.e., those who have strong positive expectations of asset price appreciation), which will push up the bidding price for the marginal consumers (Duca *et al.*, 2011; Cho, 2012). The specific linkage is shown through the effect of the loan-to-value (LTV) ratio on the housing price-to-rent ratio, the parameter b in Equation 10.2:

$$\ln\left(\frac{P}{R}\right) = a \cdot \ln(uc) + b \cdot LTV \qquad (10.2)$$

If the market for housing asset is in equilibrium, the revenue and the cost for holding an housing asset should be equal for the marginal borrower – that is, $(R/P) = uc$. The expression can be transformed to $\ln\left(\frac{P}{R}\right) = \ln(uc)$

(Muellbauer, 2012). This implies that the parameter *a* in Equation 10.2 should be negative unity if the asset market is in equilibrium. Empirical studies show, however, that *a* is far from negative 1: it is –0.16 for the USA (Duca *et al.*, 2011) and –0.07 for Korea (Cho, 2012). These results suggest that rising g^e, due to positive expectation about future housing price appreciation, has a positive impact on the housing price, but that this impact is not as strong as the equilibrium condition implies.

As to the effect of the leverage, the above studies report that the LTV effect (parameter *b*) is positive and statistically significant for both countries. In Korea, both the average LTV on home mortgages and the mortgage debt outstanding (as a ratio to GDP) went up remarkably after the AFC, which led to a strong demand for home purchases and, hence, a run-up in housing prices, especially in the hottest sub-markets in Seoul between 2003 and 2007. In response, the government tried to discourage speculative demand by imposing lending restrictions, such as the LTV·DTI ceilings and raised taxes on capital gains, as well as introducing a new tax on holding expensive houses and on owning two or more houses.

The recent global financial crisis has had a major impact on the behavior of housing consumers, for a reason that is different from the past episode of the AFC. The user cost did go up as a result of the outbreak of the crisis, despite the low and declining market interest rates (see Figure 10.10). This was due to a fundamental change in the consumers' attitude to home ownership. As the housing supply ratio (number of housing units divided by number of households) exceeds 100% nationally, the expectation of future housing price appreciation naturally became more modest.

The more important cause of changing expectations is the prospect for demographic changes and the slowdown of economic growth. The fear that the rapidly aging population and the retirement of baby-boomers may lead to increasing the supply of existing houses on the market, while the slowdown of economic growth will reduce demand for housing, has made many potential home buyers believe that housing price can only come down in the future. Consequently, many of them decided not to own houses and remain as renters (*chonsei* tenants, to be more precise), exerting pressure on the rental market. For the first time, there is a substantially large number of renters by choice, and not by default, as when households cannot afford to buy a home.

At the same time that the demand for rental housing under a *chonsei* contract is increasing, the slowdown of housing price appreciation, and the interest, results in a decrease in the supply of *chonsei*. units As a result, *chonsei* deposits have been rising in recent years, while housing prices remained soft, leading to a continuous rise in the ratio of *chonsei* deposit to purchase price. The private rental housing market in Korea has been dominated by pure *chonsei* contracts (with a large lump sum up-front deposit and no monthly rents during the lease period) for many years. However, the share of the hybrid type, featuring a varying amount of deposit and monthly rents, has been rising fast for the past ten years or so. The pace of conversion from a *chonsei* lease to the hybrid lease accelerated after the global financial crisis of 2007–09. However, pure monthly rental contracts, with a security deposit equivalent to one- or two- months' rent, remain rare in Korea.

The rental market is in transition, and the extent to which the conversion from *chonsei* to the hybrid contract will continue remains to be seen. The demand for *chonsei* is still strong, given very low out-of-pocket expense on the part of renters (plus no tax liability against the benefit from local public services). In terms of the user cost, *chonsei* is the lowest, followed by ownership and hybrid rental lease. In addition, *chonsei* lending (i.e., two year loans to finance the *chonsei* deposits) has rapidly expanded, which has made *chonsei* more attractive relative to other tenure types (owning and hybrid rental). Going forward, it is a key policy issue to manage a soft landing for the ongoing transition from the *chonsei*-based system to a more transparent monthly rental system.

10.4.2 Mortgage lenders

The pro-cyclical behavior of mortgage lenders has long been recognized as an amplifier of real estate cycles in the US[14]. In Korea, a similar lending behavior was more pronounced in the construction lending sector, which will be discussed in the next section. In the residential mortgage lending, however, such pro-cyclical lending appears to be less obvious, possibly due to the lending restrictions imposed by government from the outset of the expansion of mortgage lending. Nonetheless, there are several characteristics of the lenders that are worth discussing.

The first issue is the allocation of the risks associated with mortgage lending. Market-based mortgage lending was very limited prior to the 1997 Asian Financial Crisis (Cho and Kim, 2011). The mortgage lending sector was dominated by the National Housing Fund (NHF) and the Korea Housing Bank, which was later privatized and then merged to Kookmin Bank (KB), to become the largest commercial bank in Korea. The average loan amount was small, and the typical LTV ratio was 30% or less. Non-price mechanisms were used to ration credit among potential borrowers. Then mortgage lending rates were deregulated in phases, and this deregulation was completed after the AFC.

Commercial banks then shifted their operational focus from business lending to consumer lending, as the demand for loans by the corporations fell as

---

[14] For example, as early as the 1930s, Hoyt (1933) depicted 30 steps of real estate boom-busts in Chicago from 1833 to 1933, in which the pro-cyclical credit supplies by lenders were shown to be the key contributors to the heightened market volatility.

a result of corporate restructuring, which required the lowering of leverage. The banks quickly became dominant players in the market for credit cards and residential mortgage markets. A positive outcome of this shift was the extension of loans to marginal borrowers, making home purchase more affordable to them. However, a negative consequence was that most lending risks, particularly the interest rate risk, were transferred to the borrowers. That is, for a long while, banks offered short-maturity adjustable rate mortgages (ARMs) with pre-payment penalties, assigning both upside and downside interest rate risks to the borrowers. Regarding credit risk, lenders have been fairly conservative and have used relatively low LTV caps to keep credit risks low. Devising an appropriate risk-sharing mechanism among the private lenders, the guarantors and the borrowers for both credit risk and interest rate risk remains a challenge.

The second issue is the relationship between funding mechanisms and the composition of the loan products. Figure 2.3 has shown that there is a negative correlation between the share of ARMs and the share of capital market funding of mortgages. Bank deposits remain the primary source of funds for residential mortgage lending, however, although MBS-financing by the Korea Housing Finance Corporation (KHFC) has been increasing in recent years. Government has been encouraging lenders to increase their supply of long-term fixed-rate mortgages (FRM) to enhance the stability of the mortgage lending sector.

In June, 2011, the Financial Supervisory Committee assigned mortgage lenders a specific target to increase the share of FRM loans in the mortgage debt outstanding to 30% by 2016. It also assigned higher risk weights for non-amortizing ARMs in computing the regulatory capital. Substantial progress has been made since then, so that the share of FRM rose to 18% by 2013. In order to raise the share of FRMs further, the wholesale funding through MBS, covered bonds or other debt-financing instruments should be increased.

It remains to be seen how the lending market, on both the supply side and the demand side, will adjust to FRMs under a high and volatile interest rate environment (e.g., before the AFC in Korea and early 1980s in the US), as opposed to a low and stable interest rate environment (e.g., the post-GFC period). According to the US experience, FRM has been the product of choice by market participants, especially when the lending rates were low and stable (e.g., the 3-6-3 rule for lenders in 1950s and 1960s – paying 3% for deposits, lending at 6%, and gaining a 3% spread), whereas ARM gained popularity when the rates were high and volatile. Given the short history of market-based mortgage lending in Korea (mostly in the low rate environment in 2000s), it appears to be necessary for policymakers to strategize to find an optimal composition between ARM and FRM under different interest rate scenarios.

The third point concerns the regulation of mortgage lending to enhance for housing market stability. The primary tools employed in Korea are ceilings on LTV and DTI, introduced during the housing price boom in the early- to mid-2000s. An effective policy mix can be considered which combines these tools with other that apply to the portfolio management side (e.g., exposure limits, low reserves, risk weights in computing regulatory capital) (Crowe *et al.*, 2011; Kuttner and Shim, 2013).

10.4.3   Developers, builders and the boom-bust in project finance (PF)

Developers are known for their myopic decision-making. Their behavior, and the inherent inefficiency due to construction time lag, may amplify construction cycles (Wheaton, 1999). In Korea, there are two additional institutional characteristics that make the home building industry a critical contributor to housing price and output cycles. First, the pre-sale system makes it more likely to overinvest in development projects when market conditions are favorable, often resulting in a large inventory of unsold new housing units when the market turns around.

Second, the division of development projects into two phases, each undertaken by separate business entities, with the initial phase of permit acquisition, financing, land development, and marketing, separate from the phase of actual construction, amplifies housing cycles. This current practice of separation began after the AFC. Prior to 1997, construction companies used to purchase land and construct housing with loans, and then market the completed housing units. After the AFC, construction companies tried to reduce the risks from development projects by becoming contractors, to separate developers who purchase land with project financing (PF). The problem is that these developers are small and poorly capitalized. Hence, they depend too much on debt financing with a guaranty by the contractors.

There is a moral hazard problem with the developers who have a minimal stake. The excess supply of housing and the outbreak of the global financial crisis led to the failure of many projects that started with PF financing during the housing boom, imposing financial trouble on the contractors, who had to repay the loans taken by the developers with their guaranty. Many contractors, and several mutual savings banks, went bankrupt. This episode is referred to as the real estate PF lending crisis.

The fallout of the PF lending boom-bust was severe. As shown in Figure 10.11, the number of so-called "zombie companies", with revenue smaller than their debt servicing requirements, has risen greatly after the 2009 GFC, both in absolute numbers and as a percentage of publicly-listed construction firms, reaching a level that was higher than what prevailed after the AFC.

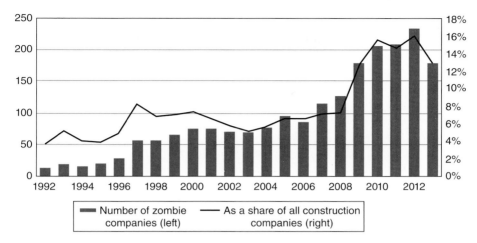

Figure 10.11 Share of "zombie" companies among listed construction firms, 1992–2012. *Source*: Korea (Enterprise Credit) Ratings.

There are several other contributing factors to the boom-bust in construction financing. First, the large scale housing development projects in the Seoul Capital Region, known as the second-generation new towns projects, were not as successful as the first-generation new towns developed in the early 1990s. The main reason was that the demand was weak, due to the poor access to Seoul and, hence, the projects were not profitable, leading to the failures of developers and financiers. Second, the multiple phases of development project discussed earlier incentivized the small developers to take excessive risks with maximum leverage, making the early stage of the projects an extremely high-risk-high-return business. Going forward, various policy remedies are being considered to make the construction sector more efficient and more stable, with such measures as requirement of proper capital on developers, and risk-ratings of large construction projects.

10.4.4 Central bank

For a long time, the Bank of Korea (BOK), the nation's central bank, was an outsider in housing policy in Korea. During and after the AFC, however, BOK played a critical role by instituting two regulatory changes which facilitated the expansion of residential mortgage lending. First, it liberalized the lending rates and the deposit rates charged by the financial institutions, based on a long, gradual process of deregulation that started in 1991 and accelerated after the AFC. Second, it lifted the restrictions on real estate lending by commercial banks and other financial institutions in February 1998, almost immediately after the outbreak of the AFC. Prior to this policy

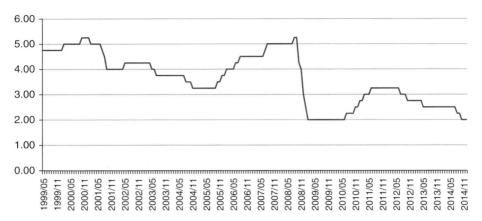

Figure 10.12   The base interest rate set by the Bank of Korea.
Source: Bank of Korea.

move, banks were not allowed to make loans to finance land purchases or the purchases and construction of houses that exceed 100 square meters of floor space. Taken together, the two deregulations strongly induced the major commercial banks (CBs) and non-bank deposit-taking financial institutions to enter the mortgage-lending business.

BOK adopted inflation targeting in 1998 and used the *call rate* as the major instrument until it switched to the *base rate*, starting from March 2008. During the housing boom of the early 2000s, BOK closely monitored the behavior of housing prices, in conjunction with inflation and household debt, in setting the interest rate. Although BOK raised the policy interest rate during the 2005–2007 housing boom, it is not clear whether housing prices were a major factor affecting the BOK's monetary policy decisions. Figure 10.12 shows the trend of the policy interest rate of the bank. The bank's monthly statements of its interest rate policy decisions, the trend of the price and the trading volume of housing are discussed in the context of overall prices, but often in a way that is inconsistent with the decisions over the interest rate adjustment. Thus, it appears that housing price is a factor, but not a critical one, for the BOK's monetary policy decisions.

After the global financial crisis, two particular policy areas emerged, in which BOK, along with other regulatory authorities, can play a bigger role. The first is macro-prudential regulation, aimed at ensuring the overall stability of the financial system, rather than financial soundness of individual FIs, by preventing housing-driven systemic shocks. The second is consumer protection designed to protect financial consumers from fraudulent and other improper lending practices. Discussions as to who will be in charge for each policy regime, as well as what policy instruments should be utilized on both the demand-side and the supply-side of the lending system, are still at an early stage in Korea. Currently, the Financial Service Commission is responsible for the regulations of loan-to-value (LTV) ratios and of debt service-to-income (DTI) ratios on consumer credit.

Another area in which the BOK is increasingly interested is monitoring the size and composition of household debt. The current level of aggregate household debt, which is about 1000 trillion KRW (US $1=1100 KRW), as of September 2014, is considered excessive and detrimental to speedy economic recovery. Household debt consists of consumer loans collateralized by housing (mortgage loans and home-equity loans) and other loans without collateral. The former comprises only about 60% of the household debt issued by banks and non-bank deposit-taking financial institutions, while the remainder includes line of credit on savings accounts. About one-half of the loans collateralized with housing are used for home purchases, and the rest is used to finance working capital and other funding needs.

Nevertheless, the concern over the sheer size of the household debt operates as an obstacle in expanding home mortgage service to more marginal borrowers, in order to enhance financial inclusion. Many market observers speculate that relaxing residential mortgage underwriting criteria (by raising the LTV caps, for example) would exacerbate risks in the consumer lending sector. Thorough research is warranted for each segment of the sector, such as credit card debt, home mortgage sector, and non-residential mortgage sector.

10.4.5 Central government

Traditionally, the Ministry of Construction (MOC), currently called the Ministry of Land, Infrastructure and Transport (MOLIT), has played a leading role in the making of housing policy, but the Economic Planning Board (EPB), which is currently a part of the Ministry of Finance and Strategy (MOSF), and other government agencies were also involved in making decisions on significant housing issues. For example, EPB coordinated the two million units construction initiative described above. In recent years, the Ministry of Finance and Strategy (encompassing the functions of Ministry of Finance and Economic Planning and Budget) has been involved in coordinating housing policy, as well as setting real estate taxation policies. The Financial Service Commission (FSC) is responsible for mortgage lending restrictions and other financial sector-related policies and regulations. The Korea Housing Finance Corporation, which was established in 2004 as a government-owned corporation, is in charge the secondary mortgage market, by issuing mortgage backed securities (MBS) with its own guaranty, as well as providing guaranty on reverse mortgages (called housing pension).

MOLIT is still in charge of regulating the housing market, the National Housing Fund, and other policies towards the real estate industry, including the REITs and real estate brokerage. As regulator, the Ministry sets and implements various regulations, ranging from land development to the pricing and allocation of new housing to eligible households. This heavily interventionist approach into the housing market is believed to have made housing supply very inelastic with respect to price.

MOLIT also controls the Korea Land and Housing Corporation (LH), which is charged with large-scale land development and the construction and management of public rental housing, as well as the Korea Housing Guarantee Corporation, which provides guaranty on pre-sold new housing units. NHF, the government housing fund, is being restructured to cover both the financing of housing on demand-side and supply-side and urban re-development projects. NHF has been instrumental in enhancing mortgage affordability in recent years through the introduction of new innovative products, such as the shared appreciation mortgage (SAM) in 2013, which was well accepted by the market. MOLIT launched a pilot program of demand-side housing subsidy in 2014, which was due to become a regular program starting in 2015.

10.4.6   Local governments

Local governments have not been major players in Korean housing policy. Housing policy was the purview of central government for decades. Local governments were vested with some limited power over urban planning, but they had no initiative of their own in housing policy. Until 1995, the heads of local governments (mayors and provincial governors) were officials appointed by the central government, rather than elected through popular votes. Although local government officials have been directly elected since then, and more power has been given to local entities in various areas, their role in housing policy remains limited and passive. Nonetheless, some large local governments have instituted their own housing programs. For example, the Seoul Metropolitan Government (SMG) introduced a small housing voucher program and directly supplied affordable housing units via the Seoul Housing Corporation (SH), which is the policy arm of SMG for housing development and allocation. SMG has also used its urban planning powers to require redevelopment projects to provide public rental housing.

The linkages between the housing sector and local government finance are also weak. Unlike the US and many other countries, Korean local governments have little discretion over local taxes, as rates and tax bases are determined by the central government. The first tier of local governments (i.e., Seoul, the six next largest cities and provincial governments) collect acquisition and registration taxes. Second tier local governments (i.e. autonomous districts of Seoul and six other cities, cities and counties) collect property holding tax. Transactions-related taxes comprise the largest share of tax revenue of the first-tier local government, but the contribution of these taxes varies with fluctuations in the housing market. Local property holding tax represents a small share of revenue of the second-tier local government. On the expenditure side, the housing budget comprises a very small share of total budgets (for example, it was 3.8% in 2014 for Seoul).

10.5   Looking ahead: Korean housing at a crossroads

Given the ongoing transitions in the housing market and in the economic and social environment surrounding it, housing policies should address several key challenges. First, the focus of housing policy should shift from the government-driven land and housing development, to targeted housing programs to enhance the housing welfare of low-income and the disadvantaged. In particular, public rental housing, and housing vouchers tailored for old age groups, might be needed, considering the rapid population aging and expected rise in poverty among the elderly. The location and the design of public rental housing targeted to the elderly should accommodate the tendency of aging in place.

Second, ways should be found for utilizing real estate assets held by the elderly to supplement their income to finance their retirement. This is most relevant in Korea, in which 82% of wealth held by persons 70 years of age or older is in real estate, 42% in primary residence, 30% in non-residential properties, and 10% in non-residing homes. Unlocking home equity via reverse mortgage, and ensuring stable cash flow from income-generating real estate via professional asset management enterprises (e.g., REITs), are candidates for policy focus to mitigate economy-wide shocks from population aging.

Third, affordable housing finance products should be developed, along with proper risk assessment and risk-sharing arrangements, to assist home purchases by low- and moderate-income families. To that end, innovative financing arrangements (e.g., Shared Appreciation Mortgage (SAM) and Equity Sharing Mortgage (ESM)) can be considered.

Fourth, reforming the private rental housing sector in structural transition is an important task. Specifically, proper market infrastructure for monthly rental system should be developed, including fair market rent, and risk control mechanism for delinquency on monthly rents. In addition, the *chonsei* system should be made efficient and transparent by incentivizing the non-registered *chonsei* suppliers to register, and by imposing proper taxation scheme on rental income.

Finally, policies toward housing market stabilization should be considered in the context of managing "excessive" volatility in price and quantity cycles, which can inflict systemic risk onto the macroeconomy. To that end, specific market indicators, along with their thresholds to trigger policy actions, can be designed. In addition, governance structure for macro-prudential regulations should also be developed, as well as effective policy mixes in dealing with market volatility.

Part V
Conclusions

11

Overall Findings and Outlook for East Asian Housing

11.1 Distinctive characteristics of East Asian housing systems

11.1.1 East Asian housing cycles differ significantly from Western cycles

The original impetus of the present study was to understand how East Asian housing cycles might differ from US and other Western housing cycles. In the process, we expected also to identify the most significant individual features of each of these six systems.

A practical motivation is that the six East Asian housing systems of China, Japan, South Korea, Taiwan, Hong Kong and Singapore produce about one third or more of the world's annual housing output in value terms, out of some 188 countries, based on the number of countries that were members of the IMF in 2014[1]. Therefore, it is productive to fill the gaps in our understanding of the behavior of these six housing systems. Looking at six countries in a genuinely comparative manner has helped us to differentiate country idiosyncrasies from common behavioral elements. As Asian research continues to progress rapidly, and policy needs keep diversifying, we hope that the present study will motivate individual readers to sharpen their own

---

[1] The share of the six East Asian economies in total world investment in current US dollars has varied from 30% to 36.4 % between 2000 and 2013 (*IMF World Outlook Database*, 2014). The share of housing in national investment varies by country and over time. The housing share of total national investment is higher in middle- and high-income countries than in low-income countries. This is why we expect the EA share of global housing to be at least 30% of global housing investment.

Dynamics of Housing in East Asia, First Edition. Bertrand Renaud,
Kyung-Hwan Kim and Man Cho.
© 2016 John Wiley & Sons, Ltd. Published 2016 by John Wiley & Sons, Ltd.

analytical understanding of each of these six East Asian housing systems, and that they will contribute further to our shared understanding of each.

Our results show that, during the global housing boom of 1995–2007, both the duration and depth of EA cycles have differed significantly from Western markets. Due to an apparently better degree of market pricing efficiency, the duration of the East Asian housing booms has been much shorter, and the degree of mean reversion to longer term price trends has been faster, than comparator US markets. Comparisons of China with the five other EA housing cycles are constrained by data coverage that is limited to the past decade only.

The second finding is that the operations of EA housing systems are marked by a higher degree of government intervention than in Western housing markets, in the three key areas of land use regulations, taxation, and housing finance. However, the range of housing policy experiences is still wide across the six systems. The highest degree of intervention is in Singapore. At the other end of the housing policy spectrum, Taiwan has been following a distinctive policy of non-intervention in housing markets. Once the institutions of the Taiwanese housing sector were put in place nationally, notably through the national constitution itself, local governments played a leading role, in contrast with the leading role of central governments in the other five East Asian economies.

Another important difference between East Asian and Western housing systems during the great housing boom of 1995–2007 are the early experiments with of macroprudential policies and current account surpluses, in response to negative regional experiences during the 1997–98 Asian Financial Crisis. These macroprudential policies have mitigated the pro-cyclicality that has been strongly in evidence in countries like the USA, Spain and Ireland between current account deficits and financial vulnerabilities, during the global housing boom of 1995–2007. Being only a comparative analysis of the six EA housing systems, the investigation did not extend to the major global issue of how these successful defensive East Asian policies have also contributed to the large imbalances that played a major role in the GFC (Wolf, 2014).

The correlation of house price movements across East Asian cities appears to have increased during the GFC, over what it was during the AFC. Movements in GDP and in private credit provision show comparable patterns with those of housing prices in each country. The greater housing price correlation across the six economies during the GFC probably reflects expanding channels of contagion through the globalization of financial markets, as well as greater trade and supply chains integration across Asia. The cyclical analysis also suggests that regional spillovers effects may have been developing during the last decade, and that a "China effect" may have affected housing prices in Hong Kong, Singapore and Taiwan, but the early evidence remains mixed (Kim and Park, 2013, 2014).

To improve our understanding of cyclical differences between EA and western housing systems, we have examined the individual impacts on each housing system of the 1997–98 Asian Financial Crisis (AFC) and the 2007–2009 Global Financial Crisis (GFC). During the AFC, housing prices in Hong Kong and Singapore experienced the deepest downturns, followed by Seoul and Tokyo. During the GFC, housing prices in all six EA primate cities fell. The ranking of markets by depth of housing price, declining from the most pronounced to the shallowest, was: Singapore, Hong Kong, Tokyo, Beijing, Seoul, and Taipei. All six capital cities show a fast price recovery after the GFC.

11.1.2   The foundations of East Asian housing systems were laid during the growth take-offs

There is a unity of analysis in the comparison of the six East Asian housing systems. First, they share three characteristics that differentiate them from Western economies and have played a major role in their urbanization. These are: very high rural and national population densities; a deep Sinical heritage, which has had a lasting impact on public and private institutions and norms of public and private behavior[2]; and the role of the "developmental state" during their growth take-off decades.

In addition, the individual experience of the six East Asian economies fits well the modern research on growth and development that distinguishes two main stages in the long-term development of an economy: first, a rapid growth take-off stage, then a steady-state growth stage, when an economy becomes fully urbanized and turns into a high income economy. Between these two stages lies a critical growth transition that the first five East Asian economies were actually *the only ones* to cross successfully in the post-World War II era among all developing economies. The sixth East Asian economy, China, is only now going through this politically and economically difficult and risky transition.

The growth take-off stage, with its strong dimension of "catching up" with Western high-income economies, went particularly well across East Asia but, seen in a global context, this stage is the easier part of long-term development. The reason why the "middle-income trap" has not been avoided by other countries is that *"as successful policies change the conditions that originally made them successful, at some point they can become counterproductive and must be reversed.[3]"* Outside the five East Asian economies, the political and economic elites that emerged during the rapid

---

[2] *"China was the first world civilization to establish a non-patrimonial modern state, which it did some eighteen centuries before similar political units appeared in Europe"* (Fukuyama, 2014, p. 10).
[3] Albert O. Hirschman, quoted in Pettis (2014b).

take-off have strongly resisted these needed institutional and policy reforms. It is too early to tell whether China will manage its growth transition successfully. Frequently voiced expectations of China's economic convergence with past East Asian experiences are not a foregone conclusion.

It is during the high growth take-off stage that East Asian cities have moved from a slow pre-industrial von Thünen urban dynamics based primarily on agricultural markets with high transportation costs and limited economies of scale, to a new Krugman urban economic geography based on industrialization, economies of scale and rapidly falling transportation and communication costs, promoted by public infrastructure investment policies. Rapid industrialization and rapid urbanization have been the two sides of the same development coin in East Asia, because rapid increases in labor productivity and rising labor incomes have fueled the demand for urban housing.

In each of the six economies, we have shown the rapid transition from traditional vernacular housing to organized real estate and housing markets during the growth take-off stage. Given the path dependency of institutions, we also found that the institutional organization of each housing systems that emerged during the take-off retains considerable explanatory power on how these housing systems work today. However, the development of housing institutions was far from identical across different countries. During the post-World War II era, East Asian countries adopted very significantly different housing strategies that have left their marks on today's housing systems.

Four very distinct housing strategies were adopted across East Asia during the period 1950–1980. In order to support rapid industrialization, Japan and South Korea adopted housing policies of household demand redirection and relative under-investment in housing. These policies can be seen as a modified version of the policy priorities of a war economy in the Japan of the 1930s, and the desire to achieve the fastest rates of industrialization. Under their new communist regimes, China and North Korea adopted the central planning's view of housing as a social good to be distributed by the state.

The two precarious city economies of Singapore and Hong Kong implemented policies of large-scale public housing programs in order to provide labor force stability in a small open economy. However, these housing policies were quite different again. In Singapore, large-scale public housing programs were designed to remedy private market supply failures and to support a deliberate strategic choice of creating a new nation of home-owning citizens. In contrast, in Hong Kong, the successful public *rental* housing programs had started with a historical accident (the Christmas Eve fire of 1953), and remained a pragmatic choice of the British colonial administration, which was merely aiming to stabilize a labor force of immigrants. The result is that Hong Kong still has today a dual housing system, with a massive public rental sector that once represented as much as 50% of the entire housing stock and remains over 30% today.

Alone in East Asia, Taiwan followed non-interventionist housing policies, relying on market mechanisms. The foundations of these policies are embedded in the national constitution. The exceptional development policies for the times implemented by Taiwan in the 1960s made this strategic housing choice possible and successful.

The "catch-up" industrialization that is behind the growth take-off stage of most countries led, in East Asia, to exceptionally high rates of urbanization. The resulting pressures on the emerging real estate markets of fast growing East Asian cities led, towards the end of the high growth take-off, to the highest rates of land price appreciation in the history of these countries. What has been happening to land prices in China during its great housing boom of 1998–2012 is comparable to what had happened in Japan, South Korea and Taiwan several decades earlier, but Chinese land price inflation has been amplified by the institutional legacies of the central planning era.

Because all five East Asian economies successfully managed their growth transition past the middle-income stage of about $13,000 *per capita* in PPP dollars, they have now reached a high-income status, and real estate assets have now become the largest asset class in these economies. At that stage, mismanaging this asset class can become extremely costly, as in the case of Japan during its massive real estate boom and bust of 1985–1991. The outcome has been a new and severe "balance-sheet recession", which was poorly understood, and led to two decades of very slow growth and low deflation (Koo, 2009). The level of Japanese land prices has yet to recover back to what it was in 1985, before the start of the boom, as seen in Chapter 5.

11.1.3   The behavior of the six drivers of housing cycles differs in China and in Korea

To understand better the drivers of East Asia housing cycles and to complement the quantitative analysis of cycles of Chapters 7 and 8, we have focused later on the six key actors that shape all housing cycles: households, mortgage lenders, developers-builders, the central bank, the central government, and local governments. To contain the length of this analysis, we chose two contrasting housing systems in terms of stage of urban development: China and Korea.

The rationale for selecting China was two-fold. First, there is great interest in understanding how the six players in the first market-based Chinese housing cycle might adjust to the housing correction that is expected to follow the great housing boom. Second, China's economy has now grown so large that the interactions between housing and the performance of the wider economy have systemic impacts on the global economy. The transfer of resources from rural areas to cities that characterizes the stage of the growth take-off of a country was particularly massive and fast in China, where cities and their housing systems grew exceptionally rapidly during the great housing boom of 1998–2012, which is when the spillover effects on global commodity markets reached their peak.

The behavior of the six drivers behind a housing boom has differed in China from Western market experiences, because the Chinese economy is still undergoing multiple transitions from plan to market. The great housing boom of 1997–2012 has not led to a national bubble, because of the great diversity of city conditions. China has a population that is 4.3 times larger than that of the USA, and cyclical conditions have varied significantly across the various tiers of the Chinese system of some 660 cities. Evidence of bubbles after 2005 has been found only in a limited number of large eastern cities where there has been rapid industrialization. During the housing correction that started in late 2013, "lower tier" cities are the main concern, because of supply-driven overinvestment in housing, but housing price bubbles have not yet been tested for them. Since the fundamental housing reforms of 1998, the national share of rental housing has become very small, and is about 15%. While there is no normative economic rationale for an optimal housing tenure balance between owning and renting, international experience suggests that the unusually very low share of rental housing in China will probably be an amplifying factor in future Chinese housing cycles.

Structural legacies from the central planning era still differentiate the Chinese housing cycle from other East Asian cycles. These structural legacies affect four major areas and have contributed to the significant deterioration of access to housing for the majority of the Chinese urban population. The corporate structure and the privatization of SOEs after 1998 has played a major role in the rapid deterioration of the urban income distribution in favor of the very highest income group which, in turn, has skewed the housing supply in favor of high-priced housing units. The discriminatory *hukou* registration system also prevents access to housing and other important urban services, such as education and health services for about one-third of the population actually present in the largest cities. The spatial structure of Chinese cities, and the efficiency of land markets and urban planning policies, are also significantly affected by the major difference in property rights between rural land and urban land. The extraordinary scale of Beijing's new Seventh Ring, with its 900 kilometers of roads, illustrates the unique dynamics of spatial development of Chinese metropolitan areas.

Finally, Chinese local government incentives, resulting from flawed intergovernmental fiscal relations, have played a leading role in the great housing boom, an outcome that differs profoundly from the five other EA housing cycles and also Western experiences, where local governments played a limited role. It is the behavior of local governments that primarily explains the paradox of Chinese *overinvestment* in housing – especially after 2005 – which is coexisting with financial repression policies comparable to those that have led, in Japan and Korea, to *underinvestment* in housing. Given the leading role played by local governments and by high-net-worth households in China's great housing boom, even a large housing price correction is not expected to induce an economy-wide recession, given the large fiscal reserves of the central government and the financial reserves of the central bank. These, and the net worth of high-income households where national wealth is concentrated, can act as buffers to sharp declines in land and housing prices.

Korea's housing experience contrasts with that of China in many important ways. First, Korea is now a fully urbanized, high-income economy. Korea's share of urban population was 90% in 2012 when China had just reached its 50% marker. Korea's *per capita* GDP in PPP dollars is projected by the IMF to equal, and then overtake, that of Japan before the end of the decade, rising from PPP$35,400 in 2014 to around PPP$46,500 (IMF, October 2014). Meanwhile, China is projected to move from PPP$12,900, in 2014, to around PPP$19,000.

Housing is now a major sector of the Korean economy, whose performance is closely linked to that of the wider economy. However, Korean housing cycles have, historically, been led by macroeconomic conditions, rather that the reverse, in contrast to China after 2005, Japan during its 1995 boom, and many Western economies during the global housing boom of 1995–2007. Now that Korea is a fully urbanized economy, the share of total (real estate plus civil engineering) construction investment in GDP has been gradually declining since the 1990s, to about 13% in 2013.

Real estate assets are by far the largest asset class in the Korean economy, representing 74% of total Korean national wealth in 2011, compared with 35% or less in the USA. The dominance of real estate assets in the economy explains the unusually strong emphasis on housing price stability in Korean government policies, with some administrations going as far as aiming at zero real housing price movements. Contrary to public sensitivity and Korean media reports, housing price volatility in Korea has been quite low compared to the five other East Asian housing systems and to other OECD countries.

The Korean housing tenure breakdown in the 2010 census was 61.3% owners and 38.7% renters. Among the different possible forms of landlord-renter relationships, the Korean rental market is entirely dominated by small individual landlords owning a small number of rental units. There are no large private corporate landlords in Korea, and the share of public rental housing remains quite low. However, because of the prevalence of the unusual Korean *chonsei* rental contracts, which are driven by the asset value of the rented property, this large Korean rental market does not exercise the stabilizing influence on the price of housing services than one would expect from Korea's tenure breakdown.

In contrast with other housing systems, where rental markets are priced according to familiar monthly rental contracts, in Korea rents have been more volatile than housing prices. The paradoxical and puzzling result is that Korea is an economy of a low dispersion of housing price volatility, which coincides with an extremely high degree of social sensitivity to housing price movements. Too many, and too frequent, policy interventions in Korea have made supply very inelastic, which was also shown in our KDI monograph using a set of indicators that affect supply responsiveness. However, Korea's housing price volatility was moderate. This raises the question of whether demand shock in Korean housing market was smaller than that elsewhere. It is, indeed, a puzzle.

In contrast to this low degree of *price* volatility, the annual *output* of new housing units has been historically volatile in Korea over the past four decades. This outcome can be explained by the individual performance of each of the six players in the housing cycle. Until the financial liberalization of 1975, which overlapped with the 1997 AFC, the central bank essentially played no active role in housing and real estate investment. The driving force in housing output cycles was the central government, through its Ministry of Construction (MOC) and its various avatars over time. Until the political and democratic reforms of the 1980s, local governments played an entirely passive role in housing. Up to now, their housing role remains minimal, even in the local supply of social rental housing.

Until 1997, household finance in Korea was monopolized by two "special circuits" housing finance institutions, which also fell under the direct control of MOC. Thus, the Korean government had achieved a high degree of control over the three key pillars of a housing system, through control over urban land supply, the supply of mortgage finance, and a tightly regulated real estate industry. Unfortunately, and quite different from Singapore, there was no close integration in Korea between housing policies and macroeconomic policies. In fact, communications between MOC, which was relying on physical planning criteria, and the economic ministries, led by the Economic Planning Board were mostly *ad hoc* and occasionally adversarial. There was, however, a national consensus in favor of a tight regulation of urban land supply, which has led to a very inelastic housing supply.

It was only after the 1997 AFC that private commercial banks entered the Korean mortgage finance market. To this day, these mortgage lenders fund their loans with retail deposits, and remain portfolio lenders, holding their mortgage loans on their balance sheets. The role of residential mortgage securitization remains small. The mortgage market has deepened, and the share of outstanding loan to GDP is currently on the OECD trend line of mortgage market depth in relation to *per capita* income. The public institutions that emerged during Korea's urban growth take-off before 1980 still control the real estate development process today. The Land and Housing Corporation (in its present corporate form since 2009) still controls the supply of multi-family housing, which is the essential type of new housing supply. The high degree of government intervention in housing that was very high during the decades of rapid urbanization still remains high today. Also, because the ROK government has neither the risk incentives, nor the ability to forecast housing market conditions in a timely and stable way, the short-term dynamics of Korean housing policies is casually described as a "hot-bath-cold-bath" approach.

The two cases of China and Korea show that an explicit focus on the incentives and behavior of the six drivers of housing cycles yields important insights into these drivers and into the leading sources of housing price and output volatility over time. The country chapters on Japan, Taiwan, Hong Kong and Singapore have also suggested what a six-player analysis might reveal more precisely about the balance of forces shaping each country's specific housing cycles. A recurring conclusion across the six country analyses is that each of these six East Asian housing systems has reached another new crossroad, through the joint impact of domestic structural changes and the rebalancing of the global economy in the aftermath of the global financial crisis. In closing, we therefore outline five new structural factors shaping the outlook for East Asian housing.

11.2 Issues and outlook for East Asian housing systems

Structural issues cloud the outlook of the six East Asian housing systems, and create considerable uncertainty about the future of the economies within which these housing systems operate. These issues include: population aging; increasing income and wealth inequality; high levels of debt; slower economic growth as "the new normal," with even some international discussions of a global secular stagnation; and climate change and environmental sustainability issues accentuated by the high East Asian urban densities.

These five structural issues are interactive, and they also have country-specific dimensions. Unraveling these interactions amounts to a broad new research agenda. In these concluding comments, we can merely suggest how these structural changes are likely to individually affect East Asian housing cycles. These structural changes point to a different macroeconomic and housing future, where quality indicators will matter as much as, if not more than, quantitative ones.

These structural changes will trigger some rather radical departures in strategies and policies. Sooner or later, East Asia housing systems, and the broader economies within which they operate, will also develop new institutional arrangements. Different, and more suitable, socio-economic performance indicators are likely to emerge and be used for policymaking. Such trends are already suggested by the search for more suitable alternatives to GDP indicators (Stiglitz *et al.*, 2014). Some economists have warned about "the tyranny of growth" to refer to an excessive policy focus in East Asia on quantitative GDP growth rate figures, rather than on the quality of growth (Eichengreen, 2014).

11.2.1   *Population aging: East Asia steps into the unknown*

East Asia is one of the three main engines of the global economy, along with Western Europe and North America. East Asia is also the region of the world with the most rapidly aging population. Almost no population growth is projected for the East Asia region between 2014 and 2030, with an absolute decline to a smaller population projected by 2050 (Population Reference Bureau, 2014). In Western Europe, "aged" population conditions exist also, especially in Germany. Across Eastern Europe and Russia, absolute population declines are uniformly projected, with the modest exception of the Czech Republic. In contrast, Sub-Saharan African has the youngest and most rapidly growing population.

Population aging is a gradual structural change that is difficult to reverse, and has major long-term implications for the internal organization and performance of East Asian housing systems. Because it is so gradual, population aging is still not integrated into macroeconomic analyses, and is only addressed in special-purpose analyses. However, should we not expect multiple impacts of aging that are directly relevant to macroeconomic management? For housing, should we not expect housing booms to become less frequent, and of smaller amplitude, wherever population aging is occurring? Should we not also expect smaller volumes of new annual housing output, together with a significant restructuring of the existing housing stock?

What differentiates East Asia from other regions of the world are the speed and the magnitude of the demographic changes that have been occurring, especially in Japan, which is leading the world into this unknown territory in which entirely new policies are needed. What has, so far, been unique to Japan, but now seems to be happening also to the rest of East Asia, is the speed of aging. An "aging" society is defined as having at least 7% of its population older than 65. An "aged" society has more than 14% of its population above 65. It took only 24 years for Japan to move from "aging" to aged. In contrast, for Germany it took 40 years to transit from aging to aged, it took 47 years to the UK, and it took 115 years for France, which had been the first society to reach the "aging" stage, in 1864 (Akihiko, 2006).

Demographic comparisons across the six East Asian economies require a joint look at the three drivers of aging in a given society: first, declining total fertility rates (TFR); second, increases in life expectancy; and third, variations in birth and death and rates, which create differences in age cohorts that cause baby booms and echo booms, and also the reverse over time. These cohort variations in birth rates and death rates might be seen as generating fluctuations along the long-term trends dominated by total fertility rates and life expectancy.

After rising steeply during the 1960s and 1970s, the East Asian "demographic dividend" that was a major component of the very rapid growth take-offs has now transitioned into a "demographic deficit", with very sharp turning points in dependency ratios around 2010 across all of East Asia, and much earlier in Japan *circa* 1990.

The *composition* of East Asian populations is changing very rapidly by world experience. As Table 11.1 shows, total fertility rates (TFR) have been falling sharply across the six countries, well below the replacement rate of 2.1 that would stabilize the population. Two important drivers of falling TFRs are the critical impact of the status of women, and the structure of East Asian economies, where a low share of households in aggregate consumption suggests relatively stringent household living conditions for a given *per capita* income of the economy. The other major dimensions of population aging are high and rising life expectancies, due to steadily improving health conditions. Simply put, East Asians have fewer and fewer children, and live longer and longer. The net effect is a rapidly rising share of people older than 65 (Table 11.1) and the falling ratio of the active labor force available to support the rest of the population.

Table 11.1   Population aging across East Asia, 1970–2014.

		1970	1980	1990	2000	2005	2010	2013
Total fertility rate (person)	China	5.5	2.6	2.3	1.7	1.7	1.6	1.60
	Japan	2.1	1.8	1.5	1.4	1.3	1.4	1.40
	Korea (Rep. of)	4.5	2.8	1.6	1.5	1.1	1.2	1.20
	Hong Kong	3.4	2.0	1.3	1.0	1.0	1.1	1.10
	Singapore	3.1	1.7	1.9	n/a	1.3	1.2	1.20
	Taiwan	n/a	2.5	1.8	1.7	1.1	0.9	1.10
Share of population aged 65 and over (%)	China	4.0	5.2	5.9	7.0	7.6	8.2	10.0
	Japan	7.0	9.0	11.9	17.2	19.9	22.7	26.0
	Korea (Rep. of)	3.3	3.9	5.0	7.3	9.3	11.1	12.0
	Hong Kong	3.9	5.9	8.7	11.0	12.2	12.7	15.0
	Singapore	9.9	4.7	5.6	7.4	8.5	9.0	11.0
	Taiwan	2.8	4.4	6.2	8.6	9.7	10.7	12.0

Sources: World Health Organization and Population Reference Bureau.

Japan has been leading East Asia, and the world, in the speed of its population aging. Its population started shrinking by the census of 2005. Japan's demographic conditions foreshadow a startling demographic future for the rest of East Asia. Japan's TFR had already fallen below the replacement TRF of 2.1 early in the 1970s (Table 11.1). On the other hand, Japan also has the world's highest overall life expectancy at birth, of 84.6 years in 2012, with women outliving men by several years. The number of Japanese under the age of 60 peaked in 1985, and has since dropped by more than 17%. There are now only as many Japanese under the age of 60 as there were half a century ago, in the year 1960. In 2014, Japan had the large percentage of population above 65 in the world, at 26%.

Since 2005, Japanese government statisticians have been dividing people over the age of 90 into three separate categories: 90–94, 95–99, and 100+. At the end of 2010, there were about 1.4 million Japanese who were at least 90 years old, and about 44 000 who were at least 100 years old. Most striking of all, however, is the disappearance of young Japanese. The number of Japanese under the age of 15 has already collapsed by more than 40% since 1980. In January 2015, the number of births in Japan fell to the lowest value on record, of 1 million. The number of deaths increased to 1.27 million and outnumbered the number of births by the widest margin ever. The Japanese rate of rural population decline is particularly fast, and is still falling.

In 2013, Taiwan had the lowest total fertility rate in the world, followed by Portugal and then Hong Kong, Singapore and South Korea – all with TFRs very close to that of Taiwan's. Across East Asia, life expectancy is close to Japan's and consistently above 80 years, with the exception of China at, 76 years in 2012. The net impact of the resulting aging is a working age population that is shrinking throughout East Asia, with the most extreme case found in Japan, where the absolute size of the working population is already back to what it was in 1950. The decline in working age population is now accelerating in Taiwan, Korea and also in China, where the size of the labor force began shrinking in 2012. One likely consequence is an increase in the labor-force participation of women, and also a rise in their employment status, especially in South Korea and in Japan, where female participation rates are the lowest by far among OECD countries (Nakone and Steinberg, 2012; Toshiaki, 2010).

In a discussion that focuses directly on demographic changes and macroeconomic performance, Nishimura (2011) makes a series of important observations that apply not only to East Asia, but also globally: "*There is a remarkable correlation between asset market bubbles that cause macroeconomic crisis and demographical changes. Japan, the United States, Spain and Ireland are examples of countries affected by a financial crisis. In these countries, the formation of bubbles in asset markets seems to have coincided […] with a growing ratio of working population to the non-working (dependent) population."* Conversely, *"busts in asset markets seem to happen when this ratio declines noticeably. The bubble we have experienced coincided closely with the turning point in demographic trends. We are in the midst of a balance sheet adjustment process after the worldwide financial bubble burst, at a time when the population is aging. This is not the balance sheet adjustment of the past, which took place when the population was young and growing. This is a balance sheet adjustment when the demography is rapidly tilting toward the old. [...] With the change (though gradual) in one of the long-run macroeconomic fundamentals [...] macroeconomic policy challenges are also likely to have changed accordingly. Current sophisticated mainstream macroeconomic models are not particularly suited to examining the brute force of demographic factors, globalization and aging on asset prices as stores of value"* (Nishimura, 2011; Ito and Rose, 2010; and Akihiko, 2006).

Continuing population expansion has been the underlying assumption of economics until now. Does rapid population aging simply means that existing economic analyses and policy formulae merely have to be run in reverse? Looking at Japan, is there now a fundamental analytical and policy discontinuity between what needs to be done during the decades of rapid aging years of a country, and the next period of actually shrinking population? The far-reaching socioeconomic structural transformations caused by this unprecedented demographic change of a shrinking population remain largely unknown policy territory. Demographic projections for South Korea are that it will enter the shrinking population stage before 2020.

Population aging raises new questions about shifts in the demand for housing services and the demand for housing assets. In terms of housing services, how does aging affect the composition of the housing stock and the balance between new housing supply and the retrofitting of the existing housing stock for aging in place? In terms of portfolio composition, what will, or should be, the balance between housing assets and financial assets in funding retirement when the ratio of active population to older population falls rapidly, to levels never experienced in the past? At the same time, longer life expectations creates periods of retirement of much longer lengths than in the past, which creates concerns about the depletion of retirement assets. Also, how do these effects vary across age cohorts and across income deciles? Are we likely to observe sharper intergenerational conflicts of interest over housing? Will the wealth accumulation needed to finance retirement become much longer, partly because the rate of appreciation of housing assets is slowing down, in sharp contrast to past decades?

How will the portfolio choices between financial assets and real estate assets be affected by the prospect of long periods of aging after retirement? What might be the choices between slowly appreciating domestic housing assets and foreign financial assets with better rates of return? These choices have a new dimension that is different from earlier decades, because the global economy is now an integrated system of open economies. Portfolio choices between these two broad asset classes are likely to be easier to make for the upper income deciles that already have the largest and the most diversified portfolios. The ability of the other household deciles to unlock their housing wealth through reverse mortgages and other forms of lease-back arrangements is a challenge for every East Asian economy. Then, among the lower income deciles, the supply of housing for the elderly poor is a policy issue that particularly sharp in the East, and particularly acute in countries like Korea, where the share of elderly poor aged over 65 years is already among the highest in the world.

The earliest quantitative evidence on the *incremental* impact of aging on real estate prices comes from Japan over the past 35 years (1976–2010) across its 47 prefectures. This 35-year period includes the baby boom of the 1970s, the echo boom of the late 1980s, and the rapid demographic aging, with the stunning rise of the old-age dependency ratio of people older than 65 to the population aged 20–64. Nationally, the impact of aging on real estate prices over that 35-year period is estimated at –3.7% per year. Spatially, the negative impact of aging on real estate prices has been most pronounced in rural areas (Saita *et al.*, 2014). This negative incremental impact of aging on housing prices strongly suggests that younger generations will have lower expectations than their parents regarding housing price appreciation.

11.2.2   *Worsening income and wealth inequality*

Inequality became a major policy issue in the aftermath of the Global Financial Crisis, when it worsened in many high-income economies. Prevailing concerns have been heightened by new long-term cross-country findings reported by Piketty and his colleagues in 2014. In addition to its immediate social dimensions, there are two leading questions about the impact of inequality: one is economic, the other is political. First, what are the links between rising inequality and the increasing fragility of economic growth: does inequality impair the growth of an economy? Second, does inequality also impair the effective governance of a society?

Recent analyses at the IMF, based on the best available comparative data, suggest that high levels of net inequality (after adjusting for the effects of redistributive policies) do, indeed, impair economic growth by making it more volatile and less sustainable (Ostry *et al.*, 2014). On the other hand, income redistribution programs designed to mitigate high levels of inequal-ity do not affect growth negatively, except at the very tail end of the country distribution, when they reach quantitative extremes. Ostry *et al.* (2014) find that the old academic view (Okun, 1975), that there is a "big trade-off" between equality and efficiency or equity and growth, does not seem to be supported by the available evidence.

Does inequality undermine effective public governance? And does rising inequality corrode the quality of public institutions and policies? Recent analyses of global experience with governance argue that there is no empirical support for the frequent claim that the median voter is decisive in political choices (Beesley and Persson, 2011). On the other hand, evidence shows that inequality limits the demands for social action which, over time, reduces the capacity of the state to act and weakens its legal capacity, fiscal capacity, and capacity to deliver public goods. Beesley and Perrson also find evidence that, from time to time, the values of citizens can shift markedly. How can a capitalist society avoid becoming a democracy for an insignificant minority of the very rich? This is a growing worldwide debate.

Inequality has increased across the six East Asian societies during the past quarter-century, whether it is measured by Gini coefficients or by the ratio of the top to the bottom income deciles. This new phenomenon contrasts with the growth take-off decades before 1980, when East Asian economies grew very rapidly and maintained a low degree of inequality. Taiwan even succeeded in achieving very high growth rates while actually improving its income distribution. Today, rising income inequality is not limited to the case of China, where the national income distribution has become comparable to the USA, which itself is the worst case of income and wealth inequality among high-income economies.

Income inequality has risen in the high-income economies of the Hong Kong SAR, South Korea, Singapore and Taiwan, especially after the GFC (Balakrishnan *et al.*, 2013). China and Hong Kong have the worst record in East Asia. Based on its census data, Hong Kong's Gini coefficient of its income distribution has worsened from, 0.43 in 1971 to 0.537 in 2011. This increase of 25% is very large for a high-income economy (Chen, 2014), which raises the question of the possible relationship between rapidly rising inequality and the Hong Kong SAR's flawed governance structure, inherited from its colonial past, with the continuing dominance of a small oligopoly of large corporations?

However, the level of inequality remains the lowest in East Asia among the main regions of the world. Also, China's impressive growth performance over the past three decades has made the greatest contribution to the decline in global absolute poverty. What causes some concern is that increasing income and wealth inequality might make it more difficult to sustain growth throughout East Asia over the long term, and also that the quality of governance will erode.

The main channel of increasing *income* inequality in East Asia has been the structure of labor markets. The structural factors behind rising income inequality differ across the six East Asian economies. In Japan and in Korea, two labor market dualities are important (Hirayama, 2011; Katz, 2014). One duality is the presence of very high productivity and capital-intensive giant international firms, like Sony and Samsung, coexisting with a large number of low-productivity SMEs, where almost 90% of the population works. The other duality is the rapid increase in short-term contracts, part-time workers and temporary employees, especially since the 1997 Asian Financial Crisis.

In China, the interactions between SOEs reforms after 1998, and the Hukou system, have been discussed in Chapter 9. In Taiwan, the transformation of production and supply chains across Asia is leaving a growing segment of the labor force with stagnant wages (Liu and Shih, 2013). In Singapore, with the shift to the production of high value-added goods and services during the past decade, "*the bottom three income deciles have experienced real income decline. The next two deciles have hardly experienced any real income growth* [...] *Stagnation for the bulk of the workforce has been accompanied by the rise of the superrich, with the incomes of the top 1–2% especially rising very sharply*" (Bhaskaran *et al.*, 2012). Social mobility "has declined and is no longer adequate." In contrast to Hong Kong, Singapore has fully developed parliamentary institutions, and there is a governance concern that "*coherent policies that all segments of society can rally behind will become much more difficult to achieve* [...] *as different income groups begin to see their interests as competing and conflicting.*"

The distribution of *wealth* is more skewed than that of income. A major channel of wealth inequality in East Asia is housing and the real estate sector. As already noted in the case of Korea, real estate represents a very high percentage of total private assets across East Asia. Recent East Asian magnitudes of the share of housing in total household wealth are 78% in Korea, 46.5% in Japan, and 47% in Singapore. Comparative magnitude in Western economies around 2010 are over 70% (including other real estate) in France, over 55% in the UK, over 40% in the Netherlands and about 35% in the USA (OECD (*Factbook*), 2012, 2013a, 2014). During the growth take-off decades, the real, risk-adjusted return to housing assets was the highest in East Asian economies. Historically, the ability to own urban housing has played a central role in the accumulation of wealth, usually with intra-family assistance, because mortgage markets took a long time to develop.

The diversification of East Asian household portfolios away from real estate into financial assets was constrained by public financial policies and the relatively late development of public and private pension systems. Usually, only the top two income deciles have developed relatively diversified asset portfolios. It is also within these upper income deciles that owning two or more houses is frequent. The tenure breakdown between owners and renters at the national level and within large cities is merely a suggestive initial indicator of the degree of wealth inequality. It should also be remembered that the burst of the Japanese real estate bubble in 1991 caused very large wealth losses for households, which has been an important factor in the chronically weak Japanese consumer demand, and now in the housing demand as well. In Asia, the Singaporean society has the most diversified household balance-sheets between housing and financial assets.

11.2.3 *Rising household debt levels across East Asia*

There were five main drivers in the run-up of household debt that occurred before the Global Financial Crisis of 2007: financial liberalization and deregulation; financial innovation and the loosening in credit standards; the decline in borrowing costs; the global housing price boom; and the rise in income inequality, where high income households invested heavily in housing, while middle- and lower-income households accumulated debt to gain access to housing ownership as housing prices rose (Hunt, 2014).

What was unexpected is that the level of household debt has continued to rise across East Asia and in most OECD countries since 2007. Presently, mortgage loans remain the main component of housing debt, representing more than 80% of total household debt in most OECD countries – often 90% or more. As its indebtedness rises, the household sector becomes increasingly sensitive to changes in income and interest rates, which modify the debt-income ratio through which the impact of such shocks is amplified. Because high levels of household debts are directly linked to housing price movements, these may also amplify economic downturns.

Conditions vary across the six EA economies. In Korea, for instance, household debt collateralized by housing represents just over 50% of total household debt. In addition, only half of these loans collateralized by housing are for home purchases. Therefore, only 25% of household debt is directly related to housing market. Many small business owners rely on so-called housing loans for working capital, or for big ticket consumption, such as college tuition.

Differences in the degree and composition of financial leverage of each East Asian economy, as a ratio to GDP in mid-2014, are shown in Table 11.2. Japan and Singapore are two of the most highly leveraged economies in the world. However, their source of indebtedness is quite different. Japan's government debt has risen sharply during the two lost decades, as the government fruitlessly attempted to stimulate the economy through public spending, funded by domestic debt. This process has now reached its feasible financial limits. Meanwhile, Japanese households have been steadily deleveraging since the severe housing price bust of 1991, in order to rebuild their badly damaged balance sheets. Japan now has one of the least leveraged household sector in East Asia, with China. In contrast, Korea and Taiwan have the most leveraged household sectors in East Asia. For comparison, Table 11.2 provide the level and composition of leverage in the real economies (excluding financial institutions) of Canada, Germany and the USA. Most of the data, including the global averages presented in Table 11.2, are

Table 11.2 East Asia, financial leverage by sectors (percentage of GDP, 2014Q2).

	China	Japan	South Korea	Singapore	Taiwan	Canada	Germany	USA	Global
Households	38	65	81	76	86	92	54	77	40
Non-financial corporations	125	101	105	201	141	60	54	67	56
Government	55	234	44	105	41	70	80	89	58
Real economy leverage	217	400	231	382	268	222	188	233	154

Sources: McKinsey Global Institute: Global Debt Report, February 2015; Central Bank of the Republic of China (Taiwan), 2013Q4.

based on a 2015 study of the dynamics of debt in 47 economies throughout the world (22 advanced and 25 developing economies) in the aftermath of the Global Financial Crisis of 2007 (McKinsey Global Institute, 2015).

In contrast to Japan, the cause of high leverage in the Singapore economy is the non-financial corporate sector, which is a source of productivity and growth. Singapore also has the highest share of homeowners in East Asia, at 90%, which explains the aggregate leverage of the household sector. Housing loans represented 74% of total household liabilities in 2014Q3. The balance of 26% of household debt consisted of credit card debt and car loans. However, Singaporean household balance sheets are healthy, and total household net wealth represents more than 380% of GDP in 2014Q3, with property assets representing slightly less than half (at 47%) of total household assets – because, as noted, Singapore has the most diversified household balance sheets in Asia. To prevent excessive household debt leverage, Singapore has permanently introduced the Total Debt Servicing Ratio (TDSR) as part of its macro-prudential framework (MAS, 2014).

What matters for financial sector stability is the total size of household debt and the aggregate debt-income ratio for the household sector. On the other hand, for social stability and social cohesion, the distribution of household debt across household income deciles is most important, especially as income inequality is rising. Worsening social problems, income inequality, and aging interact, as well. This phenomenon is gathering momentum in East Asian and other countries where social protection and pension systems are not well developed. The situation is particularly serious in South Korea, where 45% of people older than 65 fell below the poverty line in the mid-2000s (OECD, 2013b; Jones and Urasawa, 2014). In Japan and in the USA, the percentages of poor old people were 22.0% and 22.4%, respectively. The situation was significantly better in Canada (5.9%), Germany (8.4%) and France (8.8%). This is one of the reasons why significant institutional changes should be expected in East Asia.

11.2.4 Slower GDP growth as the "new normal"

Discussions of slower global economic growth as "the new normal" dominate the media. These discussions are fed by the secular decline of nominal and real growth rates in the largest Western economies, and in Japan since the 1970s. The core of the argument is that, to compensate for shrinking work forces, labor productivity rates would have to rise sharply to generate growth rates matching historical ones. Then, some economists strongly argue that an acceleration in innovation is unlikely to generate these needed gains in productivity (Gordon, 2012).

The performance of the Chinese economy will play a central role in the "new normal", because China's contribution to global GDP growth, which was only 5% in the early 1990s, has now grown to 40% since 2010. The ongoing rebalancing of China's economy toward greater consumption demand, as well as a better spatial distribution of economic activities, will have a widespread impact across East Asia and globally. The internal rebalancing will not happen at the exceptionally high growth rates of the first decade of the 21st century during the great housing boom. Regaining control over the high level of public, private and financial sector debt accumulated during the period 2007–2104 will lead to slower economic growth.

Globally, the new normal is likely to be characterized by six chronic conditions: a deficient aggregate demand; stagnant productivity; fragile financial conditions; unstable politics; tense geopolitics; and an overload of challenging issues (Wolf, 2015). Such an environment might stimulate East Asian societies to redefine what constitutes social and economic well-being and social progress for policy making (Stiglitz *et al.*, 2014). In earlier decades, East Asian societies prioritized high GDP growth rates. However, with the combined impacts of the 2007 Global Financial Crisis, population aging, and economic and environmental disruptions of various sorts, there are increasingly frequent debates about the continuing merits of "organizing a government's policy strategy around numerical targets for economic growth" (Eichengreen, 2014).

11.2.5   Green growth differences between developed and emerging East Asian cities

Looking at our global environmental future, Nobel Prize winner George Akerlof wrote recently: *"There are two inconvenient truths. The first is global warning itself. The second is that we aren't yet telling ourselves the stories that compel us to combat it"* (Akerlof *et al.*, 2014). The integrated policy treatment of economic policies and environment policies remains a work in progress at the decision-making level, even if there is now a widespread awareness of environmental issues among the general public because of the very high population densities of East Asia. Because most of economic growth now originates in cities, issues of green economic growth and urban green growth are coterminous. However, the actual contents of "urban green growth" policies have to differ markedly between the five high-income East Asian societies that are fully urbanized, and middle-income China, which is now going through its peak rates of urbanization. China has announced ambitious plan to push for smart cities. One point is that EA countries, including China, have a strong information and communication technology base, which can help to better manage urban services and infrastructure.

The basic categories of environmental issues are essentially the same across East Asia. They cover: energy; transport and land use; energy-efficient (green) buildings (especially in Singapore); and the management of solid waste, water pollution and air pollution. Actions to reduce the negative environmental externalities of economic growth and the impact on natural resources and environmental services, and also to lower the long-term costs to the economy of national environmental policies, will differ across East Asia, depending on the level of urbanization. The ability to retro-fit the existing physical infrastructure of the large developed cities of Japan, Korea, Taiwan and parts of urban China will be financially much more costly than managing the development of the new parts of Chinese cities. There will be wider options for urban form and land use planning in the new urban areas of China (OECD, 2013b, 2013c).

East Asian cities and their metropolitan areas may be at the cutting edge of green growth, but they cannot meet their economic and environmental goals entirely on their own. They need the support of higher levels of government to thrive over the long run. This means that issues of bureaucratic incentives, risk and information arise, across levels of government and, horizontally, across government units. Unsurprisingly, in Singapore, where these problems of intergovernmental coordination are minimized, because there is essentially only one level of government, there is a long experience in the systemic coordination of macroeconomic policies and urban policies. Already, considerable progress has been made in facing the new problems of green high-density urban development and redevelopment (Widness, 2013). As a result, Singapore is one of the important experimental laboratories for East Asia on managing green growth in high-density cities.

11.2.6   *Far-reaching East Asian reforms appear inevitable*

The five interactive trends that have just been sketched out strongly suggest that the successful East Asian economies of the future will be those that are able to implement far-reaching social, economic and financial reforms addressing these new issues. East Asian definitions of social well-being and social progress will be different, and so will be the measurement indicators. Because the political reform process will not be easy, the sooner this process starts, the better are the chances of long-term success. Because housing assets are, by now, such a massive component of the total wealth of every East Asian economy, the restructuring of the housing sector will have to be a major component of these far-reaching reforms.

Improving the governance of the housing sector and consensus building in designing and implementing housing reforms will be a major task. As a result of aging, worsening inequality and the slowdown of growth, conflicts of interests among income groups, age groups, and regions over housing policy will be more difficult to reconcile. One dimension of the new housing governance will be the leading role of cities and large metropolitan regions in modifying the old policy paradigms, which have traditionally been dominated by central governments in East Asia. However, cities cannot do it alone, and they will need the positive support of these central governments yet, as fiscal resources become scarce, the room for central government action will be constrained. Successful East Asian societies will, therefore, be those that can properly restructure their intergovernmental relations. To develop a new housing policy governance, there is also a clear need to improve the dialogue between macroeconomists and policymakers (including the central bank) on the one hand, and housing and urban professionals and policy makers on the other.

References

Abraham, Jesse M. and Patric H. Hendershott (1996). Bubbles in metropolitan housing markets. *Journal of Housing Research* **7**, 191–207.

Adelman, Irma and Cynthia Taft Morris (1967). *Society, Politics & Economic Development: A Quantitative Approach* The Johns Hopkins University Press, Baltimore, MD.

Ahuja, Ashvin, Lillian Cheung, Gaofeng Han, Nathan Porter and Wenlang Zhang (2010). *Are house prices rising too fast in China?* IMF Working Paper 10/274: http://www.imf.org/external/pubs/ft/wp/2010/wp10274.pdf.

Aizenman, Joshua and Yothin Jinjarak (2008). *Current account patterns and national real estate markets*. NBER Working Paper 13921. Cambridge, MA.

Aizenman, Joshua and Yothin Jinjarak (2013). *Real estate valuation, current account and credit growth patterns, before and after the 2008–9 crisis*. NBER Working Paper 19190 : http://www.nber.org/papers/w19190.

Aizenman, Joshua, Menzie D. Chinn and Hiro Ito (2010). *Surfing the waves of globalization: Asia and financial globalization in the context of the trilemma*. NBER Working Paper 15876 : http://web.pdx.edu/~ito/w15876.pdf.

Akamatsu, Kaname (1961). A theory of unbalanced growth in the world economy. *Weltwirtschaftliches Archiv* **86**(1), 196–217.

Akerlof, George A., Paul Krugman, Robert Solow, Michael Spence and Joseph E. Stiglitz (2014). Looming ahead. *IMF Finance and Development* **51**(3), 14–19.

Akihiko, Matsutani (2006). *Shrinking Population Economics. Lessons from Japan.* International House of Japan, Tokyo.

Allen, Franklin and Douglas Gale (2000). *Comparing Financial Systems.* MIT Press, Cambridge MA.

Allen, Franklin, Jun Qian and Meijun Qian (2008). China's Financial System: Past, Present and Future. In: Brandt, L. and Rawski, T. (eds) *China's Great Economic Transformation.* Cambridge University Press, Cambridge MA.

Allen, Franklin, Jun Qian, Chenying Zhang and Mengxin Zhao (2012). China's financial system: opportunities and challenges. (NBER Capitalizing China Project): http://www.nber.org/chapters/c12071.pdf.

Alloway, Tracy (2011, June 07). China's uncollateralised, cash flow-less, local government loans. *Financial Times:* http://ftalphaville.ft.com//2011/06/07/586896/chinas-uncollateralised-cash-flow-less-local-government-loans/.

Ambrose, Brent W. and Joe Peek (2008). Credit availability and the structure of the US homebuilding industry. *Real Estate Economics* **36**(4), 659–692.

Ambrose, Brent W. (2009). *Housing after the fall: reassessing the future of the American dream.* IRES Working Paper. Institute for Real Estate Studies, Pennsylvania State University, State College, PA.: http://merage.uci.edu/ResearchAndCenters/CRE/Resources/Documents/Ambrose.pdf.

Ambrose, Brent W. (2010). The homebuilding industry: how did we get here. *Institute for Real Estate Studies, Real Estate Research at Penn State* **2**: http://www.smeal.psu.edu/ires/realestateresearchatpennstate-2.pdf.

André, Christophe (2010). *A bird's eye view of 18 OECD housing markets.* OECD Economics Working Paper 746. Paris.

Dynamics of Housing in East Asia, First Edition. Bertrand Renaud,
Kyung-Hwan Kim and Man Cho.
© 2016 John Wiley & Sons, Ltd. Published 2016 by John Wiley & Sons, Ltd.

André, Christophe, Rangan Gupta and Patrick T. Kanda (2012). *Do house prices impact consumption and interest rate? Evidence from OECD countries using an agnostic identification procedure.* (OECD Economics Working Paper 947. Paris. http://www.oecd-ilibrary.org/economics/do-house-prices-impact-consumption-and-interest-rate_5k9d192klphd-en.

Aregger, Nicole, Martin Brown and Enzo Rossi (2012). *Can a Transaction Tax or Capital Gains Tax Smooth House Prices?* University of Berne.

Atkins, Ralph and Keith Fray (2013). *Rapid Fall in Capital Flows Poses Growth Risk.* Mckinsey Global Institute, January 6. http://www.mckinsey.com/insights/global_capital_markets/financial_globalization.

Authers, John (2010). *The Fearful Rise of Markets: Global Bubbles, Synchronized Meltdowns and How to Prevent Them in the Future.* Financial Times Press, London.

Aziz, Jahangir (2006). *Rebalancing China's economy: what does growth theory tell us?* IMF Working Paper WP/06/291: http://www.imf.org/external/pubs/ft/wp/2006/wp06291.pdf.

Balakrishnan, Ravi, Chad Steinberg and Murtaza Syed (2013). *The elusive quest for inclusive growth: growth, poverty, and inequality in Asia.* IMF Staff Working Paper WP/13/152. Washington, D.C.

Ball, Laurence, David Furceri, Daniel Leigh and Prakash Loungani (2013). *Distributional effects of fiscal consolidation.* IMF Working Paper 13/151. Washington, D.C.

Ban, Sung Hwan, Pal Yong Moon and Dwight H. Perkins (1982). *Rural Development (Studies in the Modernization of the Republic of Korea, 1945–1975).* Harvard University Press, Cambridge, MA.

Bardhan, Ashok, Robert Edelstein and Cynthia Kroll (2011). *Global Housing Markets: Crises, Policies, and Institutions.* John Wiley and Sons, Hoboken, NJ.

Bhaskaran, Manu, Ho Seng Chee *et al.* (2012). *Inequality and the Need for a New Social Compact.* Background paper presented at Singapore Perspectives 2012, Institute of Policy Studies, Lee Kwan Yew school of Public Policy, National University of Singapore, Singapore.

Batchvarov, Alexander *et al.* (2003). *Merrill Lynch Guide to International Mortgage Markets and Mortgage Backed Securities.* Merrill Lynch, London.

Beesley, Timothy and Torsten Persson (2011). *Pillars of Prosperity: The Political Economics of Development Clusters.* Princeton University Press, Princeton, NJ.

Beim, David O. and Charles W. Calomiris (2001). *Emerging Financial Markets.* McGraw-Hill, New York.

Bernanke, Ben S. (2004). *The Great Moderation.* Remarks at the meetings of the Eastern Economic Association, Washington D.C., February 20. http://www.federalreserve.gov/boarddocs/speeches/2004/20040220/default.htm.

Bernanke, Ben S. (2010). *Monetary Policy and the Housing Bubble.* Speech at American Economic Association Meetings, January 3. http://www.federalreserve.gov/newsevents/speech/bernanke20100103a.htm.

Bertaud, Alain (1997, August 30). *Urbanization in China: Land Use Efficiency Issues* : http://alain-bertaud.com/AB_Files/AB_China_land_use_report_6.pdf.

Bertaud, Alain and Bertrand Renaud (1994). *Cities without land markets: lessons of the failed socialist experiment world* (Bank Discussion Paper 22, 47). http://www.wds.worldbank.org/servlet/WDSContentServer/WDSP/IB/1994/03/01/000009265_3970716144550/Rendered/PDF/multi_page.pdf.

Bertaud, Alain and Bertrand Renaud (1997). Socialist cities without land markets. *Journal of Urban Economics* **41**(1), 379–400.

Bertaud, Alain, Jan K. Brueckner and Yuming Fu (2009). Managing urban development in Chinese cities. In: Song, Y. and Ding, C.R. (eds). *Smart Urban Growth in China.* Lincoln Institute of Land Policy Press, Cambridge, MA.

Birch, E.L. and Wachter, S.M. (eds, 2011). *Global Urbanization.* University of Pennsylvania Press.

Bird, Richard and Christine Wong (2005). *China's fiscal system: a work in progress.* Working Paper 07-11. University of Toronto Rotman School of Management, Toronto, Canada.: http://papers.ssrn.com/sol3/papers.cfm?abstract_id=875416.

Bourassa, Steven C. and Chien Wen Peng (2011). Why is Taiwan's homeownership rate so high? *Urban Studies* **48**(13), 2887–2904.

Blanchard, Olivier J. and Stanley Fischer (eds, 1992). *NBER Macroeconomics Annual 1992*, 7. MIT Press, Cambridge, MA.

Bloom, David E. and Jeffrey G. Williamson (1997). *Demographic transitions and economic miracles in emerging Asia*. NBER Working Paper 6268. Cambridge, MA.

Borstt, Nicholas (2011, November 1). *China shadow banking primer*. China Economic Watch. Peterson International Economic Institute, Washington, D.C.: http://www.piie.com/blogs/china/?p=587.

Bracke, Philippe (2011). *How long do housing cycles last? A duration analysis for 19 OECD countries*. IMF Working Paper 11/231: http://www.imf.org/external/pubs/ft/wp/2011/wp11231.pdf.

Brandt, Loren and Thomas G. Rawski (eds, 2008). *China's Great Economic Transformation*. Cambridge University Press, Cambridge.

Bristow, Roger (1987). *Land-use Planning in Hong Kong. History, Policies and Procedures*. Oxford University Press, Hong Kong.

Brueckner, Jan K., Jacques Francois Thisse and Yves Zenou (1999). Why is central Paris rich and downtown Detroit poor? An amenity-based theory. *European Economic Review* **43**, 91–107.

Brueckner, Jan K. (1986). A Modern Analysis of Site Value Taxation, *National Tax Journal*, V.39, N.2, March, 49–58.

Brueckner, Jan K. (2011). *Lectures on Urban Economics*. MIT Press, Cambridge, MA.

Brunnermeier, Markus K. and Martin Oehmke (2012). *Bubbles, Financial Crises, and Systemic Risk (Mimeo)*. Princeton University, Princeton, NJ.

Brülhart, Marius and Federica Sbergami (2009). Agglomeration and growth: Cross-country evidence. *Journal of Urban Economcis* **66**(1), 48–63.

Burns, Leland S. and Leo Grebler (1978). *The Housing of Nations: Analysis and Policy in a Comparative Framework*. John Wiley and Sons, New York.

Butler, Stephen B. (2009). Developing land markets within the constraint of state ownership in Vietnam. In: Ingram, G. and Hong, Y.H. (eds). *Property Rights and Land Policies*. Lincoln Institute Press, Cambridge, MA.

Cai, , Hongbin, J. Vernon Henderson and Qinghua Zhang (2009). *China's land market auctions: evidence of corruption*. NBER Working Paper 15067. Cambridge, MA.

Campbell, Sean D., Morris A. Davis, Joshua Gallin and Robert F. Martin (2006). *A trend and variance decomposition of the rent-price ratio in housing markets*. US Federal Reserve Board Finance and Economics WP 2006-29: http://www.federalreserve.gov/pubs/feds/2006/200629/200629pap.pdf.

Capozza, Dennis R., Patric H. Hendershott and Charlotte Mack (2004). An anatomy of price dynamics in illiquid markets: analysis and evidence from local housing markets. *Real Estate Economics* **32**(1), 1–32.

Cargill, Thomas F. and Hal Stewart Scott (2005). Japan's postal savings showdown. *The Financial Regulator* 78–86.

Case, Karl E. and Robert J. Shiller (1989). The efficiency of the market for single family homes. *American Economic Review* **79**(1), 125–137.

Castells, Manuel, Goh Lee and R. Yin Wang Kwok (1990). *The Shek Kip Mei Syndrome. Economic Development and Public Housing in Hong Kong and Singapore* Pion Limited, London.

Chamon, Marcos D. and Eswar S. Prasad (2008). *Why are saving rates of urban households in China rising?* Brookings Global Economy and Development Paper 31.

Chamon, Marcos, Kai Liu and Eswar Prasad (2010). *Income uncertainty and household savings in China*. IMF Working Paper 10/239: http://www.imf.org/external/pubs/ft/wp/2010/wp10289.pdf.

Chan, Nelson (2003). Land acquisition compensation in China-problems and answers. *International Real Estate Review* **6**(1), 136–152.

Chan, Edwin HW and Gilbert Kwok (1999). Foreign participation in housing development in mainland China: legal concerns on property ownership. *Review of Regional and Urban Development Studies* **11**(3), 154–167.

Chan, Kam Wing, J. Vernon Henderson and Kai Yuen Tsui (2008). Spatial dimensions of Chinese economic development. In: Brandt, L. and Rawksi, T. (eds). *China's Great Economic Transformation*, 776–828. Cambridge University Press, Cambridge.

Chan, Su Han, Fang Fang and Jing Yang (2008). Presales, financing constraints and developers' production decisions. *Journal of Real Estate Research* **30**, 345–375.

Chang, C.O. and Chen, M.C. (2011). *Construction Financing in Taiwan: Current State and Policy Regime*. Paper presented at KDI conference: A new housing paradigm, December 6, Seoul.

Chang, Chin Oh and Ming Chi Chen (2012). Taiwan: housing bubbles and affordability. In: Bardhan, A., Edelstein, R. and Kroll, C. (eds). *Global Housing Markets: Crises, Policies, and Institutions.* John Wiley and Sons, Hoboken, NJ.

Chang, Chin Oh and Charles W.R. Ward (1993). Forward pricing and the housing market: the pre-sales housing system in Taiwan. *Journal of Property Research* **10**, 217–227.

Chang, Ha Joon (2007). *The East Asian Development Experience.* MacMillan, London.

Chen, Jie (2010). *A Study on the Reforms of Housing Provident Funds.* Report to China's Ministry of Housing and Urban Development, Beijing.

Chen, Jie (2011). Home mortgage and real estate market in Shanghai. In: Bardhan, A., Edelstein, R. and Kroll, C. (eds). *Global Housing Markets: Crises, Policies, and Institutions.* John Wiley and Sons, Hoboken NJ.

Chen, Jie and Aiyong Zhu (2008). *The relationship between housing investment and economic growth in China: a panel analysis using quarterly provincial data.* WP 2008/17. Uppsala University, Uppsala. http://www.nek.uu.se/.

Chen, Kaiji and Yi Wen (2014). *The great housing boom of China.* Working Paper 2104-022A. Federal Reserve Bank of St. Louis, St. Louis, MO.

Chen, Liyan (2014). Beyond the umbrella movement: Hong Kong's struggle with inequality in 8 charts. *Forbes*, October 08. http://www.forbes.com.

Chen, Ming Chi and Kanak Patel (1998). Housing price dynamics and granger causality: an analysis of Taipei new dwelling market. *Journal of the Asian Real Estate Society* **1**(1), 101–126.

Chen, Nan Kuan and Hung Jen Wang (2003). *Does Collateral Value Affect Business Investment? An empirical study of Taiwan.* The Institute of Economics, Academia Sinica, Taipei.

Chen, Yu Fu, Michael Funke and Aaron Nikolai Mehrotra (2011). *What drives consumption in mainland China? The role of property price dynamics.* (SIRE Discussion Paper 2011-50). (Shorter version as Hong Kong HKIMR paper 15/2011). Scottish Institute for Research in Economics, Glasgow. http://ideas.repec.org/p/edn/sirdps/283.html.

Chen, Yen Jong and Yu Chuan Hsu (2002). *Estimating the Elasticity on the Choice Probability of Taiwan Rental Housing.* Paper presented at the AsRES-AREUEA Joint International Conference, Seoul.

Cheng, Chen (1961). *Land Reform in Taiwan.* China Publishing Company, Taipei.

Chinascope Financial (2012). The main target of China's housing regulations is the home price-to-income ratio. *Chinascope Financial*, April 16. http://seekingalpha.com/article/500181-the-main-target-of-china-s-housing-regulations-home-price-to-income-ratios.

Chinloy, Peter (1993). Elective mortgage prepayment: termination and curtailment. *Real Estate Economics* **21**(3), 313–332.

Chinloy, Peter, Man Cho and Isaac F. Megbolugbe (1996). Appraisals, transaction incentives, and smoothing. *Journal of Real Estate Finance and Economics* **14**, 89–112.

Chiquier, Loic and Michael J. Lea (eds, 2009). *Housing Finance Policy in Emerging Markets.* The World Bank, Washington, DC.

Cho, Lee Jay and Yoon Hyung Kim (1994). *Korea's Political Economy: an Institutional Perspective.* Westview Press, Boulder Co.

Cho, Man (1996). House price dynamic: a survey of theoretical and empirical issues. *Journal of Housing Research* **7**(2), 145–172.

Cho, Man (2012). *Housing Price Dynamics: The East Asian Experiences.* Paper Presented at the KDI Conference on Real Estate Driven Systemic Risk: Country Cases & Their Policy Implications, December 13–14, Seoul.

Cho, Man (2014a). *Social housing development policy in Vietnam: Lessons from the Korean experience and policy recommendations.* KDI KSP Report, April. Korea Development Institute. Seoul.

Cho, Man (2014b). *Enhancing housing affordability: The Korean Case.* KDI School Working Paper, September. Korea Development Institute. Seoul.

Cho, Man (2014). Housing price and mortgage credit cycles: Tales of two countries. In: Wachter, S. Cho, M and Tcha, M.J. (eds). *The Global Financial Crisis and Housing-A New Policy Paradigm*, pp. 82–111. Edward Elgar Publishers, Cheltenham, UK.

Cho, Man and Kyung Hwan Kim (2010). Three pillars of mortgage credit risk management: a conceptual framework and the case of Korea. *Housing Finance International* **24**, 17–23.

Cho, Man and Kyung Hwan Kim (2011). *Housing Sector Reform: Contrasting Real Sector vs. Financial Sector.* KDI-OECD Making Reform Happen Project, Korea Development Institute, May, Seoul.

Cho, Man and Kyung Hwan Kim (2012). Price dynamics in housing markets. In: Smith, S. *et al.* (eds). *International Encyclopedia of Housing and Home*, Vol. **5**. Elsevier, Oxford.

Cho, Man and Kyung Hwan Kim (2012). Mortgage market in Korea: Current state and future challenges. In: Smith, S. *et al.* (eds). *International Encyclopedia for Housing and Home*, Vol. 4. Elsevier, Oxford.

Cho, Man and Son, J.Y. (2014). *Empirical Analyses on Demand-Supply Mismatches in Local Housing Markets of Korea.* Korea Development Institute (in Korean).

Cho, Man and Moon Joong Tcha (2012). *In search of new paradigm in housing policy in the post crisis era.* KDI Research Report. Korea Development Institute, Seoul.

Cho, Man, Cho, Y., Kim, K.H. and Phang, S.Y. (2011). *Housing Supply Elasticity and Housing Price Dynamics: The Case of Global Cities.* Paper presented at the AsRES-AREUEA International Conference, July, Jeju.

Cho, Man, Kyung Hwan Kim and Bertrand Renaud (2012). *Real estate volatility and economic stability: an east Asian perspective.* KDI Research Monograph 2012-1. Korea Development Institute. Seoul.

Cho, Man, Min, I.S. and Kim, H.A. (2012). *Linking Housing Price and Mortgage Credit Cycles: An Investigation via Consumer Credit Index.* Mimeo. Korea Development Institute. Seoul.

Cho, Man, In Ho Song and Hyun Ah Kim (2013). A study on linkages between housing financial and the real sectors. *Housing Studies Review* **21**(2), 5–22. (in Korean).

Cho, Yoon Je (2002). *Financial repression, liberalization, crisis and restructuring: Lessons of Korea's financial sector policies.* ADB Institute Research Paper Series 47.Tokyo.

Choi, Songsu (1998). A housing market in the making: Zhu Ronji jumpstarts China's stalled housing reforms. *China Business Review*, November 1: https://www.chinabusinessreview.com/public/9811/choi.html.

Choy, Lennon Hungtat (2007). *Pricing under information asymmetry: an analysis of the housing presale market from the new institutional economics perspective.* University of Hong Kong, Hong Kong.

Chung, Eui Chul (2010). Consumer sentiment and housing market activities: Impact on sales price of housing. *Journal of the Korea Real Estate Analyst Association* **16**(3). (in Korean).

Clemens, Ulrich, Steffen Dyck and Tobias Just (2011, April 28). *China's Housing Markets: Regulatory Interventions Mitigate Risk of Severe Bust.* Deutsche Bank Research, Frankfurt: http://www.dbresearch.com.

Cole, David Chamberlin and Young Chul Park (1983). *Financial Development in Korea, 1945–1978.* Harvard University Press, Cambridge MA.

Commission on Growth and Development (2008). *The Growth Report, Strategies for Sustained Growth and Inclusive Development.* The World Bank, Washington D.C.: http://www.growthcommission.org/index.php?option=com_content&task=view&id=96&Itemid=169.

Cooper, Jane (2011). China's banking success story spreads across the country. *The Banker*, September 1, London. http://www.thebanker.com/Banker-Data/Banker-Rankings/China-s-banking-success-story-spreads-across-the-country?ct=true.

Cooper, Jane. (2012, April 2). Are China's banks heading for a crisis? *The Banker*, London.

Craig, R. Sean and Chang Chun Hua (2011). *Determinants of property prices in Hong Kong SAR: Implications for policy*. IMF Working Paper WP/11/277. Washington, D.C.

Credit Suisse Equity Research (2010). *Analysing Chinese grey income*. Report of 6 August 2010. Credit Suisse, Asia Pacific/China: www.institutionalinvestorchina.com/arfy/./soft/./1_1732139941.pd.

Crowe, Christopher, Giovanni Dell'Ariccia, Deniz Igan and Pau Rabanal (2011). *Policies for macrofinancial stability: Options to deal with real estate booms*. IMF Staff Discussion Note SDN/11/02 Washington, D.C.

Crowe, Christopher, Giovanni Dell'Ariccia, Deniz Igan and Pau Rabanal (2011). *How to deal with real estate booms: Lessons from country experiences*. IMF Working Paper 11/91 Washington, D.C.

Dang, Tri Vi, Hinglin Wang and Aidan Yao (2014). *Chinese shadow banking: bank-centric misperceptions*. Working Paper 22/2014. Hong Kong Institute for Monetary Research, Hong Kong.

Das, Mitali and Papa N'diaye (2013). The end of cheap labor. *IMF Finance and Development* **50**(2). http://www.imf.org/external/pubs/ft/fandd/2013/06/das.htm.

Davis, E. and Zhu, H. (2004). *Bank lending and commercial property prices: Some cross country evidence*. BIS Working Paper 150, Bazel.

Deacon, T. (1997). *The Symbolic Species: The Co-Evolution of Language and the Brain*. W.W. Norton & Company, Inc., 500 Fifth Avenue, New York, NY.

De Bary, William Theodore (1988). *East Asian Civilizations: A Dialogue in Five Stages*. Harvard University Press, Cambridge MA.

De Bary, William Theodore (1991). *The Trouble with Confucianism*. Harvard University Press, Cambridge, MA.

De Bondt, Werner F.M. and Richard H. Thaler (1994). *Financial decision-making by markets and firms: A behavioral perspective*. NBER Working Paper WP4777. Cambridge, MA.

Demirgüç-Kunt, Asli and Ross Levine (2001). *Financial Structure and Economic Growth*. MIT Press, Cambridge, MA.

Deng, Guoying, Guangliang Ye and Zhigang Li (2012, January 16). *Mortgage rate and the choice of mortgage length: Quasi-experimental evidence from Chinese transaction-level data*. BBVA Research Working Paper WP 2012/02. BBVA Bank.

Deng, Yongheng and Peng, Fei (2008). The emerging mortgage markets in China. In: Ben-Shahar, D., Leung, C.K.Y. and Ong, S.E. (eds). *Mortgage Markets Worldwide*. Blackwell Publishing, West Sussex.

Deng, Yongheng and Peng Liu (2009). Mortgage prepayment and default behavior with embedded forward contract risks in China's housing market. *Journal of Real Estate Finance and Economics* **38**(6), 214–240.

Deng, Yongheng, Joseph Gyourko and Jing Wu (2010a). *Evaluating conditions in major Chinese housing markets*. NBER Working Paper 16189: http://papers.ssrn.com/sol3/papers.cfm?abstract_id=1717036.

Deng, Yongheng, Joseph Gyourko and Jing Wu (2010b). *Just How Risky Are China's Housing Markets?* http:www.voxeu.org/index.php?q=node/5353.

Deng, Yongheng, Joseph Gyourko and Jing Wu (2012). *Land and house price measurement in China*. NBER Working Paper 18403: http://www.nber.org/papers/w18403 Cambridge, MA.

Deng, Yongheng, Randall Morck, Jing Wu and Bernard Yeung (2011). *Monetary and fiscal stimuli, ownership structure, and China's housing market*. NBER Working Paper 16871. Cambridge, MA.

Denison, Edward F., and Chung, William K. (1976). *How Japan's Economy Grew So Fast: The Sources of Postwar Expansion*. The Brookings Institution, Washington, D.C. 267 pp.

Dethiers, Jean Jacques (ed, 2000). *Governance, Decentralization and Reform in China, India and Russia*. Kluwer Academic Press, Netherlands.

Diamond, Douglas Byrnne and Michael Lea (1992). Housing finance in developed countries: An international comparison of efficiency. *Journal of Housing Research* **3**(1).

Dickie, Mure (2005). *China revises up size of economy by 17%. Financial Times*, December 20, http://www.ft.com/intl/cms/s/0/09091ab6-7107-11da-89d3-0000779e2340.html #axzz1v6HuJMIH.

Dietz Dietz, Albert G. H. and Laurence S. Cutler (eds, 1971). *Industrialized Building Systems for Housing*. The MIT Press, Cambridge, MA.

Dikötter, Frank (2010). *Mao's Great Famine: The History of China's Most Devastating Catastrophe, 1958–1962*. Walker & Co., New York.

Doebele, William A. (1982). *Land Readjustment: A Different Approach to Financing Urbanization* D.C. Heath, Lexington, MA.

Dokko, Jane, Brian Doyle, Michael T. Kiley, Jinill Kim, Shane Sherlund, Jae Shim and Van Den Heuvel, S. (2009). *Monetary policy and the housing bubble*. (Finance and Economics Discussion Series 2009–49). Federal Reserve Board, Washinton D.C.: http://www.federalreserve.gov/pubs/feds/2009/200949/200949pap.pdf.

Dore, Ronald P. (1986). *Flexible Rigidities: Industrial Policy and Structural Adjustment in the Japanese Economy*. Stanford University Press.

Dübel, Hans Joachim (2012). *Transatlantic Mortgage Credit Boom and Bust: The Impact of Market Structure and Regulation*. Finpolconsult, Berlin.

Dübel, Hans Joachim (2014). Transatlantic mortgage credit boom and bust-the impact of market structure and regulation. In: Wachter, S., Cho, M. and Tcha, M.J. (eds). *The Global Financial Crisis and Housing – A New Policy Paradigm*, pp. 112–146. Edward Elgar Publishers, Cheltenham.

Duca, John V., John Muellbauer and Anthony Murphy (2011). House prices and credit constraints: making sense of the U.S. experience. *Economic Journal* **121**, 533–551.

Dunkerley, Harold (ed, 1983). *Urban Land Policies, Issues and Opportunities*. Oxford U. Press, published for the World Bank.

Duranton, Gilles (2009). Are cities engines of growth and prosperity for developing countries? In: Spence, M., Clarke-Annez, P. and Buckley, R. (eds). *Urbanization and Growth*. The World Bank, Washington, DC.

Duranton, Gilles (2011). California dreaming: The feeble case for cluster policies. *Review of Economic Analysis* **3** 3–45.

The Economist (2009). The rise of the hybrid company. *The Economist*, December 5. http://www.economist.com/node/15011307.

The Economist (2011). *Building Rome in a day: the sustainability of China's housing boom*. https://www.eiu.com/public/topical_report.aspx?campaignid=china_realestate_wp.

The Economist (2012). Special report on state capitalism. *The Economist*, January 21. http://www.economist.com/node/21542931.

The Economist (2012). Which emerging economies have the most monetary and fiscal wiggle room? *The Economist*, January 28. http://www.economist.com/blogs/freeexchange/2012/01/emerging-economies#comments.

Edelstein, Robert H. and Sau Kim Lum (2004). House Prices, Weak Effects and the Singapore Economy. *Journal of Housing Economics* **13**, 342–367.

Edwards, Sebastian (1987). *Financial deregulation and segmented capital markets: The case of Korea*. UCLA Discussion Paper 432. http://www.econ.ucla.edu/workingpapers/wp432.pdf.

Ehmer, Philipp (2011). *Structural Change in China*. Deutsche Bank Research, February 16. Deutsche Bank, Frankfurt. http://www.dbreasearch.com.

Eichengreen, Barry, Donghyun Park and Kwanho Shin (2011). *When fast growing economies slow down: International evidence and implications for China*. NBER Working Paper 16919. Cambridge, MA.

Eichengreen, Barry, Donghyun Park and Kwanho Shin (2013). *Growth slowdowns redux: new evidence on the middle-income trap*. NBER Working Paper 8673. Cambridge, MA. http://www.nber.org/papers/w18673.

Eichengreen, Barry (2014, May 9). *The Tyranny of Economic Growth*. http://Caixin.com.

Ellis, Luci (2008). *The housing meltdown: why did it happen in the United States?* BIS Working Papers 259. Basel.

Englund, Peter (1986). Transaction Costs, Capital Gains Taxes and Housing Demand, *Journal of Urban Economics* **20**, 274–290.

Englund, Peter and Yannis M. Ioannides (1997). House price dynamics: an international empirical perspective. *Journal of Housing Economics* **6**(2), 119–136.

Erlandsen, Espen, Jens Lundsgaard and Felix Huefner (2006). *The Danish Housing Market: Less Subsidy and More Flexibility*. ECO/WKP(2006)41. OECD. Paris.

Fan, Joseph, Randall Morck and Bernard Yeung (2011). *Capitalizing China*. NBER Working Paper 17687. Cambridge MA: http://www.nber.org/books/morc10-1.

Feenstra, Robert C, Ma Hong, J. Peter Neary and D.S. Prasada Rao (2012). *Who shrunk China? Puzzles in the measurement of real GDP*. NBER Working Paper WP17729 : http://www.nber.org/papers/w17729.pdf.

Fei, John C.H., Gustav Ranis and Shirley W.Y. Kuo (1979). *Growth with Equity: The Taiwan Case*. Oxford University Press, Oxford.

Fernandez-Corugedo, Emilio and John Muellbauer (2006). *Consumer credit conditions in the United Kingdom*. Working Paper 314. Bank of England, London.

Follain, James R. (ed, 1986). *Tax Reform and Real Estate*. Urban Institute Press, Washington, DC.

Forrest, Ray, Misa Izuhara and Patricia Kenneth (2000). Homeownership in Japan's troubled economy. *Housing Finance International* **15**(2), 40–46.

Forrest, Ray and Ngai Ming Yip (eds, 2011). *Housing Markets and the Global Financial Crisis*. Edward Elgar, Cheltenham.

Fostel, Ana and John Geanakoplos (2008). Leverage cycles and the anxious economy. *American Economic Review* **98**(4), 1211–1244.

Fu, Yuming, Siqi Zheng and Rongrong Ren (2011). Housing demand and migrants in Chinese cities. In: Man, J. (ed). *China's Housing Reforms and Outcomes*. Lincoln Institute Press, Cambridge, MA.

Fuest, C., Huber, B. and Nielsen, S.O. (2004). *Capital gains taxation and house price fluctuations*. Working Paper 16. Department of Economics, Copenhagen Business School, Copenhagen.

Fukuyama, Francis (2014). *Political Order and Political Decay*. Farrar, Strauss and Giroux, New York, NY. Second volume on the history of the modern state.

Furceri, David and Prakash Loungani (2013). Who let the Gini out? *IMF Finance and Development* **50**(4). Washington, D.C.

Garg, Subash Chandra (2007). Overview of Urban Infrastructure in India. In: Peterson, G.E. and Annez, P.C. (2007). *Financing Cities, Chapter 3*. Sage Publications, Los Angeles, CA.

Gatzlaff, Dean (1994). Excess returns, inflation and the efficiency of the housing market. *Real Estate Economics* **22**(4), 553–581.

Geanakoplos, John (2010). Solving the present crisis and managing the leverage cycle. *FRBNY Economic Policy Review*, August, 101–131.

Geerolf, Francois and Thomas Grjebine (2013). *House prices drive current accounts: evidence from property tax variations*. CEPREMAP Working Paper 131: http://www.cepremap.fr/depot/docweb1315.pdf.

Geltner, David, Bryan D. MacGregor and Gregory M. Schwann (2003). Appraisal smoothing and price discovery in real estate markets. *Urban Studies* **40**, 1047–1064.

Gerlach, Stefan and Wensheng Peng (2005). *Output gaps and inflation in mainland China*. Hong Kong Institute for Monetary Research Working Papers 20/2005. Hong Kong.

Gill, Inderjit and Homi Kharas (eds, 2007). *An East Asian Renaissance: Ideas for Economic Growth*. The World Bank, Washington, DC.

Gimeno, Ricardo and Carmen Martinez Carrascal (2010). The relationship between house prices and house purchase loans: The Spanish case. *Journal of Banking & Finance* **34**(8), 1849–1855.

Glaeser, Edward L. and Joseph Gyourko (2006). *Housing dynamics*. NBER Working Paper 12787. Cambridge, MA.

Glaeser, Edward L., Joseph Gyourko and Albert Saiz (2008). Housing supply and housing bubbles. *Journal of Urban Economics* **64**(2), 198–217.

Glickman, Norman J. (1979). *The Growth and Management of the Japanese Urban System*. Academic Press, New York.

Gold, Thomas (1986). *State and Society in the Taiwan Miracle*. M.E. Sharpe, Armonk, NY.

Goldstein, Morris and Lardy, Nicholas R. (2004). *What kind of landing for the Chinese economy?* Peterson Institute for International Economics Policy Brief PBO$-07: http://www.piie.com/publications/pb/pb04-7.pdf.

Goodhart, C. and L. Dai (2003). *Intervention to Save Hong Kong: Counter Speculation in Financial Markets*. Oxford University Press.

Goodhart, G. and B. Hofmann (2007). *House Prices and the Macroeconomy: Implications for Banking and Price Stability*. Oxford University Press.

Goodman, John L. (1992). National information systems for decision making in housing and mortgage finance. *Housing Finance International*, **12**(2). http://www.housing finance.org/publications/hfi-archives.

Gordon, Robert J. (2012). *Is U.S. economic growth over? Faltering innovation confronts the six headwinds*. NBER Working Paper 18315. Cambridge, MA.

Gorton, G. (2009). *Securitized banking and run on repo*. NBER Working Papers 15223. Cambridge, MA.

Gramlich, Edward M. (1994). Infrastructure investment: A review essay. *Journal of Economic Literature* **32**(3), 1176–1196: http://www1.worldbank.org/publicsector/pe/pfma06/EdwardGramlich.pdf.

Gramlich, Edward M. (2007). *Subprime Mortgages: America's Latest Boom and Bust*. The Urban Institute Press, Washington, DC.

Greef, Irene and Hass, Ralph (2002). *Housing prices, bank lending, and monetary policy*. http://128.118.178.162/eps/mac/papers/0209/0209010.pdf.

Green, Richard K., Stephen Malpezzi and Stephen K. Mayo (2005). Metropolitan-specific estimates of the price elasticity of supply of housing, and their sources. *AEA Papers and Proceedings* **95**(2), 334–339.

Grenadier, Steven R. (1996). The strategic exercise of options: development cascades and overbuilding in real estate markets. *Journal of Finance* **51**(5), 1653–1679.

Groves, R., Murie, A. and Winston, C. (eds, 2007). *Housing and the Welfare State. Perspectives from East Asia and Europe*. Ashgate Publishing, London.

Guo, Xiaoyang, Liu Hongyu and Zheng Siqi (2011). *Market Power Risk and Liquidity; Empirical Evidence for an Emerging Housing Market*. IRES, Tsinghua University, Paper presented at the Annual International AsRES Conference, July 14, Jeju, Korea.

Gürkaynak, Refet S. (2008). Econometric tests of asset price bubbles: taking stock. *Journal of Economic Surveys* **22**(1), 166–186.

Gyourko, Joseph and David Sinai (2003). The spatial distribution of housing-related ordinary income tax benefits. *Real Estate Economics* **31**(4), 527–576.

Haffner, Marietta and Michael Oxley (2011, July). *House Price Volatility and Taxation*. Paper presented at ENHR Conference, Toulouse.

Hagan-Kuwayama, Patricia (2000, May). Postal banking in the United States and Japan: A comparative analysis. *Bank of Japan Monetary and Economic Studies*, May, 73–104.

Haggard, Stephan and Yasheng Huang (2008). Political economy of private sector development in China. in Brandt and Rawksi (eds). *China's Great Economic Transformation*, Cambridge University Press, Cambridge.

Harding, Don and Adrian Pagan (2002). Dissecting the cycle: a methodological investigation. *Journal of Monetary Economics* **49**, 365–381.

Harding, Don and Adrian Pagan (2006). Synchronization of cycles. *Journal of Econometrics* **132**, 59–79.

Harding, John P, Stuart S. Rosenthal and C.F. Sirmans (2007). Depreciation of housing capital and the gains from homeownership: Estimates from a Repeat Sales Model. *Journal of Urban Economics* **61**, 193–217.

Hartzell, D., Pittman, R. and Downs, D. (1994). An Updated Look at the Size of the U.S. Real Estate Market Portfolio. *Journal of Real Estate Research* **9**(2), 197–212.

Haughwout, Andrew, Donghoon Lee, Joseph Tracy and Wilbert Van der Klaauw (2011). *Real estate investors, the leverage cycle and the housing market crisis.* Staff Report 514. Federal Reserve Bank of New York, New York.

Hausmann, Ricardo, Lant Pritchett and Dani Rodrik (2004). *Growth Accelerations.* NBER Working Paper 10566. Cambridge, MA.

He, Dong (2013). Hong Kong's Approach to Financial Stability. *International Journal of Central Banking*, 299–313.

He, Dong (2014). The effects of macroprudential policies on housing market risks: evidence from Hong Kong. Macroprudential policies: Implementation and Interactions, *Banque de France Financial Stability Review* **18**, 105–119.

He, Jia and Ming Liu (1998). Mortgage Prepayment Behavior in a Market with ARMs. *International Real Estate Review* **1**(1), 64–80.

Hebbert, Michael and Norihiko Nakai (1988). *How Tokyo grows: Land development and planning on the metropolitan fringe.* ST/ICERD Occasional Paper 11. London School of Economics, London.

Herring, Richard J. and Susan M. Wachter (2002). *Real estate booms and banking busts: an international perspective.* Working Papers 99-27. Center for Financial Institutions of Wharton School Center for Financial Institutions, University of Pennsylvania, Philadelphia, PA.

Hilbers, Paul, Alexander W. Hoffmaister, Angana Banerji and Hayian Shi (2008). *House price developments in Europe: a comparison.* IMF Working Paper 08/211. Washington, D.C.

Himmelberg, Charles, Christopher Mayer and Todd Sinai (2005). Assessing high house prices: Bubbles, fundamentals and misperceptions. *Journal of Economic Perspectives* **19**(4), 67–92.

Hirayama, Yosuke (2011). Toward a post-homeowner society? Home ownership and economic insecurity in Japan. Chapter 12 in: Forrest, R. and Yip, N.M. (eds). *Housing Markets and the Global Financial Crisis.* Edward Elgar, Cheltenham, UK.

Ho, Samuel P.S. (1978). *Economic Development in Taiwan: 1860–1970.* Yale University Press, New Haven.

Ho, Sik Ying Petula (2012). Beyond obedience and virtue. *GlobalAsia* **6**(3).

Hong, Yu-Hung and Alven H.S. Lam (1998). *Opportunies and Risks in Capturing Land Values Under Hong Kong's Leasehold System.* Working Paper WP98YH1, Lincoln Institute of Land Policy, Cambridge, MA.

Hong Kong Consumer Council (1996). *How Competitive is the Private Residential Market?* http://www.consumer.org.hk/website/wrap_en2/hse9607/hse_e.htm.

Hong Kong Monetary Authority (2010). *Half-Yearly Monetary and Financial Stability Report.* Hong Kong Monetary Authority, Hong Kong.

Hong Kong Monetary Authority (2014, September). *Monetary and Financial Stability Report.* Hong Kong Monetary Authority, Hong Kong.

Hoyt, Homer (1933). *One Hundred Years of Land Value in Chicago.* University of Chicago Press, Chicago, IL.

Hsing, You Tien (2006). Land and territorial politics in urban China. *China Quarterly* 187.

Hsing, You Tien (2010). *The Great Urban Transformation: Politics of Land and Property in China.* Oxford University Press, Oxford.

Hua, Ching Chun, Chin-Oh Chang and Chengho Hsieh (2001). The price-volume relationships between the existing and the pre-sales housing markets in Taiwan. *International Review of Real Estate Research* **4**(1), 80–94.

Huang, Yasheng (2008). *Capitalism with Chinese Characteristics: Entrepreneurship and the State.* Cambridge University Press, Cambridge.

Huang, Youqin and William A.V. Clark (2002). Housing tenure in transitional China: A multilevel analysis. *Urban Studies* **39**(1), 7–32.

Hui, Eddie Chi Man and Francis Kwan Wah Wong (1999). Housing reform in Guangzhou and Shenzhen, China. *Review of Urban and Regional Development Studies* **11**(2), 141–152.

Hui, Eddie C.M. and Vivian S.M. Ho (2002). *Relationship between the land-use planning system, land supply and housing prices in Hong Kong.* Pennsyvania State University, State College, PA.

Hunt, Chris (2014). Household debt: a cross-country perspective. *Reserve Bank of New Zealand Bulletin* **77**(4), 1–13.

Hurun Report (2011). *The Chinese Millionaire Wealth Report 2011*: http://www.hurun.net/usen/Default.aspx.

Igan, Deniz and Heedon Kang (2011). Do loan-to-value and debt-to-income limits work? Evidence from Korea. *IMF Working Papers* 11/297. Washington, DC.

Igan, Deniz, A. Kabundi, F.N.D. Simone, M. Pinheiro and N. Tamirisa (2011). Housing, credit, and real activity cycles: Characteristics and comovement. *Journal of Housing Economics* **20**, 210–231.

Ingram, Gregory K. (1982). Land in perspective: Its role in the structure of cities. In: Cullen, M. and Woolery, S. (eds). *World Congress on Land Policy, Proceedings*. D.C. Heath, Lexington, MA.

International Finance Corporation, World Bank Group (2007). *Reforming Collateral Laws and Registries: Best Practices and the Case of China*, Washington, DC.

International Monetary Fund (2004). *World Economic Outlook.* International Monetary Fund, Washington, DC.

International Monetary Fund (2010). *Integrating Stability Assessments under the Financial Sector Assessment Program into Article IV Surveillance: Background Material*. Monetary and Capital Markets Department, August 27.

International Monetary Fund (2011). Housing finance and financial stability-back to basics. in *Global Financial Stability Report: Durable Financial Stability: Getting There from Here* International Monetary Fund, Washington, DC.

International Monetary Fund (2011a). *China: 2011 Article IV consultation*. IMF Country Report 11/192. Washington, DC.

International Monetary Fund (2011b). *China: spillover report for consultation and selected issues*. IMF Country Report 11/193. Washington, DC.

International Monetary Fund (2011c). *Consolidated Spillover Report – Implications from the Analysis of the Systemic-5*. Washington, DC.

International Monetar Fund (2011d). *China: Financial system stability assessment*. IMF Country Report 11/321. Washington, DC.

International Monetary Fund (2012a). *China Economic Outlook.* IMF Beijing Resident Representative Office, Beijing. Washington, DC.

International Monetary Fund (2012b). Dealing with household debt. In: *World Economic Outlook.* International Monetary Fund, Washington, DC.

International Monetary Fund (2012c). *People's Republic of China – Hong Kong SAR Staff Report for 2012 Article IV Consultation: Discussions of Main Issues*. IMF Country Report cr13/11. Washington, DC.

International Monetary Fund (2013a). *People's Republic of China – Hong Kong SAR 2012 Article IV Consultation*. IMF Country Report cr11-348. Washington, DC.

International Monetary Fund (2013b). *Key Aspects of Macroprudential Policy – Background Paper*. Washington, DC. http://www.imf.org/external/np/pp/eng/2013/061013c.pdf.

International Monetary Fund (2013c). *Singapore: financial system stability assessment*. IMF Country Report 13/125.Washington, DC.

International Monetary Fund (2014), *World Economic Outlook. Legacies, Clouds, Uncertainties*. October, Washington D.C.

Isham, Jonathan and Daniel Kaufman (1995). *The forgotten rationale for policy reforms: The productivity of investment projects*. World Bank Policy Research Working Paper 1549. Washington, D.C.

Ishikawa, Tomohiro (2011). *Japan's bubble, deflation, and long-term stagnation*. ESRI Research Note 19. Japan Cabinet Office, Tokyo.

Ito, Takatoshi (1992). *The Japanese Economy.* MIT Press, Cambridge, MA.

Ito, Takatoshi and Keiko N. Hirono (1993). Efficiency of the Tokyo housing market. *Bank of Japan Monetary and Economic Studies* **11**(1), 1–32.

Ito, Takatoshi and Tokuo Iwaisako (1995). *Explaining asset bubbles in Japan*. NBER Working Paper 5358. Cambridge, MA.

Ito, Takatoshi and Andrew Rose (eds, 2010). *The Economic Consequences of Demographic Change in East Asia*. NBER-EASE Volume **19**. University of Chicago Press, Chicago, IL.

Jaffee, Dwight M. and John M. Quigley (2008). Mortgage guarantee programs and subprime crisis. *California Management Review* **51**(1), 117–143.

Jisheng, Yang (2010). The fatal politics of the PRC's great leap famine: the preface to Tombstone. *Journal of Contemporary China* **19**(6), 755–766.

Jisheng, Yang (2012). *Tombstone: The Great Famine 1958–1962*. Farrar, Giroux and Strauss, New York, NY.

Johnson, Chalmers (1982). *MITI and the Japanese Miracle: the Growth of Industrial Policies, 1925–1975* Stanford University Press, Stanford, CA.

Jones, Randall S. and Satoshi Urasawa (2014). *Reducing income inequality and promoting social stability in Korea*. OECD Economics Department Working Papers 1153. Paris.

Jorgenson, Dale (1961). The development of a dual economy. *Economic Journal* **71**, 309–334.

Kaganova, Olga and James McKellar (2006). *Managing Government Property Assets: International Experiences*. The Urban Institute Press, Washington, DC.

Kanaya, Akira and David Woo (2000). *The Japanese Banking System Crisis of the 1990s, Sources and Lesson*. IMF Working Paper/00/7, January.

Katz, Richard (2014). Does Korea Risk Reprising Japan's Lost Decades? *International Journal of Korean Studies* **18**(1), 177–202.

Kim, Chung Ho and Kyung-Hwan Kim (2000). Political economy of government policies on real estate in Korea. *Urban Studies* **37**(7), 1157–1169.

Kim, Joon-Kyung (2008). *Korean Households' Indebtedness and Debt Service Capacity*. Paper presented at the KDI School, Seoul.

Kim, Kyung Hwan (1987). *An Analysis of the Efficiency of Urban Housing Markets: The Case of Seoul, Korea*. Unpublished PhD dissertation. Princeton University, Princeton NJ.

Kim, Kyung Hwan (1993). Housing prices, affordability and government policy in Korea. *Journal of Real Estate Finance and Economics* **6**(1), 55–72.

Kim, Kyung Hwan (2000). Could a price bubble have caused the Korean economic crisis? In: Mera, K. and Renaud, B. (eds). *Asia's Financial Crisis and the Role of Real Estate*. M.E. Sharpe, Armonk NY, 99–114.

Kim, Kyung Hwan (2004). Housing and the Korean economy. *Journal of Housing Economics* **13**, 321–341.

Kim, Kyung Hwan (2012). The Global Financial Crisis and the Korean Housing Sector: How is this time different from the Asian Financial Crisis? In: Bardhan, A., Edelstein, R. and Kroll, C. (eds). *Global Housing Markets: Crises, Institutions and Policies*, pp. 399–419. John Wiley and Sons, Hoboken, NJ.

Kim, Kyung Hwan and Man Cho (2010). Structural changes, housing price dynamics, and housing affordability in Korea. *Housing Studies* **25**(6), 839–856.

Kim, Kyung Hwan and Man Cho (2012). *Real Estate Cycles and Government Policy: The Korean Case*. Paper presented at the KDI Conference on Real Estate Driven Systemic Risk: Country Cases & Their Policy Implications, Seoul, December 13–14.

Kim, Kyung Hwan and Man Cho (2013). *Assessing risk elements of local housing markets in China*. KDI Research Monograph, 2013-09, Korea Development Institute, Seoul (in Korean).

Kim, Kyung Hwan and Man Cho (2014). Mortgage markets international. In: Chinloy, P. and Baker, K. (eds). *Pubic Real Estate markets and Investment*, pp. 97–120. Oxford University Press, Oxford.

Kim, Kyung Hwan and Young Joon Park (2013). *International Co-movements of East Asia's Housing Price Cycles and China Effects in Greater China* (Revised 2014). Paper presented at the 2013 Asian Real Estate Society Conference, Kyoto, Japan, July. Forthcoming in *Asian Economic Papers*, Winter 2015/16.

Kim, Kyung Hwan and Bertrand Renaud (2009). The global house price boom and its unwinding: an analysis and a commentary. *Housing Studies* **24**(1), 7–24.

Kim, Kyung Hwan and Seoung Hwan Suh (1991). An analysis of optimality of housing investment in Korea. *International Economic Journal* **5**(1), 91–103.

Kim, Kyung Hwan and Seoung Hwan Suh (1993). Speculation and price bubble in the Korean and Japanese real estate markets. *Journal of Real Estate Finance and Economics* **6**(1), 73–88.

Kim, Kyung Hwan, Chang Moo Lee and Yong Man Lee (2014). Rental housing system and housing market volatility: Monthly-rent based vs. asset-based systems. In: Wachter, S., Cho, M. and Tcha, M.J. (eds) *The Global Financial Crisis and Housing – A New Policy Paradigm*, pp. 296–312. Edward Elgar Publishers, Cheltenham.

Kim, Kyung Hwan, Stephen Malpezzi and Chung Ho Kim (2008). *Property Rights, Regulations and Housing Market Performance*, Center for Free Enterprise, Seoul.

Kim, Kyung Hwan, Sock Yong Phang and Susan Wachter (2012). Price elasticity of housing supply. In: Smith, S. *et al.* (eds), *International Encyclopedia of Housing and Home*, Vol. 7. Elsevier, Oxford.

Kim, Sukkoo (1998). Economic integration and convergence: US regions, 1840–1987. *Journal of Economic History* **58**(3), 659–683.

Kim, Young Il (2014). Housing and business cycles in Korea: assessing the role of housing volume cycles. In: Wachter, S., Cho, M. and Tcha, M.J. (eds). *The Global Financial Crisis and Housing – A New Policy Paradigm*, pp. 40–61. Edward Elgar Publishers, Cheltenham.

Kindleberger, Charles P. (1978). *Manias, Panics, and Crashes: A History of Financial Crises*. Basic Books, New York.

Knight, John (2007). *China, South Africa and the Lewis model*. Oxford University CSAE WPS/2007-12. Oxford University, Oxford.

Knight, John, Quheng Deng and Shi Li (2010). *The puzzle of migrant labor shortage and rural labor surplus in China*. Oxford Department of Economics Discussion Paper 494. Oxford University, Oxford.

Koo, Anthony Y.C. (1968). *The Role of Land Reform in Economic Development: A Case Study of Taiwan*. Frederick A. Praeger, New York.

Koo, Richard C. (2009). *The Holy Grail of Macroeconomics. Lessons from Japan's Great Recession*. John Wiley Asia, Singapore.

Krugman, Paul (1991). *Geography and Trade*. MIT Press, Cambridge, MA.

Krugman, Paul (1994). The myth of Asia's miracle. *Foreign Affairs* **73**(6), 62–78.

Krugman, Paul (2008). *The Increasing Returns Revolution in Trade and Geography*. Nobel Prize Lecture, Stockholm. http://www.nobelprize.org/nobel_prizes/economics/laureates/2008/krugman_lecture.pdf.

Krugman, Paul (2009). How did economists get it so wrong? *The New York Times*, September 2. http://www.nytimes.com/2009/09/06/magazine/06Economic-t.html?pagewanted=all.

Kuo, Shirley W.Y., Gustav Ranis and John C.H. Fei (1981). *The Taiwan Success Story: Rapid Growth with Improved Income Distribution in the Republic of China, 1952–1979*. Westview Press, Boulder, CO.

Kuttner, Kenneth and Ilhyock Shim (2013). *Can non-interest rate policies stabilise housing markets? Evidence from a panel of 57 economies*. BIS Working Papers 433. Basel.

Kyongje, M-I. (Economic Daily) (2013). *Revamping home property tax codes is vital*. Seoul, Editorial, Monday, 15 July.

LaCour Little, Michael and Stephen Malpezzi (2003). Appraisal quality and residential mortgage default: evidence from Alaska. *Journal of Real Estate Finance and Economics* **27**(2), 211–233.

Lai, Rose Neng and Robert Van Order (2010). Momentum and house price growth in the United States: Anatomy of a bubble. *Real Estate Economics* **38**(4), 753–773.

Lai, Rose Neng and Robert Van Order (2014). *U.S. House Prices over the Last 30 Years: Bubbles, Regime Shifts and Market (In)Efficiency*. (Mimeo).

Lai, Rose Neng and Ko Wang (1999). Land-supply restrictions, developer strategies and housing policies: The case of Hong Kong. *International Real Estate Review* **2**(1), 143–159.

Lai, Rose Neng, Ko Wang and Yuging Zhou (2004). Sales before completion of development: pricing and strategy. *Real East Economics* **32**(2), 329–357.

Lam, Alven HS and Steve Wei Cho Tsui (1998). *Policies and mechanisms on land value capture: Taiwan case study*. Working Paper WP98AL1. Lincoln Institute of Land Policy, Cambridge, MA.

Lankov, Andrei (2013). *The Real North Korea. Life and Politics in the Failed Stalinist Utopia*. Oxford University Press, London.

Lardy, Nicholas R. (1998). *China's Unfinished Revolution*. Brookings Institution Press, Washington, DC.

Lardy, Nicholas R. (2002). *Integrating China into the Global Economy*. Brookings Institution Press, Washington, DC.

Lardy, Nicholas R. (2006). *China: toward a consumption-driven growth path*. Policy Brief 06-6. Peterson Institute for International Economics, Washington, DC. http://www.petersoninstitute.org/publications/pb/pb06-6.pdf.

Lardy, Nicholas R. (2008). *Financial repression in China* (Policy Brief 08-8). Peterson Institute for International Economics, Washington, DC. http://www.petersoninstitute.org/publications/interstitial.cfm?ResearchID=999.

Lardy, Nicholas R. (2010, June 23). *Yes, China does need that infrastructure. Wall Street Journal*: http://www.piie.com/publications/opeds/oped.cfm?ResearchID=1608.

Lardy, Nicholas R. (2012). *Sustaining China's Economic Growth after the Global Financial Crisis*. Peterson Institute for International Economics, Washington, D.C.

Lau, Lawrence (ed, 1986). *Models of Development. A Comparative Study of Economic Growth in South Korea and Taiwan*. ICS Press, San Francisco, CA.

Lau, Lawrence and Klein, L.R. (eds, 1984). *Models of Development. A Comparative Study of Economic Growth in South Korea and Taiwan*. ICS Press, San Francisco, CA.

Lea, Michael (2010). *International Comparison of Mortgage Product Offerings*. Research Institute for Housing American and the Mortgage Bankers Associations, Washington, DC.

Leamer, Edward (2007). Housing is the business cycle. *Proceedings of Federal Reserve Bank of Kansas City* 149–233.

Lee, Il Houng, Murtaza Syed and Xueyan Liu (2012). *Is China over-investing and does it matter?* IMF Working Paper WP/12/277. Washington, DC.

Lee, Jin Soon (1994). Korean land ownership and use. In: Cho, L.J. and Kim, Y.H. (eds). *Korea's Political Economy: An Institutional Perspective*. Westview Press, Boulder, CO.

Lee, Kuan Yew (2000). *From Third World to First. The Singapore Story: 1965–2000*. Harper.

Leung, Barbara, Eddie Hui and Bill Seabrooke (2007). Pricing of presales properties with asymmetric information problems. *Journal of Real Estate Portfolio Management* **13**(2), 139–152.

Leung, Barbara Y.P., Eddie C.M. Hui and Bill Seabrooke (2006). Asymmetric information in the Hong king forward property market. *International Journal of Strategic Property Management* **11**(2) 91–106.

Leung, Charles Ka Yui and Edward Chi Ho Tang (2011). Comparing two financial crises. In: Bardhan, A., Edelstein, R. and Kroll, C. (eds). *Global Housing Markets: Crises, Policies, and Institutions*, pp. 377–398. John Wiley and Sons, Hoboken, NJ.

Leung, Frank Kevin Chow and Gaofeng Han (2008). *Long-term and short-term determinants of property prices in Hong Kong*. Hong Kong Monetary Authority Working Paper 15/2008, Hong Kong.

Leventis, Andrew. (2006). *Removing appraisal bias from a repeat transactions house price index: a basic approach*. OFHEO Working Paper 06-1, Washington, DC.

Lewis, W. Arthur (1954). Economic Development with Unlimited Supplies of Labor. *The Manchester School Journal* **22**, 139–91.

Li, Jianjun and Sara Hsu (2012). Shadow banking in China. (MPRA Paper 39441). Munich University, Munich; English summary of *The Annual Report of China's Banking System* (in Chinese).

Li, William D.H. (1998). *Housing in Taiwan, Agency and Structure*. Ashgate Publishers, London.

Li, Yi Hsuan (2011). Research on public housing policy in Taiwan. In: Shrenk, M., Popovich, V. and Zeile, P. (eds). *Proceedings of Real Corp 2011, Essen, Germany*. www.corp.at/archive/CORP2011_53.pdf.

Liang, Qi and Hua Cao (2007). Property prices and bank lending in China. *Journal of Asian Economics* **18**(1), 63–75.

Lim, Chong Yah and Associates (1988). *Policy Options for the Singapore Economy.* McGraw-Hill, Singapore.

Lin, Che Chun and Tyler T. Yang (2005, June). *Customizing Mortgage Performance Models: A Taiwan Case of Mortgage Curtailment.* Paper presented at Conference on Residential Welfare and Housing Policies, June, Seoul.

Lin, Che Chun, Chu Ting Heng, Larry J. Prather and Perry Wang (2005). Mortgage curtailment and default. *International Real Estate Review* **8**(1), 95–109.

Lin, S.J. and Lin, C.C. (2001). The Taiwan area housing supply elasticity estimates. *Chinese Society of Housing Studies* **2001**, 1–12.

Lin, Jibin and Liu Yi (2007). *Characteristics of China's land system and its influence on the housing property system* (translated into English). Land Institutions and Housing Policy of Development Research Center, State Council, Beijing.

Lincoln, Edward J. (2013). *Japan post bank: Problematic issues.* Working Paper of Columbia University Center on Japanese Economy and Business, 312.

Lincoln Institute of Land Policy (2002). *Land Readjustment in Korea.* Lincoln Institute of Land Policy, Cambridge, MA.

Lindblom, Charles (1977). *Politics and Markets: The World's Political Economic Systems* Basic Books, New York.

Linneman, Peter (1986). An empirical test of the efficiency of the housing market. *Journal of Urban Economics* **20**, 140–154.

Liu, Da Nien and Hui Tzu Shih (2013). The transformation of Taiwan's status within the production and supply chain in Asia. *Taiwan-US Quarterly Analysis* **13**.

Liu, Suinian and Qungan Wu (1986). *China's Socialist Economy, an Outline History (1949–1984,)* Beijing Review, Beijing.

Lockwood, William (1954). *The Economic Development of Japan, Growth and Structural Change 1868–1938.* Princeton University Press, Princeton, NJ.

Loutskina, Elena and Philip E. Strahan (2011). Informed and uninformed investment in housing: The downside of diversification. *The Review of Financial Studies* **24**(5), 1447–1480.

Lum, Sau Kim (2011). *The impact of land supply and private housing provision on the private housing market of Singapore.* Working Paper IRES2011-005. Institute of Real Estate Studies, National University of Singapore, Singapore.

Lum, Sau Kim (2012). Government policy, housing finance, and housing production in Singapore. In: Bardhan, A., Edelstein, R. and Kroll, C. (eds). *Global Housing Markets: Crises, Policies, and Institutions*, pp. 421–446. John Wiley and Sons, Hoboken, NJ.

Ma, Guonan, Xiandong Yan and Liu Xi (2011). *China's evolving reserve requirements.* BIS Working Papers 360: http://www.bis.org/publ/work360.pdf.

Ma, Hong (1983). *New Strategy for China's Economy.* New World's Press, Beijing.

Malpezzi, Stephen (1988). *Urban housing and financial markets: some international comparisons.* INURD Working Paper. The World Bank, Washington, D.C.

Malpezzi, Stephen (1999). A simple error correction model of house prices. *Journal of Housing Economics* **8**(1), 27–62.

Malpezzi, Stephen and Duncan Maclennan (2001). The long-run price elasticity of supply of new residential construction in the United States and the United Kingdom. *Journal of Housing Economics* **10**, 278–306.

Malpezzi, Stephen and Stephen K. Mayo (1997). Getting housing incentives right: a case study of the effects of regulation, taxes, and subsidies on housing supply in Malaysia. *Land Economics* **73**, 372–391.

Malpezzi, Stephen, Mayo, Stephen and Gross, D. (1985). *Housing demand in developing countries.* World Bank Staff Working Paper 733, 122.Washington, DC.

Malpezzi, Stephen and Susan M. Wachter (2002). The role of speculation in real estate markets. *Journal of Real Estate Literature* **13**(2), 141–164.

Man, Joyce Yanyun (ed, 2011). *China's Housing Reforms and Outcomes.* Lincoln Institute Press, Cambridge, MA.

Man Joyce Yanyun and Yu Hung Hong (eds, 2011). *Local Public Finance in Transition.* Lincoln Institute of Land Policy Press, Cambridge, MA.

Mason, Andrew (ed, 2001). *Population Change and Economic Development in East Asia.* Stanford University Press, Stanford, CA.

Mason, Andrew and Tomoko Kinugasa (2008). East Asian economic development: two demographic dividends. *Journal of Asian Economics* **19**(5–6), 389–399.

Mason, Edward S., Dwight H. Perkins, Kwang Suk Kim, David C. Cole and Mahn Je Kim (1979). *The Economic and Social Modernization of the Republic of Korea.* Harvard University Press, Cambridge, MA.

McCulley, Paul (2009). The shadow banking system and Hyman Minsky's journey. *Pimco Global Central Bank Focus*: http://media.pimco-global.com/pdfs/pdf/GCBFocus.

McGregor, Richard (2010). *The Party: The Secret World of China's Communist Leaders.* Allen Lane, London.

McKinsey Global Institute (2006). *Putting China's Capital to Work: The Real Value of Financial System Reform.* http://www.mckinsey.com/Insights/MGI/Research/Financial_Markets/Putting_Chinas_capital_to_work.

McKinsey Global Institute (2008). *Mapping global markets.* Fifth Annual Report.

McKinsey Global Institute (2009). *Preparing for China's Urban Billion.* http://www.mckinsey.com/Insights/MGI/Research/Urbanization/Preparing_for_urban_billion_in_China.

McKinsey Global Institute (2010). *Debt and deleveraging: The global credit bubble and its economic consequences.* McKinsey Global Institute.

McKinsey Global Institute (2012). *Debt and Deleveraging: Uneven Progress on the Path to Growth.* McKinsey Global Institute.

McKinsey Global Institute (2015). *Debt and (Not Much) Deleveraging.* McKinsey Global Institute.

Meen, Geoffrey (1998, September). *25 Years of House Price Modelling in the UK. What Have We Learnt and Where Do We Go From Here?* Paper presented at the ENHR Conference, Cardiff.

Meen, Geoffrey (2001). *Modelling Spatial Housing Markets: Theory, Analysis and Policy.* Kluwer Academic Publishers Group.

Meen, Geoffrey (2008). Ten new propositions in UK housing macroeconomics: an overview of the first years of the century. *Urban Studies* **45**(13), 2759–2781.

Meese, Richard and Nancy Wallace (1994). Testing the present value relation for house prices: should I leave my house in San Francisco? *Journal of Urban Economics* **35**, 245–266.

Melman, Stephen (2010). *Structure of the home building industry (Special Studies).* US National Association of Homebuilders: http://housingeconomics.com.

Mera, Koichi and Eric J. Heikkila (1999). *The linkage of land price with the economy. Policy making failures of the Japanese government in the 1990s.* Paper presented at the Joint AREUEA-ASES conference, May, Hawaii.

Mera, Koichi and Bertrand Renaud (eds, 2000). *Asia's Financial Crisis and the Role of Real Estate.* M.E. Sharpe, New York, NY.

Mercer, Oliver Wyman (2005). *Risk and Funding in European Residential Mortgages: Responding to Changes in Mortgage Demand.* Mortgage Insurance Trade Association, London.

Mian, Atif R. and Amir Sufi (2009). House prices, home equity-based borrowing, and the U.S. household leverage crisis. *American Economic Review* **101**(5), 2011, 2132–2156.

Mian, Atif and Amir Sufi (2014). *House of Debt.* Chicago University Press, Chicago, IL.

Miles, David (2012). Demographics, house prices and mortgage design. *Scottish Journal of Political Economy* **59**(5), 444–466.

Mills, Edwin S. (1987). Has the United States overinvested in housing? *Real Estate Economics AREUEA Journal* **15**(1), 601–616.

Mills, Edwin S. and Katsutoshi Ohta (1976). Urbanization and Urban Problems. In: Patrick, H. and Rosovsky, H. (eds, 1976). *Asia's New Giant: How the Japanese Economy Works*, Chapter 10. The Brookings Institution, Washington, DC.

Mills, Edwin S. and Byung Nak Song (1979). *Urbanization and Urban Problems. Studies in the Modernization of the Republic of Korea, 1945–1975.* Harvard University Press, Cambridge, MA.

Minsky, Hyman (1986). *Stabilizing an Unstable Economy.* McGraw Hill, New York.

Minsky, Hyman (1992). The financial instability hypothesis. *Working Paper of Levy Institute of Bard College,* **74**.

Monetary Authority of Singapore (2011). *Financial Stability Review.* Monetary Authority of Singapore. Singapore.

Monetary Authority of Singapore (2014). *Guidelines on the Application of Total Debt Servicing Ratio for Property Loans under MAS Notices 645, 1115, 831, and 128.* June 2013, revised on 10 February 2014

Monkkonen, Paavo (2014). *Public housing and unemployment in postindustrial Hong Kong.* Working Paper WP14PM1. Lincoln Institute of Land Policy, Cambridge, MA.

Morinobu, Shigeki (2006). *The rise and fall of the land myth in Japan – some implications for Chinese land taxation.* PRI Paper 06A-08. Ministry of Finance, Policy Research Institute, Tokyo.

Muellbauer, John (2005). Property and land, taxation and the economy after the Barker review. *Economic Journal* **115**, C99–C117.

Muellbauer, John (2011). Housing markets and the macroeconomy. In: Smith, S. *et al.* (eds). *International Encyclopedia of Housing and Home.* Elsevier.

Muellbauer, John (2012). *When is a Housing Market Is Overheated enough to Threaten Stability?* Keynote address at Conference on Property Markets and Financial Stability, August 19, co-hosted by the Bank of International Settlements and the Reserve Bank of Australia, Sydney.

Muellbauer, John and Keiko Murata (2010). Consumption, land prices and the monetary mechanism in Japan. In: Hamada, K., Kashyap, A. and Weinstein, D. (eds). *Japan's Bubble, Deflation and long-term stagnation.* MIT Press, Cambridge, MA.

Muellbauer, John and Anthony Murphy (2008). Housing markets and the economy; The Assessment. *Oxford Review of Economic Policy* 24(1), 1–33.

Nabar, Malhar (2011). *Targets, interest rates, and household saving in urban China.* IMF Working Paper WP/11/2230 : http://www.imf.org/external/pubs/ft/wp/2011/wp11223.pdf.

Nabar, Malhar and Murtaza Syed (2011). *The great rebalancing act: Can investment be a lever in Asia?* IMF Working Paper WP/11/35). http://www.imf.org/external/pubs/ft/wp/2011/wp1135.pdf.

Nakamura, Takafusa (1981). *The Postwar Japanese Economy. Its Development and Structure* (Translated by Jacqueline Kaminski). University of Tokyo Press, Tokyo.

Nakone, Masato and Chad Steinberg (2012). *Can Women Save Japan?* IMF Staff Working Paper 12/248, Washington, D.C.

Nasar, Sylvia (1993). S.C. Tsiang, an economist, helped guide Taiwan's economy. *The New York Times,* November 25, New York.

Naughton, Barry (ed, 1997). *The China Circle.* Brookings Institution Press, Washington D.C.

Naughton, Barry (ed, 2007). *The Chinese Economy: Transitions and Growth.* MIT Press, Cambridge MA.

Naughton, Barry (2010). First steps toward a post-crisis economy. *China Leadership Monitor* **31**.

Naughton, Barry (2010). The turning point in housing. *China Leadership Monitor,* **33**.

Naughton, Barry (ed, 2013). *Wu, Jinglian Voice of Reform in China.* MIT Press, Cambridge, MA.

Needham, Barrie (2007). *Dutch Land-Use Planning: Planning and Managing Land-Use in the Netherlands, the Principles and the Practice.* Sdu Uitgevers, Den Haag.

Nishimura, Kiyohiko (2011). *Population decline, macroeconomic crisis and policy challenges.* Paper of Bank of Japan presented at the 75th Anniversary of Keyne's General Theory, June 19-21, Cambridge.

Nishimura, Kiyohiko (2012). How to Detect and Respond to Property Bubbles: Challenges for Policy Makers. In: Heath, A., Packer, F. and Windsor, C. (eds). *Property Markets and Financial Stability,* pp. 292–301. Reserve Bank of Australia, Sydney.

Noguchi, Yukio (1994). Land prices and house prices in Japan. In: Noguchi, Y. and Poterba, J. (eds). *Housing Markets in the U.S. and in Japan*. University of Chicago Press, Chicago.

Noguchi, Yukio and James Poterba (1994). *The Housing Markets in the U.S. and Japan*. University of Chicago Press, Chicago.

Noh, Tae Woo (2011). Memoire: critical strategies in the era of transition. *Chosun Daily News Press*, Seoul (in Korean).

Nomura Global Economics & Strategy (2011). *China Risks*. Nomura Global Economics & Strategy. http://www.nomuranow.com/research/globalresearchportal/getpub.aspx?pid=471542.

OECD (2011). *Economic Policy Reform 2011 Going for Growth*. Organisation for Economic Cooperation and Development, Paris.

OECD (2012). *Factbook 2012*. OECD Publishing, Paris.

OECD (2013a). *Factbook 2013*. OECD Publishing, Paris.

OECD (2013b). Getting older, getting poorer. In: *OECD Factbook 2013*. OECD Publishing, Paris.

OECD (2013c). *Green growth in cities*. OECD Synthesis Report 2013, OECD Publishing, Paris.

OECD (2013d). *Urbanization and green growth in China*. OECD Regional Development Working Papers, 2013/07. OECD Publishing, Paris.

OECD (2014). *Factbook 2014*. OECD Publishing, Paris.

Oikarinen, Elias (2009). Household borrowing and metropolitan housing price dynamics-empirical evidence from Helsinki. *Journal of Housing Economics* **18**(2), 126–139.

Okun, Arthur (1975). *Equality and Efficiency: The Big Tradeoff*. Brookings Institution Press, Washington, DC.

Ong, Aihwa and Li Zhang (eds, 2008). *Privatizing China: Socialism from Afar*. Cornell University Press, Ithaca, NY.

Orlik, Thomas (2011). *Understanding China's Economic Indicators*. Financial Times Press, London.

Ortalo Magné, Francois and Stephen Rady (2006). Housing market dynamics: On the contribution of income shocks and credit constraints. *Review of Economics Studies* **73**, 459–485.

Ostry, Jonathan, Andrew Berg and C.G. Tsarangides (2014). *Redistribution, inequality and growth*. IMF Staff Discussion Note, April.

Park, Chang Gui (2012). Korean national income based on chain index, 1953-2010. *Research Papers of Bank of Korea* **34**(3), 116. Bank of Korea, Seoul.

Park, Sae Woon, Doo Won Bang and Yun W. Park (2010). Price run-up in housing markets, access to bank lending and house prices in Korea. *Journal of Real Estate Finance and Economics* **40**, 332–367.

Patrick, Hugh and Henri Rosovsky (eds). *Asia's New Giant: How the Japanese Economy Works*. The Brookings Institution, Washington, DC.

Pavlidis, Efthymios, Alisa Yusupova, Ivan Paya et al. (2013). *Monitoring housing markets for episodes of exuberance: an application of the Phillips et al. (2012, 2013) GSADF Test on the Dallas Fed international housing database*. WP 0165. Globalization and Monetary Policy Institute, Federal Reserve Bank of Dallas, Dallas, TX.

Pavlov, Andrey and Susan M. Wachter (2011). Subprime lending and real estate prices. *Real Estate Economics* **39**(1), 1–17.

Peng, Ruijie and William Wheaton (1994). Effects of restrictive land supply on housing in Hong Kong: An econometric analysis. *Journal of Housing Research* **5**, 263–291.

Peppercorn, Ira Gary and Claude Taffin (2013). *Rental Housing: Lessons from International Experiences*. The World Bank, Washington, DC.

Peterson, George E. and Patricia Clarke Annez (2007). *Financing Cities*. Sage Publications for the World Bank, Los Angeles, CA.

Pettis, Michael (2011). *The contentious debate over China's economic transition*. Policy Outlook of Carnegie Endowment for International Peace, March 25. http://www.chinausfocus.com/library/think-tank-resources/us-lib/financeeconomy-us-lib/carnegie-the-contentious-debate-over-chinas-economic-transition-march-2011/.

Pettis, Michael (2011). How do we know that China is overinvesting? *China Financial Markets Monthly Letter*: http://www.mpettis.com/

Pettis, Michael (2013). *Avoiding the Fall: China's Economic Restructuring.* Carnegie Endowment for Peace, Washington, DC.

Pettis, Michael (2014a). The impact of debt on Chinese growth. *China Financial Markets Monthly Letter*, Peking University, Beijing.

Pettis, Michael (2014b). Taking stock of China's transition. *Global Source Partners Monthly Report*: http://www.globalsourcepartners.com.

Phang, Sock Yong (1992). *Housing Markets and Urban Transportation. Policy Analysis for Singapore.* McGraw-Hill Book, Singapore.

Phang, Sock Yong (2001). Housing policy, wealth formation and the Singapore economy. *Housing Studies 2001*, Special Millennium Issue.

Phang, Sock Yong (2004). House prices and aggregate consumption: do they move together? Evidence from Singapore. *Journal of Housing Economics* **13**, 101–119.

Phang, Sock Yong (2007). The Singapore model of housing and the welfare state. In: Groves, R., Murie, A. and Watson, C. (eds). *Housing and the Welfare State. Perspectives from East Asia and Europe.* Ashgate Publishing, London.

Phang, Sock Yong (2013). *Housing Finance Systems. Market Failures and Government Failures.* Palgrave-McMillan.

Phang, Sock Yong (2015). *Superstars Cities, Inequality and Housing Policy.* Celia Moh Professorial Lecture, Singapore Management University.

Phang, Sock Yong and Kyung Hwan Kim (2013). *Singapore's Housing Policies: 1960–2013.* Paper presented at the Knowledge and Learning Workshop, KDI School and World Bank Institute, November, Seoul.

Phang, Sock-Yong, Kyung-Hwan Kim and Susan Wachter (2012). Supply Elasticity of Housing. In: Smith, S.J. (Editor in Chief). *International Encyclopedia of Housing and Home.* Elsevier Ltd.

Phillips, P.C., Shi, S.P. and Yu, J. (2012). *Testing for multiple bubbles.* Cowles Foundation Discussion Papers, 1843. Cowles Foundation for Research in Economics, Yale University, New Haven, CT.

Piketty, Thomas (2014). *Capital in the Twenty First Century.* Harvard University Press, Boston, MA.

Pilling, David (2011). Hong Kong land system that time forgot. *Financial Times*, March 9.

Pistor, Katharina (2009). *The governance of China's finance. NBER Project on Capitalizing China.* Cambridge, MA. http://www.nber.org/chapters/c12073.pdf.

Pistor, Katharina (2010). Banking reforms and bank bail outs in the Chinese mirror. In: Stiglitz, J. (ed). *China's Transition to a Market Economy.* Oxford University Press, Oxford. http://policydialogue.org/files/events/Pistor_banking_reform_bail_outs.pdf.

Population Reference Bureau (2014). *2014 World Population Data Sheet.* Population Reference Bureau, Washington DC. http://www.prb.org.

Poterba, James (1984). Tax subsidies to owner-occupied housing: an asset market approach. *Quarterly Journal of Economics* **99**(4), 729–752.

Prasad, Eswar (2009 December). Rebalancing growth in Asia. *IMF Finance and Development*, 19–22 www.imf.org/external/pubs/ft/fandd/2009/12/pdf/prasad.pdf.

Prasad, Eswar (2009). *Rebalancing growth in Asia.* IZA Discussion Paper 4298. http://ftp.iza.org/dp4298.pdf.

Prasad, Eswar and Lei Sandy Ye (2012). *The Renminbi's role in the global monetary system.* Brookings Global Economy and Development Paper, Brookings Institution, December. Washington, D.C.

Pyo, Hak K. (1988). Estimates of capital stock and capital output coefficients by industries: 1953-1986. *International Economic Journal* **2**(3), 79–121.

Quan, Daniel C. and John M. Quigley (1989). Inferring an investment return series for real estate from observations on sales. *AREUEA Journal* **17**(2), 218–230.

Rabinovitch, Simon (2012). *China Details Local Debt Rollover Plan.* http://www.ft.com/intl/cms/s/0/b173008e-71bb-11e1-8497-00144feab49a.html#axzz1wMDvRChT.

Raftery, John (1991). *Principles of Building Economics.* BSP Professional Books, Oxford.

Ramsey, S. Robert (2013). *What does it mean to be East Asian?* (Unpublished). Inaugural Lecture of East Asian Humanities Lecture Series, George Washington University, Washington, D.C., October 15.

Rappoza, Kenneth (2014, April 7). *China's Foreign Assets More Than Half Its GDP.* Forbes.

Reinhart, Carmen and Kenneth Rogoff (2009). *This Time is Different: Eight Centuries of Financial Folly.* Princeton University Press, Princeton, NJ.

Reinhart, Carmen and Kenneth Rogoff (2010). Growth in a Time of Debt. *American Economic Review* **100**(2), 573–578.

Reinhart, Carmen M. and Takeshi Tashiro (2013). *Crowding Out Redefined: The Role of Reserve Accumulation.* NBER Working Paper No. 19652, November

Renaud, Bertrand (1989). Compounding financial repression with rigid urban regulations: Lessons of the Korean housing market. *Review of Urban and Regional Development Studies* **1**(1), 3–22.

Renaud, Bertrand (1990). China's 1998 urban housing reforms: origins, scope and major obstacles. In: Lim, G.C. and Chang, W. (eds). *Dynamic Transformation: Korea, NICs and Beyond.* Consortium of Development Studies, Myung-Bo Publishing, Seoul.

Renaud, Bertrand (1991). *Housing reforms in socialist economies.* World Bank Discussion Papers 125. Washington, DC.

Renaud, Bertrand (1992). The housing system of the former soviet union: Why do the Soviets need housing markets? *Housing Policy Debate* **3**(3), 877–899.

Renaud, Bertrand (1993). Confronting a distorted housing market: can Korean polices break with the past? In: Krause, L. and Park, F.K. (eds). *Social Issues in Korea.* Development Institute, Seoul.

Renaud, Bertrand (1995). The real estate economy and the design of Russian housing reforms. *Urban Studies* Part I: **32**(8); Part II: **32**(9).

Renaud, Bertrand (1997). The 1985 to 1994 global real estate boom: an overview. *Journal of Real Estate Literature* **5**(1), 13–44.

Renaud, Bertrand (2003). Speculative behavior in immature real estate markets: Lessons of the 1997 Asia financial crisis. *Urban Policy and Research* **21**(2), 151–173.

Renaud, Bertrand (2004). *Permanence and Change, East Asian Housing Policies after Fifty Years.* Keynote presentation at the International Housing Conference celebrating the 50th anniversary of the Hong Kong Housing Authority, February 24, Hong Kong.

Renaud, Bertrand (2011). A systemic view of housing policy for China's new urban era. In: Man: J.Y. (ed) *China's Housing Reform and Outcomes,* 213–247. Lincoln Institute of Land Policy, Cambridge, MA.

Renaud, Bertrand (2012). Real estate bubble and financial crisis in Dubai: Dynamics and policy response. *Journal of Real Estate Literature* **20**(1), 51–77.

Renaud, Bertrand, Joseph K. Eckert and R. Jerome Anderson (2009). Property rights and real estate privatization in Russia: A work in progress. In: Ingram, G. and Hong, Y.H. (eds). *Property Rights and Land Policies.* Lincoln Institute Press, Cambridge, MA.

Renaud, Bertrand and Kyung Hwan Kim (2007). The global housing boom and its aftermath. *Housing Finance International* **22**(2), 3–17.

Renaud, Bertrand, Frederik Pretorius and Bernabe Pasadilla (1997). *Markets at Works. Dynamics of the Residential Real Estate Market in Hong Kong.* Hong Kong University Press, Hong Kong.

Reuters (2011). Exclusive: China to clean up billions worth of local debt. *Reuters,* May 31. http://www.reuters.com/article/2011/05/31/us-china-economy-debt-idUSTRE74U26320110531.

Rey, Hélène (2014). *Global Financial Flows and Monetary Policy.* Annual Mundell-Fleming Lecture, IMF.

Riggs, Fred Warren (1964). *Administration in Developing Countries.* Houghton Mifflin, New York, NY.

Rodrik, Dani (1994). *Getting interventions right: How South Korea and Taiwan grew rich.* NBER Working Paper 4964, Cambridge, MA.

Rodrik, Dani (1996). Coordination failures and government policy: A model with applications to East Asia and Eastern Europe. *Journal of International Economics* **40**(1–2), 1–22.

Rodrik, Dani (2005). Growth strategies. In: Aghion, P. and Durlauf, S. (eds). *Handbook of Economic Growth.* Elsevier, Amsterdam.

Rodrik, Dani (2015). Economic Rules: the Rights and Wrongs of the Dismal Science: New York, W.W. Norton.

Rodrik, Dani, Subramanian, A. and Trebbi, F. (2002). *Institutions rule: The primacy of institutions over geography and integration in economic development.* NBER Working Paper 9305. Cambridge, MA.

Rosen, Harvey (1985). *Housing Behavior and the Experimental Housing-Allowance Program: What Have We learned?* http://www.nber.org/chapters/c8373.

Saita, Yumi, Chihiro Shimizu and Tsutomu Watanabe (2014). *Aging and real estate prices: Evidence from Japanese and US regional prices.* Working Paper E-68. Tokyo Center for Economic Research, Tokyo.

Samuelson, Paul A. (1958). An exact consumption-loan model of interest with or without the social contrivance of money. *Journal of Political Economy* **66**(6), 467–482.

Sánchez, Aida Caldera and Åsa Johansson (2011). *The price responsiveness of housing supply in OECD countries.* OECD Economics Department Working Papers 837, Paris.

Scitovsky, Tibor (1986). Economic development in Taiwan and South Korea, 1965–1981. In: Lau, L.J. and Klein, L. (eds). *Models of Development.* Institute for Contemporary Studies, San Francisco, CA.

Seko, Miki, Kazuto Sumita and Michio Naoi (2011). The recent financial crisis and the housing market in Japan. In: Bardhan, A., Edelstein, R. and Kroll, C. (eds). *Global Housing Markets: Crises, Policies, and Institutions,* 357–374. John Wiley and Sons, Hoboken, NJ.

Schell, Orville and John Delury (2013). *Wealth and Power: China's Long March to the Twenty-First Century.* Random House, New York, NY.

Schelling, Thomas C. (1978). *Micromotives and Macrobehavior.* W.W. Norton, New York, NY.

Shen, Bingxi and Lijuan Yan (2008). Development of consumer credit in China. *BIS Papers of Bank of International Settlements* **46**. http://www.bis.org/publ/bppdf/bispap46g.pdf.

Sheng, Andrew (1998). *The Crisis of Money in the 21st Century.* Public Lecture, April 28, City University of Hong Kong, Hong Kong.

Sheng, Andrew (2009). *From Asian to Global Financial Crisis: An Asian Regulator's View of Unfettered Finance in the 1990s and 2000s.* Cambridge University Press, Cambridge.

Shih, Victor (2010). *Looming Problem of Local Debt in China-1.6 Trillion Dollar and Rising. Blog on Elite Chinese Politics and Political Economy.* Northwestern University, Evanston, IL. http://chinesepolitics.blogspot.com/2010/02/looming-problem-of-local-debt-in-china.html.

Shih, Victor and Zhang Qi (2007). Who receives subsidies? A look at the county level in two time periods. In: Shue, V. and Wong, C. (eds). *Paying for Progress in China.* Routledge, London. http://faculty.wcas.northwestern.edu/~vsh853/papers/shih_zhang_final.pdf.

Sing, Tien Foo, I. Chun Tsai and Ming Chi Chen (2006). Price discovery and segmentation in the public and private housing markets in Singapore. *Journal of Housing Economics* **15**(4), 305–320.

Singapore Statistics (2006). *Housing Mobility 1995–2005.* Occasional Paper 10.

Skinner, G. William (1964). Marketing and social structure in rural China. *The Journal of Asian Studies* **24**(1), 3–42.

Son, Jae Young (1994). The 'Land Problem' in Korea. In: Cho, L.J. and Kim, Y.H. (eds). *Korea's Political Economy: An Institutional Perspective.* Westview Press, Boulder, CO.

Son, Jae Young (2014). Korea's development finance at the crossroads. In: Wachter, S., Cho, M. and Tcha, M.J. (eds). *The Global Financial Crisis and Housing – A New Policy Paradigm,* 208–228. Edward Elgar Publishers, Cheltenham, UK.

Son, Jae Young and Kyung-Hwan Kim (1998). Analysis of urban land shortages: The case of Korean cities. *Journal of Urban Economics* **43**, 362–384.

Son, Jae Young and Si Wook Lee (2014). *Developing a housing finance system in Mongolia.* KDI KSP Report, January, Korea Development Institute, Seoul.

Song, Yan (2012). *Infrastructure and urban development: Evidence from Chinese cities.* Paper presented at the Lincoln Institute Conference on Infrastructure and Land Policies, June 4–5, Cambridge, MA.

Spence, M., Clarke Annez, P. and Buckley, R. (eds, 2009). *Urbanization and Growth.* published by the World Bank on behalf of the Commission on Growth and Development.

Stanback, Thomas M. (1979). *Understanding the Service Economy: Employment Productivity, Location.* Johns Hopkins University Press, Baltimore, MD.

Stanbach, Thomas and Thierry Noyelle (1983). *Economic Transformation of American Cities.* Rowman & Littlefield, New York, NY.

Standard & Poor's (2012, March 7). *The worst is yet to come for Chinese developers in Asia's shaky property sector.* Industry Credit Outlook. http://static.ow.ly/docs/IndustryCreditOutlookChinaProperty_wWi.pdf.

Standard & Poor's (2014 September 29). *Slower sales and lower margins will squeeze developers.* China Property Watch: Quarterly Report.

Stephens, Mark (2011). *Tackling Housing Market Volatility in the U.K.* Joseph Rowntree Foundation, York.

Stiglitz, Joseph, Amartya Sen and Jean Paul Fitoussi (2014). *Mismeasuring Our Lives: Why GDP Doesn't Add Up.* Commission on the Measurement of Economic Performance and Social Progress, Paris.

Suh, Seoung Hwan and Kabsung Kim (2013). Global Financial Crisis and early warning system of Korean housing market. In: Wachter, S., Cho, M. and Tcha, M.J. (eds). *The Global Financial Crisis and Housing – A New Policy Paradigm,* 62-81. Edward Elgar Publishers, Cheltenham.

Susuki, Yoshio (1987). *The Japanese Financial System.* Clarendon Press, Oxford.

Tao, Zhigang and Y.C. Richard Wong (2002). Hong Kong: From an industrialized city to a center of manufacturing-related services. *Urban Studies* **39**(12), 2345–2358.

Tashiro, Takeshi (2013). *Crowding out redefined: the role of reserve accumulation.* NBER Working Paper 19652. http://www.nber.org/papers/w19652.

Taylor, John B. (2007). *Housing and monetary policy.* NBER Working Paper 13682. Cambridge, MA http://www.nber.org/papers/w13682.

Taylor, John B. (2010). *Commentary: Monetary Policy after the Fall.* Presentation at the Macroeconomic Challenges: the Decade Ahead of FR Bank of Kansas City, Jackson Hole, WY, August 28. http://www.kc.frb.org/publicat/sympos/2010/taylor-remarks.pdf.

Taylor, Lori L. (1998). Does the United States still overinvest in housing? *Economic Review of Federal Reserve Bank of Dallas* Second Quarter, 10–18.

Tirole, Jean (1985). Asset bubbles and overlapping generations. *Econometrica* **53**, 1499–1528.

Toshiaki, Tachibanaki (2010). *The New Paradox for Japanese Women: Greater Choice, Greater Inequality* (Translated by M.E. Foster). LCBT International Library Selection 26, Tokyo.

Tsatsaronis, Kostas and Haibin Zhu (2004). *What drives housing price dynamics: Cross-country evidence.* BIS Quarterly Review, March.

Tse, Raymond Y.C., E.C.M. Hui and C.H.K. Chan (2001). On the competitive land market: Evidence from Hong Kong. *Review of Urban and Regional Development Studies* **13**(1), 46–60.

Tu, Lianting (2014, October 9). *China Sets Rules for Local Government Debt Revamp.* http://www.reuters.com/article/2014/10/09/emergingmarkets-bonds-idUSL3N0S31IM20141009.

United Nations (1974). Manual VIII. *Methods for Projections of Urban and Rural Population, 1974.* Population Division, United Nations, New York, NY. http://www.un.org/esa/population/techcoop/PopProj/manual8/manual8.html.

Van den Noord, Paul (2005). Tax incentives and house price volatility in the Euro area: Theory and evidence. *Économie Internationale* **101**, 29–45.

Vogel, Ezra F. (1978). *Japan as Number One. Lessons for the United States.* Harvard University Press, Cambridge, MA.

Vogel, Ezra F. (1990). *One Step Ahead in China. Guangdong under Reform.* Harvard University Press, Cambridge, MA.

Vogel, Ezra F. (1991). *The Four Little Dragons: The Spread of Industrialization in East Asia.* Harvard University Press, Cambridge, MA.

Vogel, Ezra F. (2011). *Deng Xiaoping and the Transformation of China.* Harvard University Press, Cambridge, MA.

Von Thünen, Johann (1826). *Der Isolierte Staat in Beziehung auf Landwirthschaft und Nationalökonomie. The Isolated State* (Reprinted translation). Pergamon Press, New York.

Wachter, Susan, Man Cho and Moon Joong Tcha (eds, 2014). *The Global Financial Crisis and Housing – A New Policy Paradigm.* Edward Elgar Publishers, Hoboken, NJ.

Wade, Robert (2004). *Governing the Market* (Second paperback edition). Princeton University Press, Princeton NJ.

Walter, Carl E. and Fraser J.T. Howe (2011). *Red Capitalism: The Fragile Financial Foundations of China's Extraordinary Rise.* John Wiley and Sons, New York.

Wang, Chien An and Chin Oh Chang (2007). Relationship between the housing vacancy rate, housing price, and the moving rate at the township level in Taiwan, in 1990 and 2000. *International Real Estate Review* **10**(1), 65–82.

Wang, Fei Ling (2005). *Organizing Through Division and Exclusion: China's Hukou System.* Stanford University Press, Stanford.

Wang, Fei Ling (2005, October 7). *China's Household Registration System: Sustained Reform Needed to Protect Chinese Rural Migrants.* Testimony to US Congress Committee on China. http://www.cecc.gov/pages/news/hukou.pdf.

Wang, Ko, Yuqing Zhou, Su Han Chan and K.W. Chau (2000). Over-confidence and cycles in real estate markets: Cases in Hong Kong and Asia. *International Real Estate Review* **3**(1), 93–108.

Wang, Songtao, Su Han Chan and Bohua Xu (2012). The estimation and determinants of the price elasticity of housing supply: evidence from China. *Journal of Real Estate Research* **34**(3) 311–343.

Wang, Songtao and Siqi Zheng (2011). *Housing supply elasticity across Chinese cities, their impact on housing prices and sources.* Tsinghua University Working Paper. Tsinghua University, Beijing.

Wang, Xiaolu and Wing Thye Woo (2010). *The size and distribution of hidden Household Income in China (Revised version 25 December 2010).* China Reform Foundation, Beijing.

Wang, Ya Ping (2011). Recent housing reform practice in Chinese cities: social and spatial implications. In: Man, J.Y.Y. (ed). *China's Housing Reform and Outcomes.* Lincoln Institute of Land Policy, Cambridge, MA.

Wang, Ya Ping and Alan Murie (1999). *Housing Policy and Practice in China.* McMillan Press, London.

Watanabe, Tsutomu and Chihiro Shimizu (2012). *Sticky Housing Rents and Monetary Policy: The Japanese Experience.* Paper presented at the KDI Conference on Real Estate Driven Systemic Risk: Country Cases & Their Policy Implications, December 13–14, Seoul.

Wei, Shang Jin, Xiaobo Zhang and Yin Liu (2012). *Status competition and housing prices.* NBER Working Paper, 18000. http://www.nber.org/papers/w18000.pdf.

Werner, Richard A. (1994). Japanese Foreign Investment and the 'Land Bubble'. *Review of International Economics* **2**(2) 166–178.

Westphal, Larry, Yung W. Rhee and Gary Purcell (1981). *Korean industrial competence: Where it came from.* World Bank Working Paper, WPS 469, World Bank, Washington DC.

Wheaton, William (1999). Real estate 'cycles': Some fundamentals. *Real Estate Economics* **27**(2), 209–230.

Whitehead, Christine M.E. (1983). The Rationale for Land Government Intervention. In: Dunkerley, H. (ed, 1983). *Urban Land Policies, Issues and Opportunities,* Chapter 4. Oxford University Press, published for the World Bank.

Whiting, Susan (2011). Fiscal reform and 'land public finance': Zouping county in national context. In: Man, J.Y.Y. and Hong, Y.H. (eds). *Local Public Finance in Transition.* Lincoln Institute Press, Cambridge, MA.

Widness, Brett (2013). How Singapore builds smarter density. *Urban Land,* February 2013. Urban Land Institute and Singapore Center for Livable Cities, Washington, DC.

Williamson, Oliver (1985). *The Economic Institutions of Capitalism*. The Free Press, New York, NY.

Willis, Carol (1995). *Form Follows Finance*. Princeton Architectural Press, Princeton, NJ.

Wolf, Martin (2008). *Fixing Global Finance*. Johns Hopkins University Press, Baltimore, MD.

Wolf, Martin (2014). *The Shifts and the Shocks: What We've Learned – and Have Still to Learn – from the Financial Crisis*. Penguin Press, London.

Wolf, Martin (2015). Chronic Economic and Political Ills Defy Easy Cure. *Financial Times*, London.

Wong, Aline Kan and Yeh, Stephen Hua Kuo (1985). *Housing a Nation; 25 years of Public Housing in Singapore*. HDB, Singapore, 538 pp.

Wong, Siu Kei, C.Y. Yiu, M.K.S. Tse and K.W. Chau (2006). Do the forward sales of real estate stabilize spot prices? *Journal of Real Estate Finance and Economics* **32**, 289–304.

Wong, Yue Chim Richard (1998). *On Privatizing Public Housing*. City University of Hong Kong Press, Hong Kong.

The World Bank (1995). *Russia: Housing reform and privatization: Strategy and transition issues*. Report 14929-RU. Washington, DC.

The World Bank (1996). *World Development Report: From Plan to Market Oxford University Press, Oxford*. http://wdr.worldbank.org/worldbank/a/c.html/world_development_report_1996/abstract/WB.0-1952-1107-3.abstract1.

The World Bank (2001). *Housing reform evaluation mission*. Unpublished. Enterprise Housing and Social Security Reform Project EASUR. Washington, DC.

The World Bank (2002). *Status of housing reforms in the four project cities, recommendations*. (Unpublished). Enterprise Housing and Social Security Reform Project EASUR. Washington, DC.

The World Bank, Beijing Office (2011), *Quarterly Update*, April.

The World Bank and Development Research Center (2012). *China 2030*. Development Research Center, State Council, Beijing.

Wu, Jinglian (1992). A Suggestion that We Adopt the Authorized Expression (Tifa) Socialist Market Economy. Reprinted in translation in: Naughton, B. (ed, 2013) Wu, J. *Voice of Reform in China*. MIT Press, Cambridge, MA.

Wu, Jing, Yongheng Deng and Hongyu Liu (2011). *House price index construction in the nascent housing market: The case of China*. IRES Working Paper IRES2011-017, National University of Singapore, Singapore.

Wu, Jing, Joseph Gyourko and Yongheng Deng (2010). *Evaluating conditions in major Chinese housing markets*. NBER Working Paper 16189, Cambridge, MA.

Xinhua News Agency (2006, January 10). *China revises its GDP rate for the period 1979–2004*. Xinhua News Agency. http://www.china.org.cn/english/government/154646.htm.

Xinhua News Agency (2011, June 27). *China's local government debts exceed 10 trillion yuan*. Xinhua News Agency. http://www.chinadaily.com.cn/bizchina/2011-06/27/content_12786826.htm.

Yamamura, Kozo and Yasukichi Yasuba (eds, 1987). *The Political Economy of Japan. Volume 1. The Domestic Transformation*. Stanford University Press, Stanford, CA.

Yan, Siqi and Janet Ge (2012, January). *Backward bending new housing supply curve: evidence from China*. Paper presented at PRRES Conference, Adelaide.

Yang, Dennis Tao (2012). Saving and external imbalances in China. *Occasional Paper of Hong Kong Institute for Monetary Research* **8**, Hong Kong.

Yang, Jisheng (2010). The fatal politics of the PRC's great leap famine: the preface to Tombstone. *Journal of Contemporary China* **19**(6), 755–766.

Yang, Le (2011). *Overview of Chinese Local Government Debt*. Central Banking Seminar, Peking University, Beijing, October 1. http://ineteconomics.org/blog/china-seminar/deadly-cave-chinese-local-government-debt.

Yang, Tyler, Cary Lin and Man Cho (2011). Collateral risk in residential mortgage defaults. *Journal of Real Estate Finance and Economics* **42**, 15–142.

Yellen, Janet L. (2009). *A Minsky Meltdown: Lessons for Central Bankers*. Federal Reserve Bank of San Francisco, San Francisco, CA, April 16.

Yiu, Matthew, Jun Yu and Lu Jin (2013). Detecting bubbles in Hong Kong residential property market. *Journal of Asian Economics* **28**, 115–124.

Yoshitomi, Masaru (1996). *The 'jusen' debacle and the Japanese economy*. Working Paper 96-7. U.S-Japan Management Studies Center of Wharton School, University of Pennsylvania, Philadelphia, PA.

Young, Alwyn (1992). A tale of two cities: factor accumulation and technical change in Hong Kong and Singapore. In: Blanchard, O. and Fischer, S. (eds). *NBER Macroeconomics Annual 1992, Volume 7*. MIT Press, Cambridge, MA.

Zha, Jianying (2011). *Tide Players: The Movers and Shakers of a Rising China*. The New Press, New York.

Zhang, Longmei and Edda Zoli (2014). *Leaning against the wind: Macroprudential policy in Asia*. IMF Working Paper WP14/2. Washington, DC.

Zhang, Wenlang, Gaofeng Han and Steven Chan (2014). *How strong are the linkages between real estate and other sectors in China?* Working Paper 11/2014. Hong Kong Institute for Monetary Research, Hong Kong.

Zhang, Xiabo, Jin Yang and Shenglin Wang (2010). *China has reached the Lewis Turning Point*. IFPRI Discussion Paper 977. International Food Policy Research Institute. Washington, DC.

Zheng, Siqi, Yuming Fu and Hongyu Liu (2006). Housing-choice hindrances and urban spatial structure; Evidence from matched location and location-preference data in Chinese cities. *Journal of Urban Economics* **60**, 535–557.

Zheng, Siqi and Matthewe Kahn (2008). Land and residential property markets in a booming economy: New evidence from Beijing. *Journal of Urban Economics* **63**, 743–757.

Zhu, Rongji (2013). *Zhu Rongji on the Record, the Road to Reform 1991–1997*. Brookings Institution Press, Washington, DC.

Index of Names

Dynamics of Housing in East Asia, First Edition. Bertrand Renaud,
Kyung-Hwan Kim and Man Cho.
© 2016 John Wiley & Sons, Ltd. Published 2016 by John Wiley & Sons, Ltd.

General Index